THE
Local Historian's
ENCYCLOPEDIA

ISBN 0 9503656 7 X

Typeset by Phoenix Photosetting, Chatham
and printed and bound in Great Britain by
Biddles Ltd, Guildford and King's Lynn

Published by
Historical Publications Ltd
54 Station Road
New Barnet, Herts
(01-607 1628)

THE
Local Historian's
ENCYCLOPEDIA

John Richardson

with new sections by
BRIAN CHRISTMAS
ALEXANDER R. RUMBLE
ALFREDA WILKINSON

Section heading illustrations by
JILL DOW

HISTORICAL PUBLICATIONS

CONTENTS

NOTES ON CONTRIBUTORS

Brian Christmas is an enthusiastic genealogist and has published a number of articles on family history.

Dr Alexander Rumble has a BA in Medieval and Modern History (University of Leeds 1967), and a Ph.D in History (University College, London 1980); he also holds a Diploma in the Study of Records and Archive Administration (University of Liverpool 1968). He was Editorial Assistant for the English Place-Name Society 1973–75, and has been a Lecturer in Palaeography at the University of Manchester since 1980.

Edward Sammes recently retired from a career in the milling industry and also lectures on the history of flour milling.

Alfreda Wilkinson is an indexer of archaeological books.

ACKNOWLEDGEMENTS

I have received many helpful suggestions. In particular I would like to thank the following correspondents for their contributions or practical help: Roy Allen, Enid Ballard, David Barton, Charles Blount, Mary Bramhill, John M. Buckeridge, Alena Burton, Lyndon Cave, Ann Chiswell, Joan Coburn, Roy Edwards, John Field, John L. Gilbert, L. C. Giles, J. S. Golland, Philip D. Greenall, Sylvia Greening, E. F. Hodges, David Holman, Mrs J. Hunter, Iris Jeffery, Mrs L. E. Jerram-Burrows, Gloria Liddall, Rev. M. G. R. Morris, Lt B. Owen RN (Retd), A. P. Phillips, Miss J. C. Rowley, Horace Shooter, Duncan Stewart, R. A. Storey, J. D. Swinscoe.

Illustrations of windmills by
Richard Cook, Adam Richardson and Tom Richardson

·

The illustration on the jacket
is of Hardwick and Maple Durham,
by Joseph Farington
and published by J & J Boydell in 1793.

FOREWORD

It was with few expectations that I wrote a foreword to this Encyclopedia in 1974. It was, after all, that prime indulgence – a book that I needed for myself, for my own use in local history research, and I did not assume that too many others were of a like mind. To my surprise the Encyclopedia was well-enough liked to warrant a number of reprints.

Over the years I gathered a large file of very helpful suggestions from readers. Some sections needed enlargement, others alteration, and there were yet more that I wanted to add. My more ambitious plans would have meant a selling price too high to be popular, although I hope one day to see a further considerable expansion to include a wide range of social history entries which cover such things as recreation, costume, food, furniture and everyday items.

For the time being I have included a completely new section, much requested, on Palaeography, which has been written by Dr. Alexander Rumble, and Archaeology has been considerably enlarged by a meticulous contribution from Alfreda Wilkinson. Edward Sammes has expanded the section on watermills and windmills.

At times when I despaired of finding the tenacity to complete the task of revision, correction and rearrangement, I have been much encouraged by the enthusiasm and diligence of Brian Christmas. He originally wrote to me with some material and since then has plied me with much more, and he has also done much of the proof-reading. His speciality is genealogy but his knowledge and contribution covers many fields. To him I am much indebted. In addition, the spirit of the book has been imaginatively caught by Jill Dow's delightful drawings at the commencement of each section.

I have resisted the suggestion to rearrange the Encyclopedia into an alphabetical format. This is because I think it more useful to a researcher to be able to scan through a particular field and, perhaps, take up lines of enquiry that he or she was unaware of: alphabetical arrangements, however advantageous in other ways, do not permit this.

In the twelve years since the Encyclopedia was first published the study of local history has developed well beyond the 'highways and byways' level; the list of local organisations included in this edition shows an astonishing increase since 1974. The mobility of our Society has seemingly increased, rather than diminished, an interest in neighbourhoods. In particular the study of genealogy has inspired a wealth of societies and publications. Often it is said that this preoccupation with the past is a reflection of Society's instability or its dislike of the present; in turn this can lead to a romantic perception of previous eras. No doubt, there is *some* basis for this opinion, but more likely the new-found curiosity of present generations stems from prosaic factors such as more leisure, a wider concept of education in schools, and a revolution in printing technology which makes publications easier and relatively cheaper to produce.

Accompanying this thirst for things past has come a vociferous movement to keep them as well. The brave new world of redevelopment has lost enthusiasts and battles, and general affluence has come in time to save much from neglect or demolition. The test, however, will come if affluence disappears, because the past is expensive to maintain. In that event a simplistic choice between providing for the present or caring for the past will only be avoided if there are sufficient people who understand what the past contributes to our everyday life.

John Richardson

SECTION A

Land and Agriculture

PART ONE
LAND MEASUREMENT

A1 General. Measurement of area and distance in Saxon and medieval times varied conconsiderably over the country and within any one region. The Hide, for example, was an area which was assumed to support a peasant family for a year and its size, therefore, depended on the quality of the soil.

Generally the main units of measurement bore the same relationship to each other over England, but even so there were many exceptions. The normal relationship was:

1 Hide, Carucate or Ploughland
= 4 Virgates or Yardlands
1 Virgate or Yardland
= 2 Bovates or Oxgangs
1 Bovate or Oxgang = 10-20 Acres
1 Acre = 4 Rods × 40 Rods.

A2 Acre. The Acre, originally a stretch of land of no particular size or nature, came to mean land which was cleared for cultivation or grazing. In open field farming it was as large a strip of land as could be ploughed by a yoke of oxen in a day. The Acre was standardised by Edward I at 40 Rods long × 4 Rods wide, or 4,840 sq. yds. Even so, for a long time, there were regional variations and the Acre could mean in Ireland 7,840 sq. yds., in Westmorland 6,760 sq. yds., and in Scotland 6,084 sq. yds.

It was also a linear measure in some Midland counties of between 22 and 32 yds.

A3 Acreland. An area which varied from 8 to 20 acres.

A4 Acreme. A late-medieval term for approximately ten acres, similar to a Farthingdale.

9

A5 Arpen(t). A vineyard measure derived from France of between 100 and 160 sq. yds.

A6 Bescia. A medieval term in the fen lands for the area of turf which could be dug by one man with a spade between May 1st and August 1st. It was a variable dimension.

A7 Bovate. A variable measure related to the soil quality and the amount of land an ox could plough in a year. It was generally reckoned to be one-eighth of a Hide (qv). In some areas the normal measurement relationship (see A1) differed and the Bovate equalled one Virgate instead of one half. Alternatively known as an Oxgang.

A8 Broad Oxgang. Double a normal Oxgang (qv); equivalent to a Virgate or Yardland.

A9 Carucate. An alternative term for a Hide (qv) used mainly in Danelaw counties. In the Domesday survey it was a basis for tax assessment.

A10 Cattlegate. In parts of Leicestershire a unit of grassland having an area of 1 rood, 1 perch.

A11 Chain. When standardised, a measure of 22 yds.

A12 Davoch. A Scottish measure supposed to have averaged 416 acres.

A13 Day-Math. A Cheshire term for approximately twice a statute acre, or a day's mowing for one man.

A14 Day Work. In some areas of Yorks, Lancs and Lincs, 3 roods of land.

A15 Erws. The Welsh term for an acre.

A16 Farthingdale. A quarter of a Virgate or Yardland and therefore about 5–10 acres. It could also mean a quarter of a statute acre. Alternatively known as Fardel, Ferling, Farthing Land or Farthinghold.

A17 Ferendell. A quarter of a statute acre.

A18 Furlong. In this context, a linear measure of 220 yds. (See also under Open Field Farming).

A19 Hide. Originally the amount of land which could be ploughed in a year using one plough with an eight-ox team. The measurement therefore varied with the soil quality and could be between 60 and 180 acres. It was usually considered to hold 4 Virgates but in some areas could contain 2,3,5,6,7 or 8. In

the Domesday survey of 1086 it was used as a basis for tax assessment. Alternatively called Carucate, Husbandland, Ploughland, Ploughgate and Sulung.

A20 Hill. A Sussex land measure, amounting to half an acre.

A21 Hop Acre. The area occupied by a thousand hop plants – about half an acre.

A22 Husbandland. Generally the equivalent of a Hide (qv), but in some northern and Scottish areas could be as little as 20 acres.

A23 Irish Mile. The old measurement, before standardisation, was 6,720 ft.

A24 Knight's Fee. In this context, a variable measure which depended on the quality of soil. It was considered to be the amount of land which could support a knight and his family for a year and could vary between 4 and 48 Hides (qv).

A25 Landyard. A Somerset measure for a Rod.

A26 League. Generally a measure of about 3 miles but could be as little as 7,500 ft.

A27 Liberate. A measurement which could vary in two ways. It was an amount of land worth £1 and its area could thus vary due to the quality of the soil and the value of the pound.

A28 Lugg. A measure of 15–20 ft. Also called a Goad.

A29 Markland. An area varying between 1 and 3 acres.

A30 Math. A Herefordshire term for the area of land one man could mow in a day. Approximately 1 acre.

A31 Mile. Originally a variable measure in England between 4,854 ft and 6,600 ft. The old Scottish Mile was often 5,928 ft and the Irish Mile 6,720 ft. The standard mile of 5,280 ft was laid down in 1593.

A32 Narrow Oxgang. An Oxgang (qv); a term used to differentiate from a Broad Oxgang (qv) whtch was double the size.

A33 Nook. Two Farthingdales (qv) or nearly 20 acres. A northern or Scottish term.

A34 Oxgang. A variable measure depending on the quality of soil. It was originally the amount of land which could be cultivated in a year using one ox. It was normally considered to be one-eighth of a Hide (qv). Alternatively called a Bovate.

A35 Pace.   Approximately 5 ft or two steps.

A36 Perch.   Originally a variable measure of between 9 and 26 ft, but when standardised measured 16½ ft.

A37 Ploughland.   Equivalent to a Hide (qv). Alternatively called Ploughgate.

A38 Rod, Pole or Perch.   When standardised a measure of 16½ ft.

A39 Rood.   When standardised, a measure of 40 sq. rods. An acre consisted of 4 roods.

A40 Scottish Mile.   The old measurement, before standardisation, was usually 5,928 ft.

A41 Sulung.   A Kent term for a measure equivalent to a Hide (qv). It was divided into 4 Yokes. Alternatively spelt Suling.

A42 Tenantry Acre.   A variable measure but usually three-quarters of an acre.

A43 Verge.   In this context, a variable area of land between 15 and 30 acres.

A44 Virgate.   A variable measure depending on the quality of the soil. It was considered to be one quarter of a Hide (qv) and could measure between 15 to 60 acres, although it was generally about 30 acres. Alternatively called Yardland, Wista or Yoke.

A45 Whip Land.   Land measured out by a whip's length.

A46 Wista.   A Sussex term for a Virgate (qv).

A47 Wood Acre.   A measure of land three-eighths larger than a statute acre.

A48 Yard.   A measure which was equivalent to a quarter of an acre.

A49 Yardland.   One quarter of a Hide (qv).

A50 Yoke.   A Kent term for a quarter of a Hide (qv).

PART TWO
FIELD NAMES AND GEOGRAPHICAL FEATURES

A51 Acre.   In this context, a field of arable land.

A52 Ait.   An island in a river; an osier bed.

A53 Amad.   A hay meadow.

A54 Applegarth.   A Yorkshire term for an orchard.

A55 Assart.   A piece of woodland which has been cleared, enclosed and converted into arable land. Alternatively spelt Essart.

A56 Bache.   A stream. Alternatively spelt Batch.

A57 Bang.   A low bank serving as a boundary, or else a slope in an otherwise flat field. Alternatively called Bank or Bong.

A58 Barrow.   In this context, a grove or copse.

A59 Barth.   A sheltered pasture for young animals.

A60 Barton.   a) A barley field (from the OE *bere*, meaning barley).
   b) A farmyard.
   c) A Devonshire term for the home farm of the lord of the manor.
   d) A chicken coop.

A61 Bawn.   a) The Irish word for a cattle enclosure.
   b) A fortified enclosure.

A62 Beck.   A Danelaw county term for a stream.

A63 Belt.   A wooded stretch of land across an arable field.

A64 Berneshawe.   A barnyard.

A65 Booley.   An Irish term for a temporary enclosure used by herdsmen.

A66 Boos.   A Yorkshire term for a cowstall.

A67 Bottom.   A hollow or dell.

A68 Bourne.   A stream. In the north of England, Scotland and Ireland it is called a Burn.

A69 Brake.   Wasteland covered with brushwood.

A70 Breach. Newly cultivated land. Alternatively spelt Breech.

A71 Breck. Land enclosed from forest waste, usually on a temporary basis. Alternatively called Break or Breckland.

A72 Burgage. In this context, a small field, usually less than half an acre, a short distance from the farmhouse.

A73 Butland. Waste land.

A74 Byes. The corners or ends of fields which could not be ploughed and had to be dug by hand.

A75 Cam. A ridge on a hill, or an earthbank.

A76 Cangle. An enclosure.

A77 Cantle. A projecting corner of land.

A78 Carr. A north-country and Midland term for marshy land.

A79 Catchland. Boundary land which did not belong to any parish. The land's tithe went to the first cleric to claim it. Alternatively called Catchpole Acre.

A80 Catch-meadow. A meadow irrigated by water from a nearby slope.

A81 Chase. Hunting land reserved for the use of a local lord, or of the king.

A82 Cleugh. A deep valley or ravine. Alternatively called Clough.

A83 Close. An enclosure from the open fields.

A84 Cockshoot. A clearing cut in a wood which could be used for shooting game as it went through it. Alternatively spelt Cockshut.

A85 Coldharbour. An exposed place, or else a shelter from an exposed place.

A86 Conyger. A rabbit warren. Not until the Ground Game Act 1880 were tenant farmers permitted to kill rabbits on their own land. Alternatively called Conygree, Conyearth, Conygarth, Conyhole, Conywarren, Cunner.

A87 Co(o)mbe. A narrow valley, or hollow in the side of a hill.

A88 Cote. An enclosure for sheep or cattle.

A89 Crew(e). A small enclosure for cattle.

A90 Croft. a) Enclosed meadow or arable land, usually adjacent to a house. Alternatively called Croad, Croud, Crowd.

b) In the Highlands and Islands of Scotland, a smallholding farmed by tenants. The crofting areas were Inverness, Orkney and Shetland, Ross, Argyll, Sutherland and Caithness.

A91 Demesne. Land retained by the lord of the manor for his own use and upon which tenants gave free service according to the customs of the manor. Land which was part of the main farm of the manor.

A92 Denn. A pasture, usually for pigs.

A93 Doffhouse. A dovehouse.

A94 Dolver. An East Anglian term for land reclaimed from the fens or, more generally, marshy land.

A95 Down. A hill or expanse of hills. More particularly chalk hills permanently used for pasture.

A96 Dumble. A north-country and Midlands term for a wooded valley, or a ravine containing a stream.

A97 Dungle. A dungheap.

A98 Eddish. An enclosure. Alternatively called Etch.

A99 End. The outlying part of an estate.

A100 Ersh. A ploughed field.

A101 Ewfold. A sheepfold.

A102 Eyot(t). A small island, usually in a river.

A103 Ffridd. A Welsh term for fenced-in land near the homestead.

A104 Fit. Grassland near a river.

A105 Flash. A shallow pool.

A106 Flat(t). In this context, a piece of level ground.

A107 Flockrake. A Scottish term for a sheep pasture.

A108 Flonk. Enclosure in front of a pig-sty.

A109 Fold. A small enclosure, or else a pen, for animals.

A110 Forschel. A strip of land adjacent to a highway.

A111 Forstal. a) A small piece of waste land.
b) A paddock or farmyard.

A112 Foss(e). A ditch or trench.

A113 Freeth. A west-country and Welsh term for a hedge, especially a wattled hedge. It could also mean a gap in a hedge filled with wattle.

A114 Frith. A wooded area or a clearing in a wood.

A115 Gall. Inferior agricultural land, usually marshy.

A116 Garston. An enclosed area for cattle.

A117 Gill. A wooded valley, usually containing a stream.

A118 Glebe. Land held by a clergyman.

A119 Gospel Tree. A tree which generally marked the boundary of a parish or manor.

A120 Grange. a) Land belonging to a monastery, usually worked by tenants.
   b) A barn.

A121 Greeve. A grove. Alternatively spelt Gre(a)ve.

A122 Grip. A ditch or small watercourse.

A123 Ground. A large area of grassland lying at a distance from the farm.

A124 Gut. A stream.

A125 Gypsey. A temporary stream in a normally dry valley.

A126 Hade. A Midland term for a headland.

A127 Hafood. A Welsh term for a summer or upland pasture.

A128 Hagg. A wood, sometimes enclosed.

A129 Hale. A small corner of land. Alternatively called Hall.

A130 Half. a) A half acre.
   b) An inherited share of land.

A131 Half-Year Close. A close used for pasture in the winter.

A132 Ham. In this context: a) A narrow strip of ground by the side of a river.
   b) An enclosure, usually for pasture.

A133 Hamstal. A field adjacent to the farmhouse. Alternatively called Homestal.

A134 Hanger. A wooded hill.

A135 Hanging Field. A field on a slope.

A136 Hant. A feeding-place for cattle.

A137 Harve. An Essex term for a small plot of land near the house.

A138 Hatch. A fenced area of land.

A139 Hatchet. A field to which access is gained through a wicket gate.

A140 Haughland. A Scottish or northern term for a low-lying riverside meadow.

A141 Haw. An enclosed piece of land near a house.

A142 Hay. a) A small enclosed field; a term found in south-west England, south Wales and Northumberland.
   b) A clearing in a wood or area of scrub into which cattle were driven for identification or slaughter after being loose on a common.

A143 Headland. A strip of land at the end of a ploughed field upon which the plough turned; the headland was afterwards ploughed at right-angles. Alternatively called Hade, Harden.

A144 Heaf. A northern term for sheep pasture.

A145 Heater. An East Anglian term for a triangular piece of land.

A146 Hempland. Land, in medieval times, used for the cultvation of hemp.

A147 Hendre. A Welsh term for the land on which cattle and owners spent the winter months.

A148 Hern. An odd-shaped, small piece of land, or else land in the bend of a river. Alternatively spelt Hirn, Hyrne.

A149 Hield. A slope.

A150 Hogslease. A pig pasture. Alternatively spelt Hoggesleys.

A151 Holme. A pasture of water meadow.

A152 Holt. A grove or copse.

A153 Home Close. The field nearest the farmhouse or the close in which the house is built.

A154 Hop(e). An enclosed piece of land, especially in marshy areas.

A155 Hoppet. A small enclosure.

A156 Horselease. Meadow land used by horses.

A157 How(e). A tumulus or a natural mound.

A158 In-by Land. A northern term for the enclosed land nearest to the farmhouse. The term stems from the Scandinavian *by*, meaning farm. Alternatively called Infield.

A159 Ings. In this context, pasture by a stream.

A160 Inhams. Land enclosed from the waste. Alternatively called Inhomes.

A161 Inland. a) Land near to the farmhouse.
  b) Land enclosed and cultivated as opposed to waste or common land.

A162 Inlandes. Parts of the demesne land rented out to tenants.

A163 Innings. Marshy or flooded land which has been reclaimed. In some areas it was called Gainage if it was profitable.

A164 Intake. A piece of land which was enclosed, generally from a moor, but also from a common or waterway.

A165 Inwood. A wood in demesne land.

A166 Jack. Waste land.

A167 Keld. A northern term for a spring or a marshy area.

A168 Knap(p). A hillock.

A169 Lache. A pond.

A170 Ladder Farm. Also called a striped farm. It consisted of holdings of small ribboned fields.

A171 Laighton. A northern term for a garden. Alternatively spelt Leighton.

A172 Lake. In this context, a widespread term for a stream.

A173 Langate. A long strip of land.

A174 Laystall. An area where dung or refuse was deposited.

A175 Lea. Grassland, but quite often arable land newly laid for pasture and then ploughed up again. Alternatively spelt lay, ley, lcah, lee, ley.

A176 Lease. Meadow land, usually common. Alternatively spelt leaze.

A177 Leasow. Grassland, common or enclosed. In the west Midlands any enclosed plot; equivalent of Close or Tyning.

A178 Leat. An artificial waterway to provide water for industrial and domestic purposes. Alternatively spelt Leet.

A179 Linch Land. An unploughed strip of land serving as a boundary between fields.

A180 Lowe. Meadow land.

A181 Mailing. A northern term for a land-holding.

A182 Mains. A northern and Scottish term for demesne land.

A183 March. A border or boundary.

A184 Marksoil. A boundary mark, such as a stone.

A185 Merestake/Merestone. A boundary stake or stone.

A186 Mill Ham. A strip of ground by the side of a river.

A187 Nailbourne. A stream which ran through a normally dry valley.

A188 Nook. A secluded piece of land.

A189 Oldland. Land which was once arable but since used for pasture.

A190 Orteyard. A Cambridgeshire term for orchard.

A191 Outfield. A northern and Scottish term for land not kept in cultivation all the time, and only occasionally used for crops.

A192 Paddle. A Lincolnshire term for a riverside pasture.

A193 Park. a) Land enclosed to keep beasts for hunting – a privilege granted by the Crown.
  b) In Scotland and Ireland, land enclosed for grazing or cultivation.
  c) Demesne land, sometimes used for ornamental purposes.
  d) In south-west England, an enclosed plot of land, equivalent to a Close or Tyning.

A194 Parrock. A paddock or small enclosure.

A195 Pendicle. A Scottish term for a small piece of land sometimes attached to a large estate.

A196 Pightel. A small piece of arable land. Alternatively called Pightle, Pigtail, Pingle.

A197 Pike. A triangular piece of land.

A198 Piking. A Worcestershire term for a triangular piece of land.

A199 Pilch. A triangular piece of land.

A200 Pill. A term meaning waterway, found in Monmouthshire.

A201 Pin Fallow. Land left fallow for only part of a year, between harvest in autumn and sowing the next spring. Also called Bastard Fallow.

A202 Pingle. A Midland term for a small piece of land in the open fields, or a small enclosed field.

A203 Plack. A small field. Alternatively called Plackett or Pleck.

A204 Plashet. A marshy piece of land.

A205 Purlieu. a) Land once added unlawfully to an ancient forest.
  b) Disafforested land on the boundary of the forest.

A206 Quarter. An allotment.

A207 Quillet. A narrow strip of land, or a small croft.

A208 Rand. A Lincolnshire term for a strip of marshy land lying between a river bank and an artificial embankment running parallel to it.

A209 Rap. A west-country term for a thin strip of land.

A210 Reading. a) A clearing in a wood.
  b) Land taken in from the waste and cultivated. Alternatively called Reeding, Ridding.

A211 Reen. A major field drain which collects from smaller drains.

A212 Royd. A northern term for a clearing in a wood.

A213 Scoot. A small, oddly-shaped parcel of land.

A214 Screed. A narrow strip of land.

A215 Sentry Field. A west-country term for a field near a church which at one time had the right of Sanctuary (qv).

A216 Sheep Walk. A tract of pasture for sheep.

A217 Sherd. A clearing in a wood. Alternatively called Shord.

A218 Shieling. A Scottish term for pasture land or else for a hut built on such pasture.

A219 Shoot. A projecting nook of land.

A220 Sike. A northern term for a stream, one that usually runs dry in the summer.

A221 Slade. A valley.

A222 Slai(gh)t. Sheep pasture. Alternatively called Slei(gh)t.

A223 Slang. A narrow strip of land between fields. The term is found in the Midlands, south-west England and south Wales. Alternatively called Sling.

A224 Sling. A curved field. (See also Slang).

A225 Slip. A narrow strip of land.

A226 Slough. A marshy piece of land.

A227 Snowhill. A hill facing north which retains snow longer than other places.

A228 Spong. A Midland and East Anglian term for a narrow strip of land.

A229 Spot. A small piece of land.

A230 Stubbing A clearing; land from which tree-stumps have been removed; land which is still covered by tree-stumps. Alternatively called Stocking.

A231 Swale. Meadow land, especially in marshy areas.

A232 Swang. Swampy land.

A233 Tenement. In this context, a farm held of a superior lord; a holding of land.

A234 Thwaite. A clearing in a wood or forest.

A235 Toft. A plot of land on which a building stood, or had formerly stood. Common rights might still attach to the house even though the building had gone.

A236 Townland. The enclosed or infield part of a farm in Scotland.

A237 Township. In this context, a farm which was occupied by two farmers who worked together or divided the land between them.

A238 Tye. A small enclosure, often where three roads met.

A239 Tyning. A piece of enclosed land.

A240 Vaccary. Pasture for cattle.

A241 Velge. Fallow land.

A242 Voryer. A west-country and Welsh term for a strip of land left unploughed around the edges of an arable field.

A243 Wath. A ford, or a stream that may be forded.

A244 Waver. A village pond.

A245 Weald. A term in Kent, Surrey and Sussex for wooded country.

A246 Went. A west-country term for a part of a field, too large or hilly to be ploughed in a continuous furrow. It could also be a small part of a field separated from the rest by some barrier such as a road. Alternatively called Wentin.

A247 Wick. In this context, a dairy farm.

A248 Winterbourne. A stream running through a normally dry valley, especially in winter-time.

A249 Wong. Enclosed meadow land; low-lying land, often marshy.

A250 Wray. A nook of land. Also called Wroe.

PART THREE
OPEN FIELD FARMING

A251 General. The Open Field system of farming introduced by the Saxons is believed to have replaced the old Celtic enclosed field method in most of the country except the west, Wales and the north. Generally each locality operated a system in which there were three large fields, two of which were cultivated in any one year – the third remaining fallow. Each field was divided into strips of about one acre. There were no hedges between the strips and, usually, none between the fields either. Each farmer had strips, called Selions (qv), scattered throughout the large fields rather than in con-centrated holdings. This may have resulted from an ancient allocation of strips as they came into cultivation when woods were cleared, or else it was a way of ensuring that each farmer had a share of the good and bad land throughout the manor.

The Open Field system had drawbacks which led to its abandonment in the middle ages. Time was wasted as farmers moved from one strip to another over the whole area and, because strips were quite often reallocated each year, there was little incentive for farmers to improve the strips they temporarily held. The lack of hedges left the fields open to the spread of weeds and, furthermore, it was wasteful leaving one third of the land fallow each year.

The farmers of the open fields were able to graze their own cattle on the manor commons (see Part Four).

A252 Acre. In this context, an arable strip in a common field.

A253 Ade. A Shropshire term for a gutter or ditch which helped in the irrigation of an open arable field. Also spelt Aid.

A254 Balk. In the open fields thin, unploughed, strips called balks ran between the cultivated strips. These access paths were called waybalks or headlands if they were at right-angles to the ploughed strips or else sidebalks if parallel. More prominent balks served as grass roads and were sometimes called common or town balks. Alternatively balks were called Edges, Linchets, Meres, Reans and Walls.

A255 Broad. A wide strip of land in the common arable field.

A256 Butt. A piece of land in an open arable field which, because of the irregular shape of the field, was shorter than the normal strip.

A257 Cavel. A northern and Lincolnshire term for a division of land, or a strip in an open arable field.

A258 Champion. Open field land as distinct from land held by an individual.

A259 Co-aration. The cultivation of open fields by the community of farmers.

A260 Couture. Equivalent to a Furlong (qv). A term derived from the coulter blade of the plough.

A261 Dell. A group of Selions (qv).

A262 Fardel. A group of Selions (qv).

A263 Farren. A west-country term for a division of land in an open field.

A264 Field. The present-day fields are, more properly, closes. Before enclosure a field was a large stretch of open arable land subdivided into strips.

A265 Flat(t). A group of Selions (qv) equivalent to a Furlong (qv), or else a single Selion.

A266 Fore-Acre. A Kent term for the headland on which the plough was turned. Alternatively spelt Forical.

A267 Fother. An odd piece of land in the open field.

A268 Furhead. The headland of a field on which the plough was turned.

A269 Furlong. Originally a term to denote a furrow length in an open field, or else a rectangular block of strips. Alternatively called Couture, Dell, Flat(t), Quarentena and Sheath.
Less commonly it could mean a headland on which the plough turned.

A270 Furrow. A strip of arable land.

A271 Gore. A triangular or irregularly-shaped piece of land in an open field. It was sometimes called a Gore Acre. In Scotland it was called Gair.

A272 Headland. Untilled land, usually held in common, at the head of the strips in the open fields upon which the plough turned. Some headlands formed winding routes between the fields – the forerunners of today's lanes.

A273 Hitched Land. Part of the common arable field used especially for a different sort of crop such as turnips etc. Alternatively called Hookland.

A274 Huvvers. A Lincolnshire term for the ridges separating one tenant's land from another in the open fields.

A275 Infield–Outfield. A farming method in which the arable field, the infield, was continuously under cultivation while parts of an outlying field, the outfield, were only occasionally cultivated.

A276 Inhook. Land which was enclosed for a time in its fallow year.

A277 Laine. A southern term for an open field.

A278 Land. In this context, a Selion (qv).

A279 Lawn. In this context, a Selion (qv).

A280 Linchet. A Balk (qv).

A281 Loon. A Selion (qv).

A282 Marrows. A partnership for ploughing open field strips.

A283 Meer. A boundary strip, ditch or bank between fields or furlongs which was often marked out by boundary stones. Alternatively spelt Mere and Mear.

A284 Ming Land. A Midland term for land of different owners lying intermixed in an open field.

A285 Moss Rooms. A Cheshire term for strips of peat-moss fields which were held in common.

A286 Paull. A Selion (qv).

A287 Quarentena. Equivalent to a Furlong (qv).

A288 Quillet. An open stretch of land farmed jointly by several farmers.

A289 Rap. A Selion (qv).

A290 Rean. A Balk (qv).

A291 Ridge. A Selion (qv).

A292 Rig and Rennal. A Scottish term for an open field system.

A293 Selion. A cultivated strip in an open field. It was ploughed in such a manner that the strip became a ridge with furrows on either side acting as drains.

A294 Sheath. A north-country term for a group of Selions (qv) in an open field; equivalent to a Furlong (qv).

A295 Shot. A Selion (qv).

A296 Stadium. A Furlong (qv).

A297 Stitch. A Selion (qv). Alternatively called Stetch.

A298 Stitch-meal. Land in separated pieces; groups of Stitches (qv).

A299 Wall. A Balk or Meer (qv).

A300 Wandale. A Yorkshire term for a strip of open field.

A301 Wong. In the Danelaw counties a furrow length in an open field. Alternatively, enclosed land among the open strips.

PART FOUR
COMMONS

Common Rights

A302 Adjustment of Rights. A term used in the Commons Act 1876 to mean the determination of common rights and any modification of them.

A303 Bote. The right of manorial tenants to take material from the common for their use. See Cartbote, Estover, Firebote, Foldbote, Haybote, Housebote and Ploughbote.

A304 Cartbote. The right to take wood from the commons to make or repair carts.

A305 Cattlegait/Cattlegate. The right to pasture a fixed number of animals on the common or else on private land in which the owner of the beasts had no monetary interest. Each eligible tenant of the manor was given a fixed 'gate' on the common, that is, the number of animals he was allowed to pasture. Alternatively called Beastgate, Cowgate, Horsegate, Kinegate, Oxgate, Sheepgate or Stint.

A306 Common Appendant. The right to the use of a common which was attached to the occupancy of a piece of land.

A307 Common Appurtenant. The right to the use of a common which was based on possession of land or buildings, but did not rest on actual tenure. This could extend over several lordships and was a right usually obtained by special grant. The right could also permit the pasturing of non-commonable animals such as pigs and goats.

A308 Common in Gross. The right to the use of a common which was attached to a man's person; it was not based on his occupancy of land or buildings. The right could extend to tenants of adjoining manors.

A309 Common of Pasture. The right to pasture cattle on common land.

A310 Common of Piscary. The right to fish in manorial waters.

A311 Common of Shack. The right of tenants responsible for the yearly crop to turn their beasts on to the fields after the crop had been harvested.

A312 Common of Turbary. The right to dig on common land for peat or turf for fuel.

A313 Common of Vicinage. Where manors adjoined and where common lands merged, the right to have one's cattle stray on to the other manor's land without molestation.

A314 Commons. The right of pasturing beasts on the common land.

A315 Cow Leaze. In this context, the right to pasture cattle on the common lands.

A316 Driving. The annual right of the lord of the manor to examine animals pastured on the commons to ensure that their owners had common rights.

A317 Estover. A Norman-French term for the right to take wood from common lands for fuel or for the repair of houses or implements.

A318 Falcage. A Scottish term for the right to mow the commons.

A319 Firebote. The right to take wood from the commons for fuel. Alternatively spelt Ferbote.

A320 Foldbote. The right to take wood from the commons to make sheep folds.

A321 Freedom. The right to pasture cattle on commons.

A322 Haybote. The right to take wood from the commons to make or repair fences. Alternatively called Heybote or Hedgebote.

A323 Housebote. The right to take wood from the commons to build or repair houses.

A324 Levant and Couchant. The right to pasture cattle on the commons.

A325 Pannage. The right to feed pigs in the manorial woods, or the payment made for that right.

A326 Ploughbote. The right to take wood from the commons to make or repair ploughs.

A327 Stint. The number of cattle which a holder of common rights was allowed to pasture on the commons or on a portion of a common. Generally the word 'gate' was used in northern England, and 'stint' in the south.

A328 Stray. The right to have one's cattle stray on to the common land without molestation.

Common Terms

A329 Approvement. The enclosure of common land or waste.

A330 Carr. In this context, common land, usually of a marshy nature.

A331 Chart. A Kent and Surrey term for a rough common.

A332 Dalt. A share of the common field. Alternatively called Doat or Dole.

A333 Doles. Portions of the common meadows allocated to the tenants of the related open arable fields. The portions were sometimes allocated by lot or rotation, and tenants were entitled to the hay from their portions. Alternatively called Dales or Lot Meadows.

A334 Field Garden Allotments. Parts of a common, not more than a quarter of an acre each, let to the poor of the parish.

A335 Folk Land. Common land.

A336 Ham. In this context, a common pasture.

A337 Ings. Common meadows.

A338 Inter-Common. Common land shared by adjoining manors.

A339 Lammas Lands. Common land on which manorial tenants were permitted to pasture their beasts from Lammas Day until sowing time. Alternatively called Half-Year Land.

A340 Leaze. Common land on which manorial tenants could pasture their beasts. Alternatively spelt Lease.

A341 Lot Meadows. Portions of common meadow allocated to manorial tenants by lot. Alternatively called Doles and Rotation Meadows.

A342 Minnis. A southern term for a high common or tract of moor.

A343 Noman's Land. A small piece of common land without an owner, often on a boundary. Alternatively called Jack's Land.

A344 Playstow. A village green used for assemblies and recreation.

A345 Pleck. Waste or common land.

A346 Score. A Cheshire and Lancashire term for common pasture.

A347 Several(ty). A portion of common assigned for a period to a particular occupier.

A348 Shifting Severalties. The system of changing the occupancy of portions of the common meadow by lot or rotation.

A349 Squatter. A person who encloses common land and builds on it without the permission of the manor court.

A350 Surcharge. To overstock the common pasture with cattle.

A351 Tenantry Field. A commonly-held field.

A352 Tye. A southern term for a large common.

A353 Ward. The closing of the common meadows so that sowing may begin.

A354 Waste. Land used commonally by tenants, usually on manor boundaries.

Legislation

A355 Statute of Merton 1235. This authorised manorial lords to enclose portions of the commons and wastes provided that sufficient pasture remained for his tenants.

A356 Statute of Westminster 1285. This authorised manorial lords to enclose commons and wastes where the common rights belonged to tenants from other manors.

A357 First private Enclosure Act 1607. The first known private Act related to some parishes in Herefordshire.

A358 Enclosure Acts 1760–1797. During this period about 1500 private Enclosure Acts were passed by Parliament.

A359 General Enclosure Act 1801. This Act obviated in most cases the need for private Enclosure Acts, which were costly and time-consuming.

A360 Enclosure by Consent 1836. Legislation this year authorised enclosure if two-thirds of the interested parties agreed.

A361 Enclosure Act 1854. This Act established the Enclosure Commissioners to consider applications. The Commissioners, who reported to Parliament, were also authorised to allocate common land for 'exercise and recreation'.

A362 Metropolitan Commons Act 1866. This gave power to Enclosure Commissioners within the Metropolitan police district, on the application of 12 or more commoners or ratepayers, to authorise a scheme for the regulation of a common.

A363 Commons Preservation Society. This was formed in 1865 to safeguard commons on behalf of commoners and the public. Its major early battles were concerned with areas in the vicinity of London such as Hampstead Heath, and Wimbledon, Putney and Wandsworth Commons. Its activities were complemented on a smaller scale by the Kyrle Society (1878) and the Metropolitan Public Gardens Association (1882) which pressed for the preservation of urban open space such as burial grounds, village greens etc.

A364 Curtailment of enclosures 1876. Legislation this year prohibited enclosure of common land unless the Enclosure Commissioners considered that this would be to the benefit of the community.

A365 Commons Act 1899. This authorised District Councils to supervise commons if the lord of the manor, or tenants representing one-third in value of the common right holders, agreed.

A366 Law of Property Act 1925. This legislation gave the public right of access to any common or waste land in borough or urban districts.

A367 Commons Registration Act 1965. This legislation required the registration of all common lands and village greens in England and Wales before 2nd January 1970.

PART FIVE
CONVEYANCE OR TRANSFER OF LAND AND PROPERTY

A368 Conveyance of Freehold property.
Freehold tenures in which the owner could dispose of the property without hindrance, were conveyed by 'livery of seisin'. This involved the vendor, before a witness, presenting the purchaser with a turf from the land in question, symbolising the transfer of ownership. Usually this act was recorded on the deed of conveyance, sometimes called an indenture of feoffment. The purchaser paid an entry fee, called a Relief, to the feudal tenant-in-chief. This could sometimes be circumvented by the freeholder conveying the property to several people who, ostensibly, were the owners, but who held it for the use of the original owner. The prevalence of this legal manoeuvre caused a loss of revenue to the Crown and the introduction of the Statute of Uses 1535 which made the original freeholder the actual owner and liable for the Relief. In the same year the Statute of Enrolments made enrolment of conveyances compulsory and prohibited secret conveyancing. Alternatively the freeholder could lease his land, usually for a year, to an occupier who had entered it by a deed of grant (a Release), holding for himself a future interest (a Reversion), which was an incorporeal hereditament, and which could be conveyed without livery of seisin. Eventually a freeholder was able to sell his reversion without the necessity of a Relief. This Lease and Release procedure was in general use until 1841.

A369 Conveyance of Entailed Property. Some freehold tenures were classified as Fee Simple Conditional where inheritance could be, for example, restricted to male heirs. In 1285 this kind of tenure was made entailed and the owner was unable to sell it at all. This situation led to fictitious legal actions so that the land could be sold.

A370 Conveyance of Copyhold Property. The conveyance was recorded on the manor court rolls and a copy given to the purchaser, hence the word 'copyhold'. When a copyhold was sold it was 'surrendered' and when it was mortgaged this was termed a 'conditional surrender'. The mortgage was recorded on the court rolls but the mortgagee was not admitted to the property. On repayment of the mortgage a warrant of satisfaction was given to the mortgagor.

A371 Alienation. The transfer of property.

A372 Conditional Surrender. A term usually applied to the mortgage of copyhold property.

A373 Demise. To convey a property by lease.

A374 Enfeoff. a) To put a tenant legally in possession of a property. Alternatively spelt Infeoff.
  b) To surrender a property.

A375 Fine. A money payment made to the manorial lord by an incoming tenant.

A376 Grasson. A money payment made to the manorial lord on the transfer of a copyhold property.

A377 Quia Emptores. A Statute passed in 1289/90 which enacted that land alienated by a manorial lord was held of the Crown.

A378 Relief. A money payment made to the manorial lord by an incoming tanant.

A379 Surrender. To convey a copyhold property.

PART SIX
INHERITANCE

A380 Borough English. A custom whereby the youngest son was considered to be the legal heir, or in cases of the deceased having no issue, his youngest brother inherited. It was officially abolished in 1922–25.

A381 Chattels. Personal property. Chattels real are landholdings excluding freeholds, and chattels personal are movable goods.

A382 Corporeal Hereditaments. Tangible estate such as land, buildings etc as contrasted with Incorporeal Hereditaments such as rights and privileges.

A383 Curtesy of England. This allowed a widower to hold his deceased wife's land if they had a child still to attain his majority. The husband was allowed to retain the holding even if he remarried in the meantime. It was abolished in 1925.

A384 Devise. A term used to leave, by will, landed property. The term 'bequeath' is used in the case of personal property.

A385 Diem Clausit Extremum. The term for an order authorising an inquiry into the lands held by a Tenant-in-Chief (qv) on his death.

A386 Dower. Before the 12th century the term could denote the gift from a husband to his bride on the morning of their marriage. It came to mean that part of the estate a widow could claim for life or until her remarriage. This portion was usually one-third. A Dower House is a term for a house allocated to a widow.

A387 Escheat. The reversion to the lord or the Crown of an estate. This occurred when the tenant died without heirs, or where the heir had not yet attained his majority, or else where the tenant had committed an offence which incurred the forfeiture of his estate.

The Crown appointed Escheators to collect revenues from these escheated estates. These officers were introduced in 1195, mainly as a check on the sheriffs, and after a period of limited activity they were appointed for each county or group of counties.

Escheats were abolished in 1925.

A388 Farleu. A money payment made instead of a Heriot (qv). Alternatively called Farley.

A389 Freebench. The right of a widow to a share in her late husband's copyhold lands, either for life or until her remarriage. It corresponded to Dower in the case of freehold lands.

A390 Gavelkind. A custom by which a tenant's estate, other than the widow's dower (which could be up to a half portion), was divided in cases of intestacy equally among his sons, or for want of them, among his daughters. This custom was prevalent in Kent and in some parts of Middlesex, Dorset and Wales. Other features of the custom were that a tenant was of age at 15, and the estate could not be escheated (qv) in cases of felony but only when there were no heirs. It was abolished in 1925.

A391 Harrial. A Cumberland term for Heriot (qv).

A392 Hereditament. a) Real property which before 1926 would have descended to an heir in cases of intestacy.

b) Any property which may be inherited.

A393 Hereyeld. A Scottish term for Heriot (qv).

A394 Heriot. The obligation, derived from Saxon times, of an heir to return to the lord the military apparel of a deceased tenant, on the premise that it was originally supplied by the lord. The apparel, depending on the status of the tenant, could include a horse, harness and weapons. This obligation applied to both freemen and villeins but in later periods tended to be related to copyhold tenures only. About the time of the Norman Conquest the custom was being superseded by the gift of the best beast by the heir and this later became a money payment instead and, in effect, a fee to enter the land. It was abolished in 1922.

A395 Inquisition Post Mortem. An inquiry into the possessions, services and succession of a deceased person who held land of the Crown.

A396 Jointure. Estate or income settled on a widow for the period in which she survives her husband, or until her remarriage.

A397 Last Heir. The party, usually the Crown or the manorial lord, who received land by Escheat (qv).

A398 Livery of Seisin. The infant heir of a Tenant-in-Chief (qv) of the Crown had to sue Livery of Seisin in order to obtain possession of his father's estate. (See A368).

A399 Moiety. Usually a half portion of an estate.

A400 Mort D'Ancestor, Assize of. A system originating from the Assize of Northampton 1176, which ensured that lords admitted a tenant's heirs upon his death. At this time only close relatives were eligible to inherit automatically, but this was modified in the 13th century when more distant relations were admitted.

A401 Nonage. The condition of being under age.

A402 Personalty. Personal property which is bequeathed by testament and does not necessarily pass to the principal heir of the estate.

A403 Primer Seisin. The right of the Crown to take from the heir of a Tenant-in-Chief (qv) one full year's profits if the heir was of full age.

A404 Primogeniture. The custom or right whereby the eldest son was heir to the real estate of his father in the case of intestacy, to the exclusion of his own brothers and sisters. This was abolished in 1925.

A405 Regrant. The term commonly used in manor court rolls to denote a lord giving land back to the heirs of a deceased tenant. The regranting was normally conditional upon the payment of a fee such as a Relief (qv).

A406 Relief. A payment made by an incoming tenant to succeed to his inheritance. This payment raised up and re-established (relieved) the inheritance. In Saxon and early Norman times the term was generally used where the tenure, such as a Knight's Fee (qv), had military obligations. The payment varied with the size of the estate – eg 100 shillings for a Knight's Fee, or a year's rent for a smaller holding. The custom was abused by Crown and tenants-in-chief alike and was eventually regulated by *Magna Carta*. Reliefs were collected until 1661.

A407 Remainder. In a will, entitlement to an estate dependent upon the termination of another ownership or tenancy. The term may be applied also to personal estate.

A408 Soul Scot. An ecclesiastical Heriot (qv). In some parishes the lord of the manor took a heriot consisting of the best chattel, and the parish church was entitled to the second-best.

A409 Wardship and Marriage. The Crown was entitled to hold the land of a Tenant-in-Chief (qv) after his death until his heir had attained his majority – for a boy this was 21, and for a girl 14, except in the case of Gavelkind tenure (qv). The Crown received the revenues of the estate until the heir came of age and quite frequently farmed this wardship out to the highest bidder. The Crown was also entitled to control the marriage of a ward, as well as that of the widow.

PART SEVEN
TENANTS AND TENURES

A410 Agist. Land let out in the summer to graze cattle at a fixed price per head.

A411 Akerman. A tenant holding an acre.

A412 Al(l)odium. A term to describe some estates in Hampshire, Kent, Surrey, Sussex and Berkshire. It is thought by some authorities that the term, found in the Domesday Survey of 1086, referred to holdings which were not subject to an overlord, and for which no services were given. However, Professor Maitland in his *'Domesday Book and Beyond'* maintains that there is scant evidence for this suggestion.

A413 Allotment. In this context, a term which referred to land distributed by the Enclosure Commissioners in exchange for rights and holdings held in the open-field system. It could also mean land given to a parish or manor official.

A414 Ancient Demesne. Land which belonged to the Crown during the reigns of Edward the Confessor and William I; it is described as *terrae regis (Eduardi)* in the Domesday Survey. The tenants were exempt from the jurisdiction of the shire reeve and were not liable to serve on juries and inquests outside the manor; they were not taxed for the upkeep of roads and bridges and were free from market tolls. The tenants could only be sued or sue on matters affecting their lands in the Court of Common Pleas or in the Court of Ancient Demesne of the manor. The tenure was abolished in 1925.

A415 Anilepman. A sub-tenant on a small-holding.

A416 Basket Tenure. The tenant of this holding was required to make baskets for the Crown.

A417 Bond Tenants. A name sometimes given to copyholders or other customary tenants.

A418 Bookland. A Saxon term for land held by title deed or by 'book' of the Crown. The tenants were probably exempt from a number of public services such as defence and bridge-building. Alternatively called Charterland and Deedland.

A419 Borough English. A widespread form of tenure in which it was customary for the youngest son to inherit. It was abolished in 1924.

A420 Burgage. A tenure in an ancient borough which was held of the Crown or the lords of the borough. In Saxon times the rent was called a landgable or hawgable. The land or tenement was held subject to the customary rents and services of the borough. It was sometimes called Burgage Holding in Scotland.

A421 Chivalry. An alternative name for a Knight's Fee (qv).

A422 Copyhold. Originally a tenure dependent upon custom and the lord's will, carrying obligations to perform certain services for the lord. The Black Death in the 14th century brought about a scarcity of labour and hastened the commutation of these feudal services to money payments. The tenant was protected not by national law but by title written on the manor court rolls, of which he was provided with a copy – hence the name of the tenure. When transferring the property the tenant first surrendered it to the lord who held the fee-simple, and then the new tenant was admitted on payment of a fine. Copyhold tenure was abolished in 1922. Alternatively called Tenancy by Copy and Tenancy by the Verge.

A423 Cottier. An annual tenure, the main feature being that the land was let direct to a labourer who made the highest public bid for it.

A424 Customary Freehold. Land held by custom and not by the will of the lord – in this it differed from Copyhold tenure. The tenure was abolished in 1922. Alternatively called Frank Tenure.

A425 Demesne. Land of the manor held in the lord's own hands. The villein tenants, as part of their obligations in return for their own land holdings, had to work regularly on the demesne lands.

A426 Disseisin. Unlawful dispossession of a person's house or land.

A427 Engrossment. The drawing together of two or more holdings into one.

A428 Farm. Before its modern agricultural meaning, the term could denote land let on lease.

A429 Fee. Land or freehold property which could be inherited.

A430 Fee-Farm Rents. In this context, a term which describes a group of Crown revenues, amongst which borough rents are the most significant. The chief residents of a borough paid the Exchequer a fixed sum for the privilege of collecting and retaining the borough's revenues.

A431 Fee Simple. A freehold estate which passes without restriction to the lawful heir.

A432 Feudal Tenure. A tenure of land originally subject to military service, later commuted to money payments.

A433 Frank Fee. A tenure which required no services. Sometimes called an Improper Feud.

A434 Frankalmoign. Land granted by a layman to an ecclesiastical body which then received any income derived from it. Usually the gift was conditional upon the provision of a chantry after the donor's death, or the offer of obits and prayers for his and his decendants' souls in perpetuity. The tenure was free of manorial services except for the *Trinoda Necessitas* (qv), and was abolished in 1925.

A435 Frankmarriage. A tenure with an entailed interest. It arose in cases where a land-owner granted land to a man marrying his daughter or sister. The couple were then possessed of the land exempt from any services to the donor and this applied until the fourth generation had held the tenure.

A436 Free Warren. A franchise obtained from the Crown empowering the grantees to kill or keep game and beasts.

A437 Freehold. A tenure which was not subject to the customs of the manor or the will of the lord and which could be disposed of without restriction. Alternatively called Frank Tenement or Freeland.

A438 Glebe. Land assigned to the incumbent of a parish as part of his benefice and the endowment of the church.

A439 Glebae Adsciptitii. Villein tenants who could not be removed from their holdings as long as they performed the services due from them.

A440 Head-Right. The right granted to emigrants to acquire land where they were going to settle, usually in the USA.

A441 Joint Enfeoffment. The settlement of a property jointly on a man and his wife, a device which allowed a widow to escape paying an entry fee for the tenure on the death of her husband.

A442 King's Widow. A widow of a Tenant-in-Chief (qv). She was unable to marry again without the Crown's permission.

A443 Knight's Fee. A feudal tenure which obliged the holder to provide military assistance to the Crown. This military service would normally require a fully-armed knight and his servants for forty days a year. The tenure was quite often commuted to a money payment and was finally abolished in 1660 by the Tenures Abolition Act. Alternatively called Knight's Service.

A444 Lay Fee. Land held of a lay lord rather than of an ecclesiastical body.

A445 Leasehold. Tenure held by lease, sometimes for a fixed number of years, or for a certain number of 'lives' recorded in the original lease. When one of the 'lives' died a new name could be inserted into the lease on payment of a fee.

A446 Mesnalty. An estate held by a mesne lord who held the land directly of the Crown.

A447 Mortmain. A term meaning 'dead hand', in this case, of the Church. When land was granted by laymen to ecclesiastical bodies it became free of escheats, reliefs etc and this resulted in a loss of income to the manorial lord both at that time and for the forseeable future. When Henry III revised the *Magna Carta* in 1217 he prohibited the transfer of land to an ecclesiastical body without the lord's permission in an effort to control this 'dead hand' on income. Further legislation in 1279 added penalties for causing land to come under Mortmain.

A448 Overland. A west-country term for a tenure which had no common rights attached to it.

A449 Plight. A holding of land.

A450 Purpresture. An illegal tenure which occurred when Crown lands were encroached upon. The offence could mean the forfeiture of the encroacher's land but often the offence was merely noted and a rent levied.

A451 Quit Rent. A fixed annual rent which released a tenant from feudal services to a manorial lord.

A452 Rack-rent. The highest rent that a tenement will fetch in a year, or at least two thirds of this.

A453 Reveland. Crown land in the hands of a sheriff, reeve, bailiff or other deputy.

A454 Sac and Soc. A jurisdiction claimed by lords as part of their manorial tenure. It included a right to hold a court, and to receive manorial profits and services.

A455 Seisin. A term meaning possession rather than ownership which probably pre-dates the Norman Conquest. A grant of land was valid only when the tenant had been given livery of seisin – a symbolic gift, such as a piece of turf from the land in question, by the outgoing tenant or by the lord of the manor. The new tenant was then 'seised in deed'. Before this procedure the incoming tenant was 'seised in law'. A tenant was said to be seized of his land if he possessed it and disseized when dispossessed.

A456 Serjeanty. A tenure dependent upon a wide variety of services, some 'grand' and some 'petty'. Grand Serjeants did military service and paid fines; most serjeants performed personal services for their lord – the king, for example, might make serjeants of his tailor, physician or gamekeeper.

A457 Socage. A free tenure without the obligation of military service. The holding could be alienated by the tenant and inherited without restriction, although primogeniture was the most common rule of inheritance. The heir paid a fee to enter the land. Socage was of two kinds: free socage, where the services were honourable and fixed, and villein socage, where the services were of a humbler nature and fixed. It was abolished in 1660.

A458 Soiled Land. Land converted from freehold to copyhold tenure.

A459 Tenancy at Will. A tenure granted by the lord and at his disposal. It was mainly granted by the Crown to reward servants.

A460 Tenant-in-Chief. A tenant who held land immediately of the Crown. Alternatively known as Tenant-in-Capite.

A461 Termor. A tenant for a term of years.

A462 Tontine. A financial scheme in which subscribers to a common fund each secured an annuity during his lifetime; the value of each annuity increased as subscribers died until one person enjoyed the whole income. A tontine was a popular device in the 18th and 19th centuries to provide a public amenity, such as a village hall.

b) More generally, an 18th-century method to raise governmental funds. Money was invested by private individuals in a scheme and the surviving subscribers received a gradually increasing income.

A463 Undersettle. A sub-tenant of a small-holding.

PART EIGHT
AGRICULTURAL HISTORY

A464 Agricultural History.

17th cent.	Potatoes, turnips and red clover introduced.
c1700	Jethro Tull's seed drill and horse hoes.
c1710	James Miekle's winnowing fans in Scotland.
1716	Turnips grown on large scale in Scotland.
1747	Sugar extracted from beet in Germany.
1767	Francis Moore's steam engine for ploughing.
c1770	James Sharp's winnowing machine.
1786	Mangolds introduced from France.
1804	Guano introduced for fertilising.
1822	Rotary digging machine.
1836	Combine harvesters in USA.
1850	Horses work buttermaking churns.
1851	Reaping machine introduced.
1879	Mechanical separators for milk.
1880–95	Milking machines introduced.
1882	Bacillus of bovine TB discovered.
1886	Control of anthrax initiated.
1896	Bacillus of contagious abortion of cattle discovered.
1899	Oil-driven tractor introduced.
1910	King Edward potato introduced.

PART NINE
AGRICULTURAL ORGANISATIONS

A465 Agricultural Organisations.

1774	Bath and West of England Agricultural Society.
1791	Veterinary College in London.
1793	Board of Agriculture.
1798	Smithfield Show.
1822	Board of Agriculture wound up.
1833	Royal Jersey Agricultural and Horticultural Society.
1838	English Agricultural Society, later the Royal Agricultural Society of England.
1842	The Farmers' Club.
1843	Rothamsted Experimental Station.
1845	Royal Agricultural College at Cirencester.
1872	National Agricultural Labourers' Union.

Bibliography

1878   English Jersey Cattle Society.
1889   New Board of Agriculture.
1907   National Cattle Breeders' Association.
1908   Lincs. Farmers' Union which within a
       year was to develop into the National
       Farmers' Union.
1909   British Friesian Cattle Society.
1919   Board of Agriculture becomes Ministry
       of Agriculture.

PART TEN
BIBLIOGRAPHY

Medieval Farming Glossary, John Fisher (1968)
Hedges and Local History, M. D. Hooper (1971 repr. 1976 NCSS)
English Field Names: A Dictionary, John Field (1972, repr. 1982)
Studies of Field Systems in the British Isles, Eds. A. R. H. Baker and R. A. Butlin (1973)
The origins of open-field agriculture, ed Trevor Rowley (1981)
Studies in the Agrarian history of England in the thirteenth century, E. A. Kominsky (1956)
Trees and Woodland in the British Landscape, O. Rackham (1976)
The Making of the English Landscape, W. G. Hoskins (1955)
Interpreting the Landscape, M. A. Aston (1985)
Fieldwork in Local History, W. G. Hoskins (2nd ed 1982)
A Farm Dictionary, D. H. Chapman
The Open Fields, C. S. Orwin
The Agriculture Revolution – Changes in Agriculture 1650–1880, G. E. Mingay (1977)
Agricultural Records AD220–1958, J. M. Stratton (1969)
Ancient Fields, H. C. Bowen (1961)
History of the English Agricultural Labourer, W. Hasbach (1908)
History of the English Agricultural Labourer 1870–1920, F. E. Green (1920)
The Agrarian History of Farming in England 1500–1640, ed. Joan Thirsk
History of British Agriculture 1846–1914, C. S. Orwin and E. H. Whetham (1964)
A History of Farm Buildings in England and Wales, Nigel Harvey (1984)
Village and Farmstead: A History of Rural Settlement in England, Christopher Taylor (1983)
Old Farm Implements, P. Wright (1961)
The English Farmhouse and Cottage, M. W. Harley (1967)

Commons
The Commons Open Spaces and Footpaths Preservation Society 1865–1965, W. H. Williams (1965)
Common Lands of England and Wales, W. G. Hoskins and Sir Dudley Stamp (1963)

Enclosures
A Domesday of English Enclosure Acts and Awards, W. E. Tate, ed by M. E. Turner (1978)
Common Fields and Enclosure in England 1450–1850, J. A. Yelling (1977)
The Enclosure and Redistribution of our Land, W. H. R. Curtler (1920)
Common Land and Inclosure, E. C. K. Gonner (1966)

SECTION B
The Local Community

PART ONE
TITLES AND CLASSES OF SOCIETY

B1 Akerman. A small tenant holding an acre of land.

B2 Alien. In this context, one who had not been granted privileges by the Crown and who was unable to hold or inherit land.

B3 Armiger. Strictly speaking, a person entitled to bear a coat of arms, but also a term used to denote a Gentleman or an Esquire.

B4 Atheling. The Anglo-Saxon term to denote a relative of the king and, as a consequence, in control of large areas.

B5 Baronet. An hereditary title created in 1611, superior to that of a knight, but not of peerage rank. He is addressed as 'Sir' and after his surname the abbreviation 'Bart.' is used. His wife is addressed as Lady and his children as Mr, Miss or Mrs.

B6 Bordar. A villein cottager and one of the lowest ranks in feudal society. He had some land for subsistence but he was obliged to perform agricultural and menial services for the lord free or for a fixed sum.

B7 Burgess. (a) A citizen of a borough having full municipal rights.
(b) A Member of Parliament for a borough or corporate town.

B8 Ceorl. An Old English term for a free peasant ranking above a Serf but below a Thane or Gesith. He was obliged to do military service and keep up bridges and defences. The monetary value put on his life (wergild), was usually 200 shillings. After the Norman Conquest his status declined to that of a Bordar, or Villein. Alternatively called Carl, Carlot, Churl.

B9 Cottar. A cottager, sometimes with a smallholding. He was obliged to labour on the lord's land either free or for a fixed sum.

B10 Dame. A style of address which was once applied to the wives of baronets and knights, or else to the wives of prominent citizens, or merely to elderly women.

B11 Denizen. An alien admitted to citizenship by royal letters patent. He was able to hold and devise land, but not to inherit it; neither could he hold public office.

B12 Electioner. A person eligible to be elected to a parish office.

B13 Eorl. An Anglo-Saxon aristocrat, sometimes synonymous with Ealdorman, who was in charge of a shire.

B14 Esquire. Originally an attendant to a knight or lord and responsible for carrying shield and armour. The term later denoted a status above that of a Gentleman, but in the 19th century became merely a courtesy title.

B15 Foreigner. A resident of a town who was not a citizen or, more specifically, not a member of a guild.

B16 Franklin. A free tenant, usually of the wealthier sort; the predecessor of the Yeoman.

B17 Freeman. (a) A tenant who held his land of the lord at a fixed rent and without the obligation of feudal services.

(b) Before the Municipal Corporations Act 1835, a citizen entitled to claim a share of the profits of his city or borough, and to claim exemption from tolls. The title is now an honorary one conferred by a city or corporation.

(c) A man who has served his apprenticeship and is thus free to pursue his trade in his locality.

B18 Gebur. An Old English term for a free peasant within the strata of society called Ceorls (qv), having a status between that of Geneat and Cottar. The monetary value placed on his life (wergild) was 200 shillings. Subsequently the term was shortened to the uncomplimentary 'Boor'.

B19 Geneat. An Old English term for a free peasant within the strata of society called Ceorls (qv), having a status superior to that of a Gebur (qv). The monetary value placed on his life (wergild) was 200 shillings. In the Middle Ages his equivalent was a Radknight (qv).

B20 Gentleman. In this context, a well-born man above the rank of yeoman, usually entitled to bear a coat of arms. It was assumed that a Gentleman did not do manual work and the term gradually encompassed all those in the professions.

B21 Gesith. A companion to the king and part of his household and warband; he was rewarded with gifts of land. In the Teutonic kingdoms of England, excepting Kent, the Gesith was an aristocrat. By the 9th century the term was replaced by that of Thane. The monetary value placed on his life (wergild) was 1,200 shillings.

B22 Hold. A Scandinavian term used in Northumbria in the 10th and 11th centuries to denote a nobleman.

B23 Husbandman. A tenant farmer.

B24 Intrante. A person admitted to live and trade within a city or borough on payment of an annual fine.

B25 Knight. Knights were originally obliged to perform military service in exchange for the lands granted to them (Knight's Fees). This duty was gradually commuted to a regular fine called 'scutage'. A knight and his wife are styled Sir and Lady.

B26 Lackland. A person who owned no land.

B27 Laet. A social group in Kent in Anglo-Saxon times, between free and servile status. Its members had the rights of a free peasant but had to perform some villein services.

B28 Laird. A Scottish and north-country term for a lord or large landowner.

B29 Mesne Lord. A lord who held land directly of the Crown and who was above other lords in status.

B30 Miss and Mrs. Originally Miss was a style of address for a man's mistress. Other women, married or unmarried, in the same social class as a man who was addressed as 'Mr', were styled Mrs. By the 18th century Miss was used to denote a young spinster bride and Mrs to denote an older or married woman.

B31 Mr. An abbreviation of the word Master, and originally a style of address for a Gentleman. In 19th-century directories however, Mr. usually denotes a tradesman or someone who had no claim to be called gentry.

B32 Neife. A villein (qv).

B33 Nobility. The five ranks of peerage in descending order of precedence are Duke, Marquess, Earl, Viscount and Baron (Lord). They may be summarised as follows:

Duke: The first Dukedom in England was created in 1337 when the Black Prince was created Duke of Cornwall. The title then took precedence over other noble titles. His wife is known as a duchess, his eldest son takes his father's second title, and the younger children are addressed as Lord or Lady before their christian names. The term Duke derives from the word *dux*, meaning leader of an army.

Marquess: The first Marquess was appointed in 1385. Except on formal occasions he and his wife are referred to as Lord and Lady, and their children as Lord and Lady before their christian names. The term Marquess (Marquis in France) is derived from those barons who held and guarded lands on the borders or *marches* of a kingdom.

Earl: Before the Norman Conquest the Earl was the highest rank of nobility and acted as the king's representative in charge of a shire; subsequently the title denoted a dignity rather than a function. The wife of an earl is a countess but except on formal occasions he and his wife are addressed as Lord and Lady. His eldest son takes his father's second title, the younger sons are styled 'Honourable', and the daughters as Lady before their christian names.

Viscount: The first Viscount in the English nobility was created in 1440, but previously the term denoted a sheriff of a county acting as deputy to the Earl of the shire; the word derived from the Latin *vicecomes*. A Viscount and his wife are styled Lord and Lady.

Baron: The title Baron, more commonly styled Lord, is the most numerous rank in the nobility. A greater baron was one summoned by direct writ to the king's council, and a lesser baron was one who was summoned via the county sheriff. Peers of the realm are the successors to the greater barons. A baron and his wife are styled Lord and Lady, and his children 'The Honourable' on formal occasions and Mr, Miss and Mrs otherwise. A peeress (Baroness) in her own right who marries a commoner retains her title, but a peeress by marriage loses her title on remarriage.

B34 Peder. A Lincolnshire term for a Cottar (qv) or cottager.

B35 Radknight. A tenant who gave service on horseback to his lord as an obligation of his landholding.

B36 Regardant Villein. A person who performed the lowest manorial services but was annexed to the lord's manor rather than to his person. He was distinct in this from a Villein in Gross, who was transferable from one owner to another.

B37 Serf. An inhabitant with a status lower than that of a Villein (qv), who was annexed to the lord's person and could be sold to another person. His freedom was obtained when the lord granted a release called Manumission.

B38 Slave. In this country slaves officially became free in 1772.

B39 Socman. A free tenant.

B40 Sojourner. A temporary resident in a parish.

B41 Squire. A common term for a lord of the manor, or a principal landowner.

B42 Stranger. A new resident.

B43 Thane. An Old English term for one who was part of the king's or a lord's household and his military elite. The word seems to have superseded the term Gesith in the 9th century. The Thane had a monetary value on his life (wergild) of 1,200 shillings. Alternatively spelt Thegn.

B44 Theow. An Anglo-Saxon slave, either a conquered native or an Anglo-Saxon felon. He had no rights whatsoever.

B45 Thrall. A Slave.

B46 Vassal. A person who held land of a lord and swore fealty to him.

B47 Vavassor. A term dating from the Norman Conquest to denote a free tenant of high status but with less land than that held by a baron, and who had military obligations to his lord. The word was used in Danelaw counties. He was the forerunner of the Knight.

B48 Villein. A general term to describe an unfree tenant after the Norman Conquest. He held his land subject to a range of agricultural services and fines. He was above the status of a slave but was, excepting the Regardant Villein (qv), usually annexed to the lord's person, in which case he was termed a Villein in Gross. Neither he nor his daughter could marry without the lord's permission, nor could he bring a suit in the king's court, or acquire land that would not be taxed. Upon his death a heriot (fine) was paid by his heirs. In return he had a landholding and the right to graze a fixed number of cattle on the common pastures and to take hay from the common meadow.

The loss of population resulting from the Black Death put the Villein into a better bargaining position and his tenure gradually became Copyhold (qv).

B49 Yeoman. A free tenant, usually a prominent farmer. As he worked with his hands he could not be styled a Gentleman (qv) but his status was above that of most other copyhold tenants. He was qualified to serve on juries and vote in county elections.

PART TWO
ADMINISTRATIVE AREAS AND BODIES

B50 Bailiwick. An area under the jurisdiction of a bailiff.

B51 Barmote. A Derbyshire court which managed the affairs of the lead mines.

B52 Barony. The Irish equivalent of the English Hundred (qv). Baronies existed before the Norman Conquest virtually as small kingdoms; they were eventually divisions of counties.

B53 Bedellary. An area under the supervision of a beadle.

B54 Borough. Up to 1835 most boroughs had obtained their status by charter. Many had the right to levy a toll at the town market, to send a representative to the House of Commons and to hold a court which dealt with civil, and some criminal, matters. Often the body administering the borough was self-perpetuating and public elections did not take place. The Municipal Corporations Act 1835 laid down that in 178 boroughs councillors were in future to serve for no more than three years before facing public election; the aldermen were restricted to six years. At the same time franchise was extended to ratepayers who had lived in the borough for three years. This legislation was consolidated in the Municipal Corporations Act 1882.

B55 Burgh. The Scottish equivalent of the English Borough whose charter could derive from a king, baron or lord. Up to 1832 only royal burghs could return members to Parliament.

B56 Burh. An Old English term for a fortified area – either a town or a dwelling.

B57 Byelaw. A north-country term for a district having its own byelaw court.

B58 Cantrev. The Welsh equivalent of the English Hundred (qv). In its turn it was divided into Commote, Maenol, Trev and Gavel.

B59 Castelry. In medieval times an area which was organised for the protection of its castle.

B60 Churchtown. A west-country term for a town, village or hamlet which contained a church.

B61 Clachan. In Scotland and Ireland a village containing a church.

B62 Close Parish. A term to describe a parish which took particular care to bar itinerant strangers from obtaining Settlement Certificates there. Under the Poor Law regulations, once a settlement was granted the person could, if necessary, apply for poor relief from the parish.

B63 Colonia. There were four Coloniae in Roman Britain – Colchester, Gloucester, Lincoln and York. They were centres in which retired Roman soldiers were given land as a pension. Citizens were entitled to Roman protection and privileges, which was not the case in native townships.

B64 Constablewick. A township or tithing under the jurisdiction of a constable.

B65 Cot-town. A small village containing residents dependent on the main local farm.

B66 County. A term derived from the French word *comte* and which, after the Norman Conquest, superseded the Old English word 'shire'. Many shires followed the boundaries of the ancient kingdoms and provinces. In the 8th and 9th centuries Wessex was divided into Hants, Wilts, Berks, Somerset, Dorset and, possibly, parts of Oxfordshire. In the 10th century the kingdom of Mercia was divided to form Derbyshire, Gloucestershire, Leicestershire, Northants, Notts, Rutland, Staffs,

Warwickshire, Worcs and possibly parts of Beds, Bucks and Oxfordshire. Norfolk and Suffolk are divisions of the old East Anglian kingdoms, Sussex, Essex, Kent and Middlesex were Teutonic kingdoms, and Yorkshire roughly corresponded to the Danish kingdom of York. Cumberland was Cumbria (the land of the Welsh), and Northumberland part of the old kingdom of Northumbria. Durham was granted to St Cuthbert in AD 685 and held as a Palatinate (qv) by the Bishop of Durham until 1836. Cheshire, earlier a Roman province, became a county palatinate under William I. Lancashire was the Honor of Lancaster; in 1071 the northern part was in Yorkshire and the southern part was crown property. Westmorland, under the Normans, was held as two baronies each divided into wards. Rutland was originally a Soke (qv) in Northamptonshire, given as dower of the Queen of England during the reign of John.

The early Welsh counties were formed after the Act of Union between England and Wales in 1536. Monmouthshire has been claimed as both an English and a Welsh county, although ecclesiastically it was almost all in the ancient diocese of Llandaff. Since 1974 it has assumed its original name of Gwent and is officially part of Wales.

The Scottish counties in the Lowlands were established by Malcolm III in the 11th century, and those in the Highlands were formed in the 16th and 17th centuries.

Only six new counties in England, including London, were formed between the Norman Conquest and 1888. In 1888 also, the Isle of Ely, the Soke of Peterborough, East and West Suffolk, East and West Sussex, the Isle of Wight and the Yorkshire Ridings all became administrative counties while nominally remaining part of their original counties.

In 1964 London was enlarged by the absorption of parts of Surrey, Essex, Herts, Kent and Middlesex, and the last-named county disappeared.

In 1974 there was a major revision of county boundaries and while some disappeared others were created. The principal changes may be summarised as follows:

Anglesey: now part of Gwynedd.
Berks: northern area to Oxfordshire.
Brecon: now part of Powys.
Caernarfonshire: now part of Gwynedd.
Cambridgeshire: absorbed the Isle of Ely, Huntingdonshire and the Soke of Peterborough.

Cardiganshire: now part of Dyfed.
Carmarthenshire: now part of Dyfed.
Cheshire: absorbed southern border area of Lancashire.
Cumberland: now part of Cumbria.
Denbighshire: now part of Clwyd.
Dorset: absorbed the Bournemouth area of Hampshire.
Durham: north-east area to Tyne and Wear, south-east area to Cleveland.
Flintshire: now part of Clwyd.
Gloucestershire: south part to Avon.
Hampshire: Bournemouth area to Dorset. Isle of Wight became separate county.
Herefordshire: combined with Worcestershire.
Huntingdonshire: now part of Cambridgeshire.
Lancashire: parts around Manchester to Greater Manchester; south west to Merseyside; southern borders to Cheshire.
Leicestershire: absorbed Rutland.
Lincolnshire: northern areas to Humberside.
Merionethshire: now part of Gwynedd.
Monmouthshire: now called Gwent.
Montgomeryshire: now part of Powys.
Northants: the Soke of Peterborough to Cambridgeshire.
Northumberland: the south east, including Newcastle, to Tyne and Wear.
Oxfordshire: absorbed northern area of Berks.
Pembrokeshire: now part of Dyfed.
Radnorshire: now part of Powys.
Rutland: now part of Leicestershire.
Somerset: northern part to Avon.
Staffordshire: southern part now in West Midlands.
Warwickshire: Birmingham and Coventry area to West Midlands.
Westmorland: now part of Cumbria.
Worcestershire: part to West Midlands: remainder combined with Herefordshire.
Yorkshire: north-east to Cleveland; south-east to Humberside; remainder divided into three metropolitan counties of North, West and South Yorkshire.

The new counties may be summarised as follows:

Avon: parts of Glos and Somerset.
Cleveland: south-east Durham and north-east Yorkshire.
Clwyd: Flintshire and Denbighshire.
Cumbria: Westmorland and Cumberland.
Dyfed: Pembrokeshire, Cardiganshire, Carmarthenshire.

Greater Manchester.

Gwent: a new name for Monmouthshire.

Gwynedd: Merionethshire, Anglesey, Caernarfonshire.

Herefordshire and Worcestershire.

Humberside: south-east Yorkshire, north Lincolnshire.

Isle of Wight.

Merseyside: Liverpool and surrounding area.

Powys: Radnorshire, Brecon and Montgomeryshire.

South, West and North Yorkshire.

Tyne and Wear: south-east Northumberland and north-east Durham.

West Midlands: parts of Worcestershire, south Staffs, and Birmingham and Coventry areas.

In 1986 the metropolitan counties of Greater London, Greater Manchester, West Midlands, Merseyside, Tyne and Wear, South, North and West Yorkshire, were abolished.

B67 County Councils. These authorities were established by the Local Government Act 1888, and the administrative functions of Quarter Sessions transferred to them.

B68 Court Baron. A manorial court which enforced the customs of the manor. It was the property of the lord and was a private jurisdiction. Originally the Homage or Jury at meetings had to consist of at least two freeholders but with the decline of this form of tenure copyhold tenants formed the Homage and the Court Baron became a Customary Court Baron.

The main business of the Court included escheats (qv), surrenders and transfers of land, dower administration, the agricultural management of commons and wastes, and the rights of lord and tenants.

The Court appointed a reeve who represented the parish and collected the lord's dues, a hayward to look after fences and the common stock of animals, and other minor officials such as woodward and swineherd.

B69 Court Leet. The term usually refers to a manorial court although it could also apply to a Hundred court. It dealt with petty offences such as common nuisances or public affray, the breaking of the Assize of Bread and Ale, and with the maintenance of highways and ditches.

It was a court of record and a public jurisdiction presided over by the lord or his representative. Each male over the age of 12 or 16 (depending upon custom), was obliged to attend. If a tenant's house extended over two leets he attended the court applicable to the main bedroom of the property.

The Court met at least twice a year and apart from the duties mentioned above it appointed officials such as the constable, aletaster and pinder; it was also responsible for the View of Frankpledge (qv).

B70 Danelaw Counties. Strictly speaking, those areas of the country occupied by the Danes and Norwegians in the 9th and 10th centuries, which roughly correspond to the counties stretching from Northumberland to the south Midlands. However, the influence of the Danes was strongest in the counties of Derbyshire, Lincolnshire, Nottinghamshire and Leicestershire. (See also Five Boroughs).

B71 District Councils. These authorities were established by the Local Government Act 1894.

B72 Extra-parochial. (a) An area outside the jurisdiction of the adjoining civil or ecclesiastical parish. Its existence could arise, for example, from the purchase by an overcrowded parish of land in another parish on which to form a consecrated burial ground. No poor or church rates were paid to the parish in which the area fell, and, in theory, tithe money went to the Crown. In 1894 all Extra-parochial areas were made into parishes or incorporated into existing ones.

(b) Uninhabited land outside the bounds of any parish and exempt from church rates.

B73 Fief. An area held by grant from a superior.

B74 Field Jury. A group of tenants elected to manage the common fields.

B75 Five Boroughs. The headquarters of the Danish armies in the 9th century. They consisted of Derby, Lincoln, Nottingham, Leicester and Stamford. There is also evidence to suggest that Torksey and York were additional garrison towns. The Five Boroughs formed a federation with a general assembly as its court.

B76 Folk Moot. A town or shire assembly.

B77 Frankpledge. In Anglo-Saxon times each vill or area was divided into tithings – associations of ten or twelve households which were held corporately responsible for the behaviour of each member. The tithing was also responsible for ensuring that any member accused of an offence was available to answer the charge. This system was called Frank-pledge and at the manorial Court Leet (qv) a View of Frankpledge regulated the working of the tithings. The term will be found in court rolls into the 19th century but it had long since lost its significance in practice. Some areas, such as Westmorland, did not adopt the system and some classes of society – knights and clerks, for example – were exempt.

Representatives of tithings were called tithingmen, headboroughs, thirdboroughs and borsholders.

B78 Gemote. A Saxon term meaning a court or assembly.

B79 Green Village. A village in which the houses are grouped around a common green, as opposed to a village strung along a central road.

B80 Halmot. A Court Baron or Court Leet (qv). Alternatively spelt Hallmote, Hallmoot.

B81 Ham. A house or village.

B82 Hamil. A north-country term for a hamlet or village.

B83 Hamlet. A small village, usually without a church, under the jurisdiction of and in the same parish as another village or town. It had neither a constable or an Overseer of the Poor, and did not levy a separate rate.

B84 Hardwick. A pastoral settlement.

B85 Home. A Shropshire term for a parish consisting of several hamlets.

B86 Honour. A grouping of several Knight's Fees (qv), lordships or manors under the administration of a lord and honorial court. The court consisted of honorial barons who were the chief under-tenants. This grouping usually occurred around a castle, but in some cases the land could be widely scattered around England. Royal Honours were still to be found in the 16th century.

B87 Hundred. (a) An administrative division of a shire, probably established in the 10th century, whose influence declined as paro-chial, manorial and judicial bodies became more important. The derivation of the term remains obscure – it is thought to have origin-ally contained a hundred families or ten tithings, or else a hundred taxable hides of land. The Hundred Court, presided over by the Hundred Reeve acting on behalf of the king, usually met monthly at an open place

distinguished by a feature such as a boundary stone, barrow, tree or crossroads; it considered criminal offences, minor ecclesiastical matters and private pleas; it also levied taxes.

New hundreds were created as late as the 17th century by Justices of the Peace in Quarter Sessions, and the unit of government existed formally until the Local Government Act 1894 set up District Councils which are the success-ors of the Hundred Courts.

Alternatively called Wapentake in Danelaw counties (qv), Lathe in Kent, Rape in Sussex, Leet in East Anglia, Ward in Cumberland, Durham and Northumberland, and Liberty in the Isle of Wight.

(b) A division of a Wapentake in Derbyshire, Leicestershire, Lincolnshire and Notting-hamshire, or a division of a Lathe in Kent.

B88 Husting. A term now used in con-nection with meetings before a parliamentary election, but the Old English hustings had some legal business to pursue. In an adminis-trative sense the word is retained in the Court of Hustings in the City of London, which was established before the Norman Conquest. Similar courts, which registered deeds and wills, existed elsewhere, eg. at Boston and Winchester.

B89 Inship. A term applied to a small portion of a parish.

B90 Joclet. A Kent term for a small manor or farm.

B91 Kintra. A Scottish term for a region or district.

B92 Kirk Clachan. A Scottish village con-taining a church. Alternatively called Kirktoun.

B93 Knight's Fee. An area held by a knight for which he was obliged to perform military service to his immediate overlord.

B94 Lady Court. A court belonging to a lady of the manor.

B95 Lathe. In Kent, an administrative area equivalent to the Hundred (qv). Confusingly, it was itself divided into areas called Hun-dreds. In Norman times there were six Lathes but this was later reduced to five.

B96 Liberty. (a) An area situated outside a borough in which freemen had certain rights of pasture etc.

(b) A group of manors, the lord of which

held certain privileges of the Crown. The sheriff's authority was excluded and the lord had the return of writs. Alternatively called Soke.

(c) In the Isle of Wight another name for a Hundred (qv).

B97 Lordship. A manorial holding.

B98 Manor. An estate held by a landlord, (not necessarily a titled person), who himself was a tenant of the Crown or of a mesne lord. A manor could be part of a parish contiguous with its boundaries, or else be large enough to spread over more than one parish. The lord of the manor retained part of the land, called demesne, for his own use, while the rest was tenanted or else used for common or waste.

B99 Mayor's Brethren. A body of 24 Aldermen governing a town, together with 48 other residents, who formed a Common Council.

B100 Moot. An assembly of people which formed a legislative court, especially important in Saxon times. There were gemots, witangemots, burgmotes, hundred-motes etc. Alternatively called Mote.

B101 Open Parish. As opposed to a Close Parish (qv), one in which it was relatively easy for a stranger to obtain a Settlement Certificate.

B102 Open Vestry. A general meeting of male ratepayers which carried out the civic functions of a parish and which sometimes had authority in the expenditure of the church rate.

Open Vestries in large urban areas in the 19th century became unmanageable and sometimes open to mob leadership. Some were supplanted by Select Vestries established by Act of Parliament. Some parishes took advantage of the powers allowed in the Sturges Bourne Act 1819 to elect a Parish Committee which, confusingly, was often called a Select Vestry.

B103 Palatinate. An area administered by an earl or a bishop, such as the county palatines of Chester, Durham and Lancaster; these were abolished in 1835.

B104 Parish. Originally a township or group of townships possessing its own church and parson, to whom it paid its tithes and other ecclesiastical dues. A parish could contain one or several manors, and sometimes a manor was large enough to spread over more than one parish.

Successive Acts of Parliament, particularly in the 16th and 17th centuries, encouraged the transformation of the parish into a secular authority through its meetings of the Vestry (qv). The early parish already had the power to levy a church rate, but further legislation empowered the parish to levy a rate for poor relief and the repair of highways – two areas of activity which increased and so enhanced the importance of the parish. As this happened the functions of the manor courts, excepting those which included the transfer and inheritance of land, declined, although for a period there could be an overlap of powers between vestry and manor court.

Most vestries were Open, in that any male ratepayer could attend and vote. This was not always the best administrative solution, particularly in populous areas, and for want of an established local electoral system, some parishes opted for the establishment of Select Vestries which were self-perpetuating, undemocratic bodies. The Vestry, of whatever nature, appointed churchwardens, sexton and, subject to the approval of the Justices of the Peace, the Overseers of the Poor, the Surveyors of Highways and Constables.

In urban areas the parishes were consolidated into boroughs after the Municipal Corporations Act 1835, although London was left relatively untouched until 1855.

B105 Parish Councils. Authorities established by the Local Government Act 1894. The Act specified that such bodies should be elected in rural areas with a population of over 300. In parishes where the population numbered between 200 and 300 a parish council could be elected if a parish meeting decided so; in areas with an even smaller population a parish council could be elected if the county council agreed.

The powers of the Parish Councils were greatly expanded by the Local Government Act 1972.

B106 Portsoken. An area outside a city. Alternatively called Portsoone.

B107 Quarter. A division of a parish for the purposes of Poor Law administration.

B108 Rape. The Sussex equivalent of a Hundred (qv). There were six Rapes, each with a castle and a harbour. It was a unit of local government and assessed for tax.

B109 Regality. A Scottish term for a territorial jurisdiction granted by the Crown.

B110 Reguard. A forest court held every three years to safeguard the bounds of the forest and the Crown's interests. It consisted of 12 knights whose findings were reported to the Justices.

B111 Riding. A third of a shire, from the Old Norse *thrithing*. Yorkshire was divided into Ridings by the Danes, each with their own town courts. A similar division took place in Lincolnshire where the areas were known as Parts or Divisions. The sub-divisions of one of these, Lindsey, were also known as Ridings.

B112 Royalty. A Scottish and north-country term for an area under the jurisdiction of the Crown. An example of this could be a royal palace and its estate.

B113 Rural District Councils. Authorities established by the Local Government Act 1894.

B114 Seigniory. A lord's holding of land, usually a manor.

B115 Seigniorial Borough. A borough which received its charter from an earl or lord, and not from the Crown.

B116 Select Vestry. A self-perpetuating body of residents responsible for the civic management of a parish. Sometimes a Select Vestry was established by local residents themselves usurping the traditional Open Vestry (qv). Often in the 17th century a Select Vestry was established by Bishop's Faculty. In London a number came about as a result of the 1711 Act for building fifty new churches in the metropolis, or else from particular Church Building Acts. Other Select Vestries were formed when a sufficient body of ratepayers could obtain an Act of Parliament on the grounds that the parish was too populous to be governed by Open Vestry.

Inevitably, when Select Vestries were formed, they consisted of the wealthier members of the parish and as the Vestry was then entitled to fill any vacancies without reference to the ratepayers, this social imbalance continued and caused much resentment, especially in areas where there had previously been a strong Open Vestry.

The attraction of the Select Vestry rested on its ability to manage the affairs of a populous area better than an open meeting of ratepayers. Also, the Act establishing the Vestry could include powers that were denied Open vestries. Although the system was undemocratic it has to be remembered that no general method of local elections had yet evolved and the adoption of non-elected bodies was not considered so extraordinary.

A Select Vestry could be established with as few as twelve members whereas a parish like St Pancras in London had 122 members.

Alternatively called Twelve, Fifteen, Sixteen, Company of Four and Twenty, Ancients, Elders and Twenty.

B117 Soke. A term used in Danelaw counties (qv) to describe a jurisdiction over a number of estates and villages – there are 32 such townships in the Soke of Peterborough. It is thought that the townships were settled by Danish soldiers who owed personal allegiance to a lord and a court. The land of any particular Soke could be in a number of manors, which meant that some villages and farms were under divided lordship. The Soke was the lord's private jurisdiction and he was entitled to hold a Soke Court. His tenants were freemen.

The word was also generally used for a private jurisdiction, whether owned by barons, religious houses or guilds. Alternatively called Liberty.

B118 Swanimote. A forest court which met three times a year to manage the Crown's woodland. A fortnight before Michaelmas it would regulate the pasturing of pigs; about St Martin's Day it would meet to collect dues for this. It also met just before Midsummer when the forest was closed and the beasts fawned. Alternatively called Swanimote.

B119 Team. A Crown grant to the lord of the manor giving jurisdiction over the punishment of offenders within his manor. Alternatively spelt Theam.

B120 Tithing. (a) Originally a company of ten householders who stood security for each other within the system called Frankpledge (qv). Each male over the age of 12 was obliged to be in a Tithing.

(b) A land division, once regarded as a tenth of a Hundred (qv).

B121 Township. A division of a parish which formed a unit of local administration; it levied a separate Poor Rate and appointed a constable.

B122 Urban District Councils. Authorities established by the Local Government Act 1894.

B123 Vestry. The governing body of a parish. (See Open Vestry, Select Vestry and Parish).

B124 Vill. A division of a parish, perhaps synonymous with township, manor or tithing.

B125 Wapentake. A term used in the Dane-law counties (qv) of Derby, Leicester, Lincoln, Nottingham and York, to denote a Hundred (qv).

B126 Wardmote. A meeting of citizens of a ward.

B127 Wick. A village.

PART THREE
LOCAL OFFICIALS AND DIGNITARIES

B128 Affeeror. An officer appointed by a manorial court to assess the penalties for proven offences.

B129 Agister. A royal forest official who received payments for the pannage of commoners' pigs. In the New Forest this title survives as an officer in charge of ponies etc.

B130 Alderman. In its modern sense, one who helps to govern a local authority, whether county, corporation or borough, together with the mayor, chairman and councillors. (See also Ealdorman).

B131 Aletaster. A manorial official who tested the quality and measurement of ale and beer sold within the manor. He was the fore-runner of the Inspector of Weights and Measures (qv). Alternatively called Alefounder or Aleconner, and referred to in Latin documents as *Gustator Cervus*. Quite often his responsibilities included the testing of the quality or weight of bread.

B132 Almanac Man. An officer appointed by the Court of Sewers in Lincolnshire respon-sible for alerting inhabitants near the River Trent when high tides were expected.

B133 Aulnager. An official responsible for ensuring that any cloth was woven to the correct length and width as laid down by statute. He stamped approved cloth with the town seal. The office was abolished in 1699.

B134 Badge-Man. An official responsible for ensuring that all paupers in receipt of parish relief wore badges indicating their status and parish under the terms of an Act of 1697.

B135 Bailiff. (a) The manorial lord's repre-sentative and estate manager, but subordinate to the steward.

(b) In Colchester, at least, the name of the town's two leading citizens until 1635.

B136 Beadle. A parish officer with various duties, not necessarily the same in each local-ity. At times he was a messenger, writ-server, town crier, assistant to the constable, common driver or macebearer. In some parishes the beadle was the constable (qv). His original function was probably to bid people to parish meetings. Usually he was equipped by the parish with a coat and some form of staff of office, such as a wand. Alternatively called Beadman, Beagle, Bydel and Bedell.

B137 Bedman. A west-country term for a sexton.

B138 Bedral. A minor official in Scotland who could be a clerk, beadle or sexton.

B139 Beggar-Banger. A parish officer responsible for controlling the length of stay of any 'stranger'. In some places he was synony-mous with the constable or beadle. Alterna-tively called Bang-Beggar.

B140 Bellman. A town crier.

B141 Besswarden. A parish officer in charge of beasts on the common.

B142 Bozzler. A southern term for a sheriff's officer or a parish constable.

B143 Burgess. In this context, a word some-times used to describe a person elected by a borough to represent them in Parliament.

B144 Burleyman. A beadle or constable responsible for the enforcement of the by-laws of a manor. Alternative called Bylawman.

B145 Churchwarden. A parish officer responsible for keeping the church and repre-senting the people in parochial matters. It is a temporal post of great antiquity. Two churchwardens are usually appointed each Easter Tuesday. The main duties have been or are:

a) to manage parish property and income.
b) to represent the views of the parishioners

in parochial and collective matters.

c) the upkeep of the church fabric, the provision of facilities for worship and the allocation of pews.

d) to encourage parishioners to attend church regularly and to ensure that their children are baptised.

e) to attend the Archdeacon's court.

f) to account for the expenditure of the church rate.

g) to assist in the compilation of the parish register.

h) to report, if necessary, any failing in duty of the Incumbent.

i) to supervise the education and relief of the poor in collaboration with the Overseers of the Poor.

k) to maintain the parish arms and pay the local soldiers.

l) the control and extermination of vermin

m) to present offences within the cognizance of the church courts.

In the case of a very large parish before its sub-division into ecclesiastical districts, up to four churchwardens might be appointed to represent the various townships or villages. Alternatively called Churchman, Churchmaster, Church Reeve, Kirkmaster.

B146 Clapman. A town crier.

B147 Collector of the Poor. A parish officer responsible for collecting the poor rate, later to be superseded by the Overseer of the Poor (qv). The first Poor Law Act of 1563 enacted that 'two able persons or more shall be appointed gatherers and collectors of the charitable alms of all the residue of the people inhabiting in the parish'. A fine of twenty shillings was imposed on any parishioners who refused to act in this post. The collectors accounted for moneys each quarter.

B148 Constable. An officer appointed by the manor or parish with a wide range of duties which varied over the centuries. They included:

a) the supervision of Watch and Ward (qv) as specified by the Statute of Winchester 1285.

b) the upkeep of the stocks, lock-up or any other means of punishment and imprisonment.

c) the inspection of alehouses and the suppression of gaming-houses.

d) the apprenticing of pauper children.

e) the supervision and removal, where

necessary, of itinerant strangers and beggars.

f) collaboration with other officials in the relief of the poor.

g) the collection of the county rate and of any specially levied national tax.

h) the maintenance of the parish arms and the training of the local militia.

i) the convening of parish meetings.

j) the care of the parish bull.

k) the presentation of parishioners who did not attend church regularly.

l) assistance at shipwrecks in the locality.

m) the apprehension and detention of suspected criminals and the arrest of escaped prisoners.

n) the suppression of riots and unlawful assemblies.

o) the compilation of jurors' lists.

p) the collection of child maintenance from fathers of illegitimate children.

The constable was originally a manorial appointment made by the Court Leet (qv). As the vestries gradually became more powerful the responsibility fell on them, but for a period it was not uncommon for both manor and vestry to appoint constables within the same parish. The vestries were officially made responsible, subject to the approval of the Justices, in 1842.

Alternatively called Borsholder, Bozzler, Chief Pledge, Headborough (qv), Petty Constable, Thirdborough, Tithingman, Verderer (qv).

B149 Coroner. The office dates back to the late 12th century for certain, and possibly earlier. The Coroner had a number of duties which included inquests, treasure trove and deodands, but his main responsibility now is to hold inquests. He was a royal officer who developed gradually into a county official. Up to the Local Government Act 1888 he was appointed by the freeholders of the county but at this date his appointment was put in the hands of the county council.

B150 Countour. In the 13th and 14th centuries the officer who helped to collect and audit the county rates.

B151 Director of the Poor. A member of a board, usually established by an Act of Parliament, to administer the parish poor rate and to oversee the management of the parish workhouse. Directors were superseded by Guardians of the Poor.

B152 Distributor. An assistant to the Overseer of the Poor (qv).

B153 Dozener. A man elected by householders of a ward or street to represent them at a borough Court Leet (qv). Alternatively called Decimer.

B154 Ealdorman. Originally a royal official, often related to the king, who presided over civil matters at shire courts. He was at that time the chief personage and the king's deputy in a county. In Cnut's time he received the 'earl's penny', a third penny from the judicial profits of the shire court. After the Norman Conquest he was usually referred to as an 'Earl' a term which came to denote a status rather than a function. His administrative duties were largely taken over by the Sheriff (qv).

B155 Factor. A Scottish term for a steward of an estate, responsible for its management and the collection of rents.

B156 Feodary. An officer concerned with the inheritance of land and the obligations of Crown tenants.

B157 Field Master. A manorial officer who managed the common fields. He was sometimes synonymous with the Hayward or the Reeve. Alternatively called Fieldman, Field Reeve, Foreman of the Fields, Messor.

B158 Franklin. A free tenant farmer, quite often the manorial steward or bailiff.

B159 Gannock. A woman in charge of the parish brewhouse. A term found in Cambridgeshire.

B160 Gauger. An officer responsible for assessing and collecting excise duty.

B161 Guardians of the Poor. The Poor Law Amendment Act 1834 established Boards of Guardians to have charge of local administration of poor relief. The Boards were locally elected.

B162 Hayward. An official who supervised the repair of manor or parish fences, looked after the common stock of animals and impounded stray cattle. In some parishes he was also the Field Master (qv). Alternatively called Hedgelooker.

B163 Headborough. The head of a frankpledge (qv) or tithing (qv); a constable or his deputy. In Latin documents he is referred to as *Bosburgium* or *Decennarius*.

B164 High Constable. An officer of the Hundred, responsible for law and order and the performance of manor and parish constables. He was also assistant to the Lieutenant of the county. He was appointed by the Court Leet of the Hundred or by the Justices of the Peace. The post is mentioned in the Statute of Winchester 1285 but it is clear that it was already in existence. Alternatively called Hundred Constable.

B165 Hogringer. An officer appointed by the manor, responsible for ensuring that all pigs on the common had rings through their noses to prevent them rooting up the turf. He had power to impound pigs which were not so treated and to charge for ringing them subsequently.

B166 Incumbent. Whether rector or vicar, the Incumbent was by custom the chairman of vestry meetings but his powers were not extensive. He was charged with keeping the parish registers, a duty still with him, and for a period he was able to recommend fit people to manage alehouses and countersign constables' reports etc.

B167 Jurat. A municipal dignitary, especially of the Cinque Ports.

B168 Kirkmaster. (a) A churchwarden. Alternatively called Kirkwarden.
(b) In some parishes the term for a Select Vestryman (see Vestryman).

B169 Knocknobbler. A person appointed to drive dogs out of the church. Alternatively called Dog Whipper.

B170 Lord Lieutenant. The principal officer of a county. Originally called a Lieutenant before Tudor times, he was responsible for the upkeep and readiness of the county militia and the provision of warning beacons. He was also *Custos Rotulorum* – the keeper of the county records. His duties nowadays are mainly of a ceremonial nature.

B171 Master of the Parish. A Select Vestryman

B172 Mayor. The first Mayor was probably that of London, in 1191. By the middle of the 13th century it was general for boroughs to appoint one. His powers were governed by the provisions of the borough charters. Legislation in 1835 and 1882 relieved mayors of many of their executive duties, and the Act of 1882 allowed for the appointment of a Deputy Mayor.

B173 Meresman. A parish officer appointed to maintain the boundaries of the parish, but he could also be involved in the upkeep of roads, bridges and waterways.

B174 Moss Reeve. A bailiff who received and dealt with claims for land on swamps and mossy areas.

B175 Murenger. A Shropshire and Cheshire term for an officer appointed to supervise the upkeep of city walls.

B176 Mysgather. A tax collector.

B177 Myslayer. An assessor of taxes.

B178 Neatherd. A cowherd appointed by the community to prevent cattle straying.

B179 Overseer of the Poor. This office was established by the Poor Law Act 1597/8 and made compulsory by the Poor Relief Act 1601. It superseded the less formal office of Collector of the Poor (qv). At least two persons were appointed yearly by each vestry, subject to the approval of the Justices of the Peace, to levy a poor rate and supervise its distribution. They were unpaid and selected from among the parishioners.

Most of their duties were transferred to the Guardians of the Poor (qv) in 1834, leaving the Overseers with the duty of assessing and collecting the rate, although legislation enabled the parish to appoint paid collectors under the control of the Overseers. The office was abolished by the Rating and Valuation Act 1925.

B180 Parish Clerk. The post was a temporal one although he would normally be appointed by the Incumbent; quite frequently, in earlier times, he would be in holy orders himself. A Parish Clerk arranged baptisms and communions, acted as sexton, rang the church bell for service and even led the responses at services.

B181 Parker. An officer responsible for the care of the game on 'imparked' land.

B182 Pavior. A man paid by a town to see to the upkeep of the paving stones.

B183 Pinder. A manor or parish officer in charge of the pound or pinfold into which stray animals were put. Alternatively called Poundkeeper, Punder. The Latin term was *Custos Parci*.

B184 Ponderator. An early inspector of weights and measures, especially in market towns.

B185 Precentor. A Yorkshire term for an officer responsible for the upkeep of public footpaths.

B186 Provost. (a) An official elected by the manor, responsible for the husbandry of the commons. Walter of Henley's 13th-century *Husbandrie* remarks that he 'must cause all the hairs of the avers [cattle] to be gathered to make ropes, and have hemp sown in the court for wagon-ropes, harness etc., allowance paid for anyone who could make them'. He was also responsible for repairing hedges, ditches etc., the issue of the mares in the manor, and for stock losses.

(b) In Scotland he is the chief magistrate of a burgh.

B187 Questman. A sidesman.

B188 Reeve. Strictly speaking, a deputy. In the case of a manor, usually a man of villein status elected by his fellow tenants to organise the daily business of the manor. Because of this he was quite often their spokesman in negotiations with the lord or his representative. In return the Reeve received a payment from the tenants, sometimes a remission of rent and feudal dues, as well as special grazing rights.

He was, where no other officer was appointed, in charge of the agricultural policy of the manor, as well as responsible for the livestock. The extent of his duties varied from parish to parish and in certain areas he would have duties which in others were performed by a Hayward, Field Master or Beadle. A Reeve could be chosen either by rotation or else be a person owning a particular piece of land.

B189 Regarder. An officer who supervised a forest and presided over its triennial court (Court of Regard).

B190 Scaleraker. A north-country term for a town scavenger.

B191 Scavelman. A southern term for a man employed to scour waterways.

B192 Scavenger. An official employed to clear refuse off the streets. Alternatively called Scaleraker or Sheldrake.

B193 Searcher. A person, usually a woman, appointed by the parish to verify a death. She had no medical training although one of her duties was to ascertain the cause of death and to report any suspicious circumstances. She received a fee from the family of the deceased for a death certificate which was presented to the Sexton before burial. The office does not seem to have a basis in law and was not officially established or abolished – the post died out in the 19th century.

B194 Selectman. A member of a Select Vestry (qv).

B195 Seneschal. A steward. According to Walter of Henley's *Husbandrie* of the 13th century, a Seneschal had supervision of several manors, which he toured at least three times a year. 'He should have lands of demesne measures, should know by the perch of the country how many acres in each field for sowing (wheat, rye, barley, oats, peas, beans and dredge); ploughing (each plough should plough nine score acres – sixty for winter seed, for spring seed and in fallow), also how many acres to be ploughed by boon custom and how many by the demesne ploughs; reaping (how many acres by boon and custom and how many for money); meadows and pastures and on common. Also how stock is kept and improved. Fines imposed if loss or damage due to want of guard. No under or over stocking of manors; if lord needs money for debts, Seneschal should see from which manor he can have money at greatest advantage and smallest loss.'

B196 Sexton. An official appointed and paid by the parish, Incumbent or Churchwardens. He was responsible for gravedigging, bell-ringing and odd jobs around the church.

B197 Sheldrake. A Cumberland term for a Scavenger (qv).

B198 Sheriff. A shire-reeve. He became, as the Crown's deputy, the most important executive figure in each county, superseding the Ealdormen (qv) in this respect. Until the 14th century, when the Justices of the Peace became prominent, the Sheriff was the main agent of courts. He was also responsible for royal revenues in the shire and for the county militia before the Lord Lieutenant assumed this duty. An enquiry was held in 1170 into malpractices by sheriffs and this led to the appointment of Coroners (qv). A modern Sheriff has ceremonial and minor judicial powers.

B199 Steward. The chief agent of the lord for the management of the manor. He usually presided over the courts and kept the records.

B200 Surveyor of the Highways. A parish officer established by the Highways Act 1555. He was unpaid and appointed from among the parishioners. In 1691 the law was altered so that the inhabitants merely gave the Justices a list of landholders eligible for selection and the Justices chose, usually by rotation.

The officer was obliged to survey the highways three times a year and organise the statute labour that was provided by landholders to repair the roads, or else collect the money commutations.

Alternatively called Boonmaster, Overseer of the Highways, Stoneman, Stonewarden, Waymaker, Waywarden and Wayman.

B201 Swineherd. A man employed by the community to prevent the pigs from straying off the common.

B202 Thirdborough. A Constable (qv) or his deputy. The word is probably a corruption of the Middle English *'fridborgh'* – peace pledge.

B203 Tithingman. A term which probably originated before the Norman Conquest when a tithing – an association of ten families who stood security for each other – elected a representative as their spokesman. After the Conquest it was a term meaning constable or deputy constable.

B204 Town Husband. A colloquial term for a parish officer who collected money for the maintenance of illegitimate children from their fathers.

B205 Troner. An official in charge of the weighing of merchandise at the tron (market).

B206 Verderer. (a) An officer responsible for the preservation of the king's forest. It is thought that the post dates back to the early 11th century. There were four Verderers to each forest, elected by freeholders in the county court. The office was held for life. The Verderers attended the Court of Attachment held every 40 days and punished minor offences.

(b) In the south west he could be a petty constable.

B207 Wardman. In certain boroughs a member of a select body of burgesses representing the several wards, and empowered to choose municipal officers.

B208 Water Bailiff. An officer in seaport towns who was empowered to search ships for contraband etc.

B209 Webster. Mentioned in Walter of Henley's 13th-century *Husbandrie* as a bailiff, steward or major-domo of a great medieval lord, holding high military command.

B210 Wellmaster. An officer appointed by the Court Leet (qv) who was responsible for the supply of clean and adequate water in the area.

B211 Woodward. A forest keeper. Alternatively called Wood Reeve.

PART FOUR
CHARTERED BOROUGHS

B212 Chartered Boroughs. The following boroughs were granted charters between the years 1042 and 1660. Details of dates, grantors, extents etc. may be found in the most authoritative work on the subject called *British Borough Charters 1042–1660*, in three volumes, by Adolphus Ballard, J. Tait and H. Weinbaum.

The entries are made under the old county headings.

Beds. Bedford, Dunstable.

Berks. Abingdon, Maidenhead, Newbury, Reading, Wallingford, Windsor (New), Wokingham.

Bucks. Aylesbury, Buckingham, Colnbrook, Wycombe.

Cambs. Cambridge, Wisbech.

Cheshire. Altrincham, Chester, Congleton, Ellesmere, Frodsham, Knutsford, Macclesfield, Nantwich, Stockport.

Cornwall. Bodmin, Camelford, Dunheved, Grampound, Helston, Launceston, Liskeard, Looe (East), Looe (West), Lostwithiel, Marazion, Penknight, Penryn, Penzance, St Ives, Saltash, Tintagel, Tregony, Truro.

Cumberland. Carlisle, Egremont, Kirkby Johannis, Skynburgh.

Derby. Bakewell, Chesterfield, Derby.

Devon. Barnstaple, Bideford, Bradninch, Dartmouth, Exeter, Okehampton, Plymouth, Plympton, South Molton, Tiverton, Torrington, Totnes.

Dorset. Blandford Forum, Bridport, Dorchester, Lyme Regis, Melcombe Regis, Nova Villa (Newton), Poole, Shaftesbury, Sherborne, Weymouth.

Durham. Barnard Castle, Durham, Elvet, Gateshead, Hartlepool, Stockton-on-Tees, Sunderland, Wearmouth.

Essex. Colchester, Great Dunmow, Harwich, Maldon, Saffron Walden, Thaxted.

Glos. Berkeley, Bristol, Chipping Campden, Chipping Sodbury, Cirencester, Gloucester, St Briavels, Tewkesbury, Wotton-under-Edge.

Hants. Andover, Basingstoke, Christchurch, Petersfield, Portsmouth, Romsey, Southampton, Whitchurch, Winchester.

Hereford. Hereford, Leominster.

Herts. Berkhamstead, Hemel Hempstead, Hertford, St Albans.

Hunts. Godmanchester, Huntingdon.

Isle of Wight. Brading, Frauncheville, Newport, Newtown, Yarmouth.

Kent. Canterbury, Cinque Ports, Dover, Faversham, Folkestone, Fordwich, Gravesend, Hythe, Lydd, Maidstone, Queenborough, Rochester, Romney, Sandwich, Tenterden.

Lancs. Bolton, Clitheroe, Kirkham, Lancaster, Liverpool, Manchester, Ormskirk, Preston, Roby, Salford, Ulverston, Warrington, Warton, Wigan.

Leics. Leicester.

Lincs. Boston, Gainsborough, Grantham, Grimsby, Lincoln, Louth, Stamford, Torksey, Wainfleet.

Norfolk. Great Yarmouth, Kings Lynn, Norwich, Thetford.

Northants. Daventry, Higham Ferrers, Northampton.

Northumberland. Alnwick, Bamburgh, Berwick-upon-Tweed, Corbridge, Morpeth, Newcastle-upon-Tyne, Norham, Warenmouth.

Notts. Newark, Nottingham, Retford East, Southwell.

Oxon. Banbury, Burford, Chipping Norton, Eynsham, Henley-on-Thames, Oxford, Woodstock.

Shropshire. Baschurch, Bishops Castle, Bridgnorth, Burford, Clun, Ludlow, Newport, Oswestry, Ruyton, Shrewsbury, Wenlock.

Somerset. Axbridge, Bath, Bridgwater, Chard, Dunster, Ilchester, Langport Estover, Milborne Port, Nether Weare, Taunton, Wells, Yeovil.

Staffs. Abbots Bromley, Agardsley, Burton-on-Trent, Kinver, Leek, Lichfield, Newcastle-under-Lyme, Stafford, Tamworth, Uttoxeter, Walsall.

Suffolk. Aldborough, Bury St Edmunds, Dunwich, Eye, Hadleigh, Ipswich, Lydham, Orford, Southwold, Sudbury.

Surrey. Farnham, Godalming, Guildford, Kingston-upon-Thames.

Sussex. Arundel, Chichester, Cinque Ports, Hastings, Lewes, Pevensey, Rye, Seaford, Winchelsea (New).

Warks. Coventry, Stratford-upon-Avon, Sutton Coldfield, Warwick.

Westmorland. Appleby, Kendal.

Wilts. Calne, Chippenham, Cricklade, Devizes, Marlborough, Salisbury (New), Salisbury (Old), Wilton, Wootton Bassett.

Worcs. Bewdley, Clifton, Droitwich, Evesham, Kidderminster, Worcester.

Yorks. Beverley, Doncaster, Hedon, Helmsley, Hull, Leeds, Pontefract, Ravenserod, Richmond, Ripon, Scarborough, Sheffield, York.

Wales. Aberavon, Abergavenny, Aberystwyth, Bala, Beaumaris, Bere, Brecon, Builth, Caergwrie, Caerleon, Caerwys, Cardiff, Cardigan, Carmarthen, Caernarvon, Conway, Cowbridge, Criccieth, Deganwy, Denbigh, Dryslwyn, Flint, Harlech, Haverfordwest, Holt, Hope, Kenfig, Kidwelly, Laugharne, Llandovery, Llanfyllin, Llantrissaint, Monmouth, Montgomery, Neath, Nevin, Newborough, Newport (Mon), Newport (Pem), Newtown by Dinefwr, Newtown, Pembroke, Pwllheli, Radnor (New), Rhuddlan, Ruthin, St Clears, Swansea, Tenby, Usk, Welshpool.

PART FIVE
MANOR AND VESTRY CUSTOMS AND PROCEDURES

B213 Allegiance. The manorial tenant was obliged to pay homage and swear allegiance to his lord.

B214 Amercement. A fine paid in a manorial court. The tenant was said to be 'in mercy' of the court.

B215 Bannering. A Shropshire term for Perambulating the Bounds (qv).

B216 Biscot. A 16th and 17th century fine on landholders who did not maintain waterways running through their lands.

B217 Borchalpening. A half-penny fine paid at the View of Frankpledge (qv).

B218 Court Rolls. Transfers or grants of land were recorded on the rolls of the Court Baron. In the case of copyhold tenure a copy of the relevant minute was given to an incoming tenant and this was deemed to be a title deed. Appointments of manor officers and the punishment of minor offences were recorded in the rolls of the Court Leet and View of Frankpledge. Very early rolls might also contain details of the management of the common fields.

B219 Custumal. A statement, usually contained in the court rolls, of the customs of the manor, the services owed by free and unfree tenants, the duties of the town burgesses, and the rights and obligations of the lord. It was periodically recorded in the minutes.

B220 Defaulter. A term used in court rolls to denote an absentee from the court without an excuse.

B221 Doom. A judgement made by the jury of a manor court.

B222 Essoin. An excuse for non-attendance at a manor court, or else the tenant making it. Alternatively called Forfal.

B223 Estray. A stray animal kept in the manor pound for whom no owner could be found. Its finding was announced and if no owner claimed it within a year and a day the animal was usually taken by the lord of the manor on behalf of the Crown. An owner claiming an animal was fined and had to pay for its upkeep since it was confined.

B224 Extent. A summary of the extent, customs and valuation of the manor and its tenancies.

B225 Fealty. An oath of allegiance to the Crown made by an incoming tenant.

B226 Homage. A ceremonial pledge of loyalty and obligation made by a tenant to his lord, or else a collective term for the assembly of tenants at the manorial court which acted as a jury. The lord, in accepting the homage, also warranted protection to his tenants.

B227 House-row. The system whereby parish officers were chosen by rotation according to the position of a ratepayer's house. This method was also used in determining which house should be the next to take on a parish apprentice. It was simply a method by which the ratepayer was chosen in the order in which his house stood in the locality.

B228 Perambulation of the Bounds. The Vestry had the responsibility of walking the bounds of the parish at Rogationtide – the three days before Ascension Day. The Incumbent, parish officers, prominent vestrymen and a good many schoolchildren employed for the occasion, armed with the authority of a wand of office, checked that boundary stones were in position and that no buildings encroached, unrated, on parish territory. The custom continued well into the second half of the 19th century, long after maps made the occasion irrelevant.

B229 Pound. An enclosure maintained either by manor or vestry to confine stray animals; a fine was paid to retrieve them. Alternatively called Pinfold.

B230 Scot Ale. A dinner given to tenants on rent days.

B231 Suit of Court. The attendance which a tenant was obliged to give at the lord's manor court.

B232 Valor. A record of the values of manor lands.

B233 Waif. A piece of property which was ownerless; if unclaimed within a fixed period after due notice was given, it fell to the lord of the manor.

PART SIX
PARLIAMENTARY AND LOCAL FRANCHISE

Parliamentary Franchise

B234 The old House of Commons. Before the Reform Bill 1832 the House of Commons consisted of burgesses elected by towns, knights of the shire elected by counties and representatives elected by the universities. In the counties large tenant farmers were excluded from the franchise as a voter's qualification depended on having a freehold estate worth 40 shillings or more per annum. Franchise in the boroughs depended upon custom or charter.

B235 Reform Bill 1832. The imbalance of representation was substantially corrected by this Bill. Fifty-six 'rotten' boroughs in England were disenfranchised, thirty were reduced to one member only, and twenty-two new boroughs were created to send two members, and twenty to send one member.

B236 Representation of the People Act 1867. The franchise was reformed by a reduction of the property qualification in boroughs and counties; also enfranchised in boroughs was each man over twenty-one who occupied as owner or tenant for twelve months a separate dwelling without regard to value, or lodgings of £10 unfurnished value. The electorate was extended to 2,500,000. Some 45 constituencies were redistributed. Secret ballots were introduced in 1872.

B237 Representation of the People Act 1884. The qualification in the counties was reduced to be similar to that in towns and a further 1,500,000 men were enfranchised. A separate measure the following year equalised the ratio of population to representation throughout the country.

B238 Representation of the People Act 1918 The vote was given to any man over twenty-one who could prove six month's residence regardless of value of rent etc. Women over thirty, who were occupiers in their own right or married to men entitled to a local government vote, were given the right to vote – a discriminatory qualification to prevent women voters being in a majority in the country. Plural voting which gave as many votes to a man as he had residences in different constituencies, was abolished almost completely. University franchise was extended to graduates of provincial universities; this right to vote was additional to their residential vote. Receipt of poor law relief ceased to be a disqualification.

Registration procedures were reformed and responsibility transferred to the Clerk of a borough or county. Polls were restricted to one day only.

B239 Equal Franchise Bill 1928. Women achieved voting rights equal to those of men.

B240 Representation of the People Act 1948. The University· vote was abolished. The City of London constituency was abolished.

Local Government Franchise

B241 Vestries. Until well into the 19th century the most common form of local administration was the parish vestry. This could be an Open Vestry (qv) at which all male ratepayers could speak and vote; there were exceptions to this where ancient custom restricted participation. Some vestries were transformed into Select Vestries by Act of Parliament and membership of that Vestry was either acquired by nomination in the original Act or subsequently by co-option when a vacancy occurred – the ratepayers had no electoral right in the matter.

B242 Sturges Bourne Vestries Act 1818. This adoptive Act, which did not apply to areas governed by Select or 'close' bodies, established a system of voting according to land ownership. The scale for voting was:
Assessed to the Poor rate at over £150 – 6 votes
Assessed to the Poor rate at over £125 – 5 votes
Assessed to the Poor rate at over £100 – 4 votes
Assessed to the Poor rate at over £75 – 3 votes
Assessed to the Poor rate at over £50 – 2 votes
Assessed to the Poor rate at under £50 – 1 vote.

B243 Sturges Bourne Poor Relief Act 1819. This was an adoptive Act which enabled a parish to appoint a representative vestry or Poor Law committee to manage most of its affairs. The committee's voting powers were as laid down in the 1818 Act (see B242). Generally the wealthier members of the parish together with the incumbent, churchwardens and overseers formed such a committee.

B244 Hobhouse Vestries Act 1831. This was an adoptive Act which permitted a Select

Vestry (in the sense of being chosen by ratepayers and not being appointed by Act of Parliament). All parishioners who had paid rates for one year could cast one vote for each vacancy. On the request of five ratepayers a secret ballot could be held.

A candidate in London, or else in parishes with over 3,000 households, had to be a householder assessed at £40 or more per annum. Elsewhere a vestryman had to be assessed at £10 or more per annum. One third of the elected representatives retired each year.

B245 Municipal Corporations Act 1835. This Act followed soon after the Reform Bill 1832. The reform of the franchise for municipal elections was also long overdue and generally speaking the same basis was used in the 1835 Act as for the 1832 Bill.

The franchise was extended to each male person who had either occupied as owner or tenant a property in the parish for 2½ years, or had paid poor rates, or who had lived within 7 miles of the borough for the previous six months. Towns with a population of over 6,000 were divided into wards. Those qualified *to be selected* were:
(a) those in towns divided into four or more wards, who owned estate or property worth £1,000 or occupied land assessed at £30 or more per annum
(b) those, elsewhere, who possessed estate or property worth £500 or occupied land assessed at £15 or more per annum.

Voting was by signed voting paper. In order to vote, a tenant who paid his rates via his landlord, had to make special application. The Representation of the People Act 1867 made it easier for a tenant to do this.

B246 Metropolis Management Act 1855. This Act, applicable to London only, established the Metropolitan Board of Works as an overall local authority for the metropolis. The Board itself was mostly made up of nominations from the vestries.

In the election of vestries all parishioners rated for one year were entitled to vote. The qualification for election remained as being a householder assessed at £40 or more per annum. On the request of five ratepayers a secret ballot could be held. District Boards underneath the MBW were set up and their membership elected by the vestries.

B247 Local Government Act 1894. This Bill transferred the civil functions of vestries outside London to new parish councils and parish meetings. It also created Rural and Urban District Councils. All county and parliamentary electors were given one vote each.

In rural parishes an open meeting known as the parish meeting (to which all ratepayers and lodgers might come), would convene and in the larger parishes elect a committee to govern. Those electors, including women, who had been resident for 12 months were eligible for election.

B248 Local Government Act 1899. This Act converted London vestries established by the 1855 Metropolis Management Act into borough councils. Women were ineligible for membership, and aldermen were co-opted by councillors.

B249 Qualification for Women (County and Borough Councils) Act 1907. This Act enabled women to become councillors.

B250 Later franchise. The Representation of the People Act 1918 established a common franchise for county councils, boroughs, parishes and urban and district councils:

Men – six months occupancy of premises or land within the area.

Women – as for men, or else as the wife of a man qualified to vote, if in both cases she was over thirty.

The representation of the People Act 1928 permitted women of 21 years and over to vote. The Representation of the People Act 1945 extended local government franchise to all those registered for Parliamentary elections.

Poor Law Franchise

B251 Gilbert's Act 1782. Franchise was restricted, in the election of Guardians, to owners or occupiers of premises assessed at £5 or more, but this qualification did not apply in those areas where it would mean that less than ten people would be qualified to vote.

B252 Poor Law Amendment Act 1834. This Act defined the conditions for the elections of Guardians in Unions of parishes. The franchise was extended to owners of land in the parishes and to those ratepayers rated for one year. The owners were allowed votes as for the 1818 Vestries Act. Ratepayers were allowed votes as follows:

Assessed to the Poor rate at less than £50 – 1 vote

Assessed to the Poor rate at less than £400 – 2 votes

Assessed to the Poor rate at over £400 – 3 votes

B253 Poor Law Amendment Act 1844. Owners and ratepayers were allowed votes in the election of Guardians as follows:

Assessed to the Poor rate at less than £50 – 1 vote

Assessed to the Poor rate at less than £100 – 2 votes

Assessed to the Poor rate at less than £150 – 3 votes

Assessed to the Poor rate at less than £200 – 4 votes

Assessed to the Poor rate at less than £250 – 5 votes

Assessed to the Poor rate at above £250 – 6 votes

B254 Public Health Act 1848. This Act provided for the election of local Public Health Boards. The franchise was extended to all landowners and ratepayers. Votes were allowed as under the Poor Law Amendment Act 1844 (qv). Members of the Boards had to live in the area or within 7 miles. In boroughs the councils acted as the Boards.

Burial Board franchise

B255 Burial Act 1852. This Act applied to London. The Boards were elected by the vestries. Members had to be ratepayers. The Burial Act 1853 extended the provisions of the 1852 Act beyond London.

School Board franchise

B256 Education Act 1870. This Act allowed for the election of School Boards. The franchise, in boroughs, was extended to all burgesses, in London to all parishioners rated for one year, and elsewhere to all ratepayers. Each voter had one vote for each vacancy and if he chose could cast all his votes for one candidate.

Bibliography

PART SEVEN
BIBLIOGRAPHY

Classes of Society
Bond Men made free: medieval peasant movements and the English Rising of 1381, R. H. Hilton (1973)
The English Peasantry in the later Middle Ages, R. H. Hilton (1975)

Areas of Administration
The Manor and the Borough, Sidney and Beatrice Webb (2 vols 1908)
Life on the English Manor, H. S. Bennett (1948)
The Parish and the County, Sidney and Beatrice Webb (1906)
The Parish, J. Toulmin Smith (rev. 1857)
Liberties and Communities in Medieval England, Helen Cam (1963)
British Borough Charters 1042–1216, A. Ballard (1913)
British Borough Charters 1216–1307, A. Ballard and J. Tait (1923)
British Borough Charters 1307–1660, H. Weinbaum (1943)
Borough Customs, M. Bateson (2 vols Seldon Society 1904–6)
The Story of Early Municipal History, J. Tait (1932)
English Local Administration in the Early Middle Ages, Helen Jewell (1972)
The Medieval English Borough, J. Tait (1936)
New Towns of the Middle Ages: town plantation in England, Wales and Gascony, Maurice Beresford (1967)
Town Life in the Fifteenth Century, Alice Stopford (2 vols 1894)
Town Government in the Sixteenth Century, J. H. Thomas (1933)
Medieval Panorama, G. G. Coulton (1945)
New Towns of the Middle Ages, M. W. Beresford (1967)
English Towns 1500–1700, John Patten (1978)
Old Parish Life in London, Charles Pendrill (1937)
The English Village Community, Fredk Seebohm (1883 repr. 1971)
London Life in the Eighteenth Century, M. D. George (1930)
Social Life in the Reign of Queen Anne, John Ashton (1882)
English Landed Society in the 19th Century, F. M. L. Thompson (1963)

Franchise
Electoral Reform in England and Wales: the Development and Operation of the Parliamentary Franchise, 1832–1885. Charles Seymour (Yale University Press 1915)
The Passing of the Great Reform Bill, J. R. M. Butler (1914, repr. 1964)
Social Geography of British Elections, 1885–1910, Henry Pelling (1967)
A History of Parliamentary Elections and Electioneering in the Old Days, Joseph Grego (1886)
The English Local Government Franchise, B. Keith Lucas (1952)
Women's Suffrage and Party Politics 1866–1914, Constance Rover (1967)
The Electoral System in Britain since 1918, David E. Butler (1963)
A Handlist of British Parliamentary Poll Books, John Sims (1984)

SECTION C

Taxes, Services and Rents

PART ONE
SOME NATIONAL TAXES

C1 Armorial Bearings.   A tax was imposed from 1793 to 1882 on those carrying armorial bearings.

C2 Carriage Tax.   A tax was levied from 1747 to 1782 on the possession of a carriage.

C3 Carucage.   A tax first levied in 1194 on each carucate (hide) of land held, based upon the information contained in the Domesday Book. In areas where the term Hide was used the tax was called Hideage or Hidegeld. It was discontinued in 1224.

C4 Clocks and Watches.   A tax was levied on the possession of clocks and watches from 1797–8.

C5 Danegeld.   A tax raised, certainly by AD991, as tribute to the Danes to discourage an invasion of England. It was based upon the amount of land in each shire. Cnut later levied the tax, calling it Heregeld, to maintain a standing army, but it was abolished in 1051.

William I revived the right to raise the tax for his own revenue. In 1083/4 he raised a levy of 72 (old) pence on each hide or carucate of land. Professor Maitland's book *Domesday and Beyond* gives a list of each county's contribution in the middle of the 12th century. The tax was discontinued in 1163.

C6 Decimation.   A tax imposed on Royalists in 1655 which amounted to a 10 per cent levy on income from land.

C7 Dogs.   A tax was levied from 1796 to 1882 on the possession of dogs.

C8 Female Servants Tax.   A tax was imposed from 1785 to 1792 on households employing female servants.

C9 Food Rents.   An obligation, in Old English times, to make sufficient provision for the king and his household for a day. Generally this obligation had been commuted to a money payment by the time of the Norman Conquest.

47

C10 Free and Voluntary Present to King Charles II. Moneys supplied voluntarily by inhabitants to support the king after his restoration to the throne. It was collected in 1661, usually on town market days.

C11 Fumage. A Saxon tax on the number of chimneys in a house.

C12 Game Duty. From 1784 to 1807 all persons qualified to kill or sell game, including the manorial gamekeepers, registered with the Clerk of the Peace, who issued a certificate for which they paid a fee.

C13 Geld. An Old English term to denote an extraordinary tax based on land holdings.

C14 Guns. A tax was levied on the possession of guns from 1870–82.

C15 Hair Powder Duty. From 1795 to 1798 it was required that people using hair powder should pay duty and obtain a licence.

C16 Hearth Tax. A tax levied from 19th May 1662 until 1689 (1690 in Scotland). Its records are important to local historians as they provide an indication of the size of each assessed house at the time. Exempt from payment were those in receipt of poor relief, those inhabiting houses worth less than 20 shillings per annum and not paying parish rates, charitable institutions such as schools and almshouses, and industrial hearths with the exception of smiths' forges and bakers' ovens. The tax, paid by the occupier, was two shillings on each hearth which was collected in two instalments at Lady Day and Michaelmas. The most informative returns, many of which have been published, occur between 1662–6 and 1669–74.

C17 Horses. A tax was levied from 1784 to 1874 on the possession of horses.

C18 House-Duty. A tax was levied on inhabited houses from 1851 to 1924. It replaced the Window Tax.

C19 Income Tax. A tax first levied in 1799 to help pay for the war against France, abolished in 1802, and revived in 1803. The rate originally was 2 shillings in the £.

C20 Knight's Service. Originally the military support and other obligations due from a knight occupying a Knight's Fee (qv) to the Crown. These were later commuted to a money payment.

C21 Land Tax. A tax collected between c1692 and 1832 at the usual rate of 4 shillings in the £, by the county authorities. It was superseded by a similar tax until 1949. The records from 1780–1832 indicate the people paying tax in each county.

C22 Lay Subsidy. A tax on a person's movable items was exacted in 1181 – the so-called Saladin Tithe, at a rate of one tenth of their value. Later the tax, paid by lay people only, was standardised at one tenth for town residents and one fifteenth for country dwellers. It was last collected in 1623. Alternatively called Tenths and Fifteenths.

C23 Male Servants Tax. A tax levied from 1777 to 1852 on households employing male servants.

C24 Poll Tax. A form of personal tax which was imposed three times in the 14th century, and which was revived in 1513 and on several occasions in the 17th century. It was exacted for the last time in 1698. Some returns list not only the head of household but the family and servants as well.

C25 Purveyance. The right of the Crown to exact from a locality provisions at a rate below the market price, as the Court travelled round the country. Parish constables were responsible for arranging the transactions and also collected any payments which bought exemption from this irritating imposition.

C26 Racehorses. A tax was levied from 1784 to 1874 on the possession of racehorses.

C27 Registration Tax. A tax levied from 1694–1706 on christenings, marriages and burials recorded in parish registers. Also taxed were childless widowers, and bachelors over 25. In 1783 a tax was again placed on entries in parish registers, which resulted in an immediate fall in entries. This tax was repealed in 1794.

C28 Scutage. By the 11th century it was becoming increasingly difficult to enforce the obligation that each tenant-in-chief should provide military support for the Crown. Scutage, a term meaning 'shield-money', was introduced so that the tenants could commute the obligation. It was fixed at 20 shillings per Knight's Fee (qv).

C29 Silver Plate Tax. A tax was levied from 1756 to 1777 on the possession of silver plate.

C30 Window Tax. A tax imposed in 1696 on house occupiers to help meet the cost of reminting the damaged coinage of the realm. It replaced the Hearth Tax (qv). Each household paid a basic 2 shillings and those with between 10 and 20 windows paid a further 8 shillings. A new Act in 1747 provided that households with between 10 and 14 windows paid 6 pence per window on top of the old basic 2 shillings, and those with between 15 to 19 paid 9 pence; those above that paid one shilling per window. In 1825 those with less than 8 windows were made exempt; Scotland was exempted altogether in 1707. The tax was abolished in 1851.

PART TWO
LOCAL TAXES, SERVICES, RENTS, RATES AND OTHER DUES

C31 Aids. A Feudal Aid was a gift from a free tenant to his lord which could be exacted, according to Magna Carta, on three occasions: to pay a ransom on the lord's person, when the lord's eldest son was knighted, and when the lord's eldest daughter was married. The Statute of Westminster 1275 enacted that a Feudal Aid could not be paid until the eldest son was fifteen, and the eldest daughter was seven.

A Gracious Aid was paid by a lord or tenant-in-chief to the Crown. The amount was limited to 20 shillings for a Knight's Fee (qv) or 20 shillings for rented land worth £20 per annum. Feudal Aids were abolished by the Statute of Tenure 1660.

C32 Amober. In Wales and the border counties a payment to waive the lord's right to have sexual intercourse with the tenant's betrothed daughter before her wedding day.

C33 Arrentation. The commutation of services to a money payment.

C34 Assise rent. A free or customary rent which had become fixed.

C35 Avenage. A rent paid in oats by a tenant to his lord.

C36 Ballastage. A toll payable for the right to take ballast.

C37 Beaconage. Money paid towards the upkeep of the local beacon.

C38 Bede. A service performed by a tenant for his lord, hence Bedemad (mowing service), Bederepe (reaping service) and Bedewed (hoeing service).

C39 Benerth. A feudal service owed by a tenant to his lord, using his own plough and cart.

C40 Berbiage. A rent paid for pasturing sheep.

C41 Beverches. Services performed by unfree tenants at the lord's bidding.

C42 Bind Days. The days on which tenants were bound to work for their lord as an obligation of their tenure. Alternatively called Bailie-Days.

C43 Blancheferme. A rent or due paid to the Hundred sheriff.

C44 Bondage. A service given by a tenant to his lord as an obligation of his tenure.

C45 Boon. Service in kind or labour given by a tenant to his lord, hence Boonwork which was a day's work at specific times such as harvest or ploughing.

C46 Bord Lode. A labour service carried out by a Bordar (qv) to his lord by carrying timber from the wood to the latter's house.

C47 Brigbote. Money paid for the upkeep of the local bridges.

C48 Burgbote. Money paid for the upkeep of a borough's walls.

C49 Cane. A Scottish and north-country term for a rent paid with produce.

C50 Cess. A widespread term denoting a tax or rate.

C51 Chevage. An annual payment made by a tenant to his lord for permission to live away from the manor or, if an outsider, to live within the manor.

C52 Chief Rents. Customary rents paid by freeholders to the manorial lord.

C53 Childwite. A fine paid for fathering an illegitimate child. The fine was regarded by the lord of the manor as compensation for cheapening the value of the woman to the manor.

C54 Chiminage. A toll to pass through the lord's forest using a path cleared by him.

C55 Common Fine. Payment made by a tenant to his lord. Alternatively called Headsilver.

C56 Cornage. A rent paid by a tenant to his lord based on the number of horned cattle he possessed. Alternatively called Horngeld, Neatgeld.

C57 County Rate. The County Rate Act 1739 allowed one general rate to be levied on the parishes to take the place of a number of miscellaneous payments.

C58 Ditchsilver. A payment made by tenants to pay for the scouring of ditches.

C59 Driftland. A rent paid by tenants to drive their cattle through a manor to market.

C60 Dry Boon. A colloquial term to describe a service to the lord which was rewarded with water rather than with ale.

C61 Farm. In this context, a rent or service for a landholding.

C62 Fee-Farm Rent. A perpetual rent of at least a quarter of the value of the land imposed on an estate held in fee.

C63 Feudal Incidents. A general term for the obligations arising from a feudal tenure, such as services, aids and reliefs.

C64 Fines. Moneys or other benefits which accrued to the lord from his tenants.

C65 Foldage. The lord's right to insist that his tenants' sheep graze on his demesne land for a period so as to manure it. The lord was obliged to provide a sheep fold.

C66 Fold Course. The lord's right to graze his sheep on his tenant's land.

C67 Free Services. These were known as honourable services performed by free tenants, such as military service. Most were commuted to money payments.

C68 Furnage. A sum paid by tenants to use the lord's baking oven or, alternatively, a price paid for the privilege of owning their own.

C69 Gale. Rent, paid on Gale Days.

C70 Gavelacre. A reaping service performed by tenants for their lord. The term also applied to land ploughed by tenants for the lord.

C71 Gavelerthe. A ploughing service performed by tenants for their lord.

C72 Gavelsed. A threshing service performed by tenants for their lord.

C73 Gavol. A Saxon term for money or service due from a tenant to his lord. Alternatively called Gable or Gafol.

C74 Geld. (a) A Saxon term for money or tribute paid as compensation for a crime.
   (b) A north-country term for a tax.

C75 Gressom. A fine paid by a tenant to a lord on entry into a holding of land.

C76 Groundage. (a) A tax paid for ground on which a ship stood when docked.
   (b) A Yorkshire term for the ground rent of a leasehold property.

C77 Harrage. A variation of Average (qv).

C78 Heusire. A payment made by a tenant of a manor for the privilege of holding a manorial court.

C79 Hock Day. One of the days of a year on which rent was paid; it was the second Tuesday after Easter Sunday.

C80 Landgable. A rent paid by a tenant of an ancient borough. Alternatively called Hawgable.

C81 Leywrite. A fine paid by a villein tenant to his lord if his daughter became pregnant while still unmarried, on the grounds that the woman was of reduced value to the manor.

C82 Mail. A Scottish and north-country term for rent.

C83 Manuel Rent. Money paid to commute a feudal service.

C84 Merchet. A payment from a tenant on the occasion of the marriage of his son or daughter. Alternatively called Marchet.

C85 Millsoke. The tenant's obligation and payment to grind his corn at the lord's mill. Alternatively called Thirling Mill or Suit of Mill.

C86 Multure. A toll paid to a miller for grinding corn.

C87 Murage. A tax to pay for the upkeep of the town or city walls.

C88 Pannage. A payment made by tenants to their lord for the right to pasture their pigs in the woods.

C89 Passage. A toll on the passage of goods or passengers.

C90 Pavage. A tax to pay for the upkeep of paved roadways.

C91 Plough Duty. The obligation of landed tenants to repair highways using their own ploughs and beasts.

C92 Pontage. A toll levied to cross a bridge, which would be used for its maintenance.

C93 Quarterage. County rates.

C94 Quit Rent. A payment made by tenants to their lord to excuse themselves from the customary manor services. Abolished in 1922.

C95 Rogue Money. An annual payment from each parish to the High Constable of the Hundred for the maintenance of prisoners in the county gaol.

C96 Scot and Lot. Payments made by urban dwellers for the upkeep of the various borough facilities – the forerunners of today's rates. In some boroughs the contributors were allowed to vote in Parliamentary elections and these rights were incorporated in the Representation of the People Act 1832.

C97 Selver. A feudal term for a payment or toll.

C98 Service. A general term for a duty, obligation or due resulting from a tenant's occupancy of land or buildings belonging to a manorial lord.

A villein, or unfree tenant gave labour service on the number of days customary in the manor, and also gave produce in lieu of rent. He might also pay various other dues, such as a fine when his daughter married, or when his son went to school or went into the Church.

A free tenant was anciently obliged to perform military service.

Most services were commuted to money payments.

C99 Service Silver. A payment made by feudal tenants to their lord when his heir attained his majority.

C100 Sessions Money. A county rate.

C101 Tallage. A tax exacted by the manorial lord on his tenants, usually paid at Michaelmas. It was abolished in the 14th century as it was superseded by other forms of local taxation. Tallage was also exacted by the Crown on towns and boroughs on Ancient Demesne (qv) land.

C102 Third Penny. A Saxon term for a third part of the shire court profits, which went to the ealdorman.

C103 Toll. Originally the right to levy dues and later the description of the dues themselves. Tolls were levied at markets and for the upkeep of roads and bridges. Freedom from tolls could be purchased.

C104 Trinoda Necessitas. A term to describe the basic obligations of all villeins in feudal times. It consisted of fyrdbote (military support), burghbote (the maintenance of fortresses), and bridgebote (the upkeep of roads and bridges).

C105 Ward Money. A payment to commute a tenant's obligation to serve as a castle guard.

C106 Wardwite. A fine paid to the lord of the manor by a tenant who has failed to provide a man to perform castle-guard.

C107 Water-Gavil. A rent paid for fishing in the lord's river.

C108 Wet Boon. A colloquial term to describe an obligatory service period given by tenants to their lord which was rewarded by ale.

C109 Wite. A feudal term for a fine.

C110 Wood Penny. A payment made to the lord for the right to take wood from the commons and wastes.

PART THREE
ECCLESIASTICAL TAXES, RENTS AND DUES

C111 Altarage. A general term which covered Mortuaries (qv), Surplice Fees (qv) and other minor church income.

C112 Annates. The first year's revenues from an ecclesiastical benefice which were paid to the Pope. Henry VIII suspended their payment in 1532 as a bargaining gesture in his divorce dispute with the Pope, and in 1534 annexed them to himself. In 1704 they were paid into Queen Anne's Bounty (qv).

C113 Appropriation. An ecclesiastical benefice whose Rectorial tithes went to a religious body or ecclesiastical dignitary.

C114 Church Rates. These were levied to defray the expenses of the parish church on real property, whether owned or leased, and were based on the amount of land held. Compulsory payment was abolished in 1868.

C115 Conductio Sedilium. Pew rents.

C116 Easter Dues. The Church Rates paid at Easter.

C117 Fabric Lands. Lands given to provide funds for the upkeep of the parish church.

C118 Godbote. A fine imposed by the church for an offence against God.

C119 Hearth Penny. A penny paid by free householders on the Thursday before Easter to the Minster church.

C120 Heritor. A Scottish term to describe a landholder who was obliged to pay tithes (alternatively called Teinds) for the upkeep of the minister and his church.

C121 Lamplands. A Yorkshire term to describe those lands whose rents were used for the upkeep of the church altar lights.

C122 Lewn(e). A Church rate.

C123 Mainport. A small offering, perhaps bread, to the rector instead of certain tithes.

C124 Mortuary. In effect, an ecclesiastical Heriot (qv). When a tenant died his second best chattel was taken by the Incumbent as recompense for the tithes and other dues supposedly unpaid during the deceased's lifetime. In 1529 Parliament limited Mortuaries to moderate payments according to the value of the estate involved. Estates under the value of 10 marks were exempted in Henry VIII's reign.

C125 Parsonage. In this context, the established revenue for the upkeep of the Incumbent.

C126 Peter's Pence. A tax imposed by the Pope, in the 10th century, of a penny for each hearth or house; it was payable on Lammas Day (Aug 1st). The tax was not always actively enforced and was finally abolished in 1534 when the revenues were diverted to the Crown instead. Alternatively called Pentecostals, Romescot, Smoke Farthing and Smoke Penny.

C127 Pit Money. A burial fee.

C128 Plough Alms. Until medieval times a penny paid by each plough team to the parish priest. It was collected within a fortnight of Easter.

C129 Queen Anne's Bounty. A fund established in 1704 to receive and use the annates and other ecclesiastical dues previously annexed by Henry VIII, and which were then the property of Queen Anne, to supplement the incomes of the poorer clergy. The fund was made responsible by the Tithe Act 1925 for the collection of the tithe rent-charges (see Tithes). These were abolished by the Tithe Act 1936 and government stock was received in compensation. In 1948 Queen Anne's Bounty and the Ecclesiastical Commission were combined to form the Church Commission.

C130 Soul Scot. A gift made from the estate of a deceased person to the parish priest. It was later known as a Mortuary (qv).

C131 Spiritualities. The sources of income to a bishop or an ecclesiastical establishment which were exempt from secular control.

C132 Surplice Fees. Fees paid to the Incumbent at marriages and burials.

C133 Temporalities. Ecclesiastical holdings which were subject to secular control.

C134 Tithes. The ancient system consisted of three separate tithes: *Praedial Tithes* which were calculated on income from produce (corn, oats, wood etc), *Mixed Tithes* which were calculated on the income from a combination of stock and labour (wood, pigs, milk etc), and *Personal Tithes* assessed on income derived from labour. Income from barren heath, waste woodland and glebe land was exempt. The produce was stored in tithe barns, many of which survive today.

The tithes, theoretically a tenth part of the income, went towards the upkeep of the Incumbent of the parish church. This was straightforward where the Rector was also the Incumbent, but in cases where the Rector was a monastic institution which appointed a vicar to be in charge of the parish, the tithes were divided between Rector and Vicar. These were called Great or Rectorial Tithes and Small or Vicarial Tithes respectively. An Act of 1391 obliged monastic rectors to use some of their tithe income to support the parish poor. The Reformation complicated things further because many of the holdings of the monastic bodies fell into the hands of the Crown and then into lay hands, so that a lay person could claim the Rectorial Tithes. The Incumbent (the vicar) had the tithes most troublesome to collect – from the minor produce and labour.

Under the Tithe Commutation Act 1836 tithes could be commuted to a rent-charge, and Commissioners were appointed to negotiate fair land values with the inhabitants. The Tithe Act 1925 transferred the income to the Queen Anne's Bounty fund (qv) and the Tithe Act 1936 extinguished tithes altogether.

C135 Wax Scot. A customary payment made for the maintenance of lights in churches.

PART FOUR
BIBLIOGRAPHY

The Administration of the Window and Assessed taxes 1696–1798, H. R. Ward (1963)
English Land Tax in the 18th Century, H. R. Ward (1953)
Lay Subsidies and Poll Taxes, M. W. Beresford (1963)
History of Taxation and Taxes in England, S. Dowell (4 vols 1884)
Land Tax Assessments 1690–1950, Jeremy Gibson and Dennis Mills (rev. 1984)
The History of Local Rates in England, E. Cannan (1896)

SECTION D
Archives, Documents and Printed Records

PART ONE
GENERAL TERMS

D1 Calendar. A catalogue of documents with summaries of their contents.

D2 Cartulary. A register of lands and privileges granted by charter, occasionally in rolls but more often in book form.

D3 Charter. A document recording a grant.

D4 Chirograph. A document written in duplicate or multiplicate on the same sheet, as in the case of an Indenture.

D5 Deed Poll. A deed made by one party, needing no duplicate. It was therefore permissible to cut the edge of it clean (poll) rather than indent it (see Indenture). The term now usually describes a document which refers to a change of surname.

D6 Dorse. The reverse side of a document, hence an endorsement when wording is added on the back.

D7 Enrolment. The registering or recording of a conveyance, title or lawful act on an official document such as a Close Roll or Plea Roll (qv). This practice was encouraged by the Statute of Enrolment 1535 which not only brought in income to the Crown but ensured that a permanent record of such matters survived. The necessity for enrolment of various deeds was abolished by the Law of Property Act 1925.

D8 Inventory. A list of personal belongings, goods and chattels, usually with a valuation.

D9 Letters Close. Private letters.

D10 Letters Patent. Open letters, usually embodying a grant of a holding or privilege.

D11 Membrane. A sheet of parchment sewn with others into a roll.

D12 Muniment. A title deed, or evidence of a right or privilege.

D13 Palimpsest. a) A sheet of parchment from which the original writing has been erased and on which new material has been written.
b) A monumental brass which has been taken up and engraved on the other side.

D14 Pawn. A parchment strip containing a list of names.

D15 Pell. A parchment document recording a money payment.

D16 Ragman. A parchment document to which was attached hanging seals.

D17 Recto. The front of a leaf, or a right-hand page.

D18 Rental. A register of rents due.

D19 Roll. A document consisting of a number of single sheets (membranes) sewn end to end. The term can also be used to denote a single membrane.

D20 Starr. A term applied, before the expulsion of the Jews in 1290, to contracts between Jews and Christians. They were written in both Latin and Norman-French with an acknowledgement at the foot in Hebrew.

D21 Time Immemorial. Alternatively 'Time out of mind'. Strictly speaking, it denoted time beyond legal memory, that is, before 1189.

D22 Title Deed. A legal document providing evidence of title to land or property necessary when a transfer of ownership is to be made. The Law of Property Act 1925 made it unnecessary henceforth to prove a title back further than 30 years provided that the previous transfer had taken place during that period. This legal relaxation meant that a great many early title deeds and documents giving evidence of sale were rendered superfluous and frequently led to their disposal, unless deposited in libraries or record offices.

D23 Verso. The reverse of a leaf or a left-hand page.

PART TWO
ROMAN NUMERALS

D24 Roman Numerals.

1	I	15	XV	200	CC
2	II	16	XVI	300	CCC
3	III	17	XVII	400	CD
4	IV	18	XVIII	500	D
5	V	19	XIX	600	DC
6	VI	20	XX	700	DCC
7	VII	30	XXX	800	DCCC
8	VIII	40	XL	900	CM
9	IX	50	L	1000	M
10	X	60	LX	1500	MD
11	XI	70	LXX	1900	MCM
12	XII	80	LXXX	2000	MM
13	XIII	90	XC		
14	XIV	100	C		

A bar placed over a numeral multiplies it by 1000, eg 7000 = $\overline{\text{VII}}$, 170,000 = $\overline{\text{CLXX}}$.

PART THREE
THE CALENDAR

D25 Julian Calendar. The Roman calendar, which was at odds with the solar year, had an accumulated deficit of about two months by the time Julius Caesar revised it. The Julian Calendar began 1st January 45BC.

D26 Gregorian Calendar. By 1582 the Julian calendar was ten days adrift of the solar year. In that year Pope Gregory XIII ruled that the 5th October should be the 15th October; this was generally adhered to in Catholic countries but adjustment was made in Protestant countries such as Germany and the Netherlands in 1700. England did not alter its calendar until 1752 when the 3rd September became the 14th. This led to much grumbling that days had been lost to people's lives; more particularly eleven taxable days were lost to the government and, it is contended, the tax year was then moved from March 25th, which was then New Year's Day, to April 6th to compensate for this. At the time of this change in the English calendar 1st January was officially made New Year's Day.

Properly, documents dated between 1st January and 25th March prior to 1753 should now be referred to as bridging two years. Thus a document originally dated 25th February 1750 is referred to now as 25th February 1750/1.

D27 Quarter Days and Rent Days.

Lady Day	Mar 25	(Annunciation of the Blessed Virgin)
Michaelmas	Sep 29	(Feast of St Michael and All Angels)
Christmas	Dec 25	(Feast of the Nativity)
Midsummer	Jul 6	up to and including 1752; thereafter Jun 24

D28 Saints' and Fixed Feast Days.

Jan 1	Circumcision
Jan 6	Epiphany (Twelfth Day)
Jan 13	St Hilary the Bishop
Feb 2	Candlemas. Purification of the Blessed Virgin
Mar 1	St David
Mar 17	St Patrick
Apr 23	St George
Apr 25	St Mark
May 1	May Day. St Philip and St James the Less
Jun 24	Nativity of St John the Baptist (Midsummer)
Jun 30	St Paul
Jul 25	St James the Apostle
Aug 1	Gule of August. Lammas Day up to 1752 inclusive
Aug 13	Lammas Day 1753 onward
Aug 24	St Bartholomew the Apostle
Sep 21	St Matthew the Apostle
Sep 29	St Michael and All Angels (Michaelmas)
Oct 18	St Luke
Oct 25	St Crispin
Oct 28	St Simon and St Jude the Apostles
Nov 1	All Saints (All Hallows)
Nov 2	All Souls
Nov 11	St Martin
Nov 30	St Nicholas
Dec 21	St Thomas the Apostle
Dec 25	Christmas
Dec 26	St Stephen. Boxing Day
Dec 27	St John the Evangelist
Dec 28	Holy Innocents
Dec 29	St Thomas à Becket

D29 Movable Feast Days.

Sexegesima: Second Sunday before Lent.

Septuagesima: Third Sunday before Lent.

Palm Sunday: Sunday before Easter.

Maundy Thursday: The day before Good Friday.

Easter Sunday: First Sunday after the full moon which happens upon, or next after, the 21st day of March; and if the full moon happens upon a Sunday, Easter Day is the Sunday after. (As laid down by Act of Parliament 24 George II). The Moon referred to is not the real moon but a hypothetical moon on whose 'full' the date of Easter depends, and the lunations of this Calendar Moon consist of 29 and 30 days alternately with certain modifications to make the date of its 'full' agree as nearly as possible with that of the real moon. Present legislation is that Easter shall fall on one of the 35 days between 22nd March and 25th April. No fixed Easter Day has been agreed upon.

Rogation Days: Monday, Tuesday, Wednesday preceding Ascension Day.

Ember Days: Wednesday, Friday and Saturday after a) the first Sunday in Lent,
  b) the Feast of Pentecost,
  c) 14th September, and
  d) 13th December

Trinity Sunday: Sunday following Whit Sunday.

Ash Wednesday: the first day in Lent; it can fall at the earliest 4th February and the latest 10th March.

Ascension Day: earliest 30th April, latest 3rd June.

Advent Sunday: the Sunday nearest to 30th November.

D30 Regnal Years. It was the custom in the Middle Ages for documents to be dated by the year of the monarch's reign: thus 34 Henry II would indicate a date of 1187/88, his regnal year beginning on 19th December 1187 and ending on the following 18th December. Regnal years were used into the twentieth-century but usually, by then, the *Anno Domini* date was given as well. The following is a list of regnal year dates up to the end of the reign of George V.

William I (1066–87)
25 Dec to 24 Dec

1	1066–67	8	1073–74	15	1080–81
2	1067–68	9	1074–75	16	1081–82
3	1068–69	10	1075–76	17	1082–83
4	1069–70	11	1076–77	18	1083–84
5	1070–71	12	1077–78	19	1084–85
6	1071–72	13	1078–79	20	1085–86
7	1072–73	14	1079–80	21	1086 to death 9 Sept 1087

William II (1087–1100)
26 Sept to 25 Sept

1	1087–88	6	1092–93	11	1097–98
2	1088–89	7	1093–94	12	1098–99
3	1089–90	8	1094–95	13	1099 to death 2 Aug 1100
4	1090–91	9	1095–96		
5	1091–92	10	1096–97		

Henry I (1100–35)
5 Aug to 4 Aug

1	1100–01	13	1112–13	25	1124–25
2	1101–02	14	1113–14	26	1125–26
3	1102–03	15	1114–15	27	1126–27
4	1103–04	16	1115–16	28	1127–28
5	1104–05	17	1116–17	29	1128–29
6	1105–06	18	1117–18	30	1129–30
7	1106–07	19	1118–19	31	1130–31
8	1107–08	20	1119–20	32	1131–32
9	1108–09	21	1120–21	33	1132–33
10	1109–10	22	1121–22	34	1133–34
11	1110–11	23	1122–23	35	1134–35
12	1111–12	24	1123–24	36	1135 to death 1 Dec. 1135

Stephen (1135–54)
26 Dec to 25 Dec

1	1135–36	5	1139–40	9	1143–44
2	1136–37	6	1140–41	10	1144–45
3	1137–38	7	1141–42	11	1145–46
4	1138–39	8	1142–43	12	1146–47

13	1147–48	16	1150–51	19	1153 to death 25 Oct 1154
14	1148–49	17	1151–52		
15	1149–50	18	1152–53		

Henry II (1154–89)
19 Dec to 18 Dec

1	1154–55	13	1166–67	25	1178–79
2	1155–56	14	1167–68	26	1179–80
3	1156–57	15	1168–69	27	1180–81
4	1157–58	16	1169–70	28	1181–82
5	1158–59	17	1170–71	29	1182–83
6	1159–60	18	1171–72	30	1183–84
7	1160–61	19	1172–73	31	1184–85
8	1161–62	20	1173–74	32	1185–86
9	1162–63	21	1174–75	33	1186–87
10	1163–64	22	1175–76	34	1187–88
11	1164–65	23	1176–77	35	1188 to death 6 July 1189
12	1165–66	24	1177–78		

Richard I (1189–99)
3 Sep to 2 Sep

1	1189–90	5	1193–94	9	1197–98
2	1190–91	6	1194–95	10	1198 to death 6 Apr 1199
3	1191–92	7	1195–96		
4	1192–93	8	1196–97		

John (1199–1216)

1	27 May 1199 to 17 May 1200
2	18 May 1200 to 2 May 1201
3	3 May 1201 to 22 May 1202
4	23 May 1202 to 14 May 1203
5	15 May 1203 to 2 June 1204
6	3 June 1204 to 18 May 1205
7	19 May 1205 to 10 May 1206
8	11 May 1206 to 30 May 1207
9	31 May 1207 to 14 May 1208
10	15 May 1208 to 6 May 1209
11	7 May 1209 to 26 May 1210
12	27 May 1210 to 11 May 1211
13	12 May 1211 to 2 May 1212
14	3 May 1212 to 22 May 1213
15	23 May 1213 to 7 May 1214
16	8 May 1214 to 27 May 1215
17	28 May 1215 to 18 May 1216
18	19 May 1216 to 19 Oct 1216

Henry III (1216–1272)
28 Oct to 27 Oct

1	1216–17	9	1224–25	17	1232–33
2	1217–18	10	1225–26	18	1233–34
3	1218–19	11	1226–27	19	1234–35
4	1219–20	12	1227–28	20	1235–36
5	1220–21	13	1228–29	21	1236–37
6	1221–22	14	1229–30	22	1237–38
7	1222–23	15	1230–31	23	1238–39
8	1223–24	16	1231–32	24	1239–40

D30 *(cont)*

25	1240–41	37	1252–53	49	1264–65
26	1241–42	38	1253–54	50	1265–66
27	1242–43	39	1254–55	51	1266–67
28	1243–44	40	1255–56	52	1267–68
29	1244–45	41	1256–57	53	1268–69
30	1245–46	42	1257–58	54	1269–70
31	1246–47	43	1258–59	55	1270–71
32	1247–48	44	1259–60	56	1271–72
33	1248–49	45	1260–61	57	1272 to
34	1249–50	46	1261–62		death
35	1250–51	47	1262–63		16 Nov 1272
36	1251–52	48	1263–64		

Edward I (1272–1307)
20 Nov to 19 Nov

1	1272–73	13	1284–85	25	1296–97
2	1273–74	14	1285–86	26	1297–98
3	1274–75	15	1286–87	27	1298–99
4	1275–76	16	1287–88	28	1299–00
5	1276–77	17	1288–89	29	1300–01
6	1277–78	18	1289–90	30	1301–02
7	1278–79	19	1290–91	31	1302–03
8	1279–80	20	1291–92	32	1303–04
9	1280–81	21	1292–93	33	1304–05
10	1281–82	22	1293–94	34	1305–06
11	1282–83	23	1294–95	35	1306 to
12	1283–84	24	1295–96		death
					7 July 1307

Edward II (1307–27)
8 July to 7 July

1	1307–08	8	1314–15	15	1321–22
2	1308–09	9	1315–16	16	1322–23
3	1309–10	10	1316–17	17	1323–24
4	1310–11	11	1317–18	18	1324–25
5	1311–12	12	1318–19	19	1325–26
6	1312–13	13	1319–20	20	1326 to
7	1313–14	14	1320–21		death
					20 Jan 1327

Edward III (1327–77)
25 Jan to 24 Jan

1	1327–28	16	1342–43	31	1357–58
2	1328–29	17	1343–44	32	1358–59
3	1329–30	18	1344–45	33	1359–60
4	1330–31	19	1345–46	34	1360–61
5	1331–32	20	1346–47	35	1361–62
6	1332–33	21	1347–48	36	1362–63
7	1333–34	22	1348–49	37	1363–64
8	1334–35	23	1349–50	38	1364–65
9	1335–36	24	1350–51	39	1365–66
10	1336–37	25	1351–52	40	1366–67
11	1337–38	26	1352–53	41	1367–68
12	1338–39	27	1353–54	42	1368–69
13	1339–40	28	1354–55	43	1369–70
14	1340–41	29	1355–56	44	1370–71
15	1341–42	30	1356–57	45	1371–72

46	1372–73	49	1375–76		death 21
47	1373–74	50	1376–77		June 1377
48	1374–75	51	1377 to		

Richard II (1377–99)
22 June 21 June

1	1377–78	9	1385–86	17	1393–94
2	1378–79	10	1386–87	18	1394–95
3	1379–80	11	1387–88	19	1395–96
4	1380–81	12	1388–89	20	1396–97
5	1381–82	13	1389–90	21	1397–98
6	1382–83	14	1390–91	22	1398–99
7	1383–84	15	1391–92	23	1399 to
8	1384–85	16	1392–93		death
					29 Sept 1399

Henry IV (1399–1413)
30 Sept to 29 Sept

1	1399–00	7	1405–06	13	1411–12
2	1400–01	8	1406–07	14	1412 to
3	1401–02	9	1407–08		death
4	1402–03	10	1408–09		20 Mar 1413
5	1403–04	11	1409–10		
6	1404–05	12	1410–11		

Henry V (1413–22)
21 Mar to 20 Mar

1	1413–14	5	1417–18	9	1421–22
2	1414–15	6	1418–19	10	1422 to
3	1415–16	7	1419–20		death
4	1416–17	8	1420–21		31 Aug 1422

Henry VI (1422–61)
1 Sept to 31 Aug

1	1422–23	14	1435–36	27	1448–49
2	1423–24	15	1436–37	28	1449–50
3	1424–25	16	1437–38	29	1450–51
4	1425–26	17	1438–39	30	1451–52
5	1426–27	18	1439–40	31	1452–53
6	1427–28	19	1440–41	32	1453–54
7	1428–29	20	1441–42	33	1454–55
8	1429–30	21	1442–43	34	1455–56
9	1430–31	22	1443–44	35	1456–57
10	1431–32	23	1444–45	36	1457–58
11	1432–33	24	1445–46	37	1458–59
12	1433–34	25	1446–47	38	1459–60
13	1434–35	26	1447–48	39	1460 to
					deposition
					4 Mar 1461

Edward IV (1461–83)
4 Mar to 3 Mar

1	1461–62	6	1466–67	11	1471–72
2	1462–63	7	1467–68	12	1472–73
3	1463–64	8	1468–69	13	1473–74
4	1464–65	9	1469–70	14	1474–75
5	1465–66	10	1470–71	15	1475–76

16	1476–77	20	1480–81
17	1477–78	21	1481–82
18	1478–79	22	1482–83
19	1479–80	23	1483 to

death
9 Apr 1483

Edward V (1483)
1 9 Apr 1483 to
25 June 1483

Richard III (1483–85)
26 June to 25 June

1	1483–84	2	1484–85	3	1485 to

death
22 Aug 1485

Henry VII (1485–1509)
22 Aug to 21 Aug

1	1485–86	9	1493–94	17	1501–02
2	1486–87	10	1494–95	18	1502–03
3	1487–88	11	1495–96	19	1503–04
4	1488–89	12	1496–97	20	1504–05
5	1489–90	13	1497–98	21	1505–06
6	1490–91	14	1498–99	22	1506–07
7	1491–92	15	1499–00	23	1507–08
8	1492–93	16	1500–01	24	1508 to

death
21 Apr 1509

Henry VIII (1509–47)
22 Apr to 21 Apr

1	1509–10	14	1522–23	27	1535–36
2	1510–11	15	1523–24	28	1536–37
3	1511–12	16	1524–25	29	1537–38
4	1512–13	17	1525–26	30	1538–39
5	1513–14	18	1526–27	31	1539–40
6	1514–15	19	1527–28	32	1540–41
7	1515–16	20	1528–29	33	1541–42
8	1516–17	21	1529–30	34	1542–43
9	1517–18	22	1530–31	35	1543–44
10	1518–19	23	1531–32	36	1544–45
11	1519–20	24	1532–33	37	1545–46
12	1520–21	25	1533–34	38	1546 to
13	1521–22	26	1534–35		

death
28 Jan 1547

Edward VI (1547–53)
28 Jan to 27 Jan

1	1547–48	4	1550–51	7	1553 to
2	1548–49	5	1551–52		
3	1549–50	6	1552–53		

death
6 July 1553

Mary
1 6 July 1553 to 5 July 1554
2 6 July 1554 to 24 July 1554

Philip and Mary
1 & 2	25 July 1554 to	5 July 1555
1 & 3	6 July 1555 to	24 July 1555
2 & 3	25 July 1555 to	5 July 1556
2 & 4	6 July 1556 to	24 July 1556
3 & 4	25 July 1556 to	5 July 1557
3 & 5	6 July 1557 to	24 July 1557
4 & 5	25 July 1557 to	5 July 1558
4 & 6	6 July 1558 to	24 July 1558
5 & 6	25 July 1558 to	17 Nov 1558

Elizabeth I (1558–1603)
17 Nov to 16 Nov

1	1558–59	16	1573–74	31	1588–89
2	1559–60	17	1574–75	32	1589–90
3	1560–61	18	1575–76	33	1590–91
4	1561–62	19	1576–77	34	1591–92
5	1562–63	20	1577–78	35	1592–93
6	1563–64	21	1578–79	36	1593–94
7	1564–65	22	1579–80	37	1594–95
8	1565–66	23	1580–81	38	1595–96
9	1566–67	24	1581–82	39	1596–97
10	1567–68	25	1582–83	40	1597–98
11	1568–69	26	1583–84	41	1598–99
12	1569–70	27	1584–85	42	1599–00
13	1570–71	28	1585–86	43	1600–01
14	1571–72	29	1586–87	44	1601–02
15	1572–73	30	1587–88	45	1602 to

death
24 Mar 1603

James I (1603–25)
24 Mar to 23 Mar

1	1603–04	9	1611–12	17	1619–20
2	1604–05	10	1612–13	18	1620–21
3	1605–06	11	1613–14	19	1621–22
4	1606–07	12	1614–15	20	1622–23
5	1607–08	13	1615–16	21	1623–24
6	1608–09	14	1616–17	22	1624–25
7	1609–10	15	1617–18	23	1625 to
8	1610–11	16	1618–19		

death
27 Mar 1625

Charles I (1625–49)
27 Mar to 26 Mar

1	1625–26	9	1633–34	17	1641–42
2	1626–27	10	1634–35	18	1642–43
3	1627–28	11	1635–36	19	1643–44
4	1628–29	12	1636–37	20	1644–45
5	1629–30	13	1637–38	21	1645–46
6	1630–31	14	1638–39	22	1646–47
7	1631–32	15	1639–40	23	1647–48
8	1632–33	16	1640–41	24	1648 to

death
30 Jan 1649

D30 *(cont)*

Commonwealth (1649–1660)
Ordinary dating was used.

Charles II (1660–85)
His first regnal year was calculated from the death of his father until his own accession
29 May to 29 Jan
12 1660–61

30 Jan to 29 Jan

13	1661–62	21	1669–70	29	1677–78
14	1662–63	22	1670–71	30	1678–79
15	1663–64	23	1671–72	31	1679–80
16	1664–65	24	1672–73	32	1680–81
17	1665–66	25	1673–74	33	1681–82
18	1666–67	26	1674–75	34	1682–83
19	1667–68	27	1675–76	35	1683–84
20	1668–69	28	1676–77	36	1684–85
				37	1685 to death 6 Feb 1685

James II (1685–88)
6 Feb to 5 Feb

1	1685–86	3	1687–88	4	1688 to 11 Dec 1688
2	1686–87				

William and Mary
13 Feb to 12 Feb

1	1689–90	3	1691–92	5	1693–94
2	1690–91	4	1692–93	6	1694 to 28 Dec 1694

William III
28 Dec to 27 Dec

7	1694–95	10	1697–98	13	1700–01
8	1695–96	11	1698–99	14	1701 to death 8 Mar 1702
9	1696–97	12	1699–00		

Anne (1702–14)
8 Mar to 7 Mar

1	1702–03	6	1707–08	11	1712–13
2	1703–04	7	1708–09	12	1713–14
3	1704–05	8	1709–10	13	1714 to death 1 Aug 1714
4	1705–06	9	1710–11		
5	1706–07	10	1711–12		

George I (1714–27)
1 Aug to 31 July

1	1714–15	6	1719–20	11	1724–25
2	1715–16	7	1720–21	12	1725–26
3	1716–17	8	1721–22	13	1726 to death 11 Jun 1727
4	1717–18	9	1722–23		
5	1718–19	10	1723–24		

George II (1727–60)
11 June to 10 June

1	1727–28	13	1739–40	25	1751–52
2	1728–29	14	1740–41		11 Jun to 21 Jun
3	1729–30	15	1741–42	26	1752–53
4	1730–31	16	1742–43		22 Jun to 21 Jun
5	1731–32	17	1743–44	27	1753–54
6	1732–33	18	1744–45	28	1754–55
7	1733–34	19	1745–46	29	1755–56
8	1734–35	20	1746–47	30	1756–57
9	1735–36	21	1747–48	31	1757–58
10	1736–37	22	1748–49	32	1758–59
11	1737–38	23	1749–50	33	1759–60
12	1738–39	24	1750–51	34	1760 to death 25 Oct 1760

George III (1760–1820)
25 Oct to 24 Oct

1	1760–61	23	1782–83	45	1804–05
2	1761–62	24	1783–84	46	1805–06
3	1762–63	25	1784–85	47	1806–07
4	1763–64	26	1785–86	48	1807–08
5	1764–65	27	1786–87	49	1808–09
6	1765–66	28	1787–88	50	1809–10
7	1766–67	29	1788–89	51	1810–11
8	1767–68	30	1789–90		Regency began 6 Feb 1811
9	1768–69	31	1790–91		
10	1769–70	32	1791–92		
11	1770–71	33	1792–93		
12	1771–72	34	1793–94	52	1811–12
13	1772–73	35	1794–95	53	1812–13
14	1773–74	36	1795–96	54	1813–14
15	1774–75	37	1796–97	55	1814–15
16	1775–76	38	1797–98	56	1815–16
17	1776–77	39	1798–99	57	1816–17
18	1777–78	40	1799–00	58	1817–18
19	1778–79	41	1800–01	59	1818–19
20	1779–80	42	1801–02	60	1819 to death 24 Jan 1820
21	1780–81	43	1802–03		
22	1781–82	44	1803–04		

George IV (1820–30)
29 Jan to 28 Jan

1	1820–21	5	1824–25	9	1828–29
2	1821–22	6	1825–26	10	1829–30
3	1822–23	7	1826–27	11	1830 to death 26 Jun 1830
4	1823–24	8	1827–28		

William IV (1830–37)
26 June to 25 June

1	1830–31	4	1833–34	7	1836 to death 20 June 1837
2	1831–32	5	1834–35		
3	1832–33	6	1835–36		

The Coronation Procession of Queen Victoria

Victoria (1837–1901)
20 June to 19 June

1	1837–38	**23**	1859–60	**45**	1881–82
2	1838–39	**24**	1860–61	**46**	1882–83
3	1839–40	**25**	1861–62	**47**	1883–84
4	1840–41	**26**	1862–63	**48**	1884–85
5	1841–42	**27**	1863–64	**49**	1885–86
6	1842–43	**28**	1864–65	**50**	1886–87
7	1843–44	**29**	1865–66	**51**	1887–88
8	1844–45	**30**	1866–67	**52**	1888–89
9	1845–46	**31**	1867–68	**53**	1889–90
10	1846–47	**32**	1868–69	**54**	1890–91
11	1847–48	**33**	1869–70	**55**	1891–92
12	1848–49	**34**	1870–71	**56**	1892–93
13	1849–50	**35**	1871–72	**57**	1893–94
14	1850–51	**36**	1872–73	**58**	1894–95
15	1851–52	**37**	1873–74	**59**	1895–96
16	1852–53	**38**	1874–75	**60**	1896–97
17	1853–54	**39**	1875–76	**61**	1897–98
18	1854–55	**40**	1876–77	**62**	1898–99
19	1855–56	**41**	1877–78	**63**	1899–00
20	1856–57	**42**	1878–79	**64**	1900 to
21	1857–58	**43**	1879–80		death
22	1858–59	**44**	1880–81		22 Jan 1901

Edward VII (1901–10)
22 Jan to 21 Jan

1	1901–02	**5**	1905–06	**9**	1909–10
2	1902–03	**6**	1906–07	**10**	1910 to
3	1903–04	**7**	1907–08		death
4	1904–05	**8**	1908–09		6 May 1910

George V (1910–36)
6 May to 5 May

1	1910–11	**10**	1919–20	**19**	1928–29
2	1911–12	**11**	1920–21	**20**	1929–30
3	1912–13	**12**	1921–22	**21**	1930–31
4	1913–14	**13**	1922–23	**22**	1931–32
5	1914–15	**14**	1923–24	**23**	1932–33
6	1915–16	**15**	1924–25	**24**	1933–34
7	1916–17	**16**	1925–26	**25**	1934–35
8	1917–18	**17**	1926–27	**26**	1935 to
9	1918–19	**18**	1927–28		death
					20 Jan 1936

D31 Perpetual Calendar. From the charts below the day of the week for any year since 1753 may be found. From CHART ONE find the key number or letter for the year. Refer then to CHART TWO; use the key number or letter already obtained, refer downwards to the month in which you are interested, and obtain the calendar panel number contained in CHART THREE. The appropriate panel gives the complete month for the year in question.

CHART ONE

	1781–7	1811–4	1841–2	1871–6	1901–4	1931–1	1961–6	1991–4
	1782–4	1812–C	1842–3	1872–D	1902–5	1932–B	1962–7	1992–C
1753–7	1783–5	1813–2	1843–6	1873–5	1903–1	1933–6	1963–4	1993–2
1754–4	1784–F	1814–3	1844–D	1874–1	1904–B	1934–7	1964–C	1994–3
1755–5	1785–3	1815–6	1845–5	1875–2	1905–6	1935–4	1965–2	1995–6
1756–F	1786–6	1816–D	1846–1	1876–E	1906–7	1936–C	1966–3	1996–D
1757–3	1787–7	1817–5	1847–2	1877–7	1907–4	1937–2	1967–6	1997–5
1758–6	1788–H	1818–1	1848–E	1878–4	1908–C	1938–3	1968–D	1998–1
1759–7	1789–1	1819–2	1849–7	1879–5	1909–2	1939–6	1969–5	1999–2
1760–H	1790–2	1820–E	1850–4	1880–F	1910–3	1940–D	1970–1	2000–E
1761–1	1791–3	1821–7	1851–5	1881–3	1911–6	1941–5	1971–2	2001–7
1762–2	1792–A	1822–4	1852–F	1882–6	1912–D	1942–1	1972–E	2002–4
1763–3	1793–4	1823–5	1853–3	1883–7	1913–5	1943–2	1973–7	2003–5
1764–A	1794–5	1824–F	1854–6	1884–H	1914–1	1944–E	1974–4	2004–F
1765–4	1795–1	1825–3	1855–7	1885–1	1915–2	1945–7	1875–5	2005–3
1766–5	1796–B	1826–6	1856–H	1886–2	1916–E	1946–4	1976–F	2006–6
1767–1	1797–6	1827–7	1857–1	1887–3	1917–7	1947–5	1977–3	2007–7
1768–B	1798–7	1828–H	1858–2	1888–A	1918–4	1948–F	1978–6	2008–H
1769–6	1799–4	1829–1	1859–3	1889–4	1919–5	1949–3	1979–7	
1770–7	1800–5	1830–2	1860–A	1890–5	1920–F	1950–6	1980–H	
1771–4	1801–1	1831–3	1861–4	1891–1	1921–3	1951–7	1981–1	
1772–C	1802–2	1832–A	1862–5	1892–B	1922–6	1952–H	1982–2	
1773–2	1803–3	1833–4	1863–1	1893–6	1923–7	1953–1	1983–3	
1774–3	1804–A	1834–5	1864–B	1894–7	1924–H	1954–2	1984–A	
1775–6	1805–4	1835–1	1865–6	1895–4	1925–1	1955–3	1985–4	
1776–D	1806–5	1836–B	1866–7	1896–C	1926–2	1956–A	1986–5	
1777–5	1807–1	1837–6	1867–4	1897–2	1927–3	1957–4	1987–1	
1778–1	1808–B	1838–7	1868–C	1898–3	1928–A	1958–5	1988–B	
1779–2	1809–6	1839–4	1869–2	1899–6	1929–4	1959–1	1989–6	
1780–E	1810–7	1840–C	1870–3	1900–7	1930–5	1960–B	1990–7	

CHART TWO

	1	2	3	4	5	6	7		A	B	C	D	E	F	H
JAN.	14	20	19	16	15	18	17	JAN.	18	20	15	17	19	14	16
FEB.	11	10	9	6	5	8	7	FEB.	1	3	12	28	2	4	27
MAR.	18	17	16	20	19	15	14	MAR.	14	16	18	20	15	17	19
APR.	22	21	13	24	23	26	25	APR.	25	13	22	24	26	21	23
MAY	20	19	18	15	14	17	16	MAY	16	18	20	15	17	19	14
JUNE	24	23	22	26	25	21	13	JUNE	13	22	24	26	21	23	25
JULY	15	14	20	17	16	19	18	JULY	18	20	15	17	19	14	16
AUG.	19	18	17	14	20	16	15	AUG.	15	17	19	14	16	18	20
SEP.	23	22	21	25	24	13	26	SEP.	26	21	23	25	13	22	24
OCT.	14	20	19	16	15	18	17	OCT.	17	19	14	16	18	20	15
NOV.	25	24	23	13	26	22	21	NOV.	21	23	25	13	22	24	26
DEC.	16	15	14	18	17	20	19	DEC.	19	14	16	18	20	15	17

1	2	3	4	5	6	7		A	B	C	D	E	F	H
		COMMON YEARS								**LEAP YEARS**				

CHART THREE

No. 1

Su.	Mo.	Tu.	We.	Th.	Fr.	Sa.
			1	2	3	4
5	6	7	8	9	10	11
12	13	14	15	16	17	18
19	20	21	22	23	24	25
26	27	28	29			

No. 8

Su.	Mo.	Tu.	We.	Th.	Fr.	Sa.
			1	2	3	4
5	6	7	8	9	10	11
12	13	14	15	16	17	18
19	20	21	22	23	24	25
26	27	28				

No. 15

Su.	Mo.	Tu.	We.	Th.	Fr.	Sa.
			1	2	3	4
5	6	7	8	9	10	11
12	13	14	15	16	17	18
19	20	21	22	23	24	25
26	27	28	29	30	31	

No. 22

Su.	Mo.	Tu.	We.	Th.	Fr.	Sa.
			1	2	3	4
5	6	7	8	9	10	11
12	13	14	15	16	17	18
19	20	21	22	23	24	25
26	27	28	29	30		

No. 2

Su.	Mo.	Tu.	We.	Th.	Fr.	Sa.
		1	2	3	4	5
6	7	8	9	10	11	12
13	14	15	16	17	18	19
20	21	22	23	24	25	26
27	28	29				

No. 9

Su.	Mo.	Tu.	We.	Th.	Fr.	Sa.
		1	2	3	4	5
6	7	8	9	10	11	12
13	14	15	16	17	18	19
20	21	22	23	24	25	26
27	28					

No. 16

Su.	Mo.	Tu.	We.	Th.	Fr.	Sa.
		1	2	3	4	5
6	7	8	9	10	11	12
13	14	15	16	17	18	19
20	21	22	23	24	25	26
27	28	29	30	31		

No. 23

Su.	Mo.	Tu.	We.	Th.	Fr.	Sa.
		1	2	3	4	5
6	7	8	9	10	11	12
13	14	15	16	17	18	19
20	21	22	23	24	25	26
27	28	29	30			

No. 3

Su.	Mo.	Tu.	We.	Th.	Fr.	Sa.
	1	2	3	4	5	6
7	8	9	10	11	12	13
14	15	16	17	18	19	20
21	22	23	24	25	26	27
28	29					

No. 10

Su.	Mo.	Tu.	We.	Th.	Fr.	Sa.
	1	2	3	4	5	6
7	8	9	10	11	12	13
14	15	16	17	18	19	20
21	22	23	24	25	26	27
28						

No. 17

Su.	Mo.	Tu.	We.	Th.	Fr.	Sa.
	1	2	3	4	5	6
7	8	9	10	11	12	13
14	15	16	17	18	19	20
21	22	23	24	25	26	27
28	29	30	31			

No. 24

Su.	Mo.	Tu.	We.	Th.	Fr.	Sa.
	1	2	3	4	5	6
7	8	9	10	11	12	13
14	15	16	17	18	19	20
21	22	23	24	25	26	27
28	29	30				

No. 4

Su.	Mo.	Tu.	We.	Th.	Fr.	Sa.
1	2	3	4	5	6	7
8	9	10	11	12	13	14
15	16	17	18	19	20	21
22	23	24	25	26	27	28
29						

No. 11

Su.	Mo.	Tu.	We.	Th.	Fr.	Sa.
1	2	3	4	5	6	7
8	9	10	11	12	13	14
15	16	17	18	19	20	21
22	23	24	25	26	27	28

No. 18

Su.	Mo.	Tu.	We.	Th.	Fr.	Sa.
1	2	3	4	5	6	7
8	9	10	11	12	13	14
15	16	17	18	19	20	21
22	23	24	25	26	27	28
29	30	31				

No. 25

Su.	Mo.	Tu.	We.	Th.	Fr.	Sa.
1	2	3	4	5	6	7
8	9	10	11	12	13	14
15	16	17	18	19	20	21
22	23	24	25	26	27	28
29	30					

No. 5

Su.	Mo.	Tu.	We.	Th.	Fr.	Sa.
						1
2	3	4	5	6	7	8
9	10	11	12	13	14	15
16	17	18	19	20	21	22
23	24	25	26	27	28	

No. 12

Su.	Mo.	Tu.	We.	Th.	Fr.	Sa.
						1
2	3	4	5	6	7	8
9	10	11	12	13	14	15
16	17	18	19	20	21	22
23	24	25	26	27	28	29

No. 19

Su.	Mo.	Tu.	We.	Th.	Fr.	Sa.
						1
2	3	4	5	6	7	8
9	10	11	12	13	14	15
16	17	18	19	20	21	22
23	24	25	26	27	28	29
30	31					

No. 26

Su.	Mo.	Tu.	We.	Th.	Fr.	Sa.
						1
2	3	4	5	6	7	8
9	10	11	12	13	14	15
16	17	18	19	20	21	22
23	24	25	26	27	28	29
30						

No. 6

Su.	Mo.	Tu.	We.	Th.	Fr.	Sa.
					1	2
3	4	5	6	7	8	9
10	11	12	13	14	15	16
17	18	19	20	21	22	23
24	25	26	27	28		

No. 13

Su.	Mo.	Tu.	We.	Th.	Fr.	Sa.
					1	2
3	4	5	6	7	8	9
10	11	12	13	14	15	16
17	18	19	20	21	22	23
24	25	26	27	28	29	30

No. 20

Su.	Mo.	Tu.	We.	Th.	Fr.	Sa.
					1	2
3	4	5	6	7	8	9
10	11	12	13	14	15	16
17	18	19	20	21	22	23
24	25	26	27	28	29	30
31						

No. 27

Su.	Mo.	Tu.	We.	Th.	Fr.	Sa.
					1	2
3	4	5	6	7	8	9
10	11	12	13	14	15	16
17	18	19	20	21	22	23
24	25	26	27	28	29	

No. 7

Su.	Mo.	Tu.	We.	Th.	Fr.	Sa.
				1	2	3
4	5	6	7	8	9	10
11	12	13	14	15	16	17
18	19	20	21	22	23	24
25	26	27	28			

No. 14

Su.	Mo.	Tu.	We.	Th.	Fr.	Sa.
				1	2	3
4	5	6	7	8	9	10
11	12	13	14	15	16	17
18	19	20	21	22	23	24
25	26	27	28	29	30	31

No. 21

Su.	Mo.	Tu.	We.	Th.	Fr.	Sa.
				1	2	3
4	5	6	7	8	9	10
11	12	13	14	15	16	17
18	19	20	21	22	23	24
25	26	27	28	29	30	

No. 28

Su.	Mo.	Tu.	We.	Th.	Fr.	Sa.
				1	2	3
4	5	6	7	8	9	10
11	12	13	14	15	16	17
18	19	20	21	22	23	24
25	26	27	28	29		

PART FOUR
LATIN CHRISTIAN NAMES

D32 Latin Christian Names. The following are some common Christian names found in Latin documents, with their English equivalents. Obvious examples such as Archibaldus for Archibald, have been omitted.

Adelheidis	Adelaide
Aegidius	Giles
Aelizia	Alice
Agelwinus	Aylwin
Agna/Agneta	Agnes
Alanus	Alan
Alberedus	Alfred
Aldrida	Etheldreda/Audrey
Alecia	Alice
Alienora	Eleanor
Aloysius	Lewis
Aluredus	Alfred
Amabilia	Mabel
Amia	Amy
Andreas	Andrew
Araldus	Harold
Arcturus	Arthur
Artorius	Arthur
Audoinus	Owen
Brigitta	Bridget
Caecilius	Cecil
Caius	Kay
Cardus	Charles
Constantia	Constance
Dionisia	Denise
Dionysius	Den(n)is
Dunechanus	Duncan
Duvenaldus	Donald
Eadgitha	Edith
Eadmundus	Edmund
Eadwardus	Edward
Egidius	Giles
Elfredus	Alfred
Elias	Ellis
Emelina	Emily
Ennes	Agnes
Ethelburga	Aubrey
Etheldreda	Audrey
Eva/Eva	Eve
Eudoardus	Edward
Eustachius	Eustace
Fides	Faith
Francisca	Frances
Franciscus	Francis
Fridericus	Frederick

Galfridus	Geoffrey
Galterus	Walter
Gerusius	Gervaise
Gilebertus	Gilbert
Gladusa	Gladys
Godefridus	Godfrey
Goisfridus	Geoffrey
Goscelinus	Jocelin
Gratia	Grace
Gualterus	Walter
Guido	Guy
Guillelmus	William
Helyas	Ellis
Hendricus	Henry
Hereweccus	Harvey
Hieremias	Jeremiah
Hieronymus	Jerome
Holeus	Howell
Horatius	Horace
Hugo	Hugh
Imania	Emma
Jacobus	Jacob, James
Joceus	Joyce
Johanna	Joan, Jane
Johannes	John
Josias	Josiah
Judas	Jude
Juliana	Juliane, Gillian
Junana	Jane
Laetitia	Lettice
Laurentius	Lawrence
Leonellus	Lionel
Leuelinus	Llywelyn
Lionhardus	Leonard
Lorentius	Lawrence
Lucas	Luke
Ludovicus	Lewis
Malculinus	Malcolm
Marcus	Mark
Marta	Martha
Mattaeus	Matthew
Maya	May
Meuricius	Maurice
Milo	Miles
Moyses	Moses
Natalis	Noel
Oeneus	Owen
Patricius	Patrick
Pero	Piers
Petrus	Peter/Piers

Radulfus	Ralph
Ricardus	Richard
Riceus	Rhys/Rees
Roesia	Rose
Rohelendus	Roland
Rothericus	Roderick
Salomon	Solomon
Sescilia	Cecily
Sibella	Sybil
Sidneus	Sidney
Silvanus	Silas
Tedbaldus	Theobald
Thomasina	Thomasine/Tamsin
Tobias	Toby
Umfridus	Humphrey
Vadinus	Valentine
Villefredus	Wilfrid
Wadinus	Valentine
Wilhelmus	William
Ylaria	Hillary

PART FIVE
STATE RECORDS

D33 Association Oath Rolls. In 1696 all persons in England and Wales holding public office were required to sign a pledge of loyalty to the Crown, although the Rolls contain most residents of substance and also liverymen of the City of London. They are housed in the Public Record Office, Chancery Lane, London, WC2., or else in Quarter Sessions records at County Record Offices.

D34 Chancery Rolls. These records, running from 1199 to 1937, record royal grants of land, privileges and titles. They also contain details of various commissions, *Inquisitiones ad quod damnum* held to investigate if a grant of a market or fair infringed an existing right, and title deeds. They form part of the archives of the Court of Chancery and are housed in the Public Record Office, Chancery Lane, London, WC2.

D35 Close Rolls. These records, running from 1204/5 to 1903, contain grants of the Crown originally folded (closed) and impressed with the Great Seal. They include enclosure awards, deeds poll, quit claims, provisioning of garrisons, aids and subsidies, and pardons. The reverse sides of the membranes were used for the enrolment of deeds, conveyances, and records of livery of seisin, charities and wills. They form part of the archives of the Court of Chancery and are housed at the Public Record Office, Chancery Lane, London, WC2.

D36 Compotus Rolls. These records consist of estate accounts of royal and seigniorial officials. They are housed at the Public Record Office, Chancery Lane, London, WC2.

D37 Domesday Book. The Domesday Survey consisted, before its recent rebinding, of two volumes completed in 1086. One dealt with Essex, Norfolk and Suffolk and the other with the remainder of England with the exception of Cumberland, Durham, Northumberland and northern Westmorland; London and Winchester are also omitted. The Survey's function was not to record all the landholdings of the country but to register all taxable holdings. Therefore not all lands or buildings are noted because many, particularly those owned by religious houses, were exempt from taxation.

The taxable units were usually expressed as hides or carucates (qv), or whatever the area's land measurement term was. The annual value of a unit was assessed together with its rise and fall in the previous twenty years. Recorded too were plough teams, pasture, pannage – in short, any factor which contributed to its annual value.

The Survey was compiled hundred by hundred, vill by vill, within each shire. However, in its final assembly the entries were reorganised so that they were grouped under landholders. Thus, one parish may be shown under a number of owners.

The needs of most researchers are met by the transcription and interpretation in the appropriate volume of the *Victoria County History* or the more comprehensive county volumes published by Phillimore & Co. The original survey is housed at the Public Record Office, Chancery Lane, London, WC2.

D38 Feet of Fines. These records contain judgements as to the ownership of land and property, quite often the result of collusive actions brought by the parties to establish title in the absence of documents. The judgement, or fine, (derived from the Latin *finis*, meaning 'end'), in effect terminated doubt or dispute and registered ownership; it was written three times on the same sheet of parchment, two sections of it going to the two parties involved and the third lodged with the Court of Common Pleas. The records are housed in the Public Record Office, Chancery Lane, London, WC2 where indexed calendars for the years 1509–1798 may be consulted.

D39 Fine or Oblata Rolls. These records are concerned with the fines imposed by the Crown on subjects in receipt of particular advantages such as a charter, privilege, or the holding of the wardship of an heiress. The rolls also record the appointment of royal officials. Some have been published or calendared. They are housed at the Public Record Office, Chancery Lane, London, WC2.

D40 Hansard. Cobbett's *Parliamentary Debates* (founded in 1804) was bought by Thomas Hansard in 1811. He renamed the publication *Hansard's Parliamentary Debates*. Although it is now an official government record the name has been retained except in the period 1889 to 1943 when it was omitted from the title-page. The records may be seen in the House of Lords Library.

D41 Home Office Records. The Home Office was established in 1782. Much of its archive material, now in the Public Record Office, is concerned with law and order. There are convict transportation records and numerous lists of prisoners indicted at Quarter Sessions. The Home Office dealt with the police as from 1829, with aliens from 1793, and with naturalisation from 1844.

D42 Inquisitiones Post Mortem. On the death of one of the king's tenants-in-chief an inquest was held by the official Escheator which established the date of death, the identity and age of the heir and the extent of lands held. These records began in the reign of Henry III and many have been calendared by the Public Record Office. An heir paid a tax called a 'relief' to enter into the estate; in the case of the heir being a minor the land reverted to the Crown until he came of age.

D43 Memoranda Rolls. These records principally deal with the the accounts of the sheriffs, but they were also used to enrol private deeds. They are housed at the Public Record Office, Chancery Lane, London, WC2.

D44 Parliamentary Acts. The records of Public and Private Acts since 1500, are housed in the House of Lords Library. Many have been printed as *Statutes of the Realm* or *Statutes at Large*.

D45 Patent Rolls. These records, running from 1201 to 1920, deal with borough charters, grants of land and privileges, presentation to benefices, alienation, wardship and the appointment of officers. They are housed at the Public Record Office, Chancery Lane, London, WC2.

D46 Pipe Rolls. These are the accounts rendered by the sheriffs to the Exchequer. They include details of rent and farm and any other form of Crown revenue, together with the sheriffs' own expenses. They date from 1120 to 1831 and include the *Liber Niger Scaccarii* (the *Black Book of the Exchequer*) – a survey of England compiled in 1166.

The Pipe Rolls are so called because they were rolled around a rod or pipe. A number have been published by the Pipe Roll Society.

D47 Protestation Oath Returns 1641/2. In 1641/2 Parliament organised a signed protest against the possibility of 'an arbitrary and tyrannical government'. The returns of this protest, arranged topographically, are in the House of Lords Library, and some have been printed. Those parishes whose returns are extant are listed in the *Calendar of the Manuscripts of the House of Lords*, Volume 5.

D48 Recovery Rolls. These records relate to property conveyances since the 15th century. They are housed at the Public Record Office, Chancery Lane, London, WC2.

PART SIX
PARISH REGISTERS AND NON-PAROCHIAL REGISTERS

D49 Mandate 1538. A Mandate, formulated by Thomas Cromwell in 1538, instructed each parish to purchase a 'sure coffer', the parson to have one key and a churchwarden another. Each marriage, christening and burial was to be registered weekly by the minister with the churchwarden acting as witness; these records were then to be deposited in the newly-acquired parish chest. Quite often these early registers were simply loose sheets and the survival rate is not high.

D50 Order 1598. An Order signed by Elizabeth I this year required that all the loose leaf registers be transcribed into parchment books, especially those records since her accession – a qualification which has led to the fact that the extant records of many parishes date from 1558. Henceforth new entries were to be made in books. Under this Order both churchwardens were to witness the entries which were read out each Sunday; also, a copy was sent of the year's entries to the diocesan bishop each Easter. These copies are known as Bishops' Transcripts (qv). Early registers usually have three sections in the same volume dealing with christenings, marriages and burials, but sometimes these are all mixed together in chronological order. Most entries are single lines of brief information.

D51 Ordinance 1644/5. This Ordinance instructed that birth dates should be noted in the register as well as the parents' names. The date of death was to be noted as well as the date of burial.

D52 Registration 1653. An Act passed this year officially transferred the custody of registers to the government. It also promoted the appointment of, sometimes illiterate, Parish Registers (registrars) to keep the records. A fee of one shilling was exacted for each registration which, of course, discouraged registration. An Act of 1654 made marriages the responsibility of the Justices of the Peace rather than the clergy and those couples still opting for a religious ceremony did not, therefore, register their marriage. This legislation was revoked at the Restoration.

D53 Burial in Wool Acts, 1667 and 1678. These Acts, intended to support the wool trade, enacted that corpses should be buried in wool. The 1678 Act said that 'no corpse of any person (except those who shall die of the plague), shall be buried in any shirt, shift, sheet or shroud or anything whatsoever, made or mingled with flax, hemp, silk, hair, gold or silver, or in any stuff or thing other than what is made of sheep's wool only . . .' A relative of the deceased was required to swear an affidavit (recorded in the registers), within eight days of the event that a 'woollen burial' had taken place or else a fine of £5 was levied not only on the estate of the deceased, but on anyone connected with the burial. These Acts were repealed in 1814 but they had by then fallen into disuse.

D54 Legislation 1694. To help pay for the war with France a tax was levied on the registration of christenings, marriages and burials. This was fixed at 2/- per christening, 2/6d per

marriage and 4/- per burial of a non-pauper. The tax was higher in the case of wealthy families. In addition all births, as distinct from christenings, were to be notified to the parish incumbent for a fee of sixpence: this was because many children were being baptised by Dissenting ministers, with a consequential loss of income to the parish priest.

D55 Legislation 1711. An Act was passed ordering that proper register books should be kept with ruled and numbered pages.

D56 Hardwicke's Marriage Act 1754. This Act, limited to England and Wales, was designed to end the mounting scandal of clandestine marriages. It enacted that weddings could only be solemnised after the publication of banns which were recorded at the back of the register or in a separate book. Bound volumes of specially printed forms to register marriages were introduced at this time. The Act laid down that no marriage might be performed except by a clergyman of the Church of England, although Jews and Quakers were exempt. It also provided that minors were to obtain the consent of their parents or guardians.

D57 Stamp Act 1783. A duty of 3d was imposed on each parish register entry. The incumbent was given a 10% commission for collection.

D58 George Rose's Act 1812. From 1 January 1813 the incumbent was to keep two specially printed registers to record christenings and burials, plus the register standardised by Hardwicke's Act of 1754 to record marriages. The entries for christenings were now to include the names, addresses and occupations of the parents, and the burial entries were to state the age, address and occupation of the deceased.

D59 Marriage Act 1823. This Act declared clandestine marriages (those without banns or licence) to be valid, but the officiating minister a felon.

D60 Marriage Act 1836. Superintendent registrars were empowered to issue licences for marriage in the office of a registrar or in a non-conformist church.

D61 Banns of Marriage. Banns are the published intention of marriage which are announced on three Sundays before the actual ceremony in the parish (or each of the parishes) in which the parties reside, so that objection may be made if necessary. They derive from an order of the Lateran Council of 1215. They may be avoided by obtaining a Marriage Licence (qv). Banns were recorded separately in registers, or in separate volumes, after Hardwicke's Marriage Act 1754 (qv).

D62 Marriage Licences. These date from the early 16th century and were a device to avoid the inconvenience of banns. Licences were usually obtained from the diocese in which one of the parties resided and in which the marriage was to take place, although in certain circumstances application could be made to the Vicar-General of the province. An allegation was sworn by one of the parties that no impediment to the marriage existed.

Marriage Licence Allegations are usually now to be found in county record offices, diocesan registries, or in the library of Lambeth Palace. For more details consult *Bishops' Transcripts and Marriage Licences, Bonds and Allegations, a Guide to their Location and Indexes*, by J. S. W. Gibson, published by the Federation of Family History Societies.

D63 Bishops' Transcripts. In 1598 incumbents were instructed to send copies of the entries in their parish register to the diocesan bishop each Easter. A combination of sporadic attention to this order and the lax care of the returns has meant that the Transcripts are poor substitutes for the registers, but are sometimes useful especially, of course, where the registers have not survived. For more details as to their existence and whereabouts consult *Bishops' Transcripts and Marriage Licences, Bonds and Allegations, a Guide to their Location and Indexes*, by J. S. W. Gibson, published by the Federation of Family History Societies.

D64 Searching Parish Registers. Many parish registers have been deposited with county record offices where they are available for research; generally, microfilm or transcripts are available for the older volumes. In addition, the Society of Genealogists has a large collection of transcripts. A *National Index of Parish Registers* has been published by Phillimore.

Registers still in the care of the incumbent may be consulted under the provisions of the Parochial Registers and Records Measure 1978. This laid down a fee of £3 for the first hour or part thereof, and £2 for each subsequent hour, although this may be varied by mutual agreement with the incumbent for longer

searches. The registers must be stored in proper conditions and may be seen 'at all reasonable hours'. The incumbent may also do the search work himself although a fee should be previously agreed for this.

D65 Scottish Registers. The Presbyterian Church of Scotland registers began in 1558 but few survive from the 16th century. They are deposited at New Register House, Edinburgh. Researchers should consult a *Detailed List of Parochial Registers of Scotland* (1872).

D66 Irish Registers. Only about one third of the old parish registers escaped the 1922 fire and these, generally, had not then been deposited in Dublin. Catholic registers, which began around 1820, also survive because they had not been deposited. These old registers may be consulted at the office of the Registrar General, Custom House, Dublin.

D67 Non-Parochial Registers. In 1837 Non-Conformist religions and other bodies which had kept registers of births, deaths and marriages, were ordered to hand their registers over to the Registrar General. Jews were exempt and the Society of Friends was allowed to copy their records into digests before depositing them some years later. Further deposits were made in 1850 by when other registers had come to light. A useful guide to these is contained in *The General Register Office List of Nonparochial Registers, Main Series, and the Society of Friends Series*, which is published in Vol 42 of the publications of the List and Index Society.

D68 Baptist Registers. The old Baptist registers are now at the Public Record Office, Chancery Lane, London, WC2. The earliest known registers are as follows:

Beds 1709, Berks 1764, Bucks 1773, Cambs 1778, Cheshire 1813, Cornwall 1760, Cumberland 1797, Derbys 1753, Devon 1767, Dorset 1778, Durham 1768, Essex 1775, Glos 1651, Hants 1785, Hereford 1747, Herts 1717, Hunts 1789, Kent 1650, Lancs 1755, Leics 1752, Lincs 1703, London 1656, Middlesex 1783, Norfolk 1761, Northants 1755, Northumberland 1781, Notts 1742, Oxfordshire 1647, Rutland 1768, Shrops 1766, Somerset 1679, Staffs 1793, Suffolk 1785, Surrey 1781, Sussex 1669, Warks 1750, Wilts 1767, Worcs 1756, Yorks 1685.

Anglesey 1789, Brecon 1822, Carmarthen 1783, Denbigh 1785, Flint 1827, Glamorgan 1773, Merioneth 1800, Montgomery 1832, Pembroke 1787.

D69 Bible Christian Registers. The earliest known registers, now housed at the Public Record Office, Chancery Lane, London, WC2, are: Cornwall 1817, Devon 1818, Hants 1824, Kent 1820, Lancs 1800, London 1823, Somerset 1823, Surrey 1835, Sussex 1824.

D70 Catholic Registers. Catholics kept unofficial registers with details of births, deaths and marriages, but most of these are no older than 1778 when the first Roman Catholic Relief Bill was passed. Very few Catholic registers were handed over to the Registrar General in 1837 and most are still in the hands of the church; the Catholic Record Society has published numbers of them.

D71 Cemetery Registers. A number of prominent cemeteries, in which nonconformists could be buried, kept registers. These were deposited with the Registrar General and are now at the Public Record Office, Chancery Lane, London, WC2. These cemeteries were Bunhill Fields, London 1713–1854, Eccleshall, Sheffield 1836–38, Leeds 1835–37, Liverpool 1825–37, Walworth, London 1829–37 and Victoria Park, London 1853–76.

The registers of other large, private cemeteries such as Highgate and Kensal Green in London, are either still held by the private companies operating them or else at local authority record offices.

D72 Congregationalist Registers. The early registers are now housed at the Public Record Office, Chancery Lane, London, WC2. The earliest known registers are:

Beds 1730, Berks 1705, Bucks 1765, Cambs 1688, Cheshire 1709, Cornwall 1769, Cumberland 1700, Derbys 1703, Devon 1697, Dorset 1741, Durham 1717, Essex 1707, Glos 1712, Hants 1691, Hereford 1690, Herts 1748, Hunts 1742, Kent 1646, Lancs 1717, Leics 1733, Lincs 1774, London 1644, Middlesex 1758, Norfolk 1692, Northants 1692, Northumberland 1746, Notts 1706, Oxfordshire 1685, Rutland 1785, Shrops 1767, Somerset 1681, Staffs 1777, Suffolk 1689, Surrey 1698, Sussex 1698, Warks 1688, Westmorland 1757, Wilts 1723, Worcs 1699, Yorks 1654.

D73 Countess of Huntingdon's Connexion Registers. The old registers are now housed at the Public Record Office, Chancery Lane, London, WC2. The earliest known registers are as follows:

Berks, 1816, Cambs 1787, Cheshire 1819, Cornwall 1800, Cumberland 1789, Derbys 1787, Dorset 1822, Essex 1784, Glos 1790, Hants 1784, Hereford 1814, Herts 1806, Kent 1776, Lancs 1789, Lincs 1799, London 1783, Norfolk 1752, Oxfordshire 1790, Somerset 1788, Sussex 1781, Warks 1796, Worcs 1784.

D74 Hospital Registers. The registers of the Chelsea, Greenwich, Foundling and British Lying-in Hospitals are now at the Public Record Office, Chancery Lane, London, WC2.

D75 Huguenot Registers. The early registers are now housed at the Public Record Office, Chancery Lane, London, WC2. The Huguenot Society has published most of them.

D76 Inghamite Registers. The old registers are now housed at the Public Record Office, Chancery Lane, London, WC2. The earliest known registers are:

London 1753, Notts 1804, Westmorland 1754 and Yorks 1753.

D77 Irvingite Registers. The old registers are now housed at the Public Record Office, Chancery Lane, London, WC2. The earliest known registers are:

Cambs 1834, London 1829, Shrops 1835, Surrey 1833.

D78 Jewish Registers. The old registers were not deposited with the Registrar General. Generally most synagogues retain their own records. The most significant early ones are the marriage registers of the Spanish and Portuguese synagogue at Bevis Marks, London, EC3, which run from 1687–1837; these have been published.

D79 Methodist Registers. The old registers are now housed at the Public Record Office, London, WC2. The earliest known registers are as follows:

	Wesleyan	Primitive	New Connexion
Beds	1798		
Berks	1796	1831	
Bucks	1792	1832	
Cambs	1796	1824	
Cheshire	1793	1811	1798
Cornwall	1794	1832	1834
Cumberland	1806	1825	
Derbyshire	1794	1821	
Devon	1787		
Dorset	1796		

	Wes-leyan	Prim-itive	New Con-nexion
Durham	1797	1823	1811
Essex	1793		
Glos	1799		
Hants	1799	1833	
Herefordshire	1805	1828	
Herts	1825		
Hunts	1797		
Kent	1796		
Lancs	1784	1824	1794
Leics	1795	1820	
Lincs	1801	1825	1827
London	1779	1806	1820
Middlesex	1807		
Norfolk	1795	1822	1835
Northants	1801	1824	
Northumb.	1788	1823	1798
Notts	1787	1827	1787
Oxfordshire	1812	1835	
Rutland	1816		
Shrops	1796	1822	1829
Somerset	1780	1813	
Staffs	1795	1819	1789
Suffolk	1800	1832	
Surrey	1817		
Sussex	1795		
Warks	1802	1831	
Westmorland	1797		
Wilts	1795	1829	
Worcs	1788	1833	1829
Yorks	1753	1822	1779

In addition there are the registers of the Calvinist Methodists. The earliest known registers are:

Cheshire 1805, Glos 1762, Kent 1828, Lancs 1803, London 1738, Shrops 1821, Somerset 1775, Sussex 1825, Warks 1796.

D80 Moravian Registers. The old registers are now housed at the Public Record Office, Chancery Lane, London, WC2. The earliest known registers are:

Beds 1743, Cheshire 1784, Derbyshire 1746, Devon 1785, Glos 1757, Herefordshire 1784, Hunts 1823, Lancs 1786, London 1741, Northants 1796, Somerset 1755, Wilts 1748, Yorks 1742.

D81 New Jerusalemite Registers. The old registers are now housed at the Public Record Office, Chancery Lane, London, WC2. The earliest known registers are:

Derbyshire 1817, Essex 1813, Lancs 1803, Leics 1828, London 1816, Warks 1791, Yorks 1781.

D82 Presbyterian Registers. The old registers are housed at the Public Record Office, Chancery Lane, London, WC2. The earliest known registers are:

Berks 1723, Cheshire 1676, Cumberland 1745, Derbys 1698, Devon 1672, Dorset 1720, Durham 1688, Essex 1796, Glos 1740, Hants 1676, Herts 1729, Hunts 1820, Kent 1710, Lancs 1644, Leics 1706, Lincs 1707, London 1705, Middlesex 1727, Norfolk 1691, Northants 1820, Northumberland 1752, Notts 1690, Oxfordshire 1789, Shropshire 1692, Somerset 1694, Staffs 1726, Suffolk 1689, Sussex 1789, Warks 1695, Westmorland 1687, Wilts 1687, Worcs 1722, Yorks 1650.

D83 Prison Registers. The registers for the Fleet and King's Bench Prisons in London are at the Public Record Office, Chancery Lane, London, WC2. The Fleet records of baptisms and marriages are from 1674 to 1756.

D84 Quaker Registers. In 1837 all known registers were copied into digests and the originals sent to the Registrar General in 1840 – these are now housed in the Public Record Office, Chancery Lane, London, WC2. The Digests are held at the Society of Friends, Friends House, Euston Road, London, NW1.

D85 Swedenborgian Registers. The old registers are now housed at the Public Record Office, Chancery Lane, London, WC2. The earliest known registers are:

Lancs 1828, London 1787, Norfolk 1819, Northumberland 1808, Somerset 1830, Wilts 1834.

D86 Unitarian Registers. The old registers are now housed at the Public Record Office, Chancery Lane, London, WC2. The earliest known registers are:

Lancs 1762, Staffs 1788, Yorks 1817.

D87 Dr Williams' Library. Registers of some Presbyterian, Congregational and Baptist churches within 12 miles of London were formerly kept at this theological library in Gordon Square, London, WC1. These are now at the Public Record Office, Chancery Lane, London, WC2; they cover the period 1742–1837.

PART SEVEN
REGISTRATION OF BIRTHS, MAR-RIAGES AND DEATHS

D88 Registration in England and Wales. Since 1 July 1837 England and Wales have been divided into registration districts; copies of all birth, marriage and death certificates are sent from the district offices to the General Register Office, now located at St Catherine's House, Kingsway, London, WC2.

D89 Using the Search Room of the General Register Office. The returns from the registration districts are consolidated into quarterly indexes of births, marriages and deaths which are bound in red, green and black respectively. Up to 1865 these volumes were handwritten. The only significant changes to the format of indexes thereafter have been the introduction of the mother's maiden name in the birth index since 1911, the addition of the spouse's name against each entry in the marriage index since 1912, and the age of the deceased in the death indexes since 1866.

Searching the indexes is free but a fee is required for a copy certificate. Red, green or black application forms are supplied which have space for information contained in the indexes. The researcher will need to note the year, the quarter (denoted on the spine of the index – Mar, Jun, Sep, Dec), the registration district name, and a volume and page number related to the registration district's records.

Sometimes a researcher cannot be sure that an entry in the index is the one he is after. This could occur where the name is a common one and the date of the event, or the registration district unknown. It is possible, to avoid wasting money in obtaining a certificate for the wrong person, to detail on the reverse of the application form information that you *do* know so that the Registrar's staff can check it against the certificate requested. If the information does not tally then you will be refunded part of your fee and the certificate not sent.

Before 1912 the names of both parties to a marriage were not shown together although they were, of course, indexed separately as they are today. If the researcher knows both names for a marriage before that date it is advisable to check *both* index entries and compare registration district details so as to be sure that the correct certificate is being applied for.

Foundlings are listed after Z in the indexes.

It is possible to apply by post for this work to be done by the Registrar's staff, but the fee is considerably higher.

D90 Birth Certificates. A birth certificate gives the date and place of birth, the name and sex of the child, the parents' names and occupation of the father, the mother's maiden name, their address, and details of the informant. If the time of birth is noted, as well as the date, this could indicate a multiple birth. If a child is born out of wedlock the father's name may be included on the certificate if the parents wish, and both surnames are recorded in the indexes.

D91 Marriage Certificates. A marriage certificate gives the date, place and rites of the marriage, names, ages, occupations, marital status and addresses of the couple, the names and occupations of the fathers, and the names of the witnesses. A divorced person is described as 'single'.

D92 Death Certificates. A death certificate gives the name, address, age, sex, rank and occupation of the deceased, the cause of death and details of the informant.

D93 Adopted Children. Since 1927 a register of adopted children has been kept by the General Register Office. Certificates of birth and adoption may be obtained but they will not show the names of the natural parents or the original surname of the child. Since 1975 an adopted person over the age of 18 may apply for an *original* birth certificate. If adoption took place before 1975 the applicant will be required to have an interview with a social worker before the certificate is sent; if the adoption took place after 1975 the applicant will have the right to refuse to be interviewed and will automatically have the right to be sent the certificate.

D94 Divorces. Before 1857 a full divorce could only be obtained by a private Act of Parliament. The records of these are in the House of Lords Library. A register of divorces since 1857 is at the Divorce Registry, Somerset House, Strand, London, WC2. The applicant must know sufficient detail for the staff to search the register as the records are not for public use.

D95 Army, Navy and Air Force Registration. Births, deaths and marriages related to Army, Navy and Air Force personnel are kept at the General Register Office, St Catherine's House,

Kingsway, London, WC2, in separate registers. (See also Part 13).

D96 Registration in Scotland. The General Register of Births, Deaths and Marriages began on 1 January, 1855 and the records are held at New Register House, Edinburgh. Similar information is given on the certificates to that given on those for England and Wales (see D90–92), but in addition the Scottish birth certificate gives the marriage date of the parents, the marriage certificate gives the maiden name of the mothers of the couple, and the death certificate details the parents of the deceased.

D97 Registration in Ireland. General registration of births, marriages and deaths began in 1864 and up to and including 1921, covered the whole of Ireland. These records are in the care of the Registrar General, Custom House, Dublin who also holds those pertaining to the Republic since that date. In Northern Ireland records since partition (1922) are held by the Registrar General, Fermanagh House, Ormeau Avenue, Belfast.

PART EIGHT
CENSUS

D98 General. The censuses of England and Wales from 1801 to 1831 were concerned with numbers; names were not recorded until 1841. Each registration area was divided into enumeration districts of not more than 200 and not less than 25 inhabited houses. The individual returns were copied by census enumerators into books and it is these records which are the basis for the public record. They are housed at the Land Registry building in Portugal Street but microfilm copies are widely available at appropriate record offices and libraries.

D99 Censuses 1801, 1811, 1821 and 1831. These took place for the nights of 10/11 March, 27/28 May, 28/29 May and 30/31 May respectively. The 1801 returns give the numbers of people in each parish, the inhabited and empty houses, and a rough classification of occupations into agriculture, manufacture, commerce and handicrafts. More accurate information on occupations is given in later years. In 1831 males over twenty years were classed in seven occupational categories: agriculture, industrial labouring, manufacturing, professional, retail trades, servants and others.

D100 Census 1841. This took place for the night of 6/7 June. The names of inhabitants were recorded for the first time; for children up to the age of 14 exact ages were recorded, but those of older people are given in 5-year groups indicated by the lowest age in that group; thus, someone aged 22 is recorded as being 20. Residents were asked if they were born in the county in which they were then residing; those born in Scotland, Ireland or abroad are noted as S, I or F (for foreign parts). Occupations, often abbreviated, are given but relationships to the head of household are not. Where they were able householders filled out their own census form.

D101 Census 1851. This took place for the night of 30/31 March. Exact ages are given, as are the relationships to the head of household and marital status. Birth places if in England and Wales are given precisely, but the country only if Ireland or Scotland, and countries abroad are not detailed. The numbers of blind, deaf, dumb and lunatic are recorded; there is also a census of church congregations and accommodation.

D102 Census 1861. This took place for the night of 7/8 April. The information recorded is the same as that for 1851. In addition aliens and naturalized subjects are recorded.

D103 Census 1871. This took place for the night of 2/3 April. The information recorded is the same as that for 1861.

D104 Census 1881. This took place for the night of 3/4 April. The information recorded is the same as that for 1861.

D105 Censuses after 1881. Information after 1881 is regarded as secret and unavailable to the public. However, with the signed consent of a descendant, details for one household may be obtained provided that the information is not being used in litigation. Application should be made to the Registrar General, St Catherine's House, Kingsway, London, WC2.

PART NINE
WILLS

D106 Will and Testament. The Will concerned real estate such as land and buildings, which was regarded, technically, as the Crown's property and its disposal therefore usually bound by the customs of the manor or realm; in most of the country primogeniture determined the disposal of real estate. The Testament concerned personal estate such as furniture, belongings, crops, debts etc; this was regarded as a gift of God and bequeathable by the testator. In the case of intestacy personal estate went to the widow and children, and in the absence of children to other relatives.

D107 Ecclesiastical jurisdiction. Before 1858 most wills, where the deceased had goods worth over £5, were proved in an archdeacon's court. If the testator had estate in more than one archdeaconry jurisdiction then reverted to the diocesan bishop, either through his Consistory Court which covered the whole diocese, or his Commissary Court which had jurisdiction in such matters over a specified area of the diocese. If an estate extended over more than one diocese then probate would be given in one of the provincial courts, the Prerogative Court of Canterbury (PCC) or the Prerogative Court of York (PCY). Lastly, where an estate was in two provinces or where the death had occurred at sea or abroad, the PCC had seniority.

Parishes or groups of parishes called Peculiars, which were exempt from diocesan authority, also had jurisdiction over the wills falling within their own areas.

D108 Probate Courts. A researcher tracing a will proved before 1858 must begin with the name of the parish of the deceased; from that may be found the appropriate probate court which might be under the jurisdiction of an archdeacon, bishop or archbishop. A simplified guide for the probate courts related to each old county is given below:

Anglesey
Archdeaconry of Anglesey
Diocese of Bangor
Province of Canterbury up to 1920

Beds
Archdeaconry of Bedford
Diocese of Lincoln up to 1837
Diocese of Ely up to 1914
Province of Canterbury

Berks
Archdeaconry of Berkshire
Diocese of Salisbury up to 1836
Diocese of Oxford since
Province of Canterbury

Brecon
Archdeaconry of Brecon
Diocese of St Davids up to 1923
Province of Canterbury up to 1920

Bucks
Archdeaconry of Buckingham
Diocese of Lincoln up to 1845
Diocese of Oxford since
Province of Canterbury

Caernarvonshire
Archdeaconries of Merioneth and Bangor
Diocese of Bangor
Province of Canterbury up to 1920

Cambs
Archdeaconry of Cambridge
Diocese of Ely
Province of Canterbury

Cardiganshire
Archdeaconry of Cardigan
Diocese of St Davids
Province of Canterbury up to 1920

Carmarthenshire
Archdeaconry of Carmarthen
Diocese of St Davids
Province of Canterbury up to 1920

Cheshire
Archdeaconry of Chester
Diocese of Lichfield up to 1541
Diocese of Chester since
Province of Canterbury up to 1541
Province of York since 1541

Cornwall
Archdeaconry of Cornwall
Diocese of Exeter up to 1876
Province of Canterbury

Cumberland
Archdeaconry of Cumberland
Diocese of Carlisle
Province of York

Denbigh
Archdeaconry of St Asaph
Diocese of St Asaph
Province of Canterbury up to 1920

Derby
Archdeaconry of Derby
Diocese of Lichfield up to 1884
Province of Canterbury

D108 *(cont)*

Devon
Archdeaconries of Barnstaple,
Exeter and Totnes
Diocese of Exeter
Province of Canterbury

Dorset
Archdeaconry of Dorset
Diocese of Salisbury up to 1542
Diocese of Bristol up to 1836
Diocese of Salisbury since
Province of Canterbury

Durham
Archdeaconry of Durham
Diocese of Durham
Province of York

Essex
Archdeaconries of Essex,
Colchester and Middlesex
Diocese of London up to 1846
Diocese of Rochester up to 1877
Province of Canterbury

Flintshire
Archdeaconry of St Asaph
Diocese of St Asaph
Province of Canterbury up to 1920

Glamorgan
Archdeaconry of Llandaff
Diocese of Llandaff
Province of Canterbury up to 1920

Gloucestershire
Archdeaconry of Gloucester
Diocese of Worcester up to 1541
Diocese of Gloucester up to 1836
Diocese of Gloucester and Bristol since

Archdeaconry of Hereford
Diocese of Gloucester up to 1836
Diocese of Gloucester and Bristol since

City of Bristol
Diocese of Bristol up to 1836
Diocese of Gloucester and Bristol since
All Province of Canterbury

Hants
Archdeaconry of Winchester
Diocese of Winchester
Later divided into Diocese of Guildford and
Diocese of Portsmouth
Province of Canterbury

Hereford
Archdeaconry of Hereford
Diocese of Hereford
Province of Canterbury

Herts
Deanery of Braugham in the Archdeaconry of
Middlesex
Diocese of London up to 1845
Diocese of Rochester up to 1877

Archdeaconry of St Albans
Diocese of Lincoln up to 1845
Diocese of Rochester up to 1877

Archdeaconry of Huntingdon
Diocese of Ely up to 1845
Diocese of Rochester up to 1877
Province of Canterbury

Hunts
Archdeaconry of Huntingdon
Diocese of Lincoln up to 1837
Diocese of Ely since
Province of Canterbury

Isle of Man
Diocese of Sodor and Man
Province of York

Kent
Archdeaconry of Canterbury
Diocese of Canterbury

Archdeaconry of Maidstone
Diocese of Canterbury
Parts to Diocese of Maidstone after 1845

Archdeaconry of Rochester
Diocese of Rochester
Parts to Diocese of Maidstone after 1845
Province of Canterbury

Lancs
Archdeaconry of Richmond
Diocese of York up to 1541
Diocese of Chester since
Province of York

Archdeaconry of Chester
Diocese of Lichfield up to 1541
Diocese of Chester since
Province of Canterbury up to 1541
Province of York since

Leics
Archdeaconry of Leicester
Diocese of Lincoln up to 1837
Diocese of Peterborough up to 1926
Province of Canterbury

Lincs
Archdeaconries of Lincoln and Stow
Diocese of Lincoln
Province of Canterbury

London
Archdeaconry of City of London
Diocese of London

Archdeaconry of City of Westminster
Diocese of London up to 1540
Diocese of Westminster

Archdeaconry of Middlesex
Diocese of London
Province of Canterbury

Merioneth
Archdeaconry of Merioneth
Diocese of Bangor
Province of Canterbury up to 1920

Archdeaconry of St Asaph
Diocese of St Asaph
Province of Canterbury up to 1920

Middlesex
Archdeaconry of Middlesex
Diocese of London
Province of Canterbury

Monmouth
Archdeaconry of Monmouth
Diocese of Llandaff
Province of Canterbury up to 1920

Montgomeryshire
Archdeaconry of St Asaph
Diocese of St Asaph
Province of Canterbury up to 1920

Archdeacon of Merioneth
Diocese of Bangor
Province of Canterbury up to 1920

Norfolk
Archdeaconries of Norfolk and Norwich
Diocese of Norwich
Province of Canterbury

Northants
Archdeaconry of Northampton
Diocese of Lincoln up to 1541
Diocese of Peterborough since
Province of Canterbury

Northumberland
Archdeaconry of Northumberland
Diocese of Durham up to 1882
Province of York

Notts
Archdeaconry of Nottingham
Diocese of York up to 1839
Diocese of Lincoln up to 1884
Province of York up to 1839
Province of Canterbury up to 1934

Peculiar of Southwell
Diocese of York up to 1839
Diocese of Lincoln up to 1884
Province of York up to 1839
Province of Canterbury up to 1934

Oxon
Archdeaconry of Oxford
Diocese of Lincoln up to 1546
Diocese of Oxford since
Province of Canterbury

Pembrokeshire
Archdeaconry of St Davids
Diocese of St Davids
Province of Canterbury up to 1920

Radnorshire
Archdeaconry of Brecon
Diocese of St Davids
Province of Canterbury up to 1920

Rutland
Archdeaconry of Northampton
Diocese of Lincoln up to 1541
Diocese of Peterborough up to 1876

Archdeaconry of Oakham
Diocese of Peterborough
Province of Canterbury

Shropshire
Archdeaconry of Salop (part)
Diocese of Hereford

Archdeaconry of Salop (part)
Diocese of Lichfield
Province of Canterbury

Somerset
Archdeaconries of Bath, Wells and Taunton
Diocese of Bath and Wells
Province of Canterbury

Staffs
Archdeaconry of Stafford
Diocese of Lichfield
Province of Canterbury

Suffolk
Archdeaconries of Sudbury and Suffolk
Diocese of Norwich
Province of Canterbury

Surrey
Archdeaconry of Surrey
Diocese of Winchester (until 1847)
Large number of parishes to Diocese of London in 1846
Province of Canterbury

Sussex
Archdeaconries of Chichester and Lewes
Diocese of Chichester
Province of Canterbury

Warwickshire
Archdeaconry of Worcester
Diocese of Worcester
Province of Canterbury

Archdeaconry of Coventry
Diocese of Lichfield up to 1836
Diocese of Worcester after
Province of Canterbury

Westmorland
Barony of Appleby
Diocese of Carlisle
Province of York

Barony of Kendal
Diocese of York up to 1541
Diocese of Chester up to 1856
Diocese of Carlisle since
Province of York

Wilts
Archdeaconries of Salisbury and Wiltshire
Diocese of Salisbury
Province of Canterbury

Worcs
Archdeaconry of Worcester
Diocese of Worcester
Province of Canterbury

Yorks
Diocese of York
Province of York

D109 Locating a Will. The archives of pre-1858 wills have now mostly been decentralised and are usually to be found at county record offices. Much valuable work has been done in the complicated minutiae of tracing a will and researchers are advised to consult the following volumes: *Wills and their Whereabouts* (1974) by Anthony J. Camp and *A Simplified Guide to Probate Jurisdiction: where to look for Wills* by J. S. W. Gibson (3rd ed. 1985) published by the Federation of Family History Societies.

D110 Probate procedure. On presentation of the will the court passed a Probate Act which authorised the executors to carry out the provisions of the will; the court then endorsed the will and gave a copy to the executors. Letters of Administration were granted in cases of intestacy and the grantees were required to sign a Testamentary or Administration Bond,

usually worth twice the estimated value of the estate, which promised to administer the estate faithfully. From 1529 to 1750 executors had to produce an inventory of the effects within a year, which was compiled by two disinterested parties; these documents, where they still exist, are filed with the will in the records of the court.

D111 Nuncupative Will. A will made orally by a testator before sufficient and reliable witnesses and committed to writing after his death. The Statute of Frauds 1678 enacted that there should be three witnesses to the testator's wishes who had heard them during his last illness. Such a will could not cover freehold land nor revoke an existing written one. Nowadays, Nuncupative Wills are valid only in cases of soldiers on active service or sailors at sea.

D112 Women's Wills. Widows and single women were permitted to make wills but before 1882 a married woman was not, unless with the permission of her husband, since it was considered that her property belonged to her husband.

D113 Probation registration since 1858.
Since 1858 all copies of wills and Letters of Administration in cases of intestacy in England and Wales, have been lodged centrally and are now at the Principal Registry of the Family Division, Somerset House, Strand, London. They are indexed and many local record offices have copies of the indexes. At Somerset House wills may be consulted and photocopies made for a small charge. Copies of wills made by district registrars have mostly been deposited with local record offices.

D114 Scottish Wills. Wills in Scotland were confirmed at Commissariot courts covering areas roughly equivalent to dioceses; the earliest established was Edinburgh in 1514. Wills in Scotland are of two kinds: the 'testament testamentary' where an executor is nominated, and 'testament active' where probate is applied for by a next-of-kin or creditor. The records of these courts from 1514–1823 are at Old Register House, Edinburgh 2. From 1824 jurisdiction over wills was given to the sheriffs' courts which, generally, keep their own records, although all those for Edinburgh are still sent to Old Register House. Commissariot records up to 1800 have been indexed by the Scottish Record Society.

D115 Irish Wills. Before 1858 the Prerogative Court of Armagh had jurisdiction throughout Ireland. Abstracts of its records – most original documents were destroyed in a fire during civil disturbances in 1922 – are at the Public Record Office in Dublin. Originals which survived the fire are at the appropriate Public Record Office in Dublin or Belfast. Researchers should consult *Index to the Prerogative Wills of Ireland 1536–1810* by Sir Arthur Vicars.

Probate Terms

D116 Administration Bond. In cases of intestacy the recipient of the Letters of Administration (qv) was required to sign an Administration or Testamentary Bond which pledged to administer the estate scrupulously.

D117 Administrator. A person authorised to administer an estate, usually in cases of intestacy. Since 1925 no more than four administrators may be appointed. An Administrator could also be appointed where the will named no executor.

D118 Bona Notabilia. A term denoting goods worth at least £5.

D119 Caveat. A warning lodged by a relative, creditor or other interested party with the appropriate probate court to the effect that they had an interest in the proving of a will and that they should be notified at the time.

D120 Codicil. A signed and witnessed addition to a will.

D121 Commissary Court. A diocesan court empowered to handle probate matters falling entirely within a specified part of the diocese.

D122 Consistory Court. A diocesan court empowered to handle probate matters falling entirely within the diocese.

D123 Curation. The guardianship of a boy aged 15–20 or a girl aged 12–20.

D124 Decree. A court judgement. If the words 'by decree' or 'int.dec.' (interlocutory decree) appear in probate records it would indicate that the will had been contested and that a court had given judgement.

D125 Devise. Gift or disposition by will.

D126 Executor. The person or persons appointed by the testator to carry out the intentions of the will.

D127 Holograph Will. A will written in the testator's own hand.

D128 Intestate. Without making a will.

D129 Letters of Administration. In cases of intestacy the Probate court issued a grant, called Letters of Administration, to the next-of-kin or other person to administer the estate.

D130 Letters of Administration-with-Will-annexed. A term used where the will did not specify an executor, or where the executor was unable or unwilling to act, and the court granted Letters of Administration to the next of kin or some other person or persons, to administer the estate.

D131 Limited Probate. Probate could be granted to cover limited parts of the estate.

D132 Personalty. Personal estate, chattels, goods etc, as opposed to real estate.

D133 Probate Act. An Act passed by the Probate Court when it was satisfied with the will presented, and which enabled the executor(s) to proceed with carrying out the provisions of the will.

D134 Proved. A will is proved when probate has been granted.

D135 Renunciation. A term denoting the refusal of an executor to apply for probate.

D136 Testamentary Peculiar. A term to denote probate jurisdiction held by a Peculiar, a parish or group of parishes exempt from the authority of a bishop.

D137 Testator. A person who makes a will.

D138 Tuition. The guardianship of minors under the age of 15 (boys) and 13 (girls).

D139 Terms of relationship found in wills. Words used in older wills to denote relations do not necessarily have the same meaning today. Common ones are as follows:
Brother: This could mean a brother-in-law or stepbrother.
Cousin: This could mean any relative other than brother, uncle, aunt or parent.
Cousin german: First cousin.
Father-in-law: This could mean stepfather.
Heirs of the Body: Legitimate children.
Niece: This could mean a male or female descendant.
Relict: The widow.

PART TEN
MAPS AND MAPMAKERS

D140 Cartographer. The person who surveys or draws the map. He is often signified on old maps by one of the following words or abbreviations: *auctore, de., delt., delineavit, descipsit.*

D141 Cartouche. The panel which contains the map title, dedication, key etc. It first appeared in the 16th century and was usually highly ornamented.

D142 Circle. This symbol has, from the earliest British maps, been used to denote a settlement or town.

D143 Contours. The present method of depicting height by the use of contour lines did not come into general use in this country until well into the 19th century.

D144 Edition. An issue or reissue printed from one state (qv) of a plate or block.

D145 Engraver. The name of the engraver is quite often indicated on old maps by one of the following words or abbreviations: *caelvit, engr., fecit, incidente, sc., sculp., sculpsit.*

D146 Hachuring. A method of hill-shading on maps dating from the late 16th century.

D147 Impression. A single sheet from a plate or block.

D148 Issue. The total number of impressions from a plate or block at any one time.

D149 Orientation. Nowadays maps are usually printed with the north at the head of the sheet. In medieval times, and later, east was normally at the top because of its religious significance.

D150 Scale. The present statute mile was established in 1593 but long after that local maps were still being drawn to accepted local mile measurement.

D151 State. If alterations were made to the plate or block, the impressions from them were said to be from a different state.

Types of Map

D152 County Maps. The publication of regional or county maps began in earnest in the 16th century. Foremost amongst these were the volumes published by Christopher Saxton whose output of 34 county maps was published in 1579 as *An Atlas of England and Wales*, although they are deficient in roads. Of better quality, showing roads and distances, and using a grid reference system, were the maps of John Norden published before and after his death in 1626 which were intended to form part of his *Speculum Britanniae*, a work, unfortunately, he did not get far with. William Camden's *Britannia* of 1607, included a set of county maps, and John Speed's celebrated *The Theatre of the Empire of Great Britaine* published early in the 17th century also included a map of the county town on each county map.

For subsequent developments *County Atlases of the British Isles published after 1703*, by D. Hodson (1984), should be consulted.

D153 Enclosure Award Maps. The Enclosure Acts usually provided that a copy of the award should be left with the Clerk of the Peace for the county, and one copy deposited in the local parish archives. Some of these awards were accompanied by a map of the area. If extant these copies will be in the county record office or local authority collection.

D154 Estate Maps. The whereabouts of an Estate Map is not predictable. Many estate papers have found their way to local or county record offices but others remain in the archives of the larger landowners. The Royal Commission on Historical Manuscripts has the responsibility of locating, detailing and publishing, for the use of research, archives in family or institutional hands. Indexes of estate papers may be found at the office of the Commission at Quality House, Quality Court, Chancery Lane, London WC2.

D155 Geological Maps. The Ordnance Survey completed a 1 in. to the mile geological survey of England between 1835 and 1888. There are three kinds of geological maps:

a) Solid – describing the nature of the rocks beneath the surface.

b) Drift – describing the surface only.

c) Solid with Drift – a combination of the above two.

D156 Historical Maps. The Ordnance Survey has so far published:

a) *Ancient Britain*. This illustrates major archaeological remains above ground from pre-history to the Norman Conquest. Scale 1 in. to 10 miles.

b) *Southern Britain in the Iron Age*. This covers an area south of a line from the Isle of Man to

Scarborough, and the period 1,000 years before the Roman invasion. Scale 1 in. to 10 miles.

c) *Roman Britain*. This shows towns, villas and other settlements, roads, industrial sites etc. Scale 1 in. to 15 miles.

d) *Britain in the Dark Ages*. This covers the period from the Roman invasion to Alfred. Scale 1 in. to 15 miles.

e) *Monastic Britain*. This illustrates all monastic houses in medieval times and gives other ecclesiastical information. Scale 1 in. to 10 miles.

f) *Britain in the 17th Century*. This shows Britain after the Civil War. Scale 1 in. to 15 miles.

Roman London, on a scale of 1:2500
Britain before the Norman Conquest, on a scale of 1:625000 in two sheets.
Hadrian's Wall, in a scale of 1:31680
The Antonine Wall, in a scale of 1:25000

D157 Ordnance Survey. The Survey was established in 1791. It was called at that time the Trigonometrical Survey and gradually it mapped Great Britain at a scale of 1 in. to the mile. Between 1801 and 1873 what is known as the *First Edition* or the *Old Series* was published in 110 sheets; dating copies of this period is difficult because revisions of original maps were published still bearing the original date. Furthermore, publication could have taken place up to twenty years after the survey was made.

Reprints of many *Old Series* maps have been published by David and Charles as folded maps, and by Harry Margary of Lympne Castle, Kent in volumes. Many local and county records offices have original copies for their area and usually have them on negative so that photographic prints may be purchased.

Work on a *New Series* began in 1840 and publication commenced in the 1870s, not only of one-inch maps but also six-inch and 25-inch plans. These have all been frequently revised since and accommodated within the National Grid reference system. The largest scale published is the 50 in. to the mile plan.

D158 Road Maps. In 1675 John Ogilby published his *Britannia* which surveyed the country as a series of road maps in strips. The 100 plates each had six or seven strips showing the length of a road with geographical features marked. Ogilby used the statute mile and to measure this he invented a device called a

'wheel dimensurator' which recorded distance as it was wheeled along. Ogilby's measurements were used after 1740 when milestones were erected on main roads.

D159 Tithe Maps. Consequent upon the passing of the Tithe Commutation Act 1836 (qv), detailed parish maps were produced, accompanied by terriers, to a scale of between 13 and 26 inches to the mile. Three copies were made: one was deposited with the Tithe Redemption Commission whose archives are now at the Public Record Office, Kew, the second copy went to the appropriate bishop and the third went to the parish authorities. The Ordnance Survey published a 1 in. to the mile map which showed the parishes covered by the tithe surveys. Scotland and Ireland were not affected by the legislation.

Map Makers

D160 Henry Beighton (1687–1743). His map of Warwickshire which he surveyed in 1725 was one of the first to be based on trigonometrical principles. It also had the distinction of being an early 1 in. to the mile depiction.

D161 Emanuel Bowen (d1767). In 1720 he issued *Britannia Depicta or Ogilby Improv'd*, which contained county maps and road maps. The volume consisted of 270 plates.

D162 William Camden (1551–1623). In 1607 his *Britannia* included a set of county maps largely based on Saxton and Norden.

D163 John Cary (c1754–1835). In 1787 he issued his *New and Correct English Atlas* which, apart from being finely engraved, drew upon the many detailed county survey maps which had been made since the 1760s at the instigation of the Royal Society of Arts. The accurate depiction of roads is a strong feature of his maps.

D164 Leonard Digges (d c1571). In 1571 he published *Pantometria* in which he described his own surveying instrument, the forerunner of the theodolite.

D165 Christopher Greenwood. A prominent 19th century cartographer and publisher, his ambition was to produce a complete national atlas of 1 in. to the mile maps; this he nearly achieved.

D166 Herman Moll (1688–1745). In 1724 Moll, a Dutchman, issued a set of county maps in *A New Description of England and Wales* which largely derived from other publications but did include new descriptions of archaeological features.

D167 Robert Morden (d1703). Morden was a publisher and cartographer. He improved and updated previous county maps, inserting roads previously missed, after asking 'knowing Gentlemen in each County' to make corrections on old plans where information was wrong. He used various scales and a variety of mile measurements.

D168 John Norden (1548–1626). Norden set out to produce maps of each county but only those for Middlesex and Herts were published in his lifetime; Cornwall, Essex, Hampshire, Surrey and Sussex were printed much later. He included more roads than Saxton but the detail of these must be regarded with caution. He introduced the grid reference system whereby places could be found by a combination of number and letter, and also a triangular distance chart – a feature still used today.

D169 John Ogilby (1600–1676). Ogilby introduced road or coaching maps which divided the country into strips of roads, especially those used most frequently by the traveller.

D170 John Rocque (c1704/5–1762). Rocque issued county and town maps but his main contribution was a map of the Cities of London and Westminster on a large scale in 1746, and another one, the same year, for London and the area 10 miles around.

D171 Christopher Saxton (c1542–1611). During the period 1574–79 he published 34 county maps of England and Wales which were to form the basis for many imitations. These were gathered in a single volume in 1579 in his *Atlas of England and Wales*. Many of the plates were engraved on the Continent where techniques were more advanced. Each map measured 15 in. × 18¼ in. but used a variety of scales; roads were omitted.

D172 Charles Smith. Smith published his *New English Atlas* in 1809. The maps are similar to those of his contemporary John Cary.

D173 John Speed (1552–1629). Speed was not a surveyor and compiled his maps from research. His innovation was to include a map of the county town within each county map.

PART ELEVEN
MONUMENTAL BRASSES AND INSCRIPTIONS

D174 Monumental Brasses. In England most brasses date from the period 1300 to 1650. Apart from their decorative value they also depict the development of costume and armour. Collections of brass rubbings are held at the British Museum, the Society of Antiquaries, the Victoria and Albert Museum, the Bodleian Library and the Ashmolean Museum at Oxford, and at the Cambridge Museum of Archaeology and Ethnology.

To make a brass rubbing it is essential to make an appointment with the appropriate church official. Equipment needed is a cloth with which to clean the brass, rubbing paper and wax, masking tape to fix the paper tightly, and a plastic eraser. Proficiency is needed to make a good rubbing and, indeed, a number of churches used to many visitors, now insist on a person being experienced. It is possible to obtain some practice for a reasonable fee at establishments such as the London Brass Rubbing Centre at St James's church, Piccadilly, London, W1, which is open every day except Christmas Day.

D175 Monumental Inscriptions. Alternatively called Memorial Inscriptions, a term to denote inscriptions on plaques inside a church and on graves in the churchyard. The custom of burying prosperous people inside the church did not become popular until the 16th century. Graveyard inscriptions of great age are not usually decipherable now but researchers may find that many were copied and published in the 19th century. Many local societies are now systematically recording their own local burial grounds before there is further deterioration. The Society of Genealogists has a large library of inscriptions since they contain much information not usually found in parish registers. The Society also has Tucker's index of monumental inscription copies which are held elsewhere. Efforts were usually made, especially in urban areas, to record inscriptions when burial grounds were closed and transformed into public gardens.

PART TWELVE
QUARTER SESSIONS RECORDS

D176 General. From Tudor times until 1889 the Quarter Sessions records, usually housed in the county record offices, form the basis of much local history research. The documents concern crime, land, licensing, the militia, county rates, roads and bridges, taxes, religion, social welfare, lunatics and a host of other subjects. Some counties have records dating from even before Tudor times.

Since the 14th century the Justices of the Peace had met in each county four times a year, at Easter, Midsummer, Michaelmas and Epiphany. Usually the records were nominally in the care of a private person of some standing called a *Custos Rotulorum*, but by the 18th century the responsibility was that of the Lord Lieutenant of the county.

Many Sessions records have been calendared or printed in some way. Two publications give details of the scope of county record office holdings: *County Records* by F. G. Emmison, published by the Historical Association, and *Quarter Sessions Records for Family Historians* by J. S. W. Gibson, published by the Federation of Family History Societies. Many offices publish their own detailed guide to their holdings.

The Local Government Act 1888 transferred most of the non-judicial functions of the Quarter Sessions to the newly-created county councils.

The principal types of records lodged with the Clerk of the Peace, now in the county collections may be summarised as under.

D177 Accounts. Up to Tudor times money for the upkeep of bridges and some roads was raised by special levies, although by the time of the County Rates Act 1739 funds were being raised on a more regular basis. Two Acts of 1601 enabled counties to levy a rate for the relief of maimed soldiers and mariners. Accounts become more frequent after the 1739 Act when the Justices had to appoint a County Treasurer who presented his figures at each Quarter Sessions. His documents concern administrative expenses, rates, judicial expenses, road upkeep etc.

D178 Aliens. As from 1792 an alien arriving in this country was obliged to register with the Justices of the Peace, giving his name, address, rank and occupation. In addition, householders who received aliens had to give notice to their parish who in turn informed the Clerk of the Peace.

D179 Association Oath Rolls. The Act of Association 1696 required public office-holders to sign a declaration which was a 'Solemn Association for the better preservation of his Majesty's royal person and government'. This was lodged with the Clerk of the Peace although many records are at the Public Record Office, Chancery Lane, London, WC2.

D180 Badgers, Kidders, Drovers etc. From 1552 to 1772 this type of worker had to be licensed by Quarter Sessions. Their names and those of their sureties, sometimes with other details, were registered.

D181 Barges. Barges and other inland waterway craft were registered by the Clerk of the Peace from 1795 to 1871.

D182 Bailiffs. The names of those bailiffs present at Quarter Sessions are included in the records.

D183 Bastardy Returns. The Poor Law Amendment Act 1844 enabled a mother of an illegitimate child to apply at Petty Sessions for maintenance from its father. These applications were sent in the form of annual returns to the Clerk of the Peace.

D184 Charities. From 1786 the Clerk of the Peace sent returns of charities to Parliament, received their accounts and registered their objects, trustees etc. An Act of 1812 required details of donations based on income from land to be registered with the Clerk of the Peace.

D185 Corn Rents. Corn rents was the name given to the variable payments made in lieu of tithes when the latter were commuted in 1836. The payments were reviewed every seven years and adjusted to match the average market price of corn. Disputes as to rent at the time of the Tithe Commutation Act 1836 were settled by arbitrators: their reports and recommendations were lodged with the Clerk of the Peace.

D186 Dissenters' Meeting Houses. From 1688 Dissenters' Meeting Houses were licensed. Records included the address, type of meeting and the person certifying it.

D187 Electors. From 1762 those electing knights of the shire had to possess freehold property yielding 40 shillings or more per annum. County records might include duplicate Land Tax assessments or certificates confirming annuities.

D188 Enclosure Awards. Awards since the early part of the 18th century may be with the county record office or else with the Public Record Office or church authorities. Generally a copy, sometimes with a map and details of the people and land involved, was lodged with the Clerk of the Peace.

D189 Freemasons. The Seditious Societies Act 1799 exempted Freemasons' Lodges provided that each submitted a list of members to Quarter Sessions, together with their addresses and occupations. These records are quite often incomplete.

D190 Friendly Societies. From 1793 registers of Friendly Societies were kept by the Clerk of the Peace together with details of their meeting places and rules. These records would normally have been transferred to the Registrar of Friendly Societies after 1846.

D191 Game Duty. From 1784 to 1807 all persons qualified to kill or sell game, including manorial gamekeepers, registered with the Clerk of the Peace who issued them a certificate on payment of a fee.

D192 Gaol Delivery. Registers were kept of all prisoners delivered from gaol to stand trial at Quarter Sessions. These records include the indictments, the jurors and verdicts.

D193 Hearth Tax. Returns of this tax (qv) were lodged with the Clerk of the Peace from 1662 to 1688.

D194 High Constables. The High Constables of the Hundreds attending Quarter Sessions are listed in the records.

D195 Highways. Until 1835 the upkeep of roads was generally the responsibility of the manors, parishes or Turnpike Trusts. In 1835 an Act empowered Quarter Sessions to unite parishes into larger units for this purpose and to appoint a district surveyor. Some records may exist of Quarter Sessions involvement but county responsibility was not significant until 1894.

D196 Insolvent Debtors. Under Acts of 1670 and 1677 a debtor in gaol could petition a Justice of the Peace for a discharge if his estate was worth less than £10 per annum and if his creditors made no objection. These petitions

and any related correspondence were filed by the Clerk of the Peace.

D197 Jurors. It was the duty of parish constables from 1696 to make an annual return to the Clerk of the Peace of men between 21 and 70 qualified, by holding land worth £10 or more per annum, to serve as jurors at Quarter Sessions. The property qualification was established in 1285, varied in Acts of 1604 and 1691, and in 1730 leaseholders of property worth at least £20 per annum were also included. In 1825 jury service was limited to men aged between 21 and 60 who held property worth at least £10 per annum, leased property worth £20 or more per annum or rented property worth £30 per annum.

Lists of jurors, mostly minor freeholders, are found in the Sessions' records.

D198 Justices. The names of those Justices of the Peace present are recorded.

D199 Juvenile Offenders. Under an Act of 1847 monthly returns of juvenile offenders were compiled with details of punishments.

D200 Land Tax. A Land Tax was imposed from 1692 to 1832. The records of 1780–1832 are most useful because they contain names and the amount they paid.

D201 Licences. Numerous types of licences were issued. Records may be found of those granted to slaughter houses (after 1786), Lying-in Hospitals (after 1773), butchers (in the 17th century), printing presses (after 1799), racecourses (after 1879), gamekeepers, victuallers, Literary and Scientific Institutes etc and to establishments where music and dancing took place.

D202 Literary and Scientific Societies. After the Seditious Societies Act 1799, Literary and Scientific Societies were required to obtain a licence to hold meetings. An Act of 1843 exempted these societies from the payment of rates if they provided a certificate from the Barrister for Friendly Societies. A copy of their rules was deposited with the Clerk of the Peace.

D203 Lunatics. From 1815 returns of pauper lunatics were sent to the Clerk of the Peace. In 1832 private asylums were licensed and inspected by the Justices of the Peace.

D204 Militia Returns. The Lord Lieutenant made an annual return to Quarter Sessions giving the names of commissioned officers and stating the numbers of non-commissioned officers and other ranks. After an Act of 1854 the provision of storehouses for the militia was paid for out of county rates.

D205 Oaths of Aliegiance. An Act of 1722 made it necessary for all persons in England over 18 to swear an oath of allegiance to the Crown at Quarter Sessions.

D206 Order Books. These were the minute books of Quarter Sessions.

D207 Oyer and Terminer. A Commission of Oyer and Terminer ('hear and determine') was appointed to inquire into the more serious offences such as murder, treason, insurrection, coining etc. The records were kept by the Clerk of the Peace.

D208 Petitions. Petitions from individuals or parish representatives were heard by Quarter Sessions and kept by the Clerk of the Peace.

D209 Petty Sessions. Petty Sessions were meetings of local justices, held since Tudor times. Some records were kept by the Clerk of the Peace.

D210 Plantation Indentures. The Justices of the Peace were responsible, after 1682, for issuing indentures to those volunteering to work on the American and West Indies plantations. These records were kept by the Clerk of the Peace.

D211 Police. The County Police Act 1839 enabled counties to establish paid police forces; some did so soon afterwards, but some did not until 1856.

D212 Poor Rate Returns. The parishes sent to the Clerk of the Peace their poor rate returns; these enabled the Clerk to fix the county rate.

D213 Printing Presses. The Seditious Societies Act 1799 directed that printing presses be licensed by the Justices of the Peace. The records give names, addresses and owners. The measure was in force until 1869.

D214 Prisons. Records of the administration of prisons could occur up to 1877 when responsibility was taken out of the hands of the counties. The relevant documents should then have been transferred to the national archives but some may still remain in the county record office.

D215 Prisoners. Lists of prisoners in gaols and Houses of Correction, with details of their offences and sentences, may be found.

D216 Process Registers. These contain lists of indictments, defendants and their parishes, the verdicts and sentences.

D217 Public Undertakings. Many plans for public undertakings such as canals, turnpikes, railways, tramways, docks, gas, water and electricity companies, were deposited with the Clerk of the Peace.

D218 Recognizances. The Clerk of the Peace kept bonds which secured the appearance of defendants, prosecutors or witnesses at Quarter Sessions.

D219 Recusants. An Act of 1657 directed that people should swear an oath abjuring the papacy. Those not doing so were presented at Quarter Sessions.

D220 Removal Orders. Where the legal place of settlement for a pauper was in dispute, the matter would be referred to Quarter Sessions which would issue a Removal Order in accordance with their decision. Copies of these were kept by the Clerk of the Peace.

D221 Sacrament Certificates. From 1673 persons holding civil or military office had to produce a certificate, signed by a minister, churchwardens and two witnesses, which confirmed that he had received the Sacrament of the Lord's Supper. These were sent to Quarter Sessions within six months of taking office.

D222 Savings Banks. From 1817 banks deposited their rules, names of trustees and officers, with the Clerk of the Peace. An Act of 1828 directed that banks should obtain the approval of Justices.

D223 Sessions Books. These contain the rough minutes kept in court by the Clerk of the Peace. They contain details of those present, the indictments, verdicts and sentences.

D224 Slaughter Houses. From 1786 owners of slaughter houses had to obtain a licence from the Justices of the Peace. They had to produce a certificate from the minister and churchwardens of the parish approving of the application.

D225 Transportation. The Clerk of the Peace issued Transportation Orders and arranged contracts for the convicts' conveyance.

D226 Victuallers and Alehouses. The Alehouse Act 1552 directed that alehouse keepers be licensed by the Justices. In 1729 the annual Brewster Sessions began at which Justices licensed retailers.

D227 Tyburn Tickets. This was a colloquial name for a certificate granted by the Clerk of the Peace to a person successfully prosecuting a felon. The document exempted the person from holding a parish office; it was highly valued and saleable.

D228 Weights and Measures. Reports from Inspectors of Weights and Measures were lodged with the Clerk of the Peace.

PART THIRTEEN
ARMY, NAVY AND AIR FORCE RECORDS

D229 Records of Army Officers. The following records are held at the Public Record Office, Kew. Before embarking on research it is advisable to apply to the PRO for two free leaflets: *British Military Records as Sources for Biography and Genealogy*, and *Operational Records of the British Army 1660–1914*. It is also useful to know, if possible, the regiment of the officer concerned.

Army Lists: These contain details of commissioned officers and their regiments; they began in 1740 although there is then a gap until 1754. By the end of the 18th century they were indexed.

Commander-in-Chiefs' Memoranda. These deal with applications for commissions.

Pay Lists and Muster Rolls 1760 onward.

Pension Records 1735 onward.

Courts Martial Records 1684–1847.

Casualty Returns 1809–57. These give name, age, birthplace, next-of-kin, trade etc.

Paymaster General's Records of Full and Half Pay 1828 onward.

D230 Printed Compilations of serving Army officers. Early records have been gathered into the following publications which are available at the Public Record Office, Kew and at the National Army Museum, Chelsea.

The Army Lists of Roundheads and Cavaliers, by E. Peacock.

English Army Lists and Commission Registers 1661–1714, by Charles Dalton.

George I's Army, by Charles Dalton.

Lists of Officers of the Corps of Royal Engineers 1660–1898, by T. W. J. Connolly.

Lists of Officers of the Royal Regiment of Artillery 1716–1899, by J. Kane.

In addition a number of regiments have published histories which contain lists of serving officers.

D231 Records of Army Other Ranks. The following records may be consulted at the Public Record Office, Kew, but it is important, if possible, to know the regiment of the soldier in question. Before embarking on research it is useful to apply for the free leaflets mentioned in D229.

Description Books 1795 onward, describe age, birthplace, trade, physical features etc.

Pay Lists and Muster Rolls 1760 onwards.

Depot Musters.

Regular Soldiers' Documents 1760–1900.

Casualty Returns 1809–57. These give the name, rank, trade, birthplace, next-of-kin and a copy of a will if available.

Chelsea Hospital Pension Registers.

Discharge Certificates.

Courts Martial Records 1684–1847.

D232 Records of Army births marriages and deaths. The following records are at the General Register Office, Kingsway, London, WC2:

Chelsea Hospital Registers. These record christenings 1691–1812, marriages 1691–1765, and burials 1692–1856.

Army Chaplains' Returns 1796–1880. These record births, marriages and deaths concerning servicemen abroad.

Army Returns of Births, Marriages and Deaths 1881–1955. These concern servicemen abroad, but exclude the two World Wars (which see below).

Deaths abroad of Officers and Men in the Three Services. These relate to the two World Wars.

Army Regimental Registers. These record births, marriages and deaths concerning servicemen abroad, 1761–1924.

Reports of Officers' Marriages. In the early 19th century officers were obliged to report their marriages to their senior officers and these records give details of the parties involved etc.

Natal and South Africa Field Forces Deaths. These records relate to the Boer War 1899–1902.

Garrison Registers. These include details of births, marriages and deaths concerning servicemen.

D233 Records of Navy Officers. The following records may be consulted at the Public Record Office, Kew.

Navy Lists. These record names and commissions and have been published since 1749; they became annual in 1782.

Lists of Sea Officers 1800–

Commissioned Sea Officers of the Royal Navy 1660–1815. These lists have been published by the National Maritime Museum whose library is invaluable.

Lieutenants' Passing Certificates 1691–1832.

D234 Records of Navy Warrant Officers. The following records may be consulted at the Public Record Office, Kew.

Warrant Officers' and Seamen's Services.

Seniority Lists.

Commission and Warrant Books.

D235 Records of Navy Ratings. The following records may be consulted at the Public Record Office, Kew, but it is important, if possible, to know the name of the rating's ship. If that information is not available, but his whereabouts and the dates are known, then consult the *List Books*, 1673–1893 which detail the locations of ships.

Ships' Musters 1667 onward. These give details of a man's age, birthplace etc.

Description Books. These describe a man's physical features.

Pay Books 1669 onward.

Pension Books 1734–1885.

D236 Records of Navy births, marriages and deaths.

Bounty Papers 1675–1822. These refer to payments made to seamen or their bereaved relatives. (At the PRO, Kew).

Marine Register Books. These record the births and deaths of people of British nationality at sea since 1 July 1837. (At the General Register Office, St Catherine's House, Kingsway, London, WC2).

Greenwich Hospital Registers. These records of navy pensioners record baptisms 1720–1856, marriages 1724–54, and burials 1705–1857. They are now at the General Register Office, St Catherine's House, Kingsway, London, WC2.

D237 Records of Merchant Seamen. Except where stated the following records are at the Public Record Office, Kew. Before embarking on research it is advisable to obtain from them a free leaflet called *Records of the Registrar-General of Shipping and Seamen.*

Ships' Muster Rolls 1747 onward. These records detail the names of the crews.

Agreements and Crew Lists 1835 onward, record agreements made as to pay and duties etc. Only 10% of the records were kept as from 1861.

Registers of Seamen and Seamen's Tickets. These record the names of serving seamen from 1835.

Records of births and deaths on merchant ships from 1837–74 are held at the General Register Office, St Catherine's House, Kingsway, London, WC2 and after those dates they are housed with the Registrar-General for Shipping and Seamen, Llandaff, Cardiff.

D238 Trinity House Records. Trinity House, founded in 1529, encourages navigational skills and supervises lighthouses and buoys etc. Petitions for pensions from merchant seamen or their widows, 1780–1854, are housed at the Society of Genealogists, 14 Charterhouse Buildings, London, EC1.

D239 Lloyd's Records. Early records of Lloyd's, the marine insurers, are housed at the Guildhall Library, Aldermanbury, London, EC2. They include *Captain's Registers 1868–1947*, and *Voyage records 1740–1970*.

D240 Royal Air Force Records. The Royal Air Force, formed in 1918, superseded the Royal Flying Corps and the Royal Naval Air Force whose records are at the Public Record Office, Kew amongst the archives of the Army and Navy. *Royal Air Force Returns* 1920 onward, with details of births, deaths and marriages relating to servicemen or servicewomen, are at the General Register Office, St Catherine's House, Kingsway, London, WC2.

D241 Other Record Repositories. Important collections of army material are also held at the National Army Museum and the Imperial War Museum, both in London. Regimental histories are the speciality of the Army Museums Ogilby Trust, Connaught Barracks, Duke of Connaught Road, Aldershot. There is a considerable number of small regimental museums around the country but the most important archives outside of the public collections are at the Royal Artillery Institution, Old Royal Military Academy, Woolwich Common, London, SE18 4JJ, the Royal Army Medical College Muniment Room, Millbank, London, SW1P 4PJ, and the Royal Marines Museum, Eastney, Southsea, Hants, PO4 9PX.

Principal collections of naval material are at

the National Maritime Museum, Greenwich, London and the Naval Historical Library of the Ministry of Defence. Royal Air Force material is housed at the RAF Museum, Aerodrome Road, London, NW9 5LL.

PART FOURTEEN
LEGAL RECORDS

D242 Inns of Court. The four Inns of Court, Grays Inn and Lincoln's Inn, and Inner and Middle Temple, have all published registers of entrants and calendars of records. The Inner Temple and Lincoln's Inn have particularly good libraries which are open to approved researchers.

D243 Law List. The Law List, which records barristers and solicitors, has been published annually since 1775.

D244 Solicitors. Records concerning articles of clerkship from 1730–1835 are held at the Public Record Office, Chancery Lane, London, WC2.

D245 Court Records. The records of Quarter Sessions are usually held at the county record offices. (See Part 12).

Those of the Court of the King's Bench are at the Public Record Office, Chancery Lane, London, WC2.

The archives of the Assize Courts are at the Public Record Office, Chancery Lane with two exceptions: those for London are held at the Guildhall Library and the Corporation of London Record Office, and those for Middlesex are at the Greater London Record Office, 40 Northampton Road, London, EC1.

D246 Prisons. In 1877 prison administration was transferred from the counties to the Home Office with, theoretically, a transfer of archives. However, the county record offices may still have collections of material. Records of prisoners 1770–1894 are now at the Public Record Office, Kew but only those over 100 years old may be consulted. An index of people held for debt in London's prisons from 1775 is held by the Corporation of London Record Office.

The archives of the Howard League for Penal Reform are held at the Modern Records Centre, University of Warwick, Coventry, CV4 7AL.

PART FIFTEEN
EDUCATIONAL RECORDS

D247 Education History. The history of education is the speciality of the Institute of Education Library, University of London, 11–13 Ridgmount Street, London, WC1E 7AH.

D248 Universities. Graduates of Oxford University are listed in *Alumni Oxoniensis 1500–1886* (8 vols) by J. Foster.

Graduates of Cambridge University are listed in *Alumni Cantabrigiensis* (10 vols) by J. A. Venn.

These are supplemented by registers of admissions to many of the colleges.

Most other universities have published annual lists since their formation; a collection of these is in the library of the Society of Genealogists, 14 Charterhouse Buildings, London, EC1M 7BA.

D249 Public Schools. Many public schools have printed lists of scholars. Good archive collections, open to approved researchers, are at Eton, Harrow, Rugby, St Paul's, Westminster and Winchester.

D250 School Societies. The archives of the British and Foreign Schools Society are held at the West London Institute of Higher Education, Borough Road, Isleworth, Middlesex. The archives of the National Society may be consulted after application to the National Society for Promoting Religious Education, Church House, Dean's Yard, SW1.

D251 Local Schools. The records of Board schools and those of local education authorities generally reside in county and local record offices. School log books may also be available.

PART SIXTEEN
ELECTORAL RECORDS

D252 Poll Books. From 1696 returning officers at elections were required on demand, and for a fee, to compile for any member of the public, a return of voters and how they voted. At that time the electorate was not large. This measure was enacted because of complaints that some returning officers were partisan in their duties. In some constituencies this was enlarged into a commercial publishing venture so that numbers of copies were available for purchase; this practice continued until the General Election of 1868. Secret ballots were introduced from 1872.

Good collections of Poll Books exist at the Guildhall Library, the British Library, and the Institute of Historical Research, Senate House, University of London, and at the Bodleian Library, Oxford.

D253 Electoral Registers. These began in 1832 at a time when a property qualification was needed to vote. Therefore, the earlier registers detailed name and address of the elector and the property which qualified him. These records are generally to be found in local record offices.

PART SEVENTEEN
EMIGRATION AND IMMIGRATION RECORDS

D254 Emigration. Records relating to emigrants to America, the West Indies, the Cape Colony and Australia are to be found in the Public Record Office, Kew. Researchers are advised to apply there first for a free leaflet entitled *Emigrants: Documents in the Public Record Office.* Much useful information as to early settlers, grants of land etc is summarised in three articles in *Family Tree* magazine, Volume One, numbers 1, 2 and 3.

Many passenger lists and other papers relating to emigrants to the Americas have been published. These are succinctly detailed in *The Dictionary of Genealogy* by Terrick V. H. Fitzhugh (1985) on pages 97–8. In the same section Mr Fitzhugh notes those genealogical societies abroad who might be applied to when searching ancestors known to have emigrated. Particularly useful too is *Lists of Persons Emi-*

grating to America 1600–1700 by J. C. Hotten.

Until 1834 no British subject could go to India without the consent of the East India Company. The application records, and the permissions to trade, are housed in the India Office Library, 197 Blackfriars Road, London, SE1 8NG, where also are lists of East India Company employees up to 1794.

Transportation of convicts records are kept at the Public Record Office at Kew. A list of felons transported from the home counties to America during the period 1719 to 1744 has been published. After the American Revolution convicts were sent to Australia and Tasmania; censuses taken there list convicts and these records are at the Public Record Office.

From 1834 to 1890 the Poor Law Amendment Act encouraged the passage of poor families to the colonies at the expense of the Poor Law Unions. The records of these assisted passages are at the Public Record Office, Kew, arranged by counties; names, occupations and destinations are given.

D255 Immigrants. From 1792 an alien arriving in this country was required to register with the Clerk of the Peace, and anyone housing him had to notify his parish authorities. These records would usually be at the county record office. The Aliens Act 1836 enacted that immigrants gave name, occupation and nationality at the port of entry. These records are at the Public Record Office, Kew.

An Act of Naturalization which gave the applicant the status of a natural-born subject was expensive and only the wealthy could afford it. Records of Naturalization are at the Public Record Office, Chancery Lane, London, WC2.

A less expensive process was to become a denizen by Letters Patent, which gave status as a British subject without the full rights of a natural-born subject. Denization records are in *Patent Rolls* and *Close Rolls* at the Public Record Office, Chancery Lane, London, WC2.

PART EIGHTEEN
MANOR AND ESTATE RECORDS

D256 Manorial Records. Manorial records are usually held at county or local record offices, although many are still in private hands; other good collections are held at the Public Record Office and British Library. Researchers may consult a location index at the Historic Manuscripts Commission at Quality House, Quality Court, Chancery Lane, London, WC2, called the *Manorial Documents Register* which lists all known holdings; since 1926 it has been necessary to report any change of ownership of manorial records to the Master of the Rolls, a law not always complied with.

The principal items are the records of the Court Leet and Court Baron, the first dealing with petty crimes and manorial appointments, the second with land transfer. The two courts were usually held at one sitting and their records are noted in the same document. Originally in rolls, later in volumes, the records, with the exception of the Commonwealth period, are in Latin until 1734.

Separate from these could be rentals, and also a custumal which recites the customs, rights and obligations of a manor. The lord may also have a plan and terrier of his demesne lands.

D257 Estate Records. Inevitably such records are spread over a wide field – the local and county record offices, solicitors' offices, family libraries etc. The archives include plans, terriers, rentals, valuations, leases. Researchers should consult first at local and county record offices, and then at the National Register of Archives, Quality House, Quality Court, Chancery Lane, London, WC2 which keeps an index of many holdings which are outside of official repositories.

Some of the larger estates have their own archive offices or else have deposited them with others. The principal ones are:

Bedford Estates, 29a Montague Street, London, WC1.

Dartmouth Estate, Leeds Archives Dept, Chapeltown Road, Sheepcar, Leeds, and at the Staffordshire Record Office, Eastgate Street, Stafford.

Devonshire Estate, Chatsworth, Bakewell, Derbyshire.

Duchy of Cornwall, 10 Buckingham Gate, London SW1.

Duke of Norfolk, Arundel Castle, Arundel, West Sussex.

Grosvenor Estate, Chester Record Office, Town Hall, Chester, and at Westminster City Libraries Archives Dept, Victoria Library, Buckingham Palace Road, London, SW1.

Portland Estate, at Westminster City Library (as per *Grosvenor*).

Salisbury Estate, Hatfield House, Hatfield, Herts.

D258 Title Deeds. A title deed is a document recording the conveyance of a property which is evidence of title when the property is subsequently resold. Many early deeds were no more than a copy of an entry in court rolls where the property was copyhold (qv). Until 1925 it was necessary for the vendor to prove title back as far as possible but the Law of Property Act that year enacted that in future it would only be necessary to search back thirty years if the previous conveyance had taken place within that period. This legislation has rendered numerous title deeds superfluous and many have been thrown away or else deposited in local record offices.

PART NINETEEN
SOCIAL WELFARE RECORDS

D259 Settlement and Removal Records. The 1697 Settlement Act debarred strangers from residing in a parish unless they provided a Settlement Certificate showing that they would be taken back by their home parish if they became in need of poor relief. Removal Orders were issued when this became necessary. These records are usually in the archives of Quarter Sessions lodged with county record offices. The papers might also include examinations of the people involved.

D260 Overseers of the Poor. Until the Poor Law Amendment Act 1834 the relief of the poor was the responsibility of the parishes through their Overseers of the Poor. Records are therefore contained in vestry minutes kept at local record offices.

D261 Poor Law Records. The administration of poor relief after the Poor Law Amendment Act 1834 is mainly recorded in the archives of the Guardians of the Poor for individual parishes or unions of parishes. The records will be in local or county record offices.

D262 Workhouses. The building of work-houses began in earnest in the 18th century and reached its peak in the mid-19th century. The records are in the vestry minutes for the earlier period, and after 1834 are part of the archives of the Guardians of the Poor, which may be housed with either local or county record offices.

D263 Charities. The records of many charities are still held by their modern successors, or else they are in local and county record offices. The archives of Dr Barnardo's Homes 1867–1970 are held in the Archives Department of the University of Liverpool, and the London records of the Charity Organisation Society, which became the Family Welfare Association, are at the Greater London Record Office, 40 Northampton Road, London, EC1. The Charity Commission for England and Wales, which was set up in 1853, oversees the accounts and activities of registered charities and their archives at 14 Ryder Street, London, SW1 contain records relating to some 136,000 charities.

From 1786 the Clerk of the Peace sent returns of charities to Parliament and received copies of their accounts, objects etc. These are held in the Quarter Sessions records, usually at county record offices.

D264 Bastardy Returns. Vestry minutes contain records of proceedings against fathers for maintenance of illegitimate children. The records of Quarter Sessions, particularly since 1844 when mothers were permitted to apply for maintenance orders, are usually of more value.

D265 Foundlings. Foundlings usually became a charge on the poor rate and records of them are in vestry minutes and, inevitably, feature prominently in the parish burial registers where their status in life is often noted. The archives of the Foundling Hospital, London are at the Greater London Record Office, 40 Northampton Road, London, EC1.

D266 Dispensaries. Many towns in the 18th and 19th centuries established dispensaries, a term then to denote places to which the poor could go for medical treatment and medicine. These establishments were supported by the donations of the more affluent who had the right to nominate poor people for treatment in accordance with the amount of their dona-

tions. Records, normally held in local record offices, usually contain lists of subscribers, the accounts and details of the number of people using the dispensary etc.

PART TWENTY
PARISH AND LOCAL AUTHORITY RECORDS

D267 General. The archives held in local record offices are diverse. A good collection should contain copies of each map of the area, each general or particular history, all local newspapers, census returns, possibly copies of the parish registers, illustrations, general ephemera, rate books, vestry minutes, records of other administrative bodies such as Paving Boards, electoral registers, local directories and a selection of the burgeoning paperwork of local government in the 20th century.

Record offices vary enormously as to their care, cataloguing and presentation of this material and sometimes the researcher will need persistence to establish what is available.

D268 Vestry Minutes. Legislation from Tudor times gave more responsibilities to parishes and the vestries which ran them. Parishes administered poor relief and early records are concerned with this, the election of officials, accounts, charities and the church fabric. Local record offices may have minutes dating back to the 17th and 18th centuries but these, unlike parish registers for the same period, are largely untranscribed and indexed. They are particularly useful in tracing first mentions of street or place names.

In the 19th century the minutes are formidable in size as the vestries became responsible for public hygiene, roads, weights and measures, early building controls and street cleaning.

D269 Paving Boards. In urban areas private Acts of Parliament in the 18th and 19th centuries by estate developers permitted the owners to pave, clean and repair their own roads, and to impose a residential rate to pay for this. The Acts usually enabled the owners to put bars across appropriate roads to prevent through traffic.

The records of these Boards were usually transferred to the local authority when the parish took over their responsibilities, but the maintenance of the bars across the streets remained with the owners, who sought to keep up the value of their estates by such devices. The records relating to the demolition of such barriers are contained in later vestry minutes.

D270 Rate Books. These record the payment of the poor rate and can, in theory, date back to the 17th century but most likely they will have survived from the late 18th and early 19th centuries. Rate books are the most accurate source for establishing the age of a property, or the date of its enlargement, or the residence of a particular person. The rate books of the 19th century record the location, the name of the ratepayer and the owner of the property, the rateable value and the amount paid.

Collectors usually compiled the books on a 'route' system – that is, they began at one part of their territory and recorded property as they walked in a predetermined journey. This is very useful to local historians as it is possible to follow the gradual development of a road into blocks of terraces and villas, whereas if the collectors had assembled their books alphabetically the researcher would not necessarily know where a group of houses called, for example, Crown Terrace, belonged.

When the collector compiled a volume he usually worked from the previous one – the latter may well have names crossed out or inserted in pencil. These corrections indicate the information to go into the next volume.

D271 Charity Records. In the vogue for local history publishing in the 19th century particular attention was paid to detailing the charities, large and small, which had existed in the area. Many of them, even by then, were defunct or absorbed into the accounts of other bodies which administered them, such as the parish church. These printed histories are quite often the only record of the existence of such charities unless the vestry administered the bequest, in which case they should feature in the accounts of the vestry minutes.

D272 Church Trustees' Records. The Church Trustees administered any lands or bequests belonging to the local church. The responsibility for the church fabric or the building of new churches was often not clearly defined and was the cause of disputes between Trustees and secular vestries. Usually the records of the Church Trustees remain with the parish church.

PART TWENTY-ONE
POSTAL SERVICE RECORDS

D273 Post Office Archives. The archives of the General Post Office are housed at Freeling House, 23 Glass Hill Street, London, SE1. For telephone directories, previously part of the Post Office archives, see Part 29.

D274 Postcards. The first postcard was published in Austria in 1869, and in England in 1870. They were originally type only – pictorial ones began in the 1890s, but the illustration was confined to the same side as the message, which inhibited the picture and correspondence. In 1902 the Post Office permitted the illustration to appear on one side and the message and addressee on the other. This encouraged the 'golden age' of postcards. Topographical subjects abounded, with publishers producing short runs and selling them door-to-door; quite often these provide the only photographic record of buildings and streets for that period. Most local record offices have collections applicable to their area.

PART TWENTY-TWO
MEDICAL RECORDS

D275 History of Medicine. The Wellcome Institute for the History of Medicine was established on the death of Sir Henry Wellcome in 1936. His collection, which made up the museum, is now at the Science Museum, London; the library is also an important medical history research centre, housed at the Wellcome Institute, 183 Euston Road, London, NW1 2BP. Also here is the Contemporary Medical Archives Centre.

Glasgow University Library has a collection on 18th-century medicine with particular emphasis on William Hunter.

The Royal Society of Medicine, 1 Wimpole Street, London, W1M 8AE houses the papers of the important societies which were amalgamated to form the Society in 1907.

D276 Physicians and Doctors. Archives dealing with the history of medicine, and the internal records of the Royal College of Physicians of London, which was granted its charter in 1518, are housed in the library of the College at 11 St Andrew's Place, London, NW1 4LE. The College has also published some volumes relating to Fellows and Licentiates known as *Munk's Roll of Physicians*.

Important collections are also held at the Royal College of Physicians and Surgeons of Glasgow, 234–242 St Vincent Street, Glasgow, G2 5RJ, which was established in 1599. The Royal College of Physicians of Edinburgh, 9 Queen Street, Edinburgh, EH2 1JQ has lists of members etc since its foundation in 1681.

The *Medical Register*, which has appeared since 1858, contains biographies of practitioners.

D277 Surgeons. The Royal College of Surgeons of England was founded in 1800. Apart from the papers of leading medical men, the library houses the records of the College. Details of Fellows have been published in *Lives of the Fellows of the Royal College of Surgeons*.

D278 Apothecaries and Pharmacists. The records of the Society of Apothecaries, founded in 1617, are now at the Guildhall Library, London.

The archives of the Pharmaceutical Society, which was founded in 1841, are housed at its offices at 1 Lambeth High Street, London, SE1 7JN.

D279 Hospitals. The following major hospitals have archives which may be used by approved researchers:

Bethlem Royal Hospital, Monks Orchard Road, Beckenham, Kent BR3 3BX
King's College London, Strand, London, WC2R 2LS
Middlesex Hospital, Mortimer Street, London, W1
Royal Free Hospital, Pond Street, London, NW3
St Bartholomew's Hospital, West Smithfield, EC1
St George's Hospital, Blackshaw Road, London, SW17
St Thomas's Hospital, London, SE1 7EH

The records for *Guy's* and *Westminster* hospitals are housed at the Greater London Record Office, 40 Northampton Road, London, EC1.

PART TWENTY-THREE
TAXATION RECORDS

D280 Lay Subsidies. This term denotes a tax on movables levied from the 13th to the 17th centuries. The 1291 taxation list has been published by the Record Commissioners; the Great Subsidy rolls of 1524/5 list people over 16 years who merited taxation. Records are held at the Public Record Office, Chancery Lane, London, WC2.

D281 Poll Tax. This tax was levied a number of times between 1377 and 1697. Surviving records are at the Public Record Office, Chancery Lane, London, WC2.

D282 Free and Voluntary Present to Charles II. This 'gift' was collected in 1661; returns for over thirty English and Welsh counties survive and are housed in the Public Record Office, Chancery Lane, London, WC2.

D283 Hearth Tax. This tax was levied between 1662 to 1689. Printed lists are available of many returns and the original documents are in the Public Record Office, Chancery Lane, London, WC2. A useful guide is *The Hearth Tax, other later Stuart Tax Lists and the Association Oath Rolls*, by J. S. W. Gibson, published by the Federation of Family History Societies.

D284 Land Tax. This tax was levied from 1697 until 1832. The records from 1780 are in county record offices but some documents are at the Public Record Office, Kew. From 1772 the returns include a list of occupiers for each parish.

D285 Window Tax. This tax was levied from 1696 and abolished in 1851. Very few returns survive and these would usually be in county record offices.

D286 Customs and Excise. The library of HM Customs and Excise at King's Beam House, Mark Lane, EC3 contains records dating back to the 16th century, principally dealing with imports and exports.

PART TWENTY-FOUR
TRADE, INDUSTRY AND COMMERCE RECORDS

D287 Livery Company Records. Most of the records of the City of London livery companies, or microfilm copies of them, have been deposited with the Guildhall Library, London. The exceptions are: Air Pilots, Broderers, Clothworkers, Drapers, Fan Makers, Farmers, Haberdashers, Ironmongers, Leathersellers, Loriners, Master Mariners, Mercers, Salters, Scientific Instrument Makers, Skinners, and Vintners. The Stationers and Goldsmiths have deposited part of their archives at the Guildhall Library.

D288 Trading Companies. Records of three of the old major trading companies are located as follows:

Levant Company, at the Public Record Office, Chancery Lane, London, WC2.
East India Company, at the India Office Library, Orbit House, Blackfriars Road, SE1.
Hudson Bay Company, microfilm copies are at the Public Record Office, Kew.

D289 Apprenticeship Records. A stamp duty was levied from 1710 on apprenticeship indentures other than those for poor children. These records are at the Public Record Office, Kew. A free leaflet entitled *Apprenticeship Records as Sources for Genealogy in the Public Record Office*, may be obtained from the PRO. The Society of Genealogists has an index of these records covering the period 1710–74. Vestry minutes record the apprenticing of poor children.

The archives of the Livery Companies (see above) contain records of apprentices. In addition the Chamberlain of the City of London, Guildhall, London, EC2 has an index of freemen, (a status achieved at the end of an apprenticeship), from 1681.

D290 Bank of England. Records over 30 years old may be used by approved researchers for specific purposes. They are housed in the Museum and Historical Research Section, Bank of England, Threadneedle Street, London, EC2.

D291 Victuallers. From 1552 alehouse keepers were licensed but records are not plentiful. The annual Brewster Sessions began in 1729 but good lists of licencees exist from before that date. These records are usually in county record offices.

D292 Coal Industry. Records of the coal industry, other than those of pre-nationalised companies which were distributed to county record offices, are held at the National Coal Board Archive Centre, 200 Lichfield House, Mansfield, Notts.

D293 Steel Industry. The records of the steel industry which have been consolidated into the archives of the British Steel Corporation, are now decentralised. Researchers are advised to enquire, initially, with the Director, Secretariat, British Steel Corporation, 33 Grosvenor Place, London, SW1.

D294 Business Archives. Guidance in locating records is given by the Business Archives Council, Denmark House, 15 Tooley Street, London, SE1, and by the Business Archives Council of Scotland, Glasgow University Archives, Glasgow, G12 8QQ.

The Companies' Registration Office at Company House, 55 City Road, London, EC1 has files on companies past and present.

PART TWENTY-FIVE
RELIGIOUS RECORDS

D295 Ecclesiastical Libraries. Libraries may be used by approved researchers at Exeter, Gloucester, Hereford, Salisbury, Winchester and Worcester Cathedrals. The archives of St Paul's are at the Guildhall Library, London.

The Lambeth Palace Library contains archives relating to the Province of Canterbury. The Borthwick Institute of Historical Research, University of York, St Anthony's Hall, Peasholme Green, York, has archives of the Province of York. The latter has published a *Guide to the Genealogical Sources in the Borthwick Institute of Historical Research*. The Commissioners have records relating to church estates from 1704. These are housed at 1, Millbank, London, SW1.

The Theological College, Rosebery Crescent, Edinburgh has archives relating to the Episcopal Church in Scotland in the 16th–19th centuries.

D296 Diocesan Registries. Bishops deposited their records in the diocesan registry, although some have since been transferred to county record offices. Archives include details of church and cathedral administration, landholdings, tithes, probate, Chapter Books,

Visitation Books, Bishops' Transcripts and Marriage Licences. In 1676 each parish priest was instructed to return to either the Archbishop of Canterbury or York a census of parishioners (numbers only) together with details of those absenting themselves from worship. These returns, known as the *Compton Census*, are among diocesan records, where they survive.

D297 Baptist Records. The central repository for Baptist records and those of the Baptist Historical Society is the Baptist Union Library at 4 Southampton Row, London, WC1. Archives are also kept at the Baptist Missionary Society, 93–97 Gloucester Place, London, W1, and at Dr Williams' Library, Gordon Square, London, WC1. Much historical material is contained in *Baptist Quarterly*, the journal of the Baptist Historical Society. Researchers should also consult the *Baptist Magazine*, from 1809, and the *Baptist Handbook*.

D298 Catholic Records. For the period 1592–1691 the Recusant Rolls list many Catholics, as well as non-conformist Protestants. These records are at the Public Record Office, Chancery Lane, London, WC2, but researchers should enquire first with the Catholic Record Society to find if the appropriate Roll has been published by them. The society also publishes *Recusant History*.

A list of Catholic registers and historical records printed up to 1958 is contained in *Texts and Calendars* by E. L. C. Mullins.

In 1717 Catholics had to register their names and landholdings with the Clerk of the Peace; these archives should be in the county record office.

The Franciscan Archives (English Province) are at the Franciscan Friary, 58 St Anthony's Road, London, E7. Catholic history is also represented in the Duke of Norfolk's Library and Archives at Arundel Castle, Arundel, West Sussex. The Scottish Catholic Archives are at Columba House, 16 Drummond Place, Edinburgh. The Society of Jesus has a record office at 114 Mount Street, London, W1.

D299 Congregationalist Records. The central repository for records is the Congregational Church of England and Wales, Memorial Hall, Farringdon Road, London, EC1. The Congregational Historical Society publishes *Transactions*, and Dr Williams' Library, Gordon Square, London, WC1 has much material. Some records also exist at the library of the United Reformed Church History Society at 86 Tavistock Place, London, WC1.

D300 Huguenot Records. Most archives are kept at the joint library of the French Hospital de la Providence and of the Huguenot Society at University College, Gower Street, London, WC1. The Society has published many volumes listing naturalizations, denizations and aliens 1509–1800; other naturalizations are listed in *Index to Local and Personal Acts 1801–1947* published by HMSO.

D301 Jewish Records. Generally synagogues retain their own records. At Woburn House, Upper Woburn Place, London, WC1 is the Jewish Museum. The Jewish Historical Society, c/o University College, Gower Street, London, WC1, has published much historical material. Their library, the Mocatta Library, is here, together with the records of the Anglo-Jewish Association. The United Group of Synagogues houses its archives centrally at the United Synagogue at Woburn House noted above.

D302 Methodist Records. The central repository is the Methodist Archives and Research Centre, John Ryland's University Library of Manchester, Deansgate, Manchester. Material has been published by the Wesleyan Historical Society and by some of the other branches of Methodism. The Methodist Missionary Society has lodged its archives at the School of Oriental and African Studies, University of London, Malet Street, London, WC1. Each Methodist area has an archivist. Researchers should enquire initially with the Connexional Archivist, Methodist Church, Central Buildings, Oldham Street, Manchester.

D303 Presbyterian Records. Archives of the Presbyterian Church of England are housed in the library of the United Reformed Church History Society at 86 Tavistock Place, London, WC1. Others are held at the School of Oriental and African Studies, University of London, Malet Street, London, WC1. Material is also held at Dr Williams' Library, Gordon Square, London, WC1.

D304 Quaker Records. The central repository of records of the Society of Friends is at Friends House, Euston Road, London, NW1, but many records are held at county level. The Friends Historical Society publishes a journal.

D305 Unitarian Records. Archives are kept at the Unitarian headquarters, 1 Essex Street, London, WC2. Records are published by the Unitarian Historical Society.

D306 Missionary Society Records. The archives of the Society for Promoting Christian Knowledge are at Holy Trinity Church, Marylebone Road, London, NW1.

The archives of the United Society for the Propagation of the Gospel, 1701 onward, are at 15 Tufton Street, London, SW1.

The records of the British and Foreign Bible Society are at 146 Queen Victoria Street, London, EC4.

Those of the Church Missionary Society, 1799 onward, are at 157 Waterloo Road, London, SE1.

D307 Clerical Records. Early appointments of clergy are listed in Institution Books held at the Public Record Office, Chancery Lane, London, WC2; other information for this period may be found in diocesan registries. Appointments for the period 1800–40 are listed in *Index Ecclesiasticus* by J. Foster. Crockford's *Clerical Directory* was first issued in 1858.

PART TWENTY-SIX
THEATRICAL RECORDS

D308 Collections. A major assembly of collections of theatrical material is housed at the new Theatre Museum, Covent Garden opening in 1987.

Important collections are also held at the Royal Opera House in London, and at the Westminster City Library. The Glasgow University Library, Hillhead Street, Glasgow, G12 8QE has a collection dealing with 19th and 20th century Scottish theatre.

Most local and county record offices have collections of playbills, programmes, cuttings, etc., relating to local theatres.

D309 Publications. Useful publications, of which complete runs exist at the British Museum Newspaper Library, London, NW9, are:

The Era (from 1838)
Theatre (1877–97)
The Stage (1879 onward)

Of particular value for the London area is *London's Theatres and Music Halls 1850–1950* by

Diana Howard (1970) which gives the history of each establishment and indicates which collections have relative material.

PART TWENTY-SEVEN
POLITICAL RECORDS

D310 Principal Collections. The proceedings and enactments of the Houses of Parliament are held at the House of Lords Library.

Most collections of political material tend to be radical, socialist or concerned with trade unions. Important archives are housed at:

Marx Memorial Library, 37a Clerkenwell Green, London, EC1 0DU.

The Labour Party, 150 Walworth Road, SE17, 1JT.

National Museum of Labour History, Limehouse Town Hall, Commercial Road, London, E14.

Modern Records Centre, University of Warwick Library, Coventry, CV4 7AL.

Huddersfield Polytechnic Library, Queensgate, Huddersfield, HD1 3DH has a good regional collection.

Nuffield College Library, University of Oxford, OX1 1NF, has records of the Fabian Society and Guild Socialism as well as the papers of important political figures.

The West Sussex Record Office, West Street, Chichester, has papers relating to Cobden and 19th-century politics.

The records of the National Liberal Club are held at the University of Bristol Library, Tyndall Avenue, Bristol, BS8 1TJ.

Suffragette material is held in the Fawcett Library at the City of London Polytechnic, Old Castle Street, London, E1 7NT, and in the Museum of London's library.

An important political collection, which includes the papers of the Webbs, Lasky, John Stuart Mill etc, is held by the London School of Economics and Political Science, 10 Portugal Street, London WC2A 2HD.

PART TWENTY-EIGHT
NEWSPAPERS AND OTHER PRINTED SOURCES

D311 Newspapers. Newspapers published since 1801 are housed at the British Museum Newspaper Library, Colindale, London, NW9. Those before that date are at the British Museum, Great Russell Street, London, WC1. The Bodleian Library, Oxford, also has a collection from 1622 to 1800.

There is a '*Tercentenary Handlist of English and Welsh Newspapers 1620–1920*, published by The Times in 1920, which is arranged chronologically. Arranged geographically is a *Handlist of English Provincial Newspapers and Periodicals 1700–1760* by G. A. Cranfield.

The Times newspaper, founded in 1785 as the *Daily Universal Register*, has been indexed since 1791. Most principal libraries have sets of the indexes and microfilms of the actual newspapers.

D312 London Gazette. This newspaper first appeared in February 1665/6 as the *Oxford Gazette*. It was, and continues to be, an official publication dealing with royal engagements, church, legal, civil, naval and military appointments as well as recording business company formations and dissolutions together with bankruptcies. A complete collection is held at the Guildhall Library, London.

D313 Gentleman's Magazine. This monthly journal began publication in January 1731 and its 18th century and early 19th century editions are particularly rich in information about births, deaths and marriages and also in biographies. It also published a wide range of topographical material, some of which has been published in separate volumes. Each volume of the magazine contains an index; there are also some cumulative indexes, as well as compilation indexes of marriages, obituaries and biographies. Most principal libraries have a set.

D314 Illustrated London News. This weekly magazine began in 1842, although it is now a monthly journal. Its main strength was its coverage of London news and wealth of illustrations, but its title belies the fact that its provincial coverage was also comprehensive.

D315 Country Life. This weekly magazine began in 1897. It includes a wide range of topographical subjects and has always specialised in the description of stately homes.

D316 Notes and Queries. This monthly journal began in 1849 and ceased publication in 1962. It dealt with literature, the arts, history and topography. It is useful for detail on subjects dealt with more generally elsewhere. Most principal libraries have a set as does the Society of Genealogists in London.

D317 The Builder. This weekly magazine, first published in 1843, was devoted to architecture and construction. Many public and private buildings are described in its pages and there is an annual index. Its name was changed to *Building* in 1966. A full set is housed at the RIBA Library, Portland Place, London, W1.

D318 Building News. A weekly magazine first published in 1855; it merged with *The Architect* in 1926. It had the same function as *The Builder* above.

D319 Victoria County History. This publishing venture was begun in 1899 and is still proceeding. More properly called the *Victoria History of the Counties of England*, it is an attempt to summarise the history of each county and the principal places in them. Most importantly the volumes are based on meticulous research in archival material at the Public Record Office and elsewhere, much of which has not been published before.

D320 Lewis's Topographical Dictionaries of England and Wales. The volumes for England were published in 1831, 1833 and 1849 and for Wales in 1833. They consist of a gazetteer of each town and village but most importantly, for genealogists, they state in which parish each place lay.

D321 Local History Publications. *The Local Historian* is the official publication of the British Association for Local History. It began in 1952 as the Amateur Historian, and changed to its present name in 1968. It is published quarterly, and contains scholarly articles on a wide range of local history subjects. It is particularly useful for its book reviews and bibliography. Most main libraries have complete sets.

It may be obtained from the Association, The Mill Manager's House, Cromford Mill, Matlock, Derbyshire.

The Association also publishes *Local History News* as part of its membership entitlement;

this consists of news items and brief book reviews.

Local History was first published in July 1984 and comes out six times a year. Its articles are more localised in scope, but the publication has a wider range of news than the *Local Historian*. It may be obtained from 3 Devonshire Promenade, Lenton, Nottingham. (0602 700369).

PART TWENTY-NINE
DIRECTORIES

D322 Local Directories. From the middle of the 18th century until the 1930s local directories provide information on the nobility, gentry, trade, public buildings and services. Most local authorities have collections of these relating to their own area. The most important series was that published by Kelly's Directories from 1799 to 1939 in county or city volumes. Where necessary a volume may be consulted at Kelly's Directories Ltd, Dorset House, Stamford Street, SE1; an appointment and a search fee are required. Otherwise, good collections are held at the Guildhall Library, and the Society of Genealogists in London.

D323 Peerage Directories. *Debrett's Peerage and Baronetage* has been published since 1713.

D324 Telephone Directories. An almost complete collection of telephone directories is held at the British Telecom Museum, Baynard House, 135 Queen Victoria Street, EC4. Other collections are held at the Guildhall Library, London, the Bodleian Library, Oxford, and at the Historical Telephone Directory Library, 7th floor, 211 Old Street, EC1.

PART THIRTY
SCOTTISH AND WELSH RECORDS

D325 Scottish Record Office. This Office houses the most important state records. They include:

The General Register of Sasines, which records ownership of land in Scotland since 1617; it numbers over 50,000 volumes.

The Registers of Deeds, dating from 1554, which include indentures, contracts and writs.

Records of the Scottish central courts.

Taxation records including the Hearth Tax of 1690–93 and the Poll Tax of 1694 and 1695.

D326 Other Scottish Archives. The Royal Commission on the Ancient and Historical Monuments of Scotland has the principal collection of drawings and illustrations of buildings. It also houses the collection of aerial photographs of archaeological and architectural sites belonging to the Society of Antiquaries of Scotland. This is at 54 Melville Street, Edinburgh. The Royal Scottish Museum at Chambers Street, Edinburgh has an archaeology department. The Hay Fleming Reference Library at St Andrews Branch Library, Church Square, St Andrews, Fife has a large collection concerning the political, social and ecclesiastical history of Scotland.

D327 Welsh Records. The principal repositories of Welsh material are:

The National Library of Wales, Aberystwyth, Dyfed, which contains court records, diocesan archives and also those of the Welsh Calvinistic Methodist church, estate records and the official archives of Powys.

The Royal Commission on the Ancient and Historical Monuments of Wales at Edleston House, Queens Road, Aberystwyth, Dyfed has an extensive collection of plans, illustrations and photographs. The National Museum of Wales has collections relating to Welsh industry as well as a large print and photographic archive; this is in Bute Street, Cardiff. The Welsh Folk Museum at St Fagans, Cardiff, has the largest collection of books, photographs, recordings and ephemera of Welsh folklore and dialects.

PART THIRTY-ONE
MISCELLANEOUS RECORDS

D328 Architecture. The principal collection of architectural drawings, plans and illustrations is housed at the Royal Institute of British Architecture at 66 Portland Place, London W1 and at 21 Portman Square, London, W1. The collection also includes the papers of many architects and architectural organisations, and complete files of architectural magazines. The careers of English architects are detailed in *English Mediaevel Architects, a Biographical Dictionary* down to 1550, by John Harvey, A *Biographical Dictionary of English Architects 1660–1840*, by H. M. Colvin and *Edwardian Architecture* by A. Stuart Gray.

D329 Bills of Mortality. The Company of Parish Clerks issued a weekly statement of the numbers dead and the causes for the City of

London and adjoining parishes, from information supplied by its members. The custom prevailed from the 16th century until 1837 when the General Register Office was established, although the Guildhall Library has some for up to 1852.

D330 Costume History. The principal collection of material is at the Victoria and Albert Museum in London, although many provincial museums carry displays and material. The Costume and Fashion Research Centre at 4 Circus, Bath, an extension of the Museum of Costume there, has a large collection of illustrations and other research aids.

D331 Folklore. The collection of the Folklore Society is at University College, Gower Street, London, WC1. Collections relating to Welsh folklore are at the Welsh Folk Museum, St Fagan's, Cardiff.

D332 Freemen's Rolls. Corporate towns kept records of their freemen and guild members. These should be in the appropriate local record office.

D333 Highway Records. The Highway Act 1862 empowered Quarter Sessions to establish Highway Boards to administer highways for a combination of parishes. The Boards were abolished in 1894 and their records placed with the county record offices.

D334 Land Registration. Systematic land registration began in Middlesex and Yorkshire in the 18th century but for other parts of the country early records are found scattered among State papers, especially in the Close Rolls of Chancery and the Plea Rolls of the Courts of Common Law. The records for Middlesex and Yorkshire are in the appropriate record offices. The Land Registry was established in 1891.

D335 Lieutenancy Records. The Lord Lieutenant was a Crown appointment in each county and his importance dates from the 17th century. He was responsible for the county militia until the 19th century and records are mainly of use in this connection.

D336 Motoring. The BP Library of Motoring at the National Motor Museum, Beaulieu, Hants, has a collection of mainly printed material.

D337 Place Names. The English Place Names Society has published volumes concerning the following counties: Beds, Berks, Bucks, Cambs, Cheshire, Cornwall, Cumberland, Derbyshire, Devon, Dorset, Essex, Glos, Herts, Hunts, Middlesex, Northants, Notts, Oxfordshire, Surrey, Sussex, Warks, Westminster, Wilts and Worcestershire.

The most important general works on the subject are *English Place Names* and *English River Names*, both by Eilert Ekwall.

D338 Tithe Records. The Tithe Commutation Act 1836 allowed tithes to be commuted to a rent-charge. A large-scale map was drawn showing each piece of land involved, and the names of owners and occupiers were listed. Three copies of this survey were made. One was sent to the Public Record Office, another to the Diocesan Registry, and the third went to the parish authority. The Royal Commission on Historical Manuscripts at Quality House, Quality Court, Chancery Lane, WC2 has a register of existing tithe records.

PART THIRTY TWO
BIBLIOGRAPHY

General Works
Archives and Local History, F. G. Emmison (1966)
British Archives, J. Foster and J. Sheppard (1982)
Village Records, John West (1962)
Town Records, John West (1983)
The Local Historian and His Theme, H. P. R. Finberg (1952)
Local History in England, W. G. Hoskins (2nd ed 1982)
Fieldwork in Local History, W. G. Hoskins (1967)
The Parish Chest, W. E. Tate (rev. 1969)
Enjoying Archives, David Iredale (1973)
Sources for English Local History, W. B. Stephens (1973 rev. 1981)
Local History: A Handbook for Beginners, Philip Riden (1983)
Historical Interpretation 1066–1540, J. J. Bagley (1965)
Historical Interpretation 1540 to Present Day, J. J. Bagley (1971)
A Guide to English Historical Records, Alan Macfarlane (1983)
Texts and Calendars, E. L. C. Mullins (1958)
The Hundred and the Hundred Rolls, Helen Cam (1930)
A Handbook of British Chronology, Sir Maurice Powicke and D. and E. B. Fryde

Bibliography *(cont)*

Latin
Latin for Local History, Eileen A. Gooder (1961)
The Record Interpreter, Charles Trice Martin (1892 rev. 1982)
Revised medieval Latin word-list, R. E. Latham (1965)

State Records
Guide to the Records of Parliament, Maurice Bond (1971)
The Making of Domesday Book, V. H. Galbraith (1961)
Domesday Book and Beyond, F. W. Maitland (1960 ed)
Domesday Book, county by county publications by Phillimore & Co in 35 vols
Journals of the House of Commons from 1547
Journals of the House of Lords from 1510
Local History from Blue Books: a select list of the sessional papers of the House of Commons, W. R. Powell (1962)

Parish Registration etc
Phillimore Atlas and Index of Parish Registers, Cecil Humphery-Smith (1984)
Guide to Bishops' Registers of England and Wales, David M. Smith (1981)
Bishops' Transcripts and Marriage Licences, J. S. W. Gibson (2nd ed. 1983)
National Index of Parish Registers, D. J. Steel (12 vols)
The Parish Registers of England, J. C. Cox (1910)

Census
Census Returns 1841–1881 on Microfilm. A Directory of Local Holdings, Jeremy Gibson (4th ed. 1984)
The Population History of England 1541–1871: A Reconstruction, E. A. Wrigley and R. S. Schofield (1981)
The Development of Population Statistics, D. V. Glass
Numbering the People, D. V. Glass

Wills
Wills and Where to Find Them, Jeremy Gibson (1976)
A simplified Guide to Probate Jurisdiction: Where to look for Wills, ed. Jeremy Gibson (2nd ed. 1983)
Wills and their Whereabouts, Anthony Camp (1963)

Maps
Antique Maps and their Cartographers, Raymond Lister (1970)
Maps and Map Makers, R. V. Tooley (1970)
Maps, Geographical Magazine Vol 32 No 11 April 1960
Maps and Plans in the Public Record Office c1410–1860, HMSO (1967)
The Large Scale County Maps of the British Isles, E. M. Rodger
The Early Maps of Scotland, with an account of the Ordnance Survey, Royal Scottish Geographical Society
The Road Books and Itineraries of Great Britain 1570–1850, H. G. Fordham
The Historian's Guide to Ordnance Survey Maps, J. B. Harley (1964)
The One Inch to the Mile Maps of England and Wales, article by J. N. Harley in *Amateur Historian* Vol 5, pp 130–140
The Period Maps of the Ordnance Survey, article by C. W. Phillips in *Amateur Historian*, Vol 5 pp 166–172
The Maps of England and Wales at the Six Inch and Twenty-five Inch scales, article by J. B. Harley in *Amateur Historian* Vol 5 pp 202–211

Monumental Inscriptions
Brasses and Brass Rubbings in England, Jerome Bertram (1971)
Beginner's Guide to Brass Rubbing, Richard Busby (1969)
A List of Monumental Brasses in the British Isles, Mill Stephenson (1926 repr. 1964)

Legal
Article detailing the records of Inns of Court, D. S. Bland in *Amateur Historian* Vol 5 pp 72–6

Emigration and Immigration
The Original Lists of Persons Emigrating to America, J. C. Hotten
Topographical Dictionary of 3885 English Emigrants, C. E. Banks (1937)

Manor and Estate Records
How to Locate and Use Manorial Records, Patrick Palgrave-Moore
The Manor and Manorial Records, N. J. Hone (1906)
How to Read Old Title Deeds XVI-XIX Centuries, Julian Cornwall (1964)
Title Deeds, A. A. Dibben (1971)

Taxation
Customs Records as a Source for Historical Research, an article in *Archives* xviii p
The Lay Subsidies, article by M. W. Beresford in *Amateur Historian* Vol 3 pp 325–328 (1958) and Vol 4 pp 101–106 (1959)

Religious Records
The Records of the Established Church in England, excluding parochial records, D. M. Owen (1970)
Introduction to Ecclesiastical Records, J. S. Purvis (1953)

Newspapers and Magazines
Catalogue of English Newspapers and Periodicals in the Bodleian Library 1622–1800, T. Milford and D. M. Sutherland (1936)
Tercentenary Handlist of English and Welsh Newspapers, The *Times* (1920)
Handlist of English Provincial Newspapers and Periodicals 1700–1760, G. A. Cranfield
The Newspaper and Almanac Stamps of Great Britain and Ireland, John H. Chandler and H. Dagnall
Almanacs for Students, E. A. Fry
Index to the Marriages in the Gentleman's Magazine 1731–1768, E. A. Fry
Index to the Biographical and Obituary Notices in the Gentleman's Magazine 1731–1780

Directories
The London Directories 1677–1855, C. W. Goss (1932)
Guide to the national and provincial directories of England and Wales, excluding London, published before 1856, J. E. Norton (1950)

SECTION E

Palaeography

PART ONE
GENERAL TERMS

E1 Alphabet. The full set of individual letter-forms used to represent a language in writing. In Western Europe the Latin alphabet, in various styles or scripts (qv), has been used continuously for at least the last 2,000 years.

E2 Approach Stroke. An extra stroke of the pen, marking the parchment or paper in anticipation of the letter-form to be written.

E3 Ascender. That part of certain letter-forms (*b,d,h,l*) which rises above the height of a minim (qv). In some scripts they are closed by a loop or are thickened at the end.

E4 Autograph. An alternative term to holograph (qv), but also used for the personal signature of an individual.

E5 Base-Line. The imaginary line on which the feet of minims (qv) stand.

E6 Bastard. A term which describes a script whose origin is cursive (qv) but which has been tidied up for use in headings or in formal texts.

E7 Biting. A feature of later gothic scripts, where the curves of neighbouring letters fuse or overlap. It most often occurs with the letters *b,d,p* and a following *e* or *o*.

E8 Book Scripts. Styles of handwriting used in books, usually more formal than documentary scripts (qv).

E9 Bowl. The curved part of certain letter-forms (*a,b,d,g,o,p,q*).

E10 Calligraphic. A term used to describe handwriting of the highest formality and artistic quality.

E11 Capital. A letter in majuscule (qv) script. Nowadays this type of letter-form is used at the beginning of a sentence in prose or of a line in poetry, and for the initial letter of proper names. Consistency of usage is rarely found, however, before the 19th century.

E12 Chrismon. The symbol (✗) for Christ, based on the Greek letters *khi* and *rho*. In the early medieval period it was used as a religious sign, giving sacred protection, at the beginning of documents and inscriptions.

E13 Colophon. A short passage at the end of a written text, usually giving the name of the scribe and the date of writing. It sometimes includes an expression of relief on the part of the scribe at having finished his task and an appeal for the prayers of his readers.

E14 Corrections. The following were the main methods used to correct copying errors in medieval manuscripts.

a) Erasure: Ink was scratched away from the surface of the parchment (qv) with a sharp knife. The parchment was then smoothed again with a bone tool and the text rewritten.

b) Deletion: A line was struck through words which were incorrect. The correct version of the text was then written above.

c) Underlining or Subpuncting: In some official records and formal books, text to be omitted was merely underlined and left fully readable. Single letters were likewise distinguished by the placing of a dot beneath the line.

d) Insertion: Additional or omitted text was written in the margin or between the lines, its proper position being shown by the use of a *signe de renvoi* (qv).

E15 Court Hands. In general, these were the official styles of script used in the records of the medieval and early modern courts of law prior to 1733. 'Court hand' is also sometimes found as a (now outdated) term for *gothic cursive anglicana* script (see E73).

E16 Curlicue. A curled flourish which was used as a decoration to a page of calligraphic writing.

E17 Current. A term used to describe handwriting done in haste, usually with a resulting lack of clarity.

E18 Cursive Scripts. Styles of writing which do not call for the pen to be lifted from the page between individual letters within a word. These scripts have loops on the ascenders (qv) and frequent ligatures (qv).

E19 Decorated Initial. An initial capital (qv) which has been embellished by the use of coloured ink.

E20 Departmental Hands. Differentiated styles of documentary script (qv) which were evolved for use in particular Departments of State. These were used, in gradually fossilized form, from the late 15th to the 18th centuries.

E21 Descender. That part of certain letters $(g,j,p,q,y$ and sometimes others) which descends below the base-line (qv).

E22 Diminuendo. The use, in descending order, of varying sizes of script in neighbouring lines at the beginning of a text. Thus the first line might be in square capitals (E79), the second line in rustic capitals (E80), and the third and following lines in minuscule (qv) script.

E23 Display Script. Embellished, usually majuscule (qv), script employed at the beginning of a text or to highlight a particular passage.

E24 Documentary Scripts. Styles of handwriting used in the writing of documents, usually less formal and with more abbreviations than book scripts (qv).

E25 Duct. The progress of the writing-implement across the writing-surface, reflecting the implement's design, the angle at which it was held, and the competence of the writer.

E26 Endorsement. Something written on the back (dorse) of a document. These are sometimes archival references or notes, but occasionally record a transaction subsequent to that on the face of the document.

E27 Engrossing. A term employed to describe a very formal grade of handwriting used for the fair-copying of documents.

E28 Facsimile. An exact reproduction of an existing manuscript, copying its layout, letter-forms and text. Nowadays produced by photographic means, formerly by engraving, and earlier by actual imitative rewriting.

E29 Gloss. A commentary on a text, explaining words or allusions. Glosses were either added in the margin or between the written lines of the main text.

E30 Hand. The distinctive way in which an individual writer interprets a script (qv), reflected in the use of a combination of peculiarities of letter-form, abbreviations, and punctuation-marks.

E31 Historiated Initial. An initial capital (qv) within which has been drawn a scene illustrating events described in the text.

E32 Holograph. A manuscript of a text written entirely in its author's own handwriting.

E33 Hybrid. A term used to describe a hand (qv) containing letter-forms from more than one script (qv).

E34 Illumination. The embellishment of a written text by the application of gold or silver, burnished to give a shining appearance. This technique was mostly used in books of some luxury, but is also found in some important royal charters.

E35 Incipit. The opening words of a chapter or book.

E36 Ink. The liquid used to write medieval and early modern texts was usually made from a mixture of oak-galls, iron sulphate, and gum Arabic. Another variety, blacker in colour but less stable, could also be made from a mixture of carbon, gum and water.

E37 Insular. A term used to describe manuscripts produced within the British Isles rather than on the Continent.

E38 Letter or Letter-Form. A single unit of the alphabet (qv), each one representing a specific sound.

E39 Ligature. A line joining neighbouring letter-forms. Some ligatures are found in several different scripts, for example those joining *c* and *t*, *s* and *t*. Many more are used in cursive scripts (qv) than in formal styles of writing.

E40 Line-Filler. A series of strokes of the pen, or a design, whose function was to fill space at the end of a line of writing. This prevented the unauthorised addition of words to a document. In books, line-fillers were used to give a tidy appearance to a page whose lines of text were of unequal length.

E41 Majuscule. A term used to describe scripts in which all the letter-forms are of the same height. (See E79–82).

E42 Manuscript. A handwritten text.

E43 Miniature. A full-page illustration to a text, originally in red lead (minium), but later in various colours, often with illumination (qv).

E44 Minim. The individual vertical stroke that is the basis of the letters *i,m,n,u*. The bowl (qv) of several other letter-forms in minuscule script is generally of the same height as the minims.

E45 Minuscule. A term that describes scripts some of whose letter-forms have ascenders and descenders (qv). (See E69–78).

E46 Notary. A type of professional scribe, particularly one licensed to write on behalf of the Papacy. Each notary had his own notarial-sign, a symbol which he drew at the foot of the documents he wrote, in order to show their authenticity.

E47 Numerals. Roman numerals were used as normal throughout the medieval and early modern periods. In numbers such as *ii, iii, vii, xiii*, the last stroke was usually made into a *j* to show that the succession of vertical strokes was complete. Arabic numerals do occur in England from the 13th century but are not common until the 17th. The following medieval forms should be noted: $\mathcal{Q}$ (4), $\mathcal{Y}$ (5), Λ (7).

E48 Opening. The two facing pages of an open book, normally designed as an artistic unit.

E49 Paper. This was imported into England from the Continent for use as a writing-surface from the 14th century. It was not manufactured here however until the late 15th century, and not on any scale until the late 17th when Huguenot immigrants specialised in its production.

E50 Parchment. The treated skins of sheep or goats, used as a writing-surface. The lighter, flesh-side was preferred to the darker, hair-side for the writing of documents such as deeds, but both sides were used in the writing of rolls and books. In the latter, the parchment was usually so arranged that flesh faced flesh across an opening, and hair faced hair, giving no great contrast in appearance to the reader.

E51 Pen. In Classical and early medieval times, pens were made from dried reeds. From the 11th century until the 19th, however, the normal writing-implement was a quill-pen made from a feather of a goose. Sometimes the feathers of swans, ravens, crows or turkeys might be used instead. The widespread use of a metal pen dates from the mid 19th century, and the cheap fountain-pen from the end of the same century.

E52 Pricking. The practice of making a pattern of small holes in sheets of parchment in order to guide the ruling (qv).

E53 Punctuation. The punctuation of medieval and early modern manuscripts is often more consistent than is generally recognised, although the systems employed are not the same as those in modern texts. The most common marks of punctuation are the following.

a) The Point. In form like the modern full stop, although sometimes placed above the base-line (qv) rather than on it. In early medieval texts this marked the smallest pause. It was also used to separate numerals, and some abbreviations, from other words in a sentence.

b) The Punctus Elevatus (✓). Normally marking a moderate pause and sometimes used like a modern semi-colon.

c) The Punctus Interrogativus (⸮). Indicating a question.

d) The Virgule (✓). In later medieval manuscripts this marked a lesser pause than that shown by the point (qv).

e) The Semi-Colon (;). In the early medieval period this often marked a major pause, such as at the end of a paragraph. It began to be used in its modern way by the early 17th century.

f) The Capitulum Mark (¢ or ℂ). This originally marked the start of a fresh chapter, but was later also used to distinguish a new verse or sub-section of text.

g) The Paragraphos (¶ or ∥ or Γ). This usually indicated the start of a paragraph, but it was also used as a symbol to introduce words run over from one line to the end of the next.

E54 Quire. A number of folded sheets of parchment put together to form a booklet, a group of which were bound together to form a book.

E55 Rubric. A heading within a text, usually in red ink.

E56 Ruling. The lines, guided by the pricking (qv), which were incised or drawn upon the writing-surface in order to guide the writing and to keep it within certain margins. In England before c1150 ruling was done with the dry point of a sharp implement. From c1150 to c1400 lead was used, but from c1400 ruling was more commonly made in ink.

E57 Script. A model style of handwriting.

E58 Scriptorium. A medieval writing-office, often based at an episcopal or monastic centre.

E59 Serif. A short horizontal or oblique stroke added at an extremity of a letter.

E60 Set. A term used to describe a very formal grade of handwriting.

E61 Signe de Renvoi. A symbol of any sort, used in glossing or correcting a text, which was added both before a gloss (qv) or marginal correction and near the point to which the gloss or correction was meant to refer.

E62 Stem. A vertical stroke in a majuscule (qv) letter.

E63 Suprascript. A term used to describe a symbol, letter, or word written above a letter-form or above a word. Associated with abbreviations, glosses and corrections.

E64 Transcription. The copying of a text into one's own handwriting. The transcription of texts written in former styles of handwriting needs to be done with the greatest accuracy. The spelling and punctuation of the original should be retained and an indication given of places where one has extended an abbreviated form. A good transcription may be used as a firm base for an edition.

E65 Vellum. Fine quality parchment (qv), made from the skin of calves, lambs, or kids. For the most luxurious books the skin of unborn or aborted animals was used.

E66 Versal Letter. The initial letter to a verse or paragraph of text, embellished to make it stand out.

E67 Watermark. A symbol or a pattern of lines within a sheet of paper, usually only visible when held up to the light. These may be used to date and locate the manufacture of paper and can be important in the detection of forgery.

PART TWO
SCRIPTS IN ENGLAND
11TH–19TH CENTURIES

E68 General. A number of scripts, each using the Latin alphabet but with variations in the forms of particular letters, either succeeded each other or co-existed at various times in this period. Some changes in letter-form occurred because of periodic revivals in Classical ideas and designs. Others were the result of the need to produce a large number of documents speedily, as royal central and local government developed. Book scripts were affected by developments in documentary scripts, since most scribes could write either to order. In Roman and early medieval times whole texts were often written in majuscule scripts. From the 8th century minuscules were used for the main text and majuscule letters were reserved for headings and individual capitals. The advent of printing for books, and the spread of lay literacy, resulted in a rise in the proportion of informal to formal written texts from c1500.

Minuscule Scripts. In the following examples the letters *a,b,c,d,e,f,g,h,l,m,p,q,r, s,t,x,y* are illustrated, also *k* and *w* when found. The letters *i,n,o,u* differ little from script to script and are not shown. It should be noted however that a long form of *i* occurs in certain positions in medieval scripts (but does not always represent the sound of a modern *j*); a v-shaped form of *u* is also found in initial position, but elsewhere the letter *u* stands for both *u* and *v* sounds. The letter *z* is rare but is similar in shape to its modern form.

In all scripts, but particularly E71, E73–75, E77, a fair amount of variation in actual letterforms between individual hands may be expected, and thus differing degrees of legibility. Some alternative forms are shown for certain letters.

E69 Square Anglo-Saxon Minuscule.

a b c d e f g h l m p q r / f r s / t x / f y /

This type of insular minuscule script was developed at Winchester c900. It was used for both Latin and English texts up to c950, and thereafter for English texts alone up to c1100. The following special letters were used in Old English, equivalent to the sounds shown.

æ Æ 'ash' = a short 'a' sound
Þ 'thorn' = th
ð Ð 'eth' = th
ƿ 'wynn' = w

E70 Caroline Minuscule.

a b c d e f g h l m p q r f t x y

A clear, Classically-inspired script which was developed at the court of Charlemagne c800. It was imported into England c950 and from it developed E71–73.

E71 Protogothic Semicursive.

a b c d e f g h l m p q r f t & x y

A documentary script used in the 12th century royal Chancery.

E72 Gothic Textura.

a b c / ð d / e f g h k l m p q r / s f / t ƿ x y

The script used for the finest books c1200–1550. Varieties differ according to the way that minims (qv) are completed – some have ends which are squared, others have those which are rounded, half-rounded, or diamond-shaped.

E73 Gothic Cursive Anglicana. This was used in documents c1200–1600, in books c1250–1500.

a b c d e f g h k l m p q v / f ð / t & x y

E74 Gothic Cursive Secretary. A script which probably originated in Italy and came via France to England in the late 14th century.

a b c d e f g h k l m p q z / f ð / t ƿ x y

E75 Tudor Secretary. A development from E74, with many more ligatures. It was the usual script for most purposes in the 16th century.

a b t l ɔ f g ʃ ƒ l
m p q / v ʋ / ʃ ʆ / t ꝏ
ƺ ɣ

E76 Italic. This represented a deliberate revival of Classical and Carolingian shapes. It was used by well-educated individuals in 16th-century England. It was revived at the beginning of the 20th century by modern calligraphers.

a b c d e f g h k l m p q
r / ʃ s / t w x y

E77 Mixed Hand. A mixture of E75 and E76 used c1600–1650.

a b c d e ʒ g h k l m
p q / ʋ r / ʃ s / t w x y

E78 Round Hand. A cursive script developed from E76. It is found in formal writing from the mid 17th century to the early 20th. Also known as Copperplate, because it could be learnt from copy books printed from engraved copper plates.

a b c d e f g h k l m p q
ɹ / s f / t w x y

Majuscule Scripts and Capital Letters. In the following examples the letters *A,B,C,D,E,F, G,H,I,L,M,N,P,Q,R,S,T* are illustrated, also *W* when found. In E83 some alternative forms are shown.

E79 Square Capital Script. A script used by the Romans for inscriptions carved in stone, having straight lines and sharp angles. It was employed in later periods for initial capitals and for headings in books.

ABCDEFGHIL MNPQRST

E80 Rustic Capital Script. A Roman book script, its curved lines and serifs reflecting the use of a reed pen, rather than the chisel used for E79. It was later used for initial capitals and for headings.

ABCDEFGHIL MNPQRST

E81 Uncial Script. A Classical majuscule script used chiefly for ecclesiastical texts in the late Roman period. It was employed by the Anglo-Saxons for writing bibles and charters in the 7th and 8th centuries. A few letter-forms continued in use as initials in the medieval period.

ABCDEFGhI LϣNPQRST

E82 Half-Uncial Script. In the late Roman period this was a cross between majuscule and minuscule scripts but the Irish and the Anglo-Saxons used it as a majuscule one in the 7th and 8th centuries.

ɑbcdeꝼʒhi lmnpqrsꞇ

E83 Capitals in Gothic Scripts. Complicated capital letters were developed in the later medieval period for use with the various Gothic minuscule scripts (E72–74).

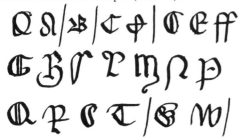

E84 Capitals in Round Hand (qv).

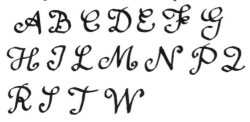

PART THREE
ABBREVIATIONS c1000–1700

E85 General. In order to save time and space a fairly consistent system of abbreviation was employed by the writers of Latin texts in medieval and early modern scripts. Words could be *contracted* by the omission of medial letters or *suspended* by the omission of the ending. Sometimes *sigla* were employed which consisted merely of the initial letter of a word or phrase, thus *eg* stands for *exempli gratia*, as still used today. Modifications of the Latin system were applied in England to vernacular texts in English or French. In all three languages a similar general sign was used to show that the text was abbreviated at a particular point. Before the 13th century this consisted merely of a short horizontal line (the *overline*) added above the letter preceding the place from which other letters had been omitted as in *ōes* for *omnes*. The overline was generally added to the ascender (qv) if *b,d,h, or l*, were the letter preceding the omission. Later this sign developed into more complicated shapes such as

ㄱ ㄱ ㄷ ㅇ

E86 Abbreviations for Specific Pairs of Letters in Latin Words. a) A vowel followed by *m* or *n*: the overline added above a final vowel means that a final *m* has been omitted. Thus *meū.* = *meum*. The overline added above a vowel in the middle of a word often means that *m* or *n* has been omitted. Thus *assūptus, frequēs* for *assumptus, frequens*.

b) Other symbols which replace pairs of letters are as follows.

ᵉ = -is
z = -ur
ᵍ = -us

E87 Abbreviations for whole Latin Words. a) **The Nomina Sacra.** The group of words associated with sacred matters were among the first to be abbreviated. These include the following:

đns = *dominus*, Lord
đs = *deus*, God
iħs xp̄s = the Greek for Jesus Christ
pr̄ ñr = *pater noster*, Our Father
scs̄ = *sanctus*, Saint, holy
sp̄s = *spiritus*, spirit

These are the nominative forms. The other grammatical cases were shown by altering the final letter of the abbreviated form.

đm = *deum* (accusative)
pr̄i ñri = *patri nostri* (genitive)

b) **The conjunction *et* 'and'.** Two alternative symbols were used in different contexts.

The *ampersand* (&), which is still used in modern typefaces.

The *tironian nota*. This was originally a part of the system of shorthand invented by Tiro, Cicero's secretary. It was used in England by the Anglo-Saxons for 'and' in the vernacular but was not adopted as the sign for Latin *et* until after the Norman Conquest. It acquired a bar through its waist in the late 12th century, but lost it in the 15th, by which time it was smaller and more curved.

7 7 7 ꝓ ᴣ

c) **Sigla** (see E85). These were used for common words or phrases, also for the name of the monarch at the beginning of some medieval documents. They are usually marked off by the use of a pair of points (See E53a). Some common examples are as follows:

.e. = *est*, it is
.i. = *id est*, that is
.s. = *scilicet*, namely

.t.   = *tunc*, then
.T.   = *Teste/Testibus*, witness(es)
.W.   = *Willelmus*, William

d) **Suprascript Letters.** In most cases the suprascript letter is the last letter of the word or syllable abbreviated.

ḥ   = *mihi*, to me
ṣ   = *sibi*, to him, to her, to them
ṭ   = *tibi*, to thee
ġ   = *igitur*, therefore
ṁ   = *modo*, now
ǔ   = *uero*, indeed

e) **Miscellaneous Common Words.**

dc̄s   = *dictus*, the said
÷   = *est*, it is
fc̄m   = *factum*, made, done
q̄n   = *quando*, when
q̇ʋ   = *quia*, because
ꝗ   = *quod*, that
q̄m   = *quoniam*, whereas
sc̄dm   = *secundum*, according to

E88 Abbreviations for Combinations of Letters which may either form a whole Latin Word or only a Syllable therein.

ꝑ/ꝑ   = *per*
p̃   = *prae/pre*
ꝓ   = *pro*
q̊ᵃ   = *qua*
q̇ⁱ   = *qui*
q̊ᵒ   = *quo*

E89 Abbreviations for Syllables within Latin Words.

b:/b;/b₃   = -*bus*
ɔ   = *com-/con-*
m̄   = -*men*-
oꝛ   = -*orum*
q:/q;/q₃   = -*que*
t̄   = -*ter*

E90 Specific Abbreviations in Middle English and Early Modern English Texts.

ꝛ ʋ   = and
ℯ   = -es/-is
oʋ   = our
ẞ   = Sir
ꝥᵗ/yᵗ   = that
ꝥᵉ/yᵉ   = the
wᶜʰ   = which
wᵗ   = with

E91 Specific Abbreviations in French Texts.

7 7 ⁊ ꝰ ʋ   = *et*, 'and'
Mon**ẞ**   = *Monsieur*
ꝑ/ꝑ   = *par*
pʋ   = *pur/pour*
ẞ   = *Sieur*

PART FOUR
BIBLIOGRAPHY

Ancient Writing and its Influence. B. L. Ullman (1969).
The Handwriting of English Documents. L. C. Hector (1966).
Examples of English Handwriting 1150–1750. H. E. P. Grieve (1954).
English Caroline Minuscule. T. A. M. Bishop (1971).
Scriptores Regis. T. A. M. Bishop (1961).
English Royal Documents, King John-Henry VI, 1199–1461. P. Chaplais (1971).
Latin Bookhands of the Later Middle Ages 1100–1500. S. H. Thomson (1969).
English Cursive Bookhands 1250–1500. M. B. Parkes (1969).
Elizabethan Handwriting. G. E. Dawson, L. Kennedy-Skipton (1968).
The Record Interpreter. C. T. Martin (1910).

SECTION F

Museums, Libraries and County Record Offices

PART ONE
GENERAL AND SPECIALIST MUSEUMS

F1 Principal General Museums.
Ashmolean Museum of Art and Archaeology, Beaumont Street, Oxford. *0865 57522*
British Museum, Great Russell Street, London, WC1. *01 636 1555*
Fitzwilliam Museum, Trumpington Street, Cambridge. *0223 69501*
Hunterian Museum and Art Gallery, University of Glasgow, Glasgow. *041 339 8855*
Manchester Museum, The University of Manchester, Oxford Road, Manchester. *061 273 3333*
Museum of London, London Wall, London, EC2. *01 600 3699*
National Museum of Antiquities of Scotland, Queen Street, Edinburgh. *031 556 8921*
National Museum of Wales, Cathays Park, Cardiff. *0222 397951*
Public Record Office Museum, Chancery Lane, London, WC2. *01 405 0741*
Royal Scottish Museum, Chambers Street, Edinburgh. *031 225 7534*
Science Museum, Exhibition Road, London, SW7. *01 589 3456*

Victoria and Albert Museum, South Kensington, London, SW7. *01 589 6371*

F2 Specialist Museums.

Agriculture and Rural Life.
Acton Scott Working Farm Museum, Wenlock Lodge, Acton Scott, Church Stretton, Salop. *06946 306*
Farmland Museum, 50 High Street, Haddenham, Cambs. *0353 740381*
Hampshire Farm Museum, Upper Hamble Country Park, Hants.
Museum of Agriculture, Wye College, Wye, Ashford, Kent. *0233 812401*
Museum of English Rural Life, University of Reading, Whiteknights, Reading. *0734 875123*
Norfolk Rural Life Museum, Beech House, Gressenhall, Dereham, Norfolk. *0362 860563*
Somerset Rural Life Museum, Abbey Farm, Chilkwell Street, Glastonbury.
Wilmington Priory Agriculture Museum, Wilmington, Polegate, East Sussex. *0323 870537*

Brewing.
Bass Museum, Horninglow Street, Burton-on-Trent. *0283 45301*

Childhood.
Bethnal Green Museum of Childhood, Cambridge Heath Road, London E2. *01 980 2415*
Museum of Childhood, 38 High Street, Edinburgh. *031 556 5447*

Clocks.
Clockmakers' Company Museum, Guildhall Library, Aldermanbury, London, EC2. *01 606 3030*
Gershom-Parkington Collection of Timekeeping Instruments, Angle Corner, Bury St Edmunds, Suffolk. *0284 63233*

Costume.
Castle Howard Costume Galleries, Castle Howard, York. *065384 333*
Gallery of English Costume, Platt Hall, Platt Fields, Rusholme, Manchester. *061 224 5217*
Museum of Costume, Bennett Street, Bath. *0225 61111*

Education.
Museum of the History of Education, The University of Leeds. *0532 431751*

Furniture.
Geffrye Museum, Kingsland Road, London, E2. *01 739 8368*
Victoria and Albert Museum, London, SW7. *01 589 6371*

Industrial History.
Beamish North of England Open Air Museum, Beamish Hall, Stanley, Co Durham.
Black Country Museum, Tipton Road, Dudley, West Midlands. *021 557 9643*
Blists Hill Open Air Museum, Coalport Road Madeley, Telford, Salop. *0952 586309*
Bradford Industrial Museum, Moorside Mills, Moorside Road, Eccleshill, Bradford. *0274 631756*
Bristol Industrial Museum, Princes Wharf, Princes Street, Bristol. *0272 299771*
Chatterly Whitfield Mining Museum, Tunstall, Stoke-on-Trent. *0782 813337*
Cheddleton Flint Mill, Leek Road, Cheddleton, Nr Leek, Staffs.
Coalbrookdale Furnace and Museum of Iron, Coalbrookdale, Telford, Salop. *0952 453418*
Industrial Museum, Wollaton Hall, Courtyard Buildings, Wollaton Park, Nottingham. *0602 284602*
Ironbridge Gorge Museum, Ironbridge, Telford, Salop. *0952 453522*
Lewis Textile Museum, Museum Street, Blackburn, Lancs. *0254 667130*

National Mining Museum, Haughton, Retford, Notts. *0623 860728*
Newcomen Engine House and Dartmouth Museum, The Butterwalk, Dartmouth, Devon. *0804 320*
Newtown Textile Museum, Commercial Street, Newtown, Powys. *0686 26243*
Peak District Mining Museum, The Pavilion, Matlock Bath, Derbys. *0629 3834*
Piece Hall Industrial Museum, Halifax, W. Yorks.
Pilkington Glass Museum, Prescot Road, St Helens. *0744 28882*
Salford Museum of Mining, Buile Hill Park, Eccles Old Road, Salford. *061736 1832*
Salt Museum, 162 London Road, Northwich, Cheshire. *0606 41331*
Sheffield Industrial Museum, Kelham Island, Alma Street, Sheffield. *0742 22106.*
Textile Machinery Museum, Tonge Moor Road, Bolton. *0204 21394*
Welsh Industrial and Maritime Museum, Bute Street, Cardiff. *0222 371805*

Inland Waterways.
Boat Museum, Dockyard Road, Ellesmere Port, Sth Wirral. *051 3555017*
Dolphin Yard Sailing Barge Museum, c/o 117 Plains Avenue, Maidstone, Kent. *0622 62531*
Waterways Museum, Stoke Bruerne, Nr Towcester, Northants. *0604 862229*
Windermere Steamboat Museum, Rayrigg Road, Windermere. *09662 5565*

Labour History.
National Museum of Labour History, Limehouse Town Hall, Commercial Road, London, E14. *01 515 3229*

Maritime.
Exeter Maritime Museum, The Quay, Exeter. *0392 58075*
Hartlepool Maritime Museum, Northgate, Hartlepool, Cleveland. *0429 272814*
Lowestoft and East Suffolk Maritime Museum, Fisherman's Cottage, Sparrows Nest Park, Lowestoft. *0502 61963*
Maritime Museum, Bucklers Hard, Hants. *059063 203*
Museum of the Royal National Lifeboat Institution, Grand Parade, Eastbourne. *0323 30717*
National Maritime Museum, Romney Road, Greenwich, London, SE10. *01 858 4422*
Swansea Maritime and Industrial Museum, Museum Square, Maritime Quarter, Swansea. *0792 50351*
Welsh Industrial and Maritime Museum, Bute Street, Cardiff. *0222 371805*

Police.
Metropolitan Police Historical Museum, Bow Street Police Station, London, WC2. *01 434 5427*

Pottery.
Coalport China Works Museum, Coalport, Telford, Salop. *0952 580650*
Gladstone Pottery Museum, Uttoxeter Road, Longton, Stoke-on-Trent. *0782 311378*
Royal Crown Derby Museum, Osmaston Road, Derby. *0332 47051*
Wedgwood Museum, Barlaston, Stoke-on-Trent. *078139 4141*

Regimental and Armed Forces.
Airborne Forces Museum, Aldershot, Hants. *0252 24431*
Artillery Museum, Rotunda, Woolwich, London, SE18. *01 856 5533*
Cheshire Military Museum, The Castle, Chester. *0244 27617*
Devonshire Regiment Museum, Wyvern Barracks, Exeter. *0392 76581*
Duke of Cornwall's Light Infantry Regimental Museum, The Keep, The Barracks, Bodmin. *0208 2810*
Gordon Highlanders Regimental Museum, Viewfield Road, Aberdeen.
Green Howards Museum, Trinity Church Square, Richmond, Nth Yorks. *0748 2133*
Guards Museum, Wellington Barracks, London, SW1. *01 735 8922*
National Army Museum, Royal Hospital Road, Chelsea, London, SW3. *01 730 0717*
National Army Museum, Sandhurst branch, Royal Military Academy, Sandhurst, Camberley, Surrey. (by appointment only) *0276 63344*
Queen Alexandra's Royal Nursing Corps Museum, Royal Pavilion, Farnborough Road, Aldershot. *0252 24431*
Royal Air Force Museum, Aerodrome Road, London, NW9. *01 205 2266*
Royal Army Medical Corps Historical Museum, Keogh Barracks, Ash Vale, Aldershot. *0252 24431*
Royal Army Ordnance Corps Museum, Deepcut, Camberley, Surrey.
Royal Army Veterinary Corps Museum, Gallwey Road, Aldershot. *0252 24431*
Royal Engineers Museum, Brompton Barracks, Chatham, Kent. *0634 44555*
Royal Fusiliers Museum, Tower of London, London, EC3. *01 709 0765*
Royal Hampshire Regimental Museum, Serle's House, Southgate Street, Winchester. *0962 63658*

Royal Leicestershire Regiment Museum, The Magazine, Oxford Street, Leicester. *0533 554100*
Royal Lincolnshire Regiment Museum, Museum of Lincolnshire Life, Burton Road, Lincoln. *0522 28448*
Royal Military Police Museum, Roussillon Barracks, Chichester. *0243 786311*
Royal Pioneer Corps Museum, Simpson Barracks, Wootton, Northampton. *0604 62742*
Royal Scots Regimental Museum, The Castle, Edinburgh. *031 336 1761*
Royal Welch Fusiliers Regimental Museum, Queens Tower, Caernarvon Castle, Caernarvon, Gwynedd. *0286 3362*
South Wales Borderers and Monmouthshire Regiment Museum, The Barracks, Brecon, Powys. *0878 3111*
Staffordshire Regiment Museum, Whittington Barracks, Lichfield. *0543 433333*
Welch Regiment Museum, Cardiff Castle, Cardiff. *0222 29367*

Roman Remains.
Chedworth Roman Villa Museum, Yanworth, Cheltenham, Glos. *024289 256*
Roman Baths Museum, Pump Room, Stall Street, Bath. *0225 61111*
Roman Palace and Museum, Salthill Road, Fishbourne, Chichester. *0243 785859*
Roman Town and Museum, Aldborough, Nth Yorks. *09012 2768*
Roman Villa Museum, Bignor, W. Sussex. *07987 259*
Roman Villa and Museum, Lullingstone Park, Lullingstone, Kent. *032 286 3467*

Theatre.
University of Bristol Theatre Collection, 29 Park Row, Bristol. *0272 303030*
Theatre Museum. Moving to Covent Garden, London in 1987.

Transport.
Bath Carriage Museum, Circus Mews, Bath. *0225 25175*
Birmingham Railway Museum, The Steam Depot, Warwick Road, Tyseley, Birmingham 11. *021 707 4696*
BL Heritage Motor Museum, Syon Park, Brentford, London. *01 560 1378*
Bressingham Steam Museum, Bressingham Hall, Diss, Norfolk. *037988 386*
Dodington Carriage Museum, Dodington House, Dodington, Chipping Sodbury. *0454 31889.*

Darlington North Road Station Railway Museum, North Road Station, Station Road, Darlington, Co. Durham. *0325 60532.*

Derby Industrial Museum (Midland Railway), Silk Mill, Silk Mill Lane, off Full Street, Derby. *0332 31111*

Duxford Airfield (Imperial War Museum), Duxford, Cambs. *0223 833963*

East Anglia Transport Museum, Chapel Road, Carlton Colville, Lowestoft. *098 683 398*

Ffestiniog Railway Museum, Harbour Station, Portmadog, Gwynedd. *0766 2340*

Great Western Railway Museum, Faringdon Road, Swindon. *0793 26161*

Lakeland Motor Museum, Cark-in-Cartmel, Cumbria. *044 853 328*

Leicester Museum of Transport, Corporation Road, Leicester. *0533 554100*

London Cab Company Museum, 1–3 Brixton Road, London SW9. *01 735 7777*

London Transport Museum, Covent Garden, London, WC2. *01 379 6344*

Midland Motor Museum, Stourbridge Road, Bridgnorth. *07462 61761*

Museum of Transport, 25 Albert Drive, Glasgow. *041 423 8000*

National Motor Museum, Beaulieu, Hants. *05990 612345*

National Railway Museum, Leeman Road, York. *0904 21261*

Newark Air Museum, Winthorpe, Newark, Notts. *0636 76302*

Sandtoft Transport Centre (trolleybuses), Sandtoft, Nr Doncaster.

Steamport Transport Museum, Derby Road, Southport. *0704 30693*

Torbay Aircraft Museum, Higher Blagdon, Nr Paignton, Devon. *0803 553540*

Totnes Motor Museum, Totnes, Devon. *0803 862777*

Tramway Museum, Crich, Matlock, Derbys. *077385 2565*

Tyrwhitt-Drake Museum of Carriages, Archbishop's Stables, Mill Street, Maidstone, Kent. *0622 54497*

Yorkshire Museum of Carriages and Horse Drawn Vehicles, Yore Mill, Aysgarth Falls, Aysgarth, North Yorks. *0748 3325*

PART TWO
GENERAL AND SPECIALIST LIBRARIES

F3 Important Libraries for local history research.

Bodleian Library, University of Oxford, Oxford. *0865 244675*

British Library, Great Russell Street, London, WC1. *01 636 1544*

General Register Office, St Catherine's House, 10 Kingsway, London, WC2. *01 242 0262*

Guildhall Library, Aldermanbury, London, EC2. *01 606 3030*

Historic Manuscripts Commission, Quality House, Quality Court, Chancery Lane, London, WC2. *01 242 1198*

National Library of Scotland, George IV Bridge, Edinburgh. *031 226 4531*

National Library of Wales, Aberystwyth, Dyfed. *0970 3816*

National Monuments Record, Fortress House, 23 Savile Row, London, W1. *01 734 6010*

Principal Registry of the Family Division, Somerset House, (South Wing), Strand, London, WC2. *01 405 7641*

Public Record Office, Chancery Lane, London, WC2. *01 405 0741*

Public Record Office, Ruskin Avenue, Kew, Surrey. *01 876 3444*

Royal Commission on the Ancient and Historical Monuments of Scotland, 54 Melville Street, Edinburgh. *031 225 5994*

Scottish Record Office, HM General Register House, Princes Street, Edinburgh. *031 556 6585*

Society of Genealogists, 14 Charterhouse Buildings, London, EC1. *01 251 8799*

F4 Ecclesiastical Libraries.

An appointment should always be sought to use the archives of the libraries listed below:

Canterbury Cathedral, City and Diocesan Record Office, The Precincts, Canterbury. *0227 63510*

Carlisle Cathedral Library, The Cathedral, Carlisle. *0228 35169*

Church Commissioners, 1 Millbank, London, SW1. *01 222 7010*

Exeter Cathedral Library and Archives, Bishops Palace, Exeter, Devon. *0392 72894*

Gloucester Cathedral Library, 6 College Green, Gloucester. *0452 21954*

Hereford Cathedral Library, The Cathedral. *0432 58403*

Lambeth Palace Library, London, SE1. *01 928 6222*

Norwich Cathedral, Dean and Chapter's Library, The Close, Norwich. *0603 20715*
Peterborough Cathedral, Prebendal House, The Precincts, Peterborough. *0733 69441*
St George's Chapel, Aerary, Dean's Cloister, Windsor Castle. *0753 557942*
St Paul's Cathedral, c/o Guildhall Library, Aldermanbury, London, EC2. *01 606 3030*
Salisbury Cathedral, Chapter Archives, 6 The Close, Salisbury.
Winchester Cathedral Library, The Close, Winchester. *0962 68580*
Worcester Cathedral, Worcester. *0905 24874*
York Minster Library, Dean's Park, York. *0904 25308*

F5 Specialist Libraries. Many specialist libraries are noted in Section D under the various research subject headings. Additional special libraries or collections related to local history studies are listed below. Researchers are advised to telephone first for an appointment.

Architecture.
British Architectural Library, Royal Institute of British Architects, 66 Portland Place, London W1.
Drawings collections at 21 Portman Square, London, W1. *01 580 5533*
Sir John Soane's Museum, 13 Lincoln's Inn Fields, London, WC2. *01 405 2107*

Agriculture.
Country Life Museum Library, National Museum of Antiquities of Scotland, Queen Street, Edinburgh. *031 225 7534*
Institute of Agricultural History, University of Reading, Whiteknights, Reading. *0734 875123*
Rothamsted Experimental Station, Harpenden, Herts. *05827 63133*

Costume.
Costume and Fashion Research Centre, Bath Museum Services, 4 Circus, Bath. *0225 61111*
Victoria and Albert Museum Library, South Kensington, London SW7. *01 589 6371*
Welsh Folk Museum, St Fagan's, Cardiff. *0222 569441*

Heraldry.
College of Arms, Queen Victoria Street, London EC4. *01 248 2762*
Institute of Heraldic and Genealogical Studies, Northgate, Canterbury. *0227 68664*
Society of Genealogists, 14 Charterhouse Buildings, London, EC1. *01 251 8799*

Numismatics.
Joint library of the Royal and British Numismatic Societies, c/o Warburg Institute, Woburn Square, London, WC1. *01 580 9663*

Oral History.
Centre for English Cultural Tradition and Language, University of Sheffield, Western Bank, Sheffield. *0742 768555*
Welsh Folk Museum, St Fagan's, Cardiff. *0222 569441*
Tom Harrisson Mass-Observation Archives, Arts Building D, University of Sussex, Falmer, Brighton. *0273 606755*

Photographic.
Searchers for illustrative material are advised to consult *Picture Sources UK* edited by Dr Rosemary Ekins (1985).

Printing.
St Bride's Printing Library, Bride Lane, London EC4. *01 353 4660*

Publishing.
Dept of Archives, University of Reading, Whiteknights, Reading. *0734 874331*
Mark Longman Library, National Book League, Book House, 45 East Hill, London, SW18. *01 870 9055*
See also *Publishing History*, a twice-yearly journal published by Chadwyck-Healey, 20 Newmarket Road, Cambridge. *0223 311479*

Transport.
Institution of Mechanical Engineers, 1 Birdcage Walk, London, SW1. (Railways) *01 222 7899*
Ironbridge Gorge Museum Library, The Wharfage, Ironbridge, Telford, Salop. *095245 3522*
National Museum of Wales, Bute Street, Cardiff. (Welsh railways) *0222 371805*
National Railway Museum Library, Leeman Road, York. *0904 21261*
Paisley College of Technology Library, High Street, Paisley. (Scottish railways) *041 887 1241*
Science Museum Library, Exhibition Road, London SW7. (Railways) *01 589 3456*
University of Bristol Library, Tundall Avenue, Bristol. (Railways) *0272 303030*
University of Salford Library, Salford, Manchester. (Canals) *061 736 5843*

PART THREE
COUNTY RECORD OFFICES

F6 English County Record Offices.

Avon:
Bristol Record Office Council House, College Green, Bristol.

Bedfordshire:
County Hall, Bedford. *0234 63222*

Berkshire:
Shire Hall, Reading. *0734 875444*

Buckinghamshire:
County Hall, Aylesbury. *0296 5000*

Cambridgeshire:
For Cambs and Isle of Ely-
Shire Hall, Castle hill, Cambridge. *0223 317281*
For Huntingdonshire-
Grammar School Walk, Huntingdon. *0480 52181*

Cheshire:
The Castle, Chester. *0224 602574*

Cleveland:
81 Borough Road. Middlesborough.

Cornwall:
County Hall, Truro. *0872 73698*

Cumbria:
Carlisle office-
The Castle, Carlisle. *0228 23456*
Kendal office-
County Offices, Kendal. *0539 21000*
Barrow-in-Furness office-
Duke Street, Barrow-in-Furness. *0229 31269*

Derbyshire:
County Offices, Matlock. *0629 3411*

Devon:
Castle Street, Exeter. *0392 53509*

Dorset:
County Hall, Dorchester. *0305 63131*

Durham:
County Hall, Durham. *0385 64411*

Essex:
Chelmsford office-
County Hall, Chelmsford. *0245 64411*
Colchester and North-east Essex office-
Stanwell House, Stanwell Street, Colchester. (*0206 572099*)
Southend office-
Central Library, Victoria Avenue, Southend-on-Sea. *0702 612621*

Gloucestershire:
Worcester Street, Gloucester. *0452 21444*
See also Avon.

Greater London:
Greater London Record Office, 40 Northampton Road, London, EC1. *01 633 6851*
Corporation of London Record Office, Guildhall, London, EC2. *01 606 3030*
Guildhall Library, Aldermanbury, London, EC2. *01 606 3030*

Hampshire:
20 Southgate Street, Winchester. *0962 63153*

Herefordshire and Worcestershire:
Herefordshire-
The Old Barracks, Harold Street, Hereford. *0432 65441*
Worcestershire-
Shirehall, Worcester. *0905 353366*

Hertfordshire:
County Hall, Hertford. *0992 54242*

Humberside:
North Humberside-
County Hall, Beverley. *0482 867131*
South Humberside-
Town Hall Square, Grimsby. *0472 53481*

Huntingdonshire:
See Cambridgeshire.

Isle of Wight:
26 Hillside, Newport. *0983 524031*

Kent:
County Hall, Maidstone. *0622 671411*
South-east Kent-
Folkestone Central Library, Grace Hill, Folkestone. *0903 57583*

Lancashire:
Greater Manchester area-
56 Marshall Street, New Cross, Ancoats, Manchester. *061 247 3383*
Lancashire-
Bow Lane, Preston. *0772 54868*

Leicestershire:
57 New Walk, Leicester. *0533 554100*

Lincolnshire:
The Castle, Lincoln. *0522 25158*

Norfolk:
Central Library, Norwich. *0603 611277*

Northants:
Delapre Abbey, Northampton. *0604 62129*

Northumberland:
Melton Park, North Garforth, Newcastle-upon-Tyne. *0632 362680*

Nottinghamshire:
County House, High Pavement, Nottingham. *0602 54524*

Oxfordshire:
County Hall, New Road, Oxford. *0865 815203*

Shropshire:
The Shirehall, Abbey Foregate, Shrewsbury. *0743 222406*

Somerset:
Obridge Road, Taunton. *0823 87600*

Staffordshire:
County Buildings, Eastgate Street, Stafford. *0785 3121*

Suffolk:
Bury St Edmunds branch-
Schoolhall Street, Bury St Edmunds. *0284 63141*
Ipswich branch-
County Hall, St Helen's Street, Ipswich. *0473 55801*

Surrey:
Guildford branch-
Castle Arch, Guildford. *0483 573942*
Kingston-upon-Thames branch-
County Hall, Penrhyn Road, Kingston-upon-Thames. *01 546 1050*

Sussex:
West Sussex branch-
West Street, Chichester. *0243 777100*
East Sussex branch-
The Maltings, Castle Precincts, Lewes. *07916 5400*

Warwickshire:
Priory Park, Cape Road, Warwick. *0926 493431*

Westmorland:
See Cumbria.

Wiltshire:
County Hall, Trowbridge. *02214 3641*

Worcestershire:
See Hereford and Worcestershire.

Yorkshire:
North Yorkshire-
County Hall, Northallerton. *0609 3123*
South Yorkshire-
Cultural Activities Centre, Ellin Street, Sheffield. *0742 29191*
West Yorkshire-
Newstead Road, Wakefield. *0924 36711*

F7 Scottish County Record Offices.

Grampian:
Woodhill House, Ashgrove Road, West Aberdeen. *0224 682222*

Strathclyde:
30 John Street, Glasgow. *041 221 9600*

F8 Welsh County Record Offices.

Clwyd:
The Old Rectory, Hawarden, Deeside. *0244 532364*

Dyfed:
Aberystwyth branch-
Swyddfa'r Sir, Marine Terrace, Aberystwyth. *0970 617581*
Haverfordwest branch-
The Castle, Haverfordwest. *0437 3707*

Gwent:
County Hall, Cwmbran. *06333 67711*

Gwynedd:
Caernarfon branch-
County Offices, Shirehall Street, Caernarfon. (Search Room at Victoria Dock) *0286 4121*
Dolgellau branch-
Cae Penarlag, Dolgellau. *0341 422 341*
Llangefni branch-
Shire Hall, Llangefni. *0248 723262*

SECTION G

Organisations and Societies

PART ONE
NATIONAL AND REGIONAL ORGANISATIONS

G1 National and Regional Organisations.

BRITISH ASSOCIATION FOR LOCAL HISTORY
The Mill Manager's House,
Cromford Mill,
Mill Road,
Cromford, Matlock.
(062982 3768)

BRITISH RECORD SOCIETY
Dept of History,
The University, Keele,
Staffs.

BRITISH RECORDS ASSOCIATION
Master's Court,
The Charterhouse,
Charterhouse Square,
London, EC1.

CLOSE SOCIETY
(the study of maps)
c/o The Map Library, British Library,
Great Russell Street, London, WC1.

EARLY ENGLISH TEXT SOCIETY
c/o Lady Margaret Hall,
Oxford.

HARLEIAN SOCIETY
(publication of heraldic and genealogical documents)
c/o College of Arms,
Queen Victoria Street, London EC4

HISTORICAL ASSOCIATION
59a Kennington Park Road,
London, SE11.

There are nearly 90 branches of the Association, details of which may be obtained from the above address.

INSTITUTE OF HISTORICAL RESEARCH
Senate House,
University of London,
London, WC1.

LIST AND RECORD SOCIETY
(the publication of PRO search room lists and indexes)
Public Record Office,
Ruskin Avenue, Kew, Surrey.

LOCAL POPULATION STUDIES SOCIETY
c/o 17 Rosebery Square,
Rosebery Avenue,
London, EC1.

MONUMENTAL BRASS SOCIETY
c/o Society of Antiquaries of London,
Burlington House,
Piccadilly, London, W1.

ORAL HISTORY SOCIETY
Dept. of Sociology,
University of Essex,
Wivenhoe Park,
Colchester, Essex.

ROYAL COMMISSION ON HISTORICAL
MONUMENTS (ENGLAND)
National Monuments Record
Fortress House,
23 Savile Row,
London, W1.

ROYAL COMMISSION ON THE ANCIENT
AND HISTORICAL MONUMENTS OF
SCOTLAND
54 Melville Street,
Edinburgh.

ROYAL COMMISSION ON ANCIENT AND
HISTORICAL MONUMENTS (WALES)
Edleston House,
Queens Road,
Aberystwyth.

ROYAL HISTORICAL SOCIETY
University College,
Gower Street, London, WC1.

SOCIETY OF ANTIQUARIES OF LONDON
Burlington House,
Piccadilly, London, W1.

SOCIETY OF ARCHIVISTS
South Yorkshire County Record Office,
Ellin Street,
Sheffield.

SOUTHERN HISTORY SOCIETY
(covers Cornwall, Devon, Somerset, Glos,
Wilts, Dorset, Hants, Essex, Berks, Bucks,
Sussex, Surrey, Kent).
62 Elmhurst Road,
Reading, Berks.

SOUTH WALES RECORD SOCIETY
c/o Library,
University College,
PO Box 78, Cardiff.

PART TWO
SPECIALIST ORGANISATIONS

G2 Agricultural History

BRITISH AGRICULTURAL HISTORY
SOCIETY
Museum of Rural Life, Whiteknights,
University of Reading, Berks.

G3 Archaeology

BRITISH ARCHAEOLOGICAL
ASSOCIATION
61 Old Park Ridings,
Winchmore Hill, London, N21.

COUNCIL FOR BRITISH ARCHAEOLOGY
112 Kennington Road,
London, SE11.

PREHISTORIC SOCIETY
Dept of Prehistoric and Romano-British Anti-
quities,
British Museum, London, WC1.

RESCUE
The British Archaeological Trust,
15a Bull Plain,
Hertford, Herts.

ROYAL ARCHAEOLOGICAL INSTITUTE
c/o 304 Eddison House,
Grove End Road,
London, NW8.

SOCIETY FOR MEDIEVAL ARCHAEOLOGY
University College,
Gower Street, London, WC1.

SOCIETY FOR POST-MEDIEVAL
ARCHAEOLOGY
c/o Museum of London,
London Wall, London, EC2.

SOCIETY FOR THE PROMOTION OF
ROMAN STUDIES
31–34 Gordon Square, London, WC1.

SUBTERRANEA BRITANNICA
c/o 16 Honeyway,
Royston, Herts.

G4 Architectural History

NORTHERN ARCHITECTURAL HISTORY
SOCIETY
c/o 8 Holmside Place,
Heaton,
Newcastle-upon-Tyne.

SOCIETY OF ARCHITECTURAL
HISTORIANS
c/o F. Kelsall, 2nd Floor,
Chesham House,
30 Warwick Street, London, W1.

G5 Commercial History

BUSINESS ARCHIVES COUNCIL
185 Tower Bridge Road,
London, SE1.

BUSINESS ARCHIVES OF SCOTLAND
c/o Loanhead Transport Ltd
Johnstone, Strathclyde

G6 Conservation and Preservation

ANCIENT MONUMENTS BOARD FOR
SCOTLAND
3–11 Melville Street, Edinburgh.

ANCIENT MONUMENTS BOARD FOR
WALES
Welsh Office,
New Crown Building,
Cathays Park, Cardiff.

ANCIENT MONUMENTS SOCIETY
St Andrew-by-the Wardrobe,
Queen Victoria Street, London, EC4.

ARCHITECTURAL HERITAGE FUND
Civic Trust,
17 Carlton House Terrace, London, SW1.

ARCHITECTURAL HERITAGE SOCIETY OF
SCOTLAND
43b Manor Place, Edinburgh.

ASSOCIATION FOR STUDIES IN THE CON-
SERVATION OF HISTORIC BUILDINGS
Institute of Archaeology,
31–34 Gordon Square, London, WC1.

CIVIC TRUST
17 Carlton House Terrace, London, SW1.

COUNCIL FOR THE CARE OF CHURCHES
83 London Wall, London, EC2.

ENGLISH HERITAGE
Fortress House,
23 Savile Row, London, W1.

GEORGIAN GROUP
37 Spital Square, London, E1.

GEORGIAN SOCIETY FOR EAST
YORKSHIRE
c/o The White Hall,
Winestead,
Hull, Humberside.

HISTORIC BUILDINGS COUNCIL FOR
SCOTLAND
25 Drumsheugh Gardens,
Edinburgh.

HISTORIC BUILDINGS COUNCIL FOR
WALES
Room GO46,
New Crown Building,
Cathays Park, Cardiff.

HISTORIC CHURCHES PRESERVATION
TRUST
Fulham Palace, London, SW6.

HISTORIC HOUSES ASSOCIATION
38 Ebury Street, London, SW1.

NATIONAL PIERS SOCIETY
82 Speed House,
Barbican, London, EC2.

NATIONAL TRUST for places of historic interest or natural beauty
36 Queen Anne's Gate, London, SW1.

The Trust has many branches, details of which
may be obtained from the above address.

NATIONAL TRUST FOR SCOTLAND
5 Charlotte Square, Edinburgh.

REDUNDANT CHURCHES FUND
St Andrew-by-the Wardrobe,
Queen Victoria Street, London, EC4.

SAVE BRITAIN'S HERITAGE
68 Battersea High Street, London, SW11.

SCOTTISH CIVIC TRUST
24 George Square, Glasgow.

SOCIETY FOR THE PROTECTION OF
ANCIENT BUILDINGS
c/o 55 Great Ormond Street, London, WC1.

THIRTIES SOCIETY
3 Park Square West, London, NW1.

VICTORIAN SOCIETY
1 Priory Gardens, London, W4.

Details of the Society's branches may be
obtained from the above address.

G7 Costume History.

COSTUME SOCIETY
251 Popes Lane, London, W5.

FRIENDS OF FASHION
Museum of London,
London Wall, London EC2.

KENT COSTUME TRUST
The Farriers Cottage,
St Nicholas-at-Wade,
Birchington, Kent.

G8 Countryside and Footpath Protection

ASSOCIATION FOR THE PROTECTION OF
RURAL SCOTLAND
14a Napier Road,
Edinburgh.

BYWAYS AND BRIDLEWAYS TRUST
9 Queen Anne's Gate,
London, SW1.

COUNCIL FOR THE PROTECTION OF
RURAL ENGLAND
4 Hobart Place,
London SW1.

COUNCIL FOR THE PROTECTION OF
RURAL WALES
14 Broad Street,
Welshpool, Powys.

COUNTRYSIDE COMMISSION
John Dower House,
Crescent Place,
Cheltenham, Glos.

COUNTRYSIDE COMMISSION FOR
SCOTLAND
Battleby, Redgorton,
Perth, Tayside.

RAMBLERS ASSOCIATION
1–5 Wandsworth Road,
London, SW8.

SCOTTISH RIGHTS OF WAY SOCIETY
52 Plewlands Gardens
Edinburgh.

G9 Dialect and Folklore

CENTRE FOR ENGLISH CULTURAL
TRADITION AND LANGUAGE
University of Sheffield, Sheffield.

ENGLISH FOLK DANCE AND SONG
SOCIETY.
Cecil Sharp House,
2 Regents Park Road, London, NW1.

FOLKLORE SOCIETY
University College,
Gower Street, London, WC1.

INSTITUTE OF DIALECT AND FOLK LIFE
STUDIES
School of English,
University of Leeds, Leeds.

LAKELAND DIALECT SOCIETY
Knox Croft,
Thornby,
Wigton, Cumbria.

WILTSHIRE FOLK LIFE SOCIETY

YORKSHIRE DIALECT SOCIETY
Fieldhead House,
West Street,
Hoyland, Barnsley.

G10 Economic History.

ECONOMIC HISTORY SOCIETY
London School of Economics,
Houghton Street, London, WC2.

G11 Education.

HISTORY OF EDUCATION SOCIETY
History Dept,
University of London,
Institute of Education,
20 Bedford Way, London, WC1.

G12 Heraldry.

HERALDRY SOCIETY
44/45 Museum Street,
London, WC1.

The Society has branches in Bath, Birmingham, Cambridge University, the Chilterns, the East Midlands, Ireland, Lancashire, Leeds, Macclesfield, Manchester, Middlesex, Norfolk, Oxford University, Oxford, Preston, Scotland, Sherborne, and Suffolk. The up-to-date addresses may be obtained from the main Society. There is also an Ecclesiastical Heraldry Group.

INSTITUTE OF HERALDIC AND
GENEALOGICAL STUDIES
80 Northgate,
Canterbury, Kent.

G13 Horticulture.

GARDEN HISTORY SOCIETY
12 Charlbury Road,
Oxford.

G14 Industrial History.

ARKWRIGHT SOCIETY
Tawney House,
Matlock Green,
Matlock, Derbys.

ASSOCIATION FOR INDUSTRIAL
ARCHAEOLOGY
The Wharfage,
Ironbridge,
Telford, Salop.

BERKSHIRE INDUSTRIAL ARCHAEOLOGY
GROUP
7 Hollow Lane,
School Green,
Shinfield,
Reading, Berks.

BOLTON INDUSTRIAL HISTORY SOCIETY
Human History Dept,
Bolton Museum and Art Gallery,
Civic Centre,
Bolton, Lancs.

BREWERY HISTORY SOCIETY
10 Ringstead Court,
Ringstead Road,
Sutton, Surrey.

BRISTOL INDUSTRIAL ARCHAEOLOGY
SOCIETY
41 Grove Avenue,
Coombe Dingle, Bristol.

CAMBRIDGE SOCIETY FOR INDUSTRIAL
ARCHAEOLOGY
20 Harvey Goodwin Avenue,
Cambridge.

CLEVELAND INDUSTRIAL
ARCHAEOLOGY SOCIETY
5 Gresham Road,
Middlesborough, Cleveland.

EAST KENT MILLS GROUP

FURNITURE HISTORY SOCIETY
Dept of Furniture and Woodwork,
Victoria and Albert Museum,
London, SW7.

GLOUCESTERSHIRE SOCIETY FOR
INDUSTRIAL ARCHAEOLOGY
Oak House,
Hamshill, Coaley,
Dursley, Glos.

GREATER LONDON INDUSTRIAL
ARCHAEOLOGY SOCIETY
30 Gawston Drive,
Berkhamsted, Herts.

LEICESTERSHIRE INDUSTRIAL HISTORY
SOCIETY
54 Chapel Street,
Measham, Leics.

MANCHESTER REGION INDUSTRIAL
ARCHAEOLOGY SOCIETY
30 Kingsway,
Worsley, Manchester.

MEDWAY INDUSTRIAL ARCHAEOLOGY
GROUP
269 London Road,
Rainham Park,
Gillingham, Kent.

NATIONAL ASSOCIATION OF MINING
HISTORY ORGANISATIONS
38 Main Street,
Sutton,
Via Keighley, Yorks.

NORFOLK INDUSTRIAL ARCHAEOLOGY
SOCIETY
Norwich Reference Library,
Norwich.

NORTH-WESTERN SOCIETY FOR
INDUSTRIAL ARCHAEOLOGY AND
HISTORY
Merseyside County Museum,
William Brown Street,
Liverpool.

NORTHANTS INDUSTRIAL
ARCHAEOLOGY GROUP
Abington Museum,
Abington Park,
Northampton.

NOTTINGHAMSHIRE INDUSTRIAL
ARCHAEOLOGY SOCIETY
44 Wadham Road,
Woodthorpe,
Nottingham.

PEAK DISTRICT MINES HISTORICAL
SOCIETY
8 Bernard Avenue,
Hucknall, Notts.

PRINTING HISTORICAL SOCIETY
St Brides Institute,
Bride Lane,
Fleet Street,
London EC4.

SCOTTISH INDUSTRIAL ARCHAEOLOGY
UNIT
Royal Commission on the Ancient and
Historical Monuments of Scotland,
54 Melville Street,
Edinburgh.

SCOTTISH INDUSTRIAL HERITAGE
SOCIETY
Scottish Museums Council,
County House,
20 Torpmichen Street,
Edinburgh.

SOUTH CHESHIRE INDUSTRIAL
ARCHAEOLOGY SOCIETY
8 Dorset Close
Congleton, Cheshire.

SOUTH-WEST WALES INDUSTRIAL
ARCHAEOLOGY SOCIETY
17 Orpheus Road,
Ynysforgan,
Swansea.

SOUTHAMPTON UNIVERSITY
INDUSTRIAL ARCHAEOLOGY GROUP
6 Prestwood Road,
Hedge End,
Southampton, Hants.

STAFFORDSHIRE INDUSTRIAL
ARCHAEOLOGY SOCIETY
4 Longstaff Croft,
Lichfield, Staffs.

SUFFOLK INDUSTRIAL ARCHAEOLOGY
SOCIETY
Oak Tree Farm,
Hitcham, Ipswich.

SURREY INDUSTRIAL ARCHAEOLOGY
GROUP
Orchard Cottage,
Alfold Crossways,
Cranleigh, Surrey.

SUSSEX INDUSTRIAL ARCHAEOLOGY
SOCIETY
42 Palmer Avenue,
Saltdean, Brighton.

WATFORD INDUSTRIAL HISTORY
SOCIETY
13 Cromer Road,
Watford.

WELSH MINES SOCIETY
c/o Pound House,
Newent, Glos.

WEST WILTSHIRE INDUSTRIAL
ARCHAEOLOGY SOCIETY
Hope Cottage,
Station Road,
Holt,
Trowbridge, Wilts.

WORCESTER INDUSTRIAL
ARCHAEOLOGY AND HISTORY SOCIETY
9 Redfern Avenue,
Worcester.

G15 Insurance.

FIRE MARK CIRCLE
99 North End Road,
London, NW11.

INSURANCE HISTORY SOCIETY
c/o Chartered Insurance Institute,
20 Aldermanbury, London, EC2.

G16 Labour History.

INTERNATIONAL ASSOCIATION OF
LABOUR HISTORY
19 Museum Chambers,
Bury Place, London, WC1.

NORTH EAST LABOUR HISTORY SOCIETY
School of English and History,
Lipman Building,
The Polytechnic,
Newcastle-upon-Tyne.

NORTH-WEST SOCIETY FOR THE STUDY
OF LABOUR HISTORY
9 St Pauls Road,
Salford, Lancs.

SCOTTISH LABOUR HISTORY SOCIETY
21 Liberton Brae,
Edinburgh.

SOCIETY FOR THE STUDY OF LABOUR
HISTORY
Dept. of Social and Economic History,
University of Sheffield,
Sheffield.

G17 Legal and Police.

CAMBRIDGESHIRE POLICE HISTORY
SOCIETY
c/o Cambridge Police HQ,
Hinchingbrooke Park,
Huntingdon, Cambs.

POLICE HISTORY SOCIETY
c/o Norfolk Constabulary,
Martineau Lane,
Norwich, Norfolk.

SELDEN SOCIETY
Faculty of Laws,
Queen Mary College,
Mile End Road, London, E1.

G18 Medicine.

BATH MEDICAL HISTORY GROUP
35 Pulteney Street,
Bath, Avon.

BRISTOL MEDICAL HISTORY CLUB
Postgraduate Medical Centre,
Frenchey Hospital,
Bristol.

BRITISH SOCIETY FOR THE HISTORY OF
PHARMACY
Halfpenny Furze,
Mill Lane, Chalfont St Giles,
Bucks.

HISTORY OF MEDICINE SOCIETY OF
WALES
Lower Farm House,
Llysworney,
Cowbridge, Sth Glamorgan.

SOCIETY FOR THE SOCIAL HISTORY OF
MEDICINE
47 Banbury Road,
Oxford.

VETERINARY HISTORY SOCIETY
32 Belgrave Square,
London, SW1.

WELLCOME INSTITUTE FOR THE HISTORY
OF MEDICINE
183 Euston Road,
London, NW1.

G19 Military and Navy

ALDERSHOT MILITARY HISTORICAL
TRUST
Garrison Headquarters,
Cavans Road,
Aldershot, Hants.

MEDWAY MILITARY RESEARCH GROUP

MILITARY HISTORICAL SOCIETY
Duke of Yorks Headquarters,
London, SW3.

NAVY RECORDS SOCIETY
Royal Naval College, Greenwich,
London, SE10.

ROMAN MILITARY RESEARCH SOCIETY
Midfield Court,
Thorplands, Northampton.

SOCIETY FOR ARMY HISTORICAL
RESEARCH
National Army Museum,
Royal Hospital Road, London, SW3.

G20 Population History

The Local Population Studies Society
c/o Dr. Malcolm T. Smith,
Dept of Anthropology, University of Durham,
43 Old Elvet, Durham.

G21 Postal History.

DERBYSHIRE POSTAL HISTORY SOCIETY
164 Smedley Street,
Matlock, Derbys.

EAST ANGLIAN POSTAL HISTORY STUDY
GROUP
76 Rushmere Road,
Ipswich, Suffolk.

KENT POSTAL HISTORY GROUP
296 Lonsdale Drive,
Gillingham, Kent.

POSTAL HISTORY SOCIETY
Lower Street Farmhouse,
Hildenborough,
Tonbridge, Kent.

G22 Religous History.

BAPTIST HISTORICAL SOCIETY
4 Southampton Row,
London, WC1.

CATHOLIC ARCHIVES SOCIETY
4a Polstead Road,
Oxford.

CATHOLIC RECORD SOCIETY
114 Mount Street,
London, W1.

CORNISH METHODIST HISTORICAL
ASSOCIATION
Park View,
Ponsanooth,
Truro, Cornwall.

ECCLESIASTICAL HISTORY SOCIETY
Dept of History,
Birkbeck College,
Malet Street, London, WC1.

FRIENDS HISTORICAL SOCIETY
Society of Friends,
Friends House,
Euston Road, London, NW1.

HISTORICAL SOCIETY OF THE CHURCH
IN WALES
Trinity College,
Carmarthen.

G22 *(cont)*

HISTORICAL SOCIETY OF THE
METHODIST CHURCH IN WALES
Llys Myfyr,
Pwllheli,
Gwynedd.

HISTORICAL SOCIETY OF THE
PRESBYTERIAN CHURCH IN WALES
Ymans,
Heol Caradog,
Aberystwyth, Dyfed.

HUGUENOT SOCIETY
67 Victoria Road,
London, W8.

INDEPENDENT METHODIST CHURCHES
HISTORICAL SOCIETY
Providence Independent Methodist Church,
Albert Road,
Colne, Lancs.

JEWISH HISTORICAL SOCIETY
University College,
Gower Street,
London, WC1.

KENT RECUSANT HISTORY SOCIETY
The Old Manse,
Wingham,
Kent.

LINCOLNSHIRE METHODIST HISTORY
SOCIETY
3a Church Road,
Upton,
Gainsborough, Lincs.

METHODIST HISTORICAL SOCIETY
(Plymouth and Devon Branch)
11 Station Road,
Topsham, Exeter.

NORTH-EAST CATHOLIC HISTORY
SOCIETY
16 Spital Terrace,
Gosforth,
Newcastle-upon-Tyne.

NORTH-WEST CATHOLIC HISTORY
SOCIETY
282 Whelley,
Wigan, Lancs.

SCOTTISH CHURCH HISTORY SOCIETY
New College Library,
Mound Place,
Edinburgh.

STAFFORDSHIRE CATHOLIC HISTORY
SOCIETY
The Dell, Oakmoor,
Stoke-on-Trent.

STRICT BAPTISTS HISTORICAL SOCIETY
26 Denmark Street,
Bedford.

UNITARIAN HISTORICAL SOCIETY
6 Ventnor Terrace,
Edinburgh.

UNITED REFORMED CHURCH HISTORY
SOCIETY
86 Tavistock Place,
London, WC1.

WELSH BAPTIST HISTORICAL SOCIETY
13 Ty'r From Avenue,
Llanelli, Dyfed.

WESLEY HISTORICAL SOCIETY
34 Spiceland Road,
Northfield,
Birmingham.

WESLEY HISTORICAL SOCIETY
(East Anglia)
8 St Andrews Close,
Holt, Norfolk.

WESLEY HISTORICAL SOCIETY
(Lancs and Cheshire)
26 Roe Cross Green,
Mottram,
Hyde, Cheshire.

WESLEY HISTORICAL SOCIETY
(North -east)
22 Nilverton Avenue,
Sunderland.

WESLEY HISTORICAL SOCIETY
(West Midlands)
34 Spicelands Road,
Northfield,
Birmingham.

WESLEY HISTORICAL SOCIETY
(Yorkshire)
4 Lynwood Grove,
Leeds.

G23 Transport History.

ASSOCIATION OF RAILWAY
PRESERVATION SOCIETIES
Sheringham Station,
Sheringham,
Norfolk.

CROYDON AIRPORT SOCIETY
Sutton Central Library,
St Nicholas Way,
Sutton, Surrey.

EAST KENT RAILWAY SOCIETY

KENT AVIATION AND RESEARCH
SOCIETY

LEEDS TRANSPORT HISTORICAL SOCIETY
4 Maplewood Paddock,
York.

MIDLAND RAILWAY TRUST LTD
Butterley Station,
Ripley, Derbys.

NORTH-EAST BUS PRESERVATION
SOCIETY
3 The Path,
Low Fell, Gateshead.

NORTH-EASTERN LOCOMOTIVE
PRESERVATION GROUP
88 Featherstone Road,
Newton Hall, Durham.

NORTH YORKSHIRE MOORS HISTORICAL
RAILWAY TRUST
Pickering Station,
Pickering,
North Yorks.

NORTHAMPTON AIRCRAFT RESEARCH
GROUP
88 Hunter Street,
Northampton.

OLD UNION CANAL SOCIETY
1 The Green,
Lubenham,
Market Harborough, Leics.

RAILWAY AND CANAL HISTORICAL
SOCIETY
64 Grove Avenue,
London, W7.

RAILWAY AND CANAL HISTORICAL
SOCIETY
(East Midlands)
75 Brendon Road,
Wollaton, Notts.

RAILWAY AND CANAL HISTORICAL
SOCIETY
(London)
4 Sudbury Croft,
Wembley, Middx.

RAILWAY AND CANAL HISTORICAL
SOCIETY
(North east)
27 Carr Lane,
Acomb, York.

RAILWAY AND CANAL HISTORICAL
SOCIETY
(Northwest)
Fron Fawnog, Haford Road,
Gwernymydd, Mold, Clwyd.

RAILWAY AND CANAL HISTORICAL
SOCIETY
(West Midlands)
9 Berberry Close,
Birmingham.

RAILWAY CORRESPONDENCE AND
TRAVEL SOCIETY
158a North View Road,
London, N8.

SCOTTISH TRAMWAY MUSEUM SOCIETY
PO Box 78,
Glasgow.

SOUTHAMPTON CANAL SOCIETY
4 Somerset Avenue,
Bitterne,
Southampton, Hants.

TRAMWAY MUSEUM SOCIETY
National Tramway Museum,
Crich, Matlock,
Derbys.

TRANSPORT TRUST
Marylebone Station Offices,
London, NW1.

TREVITHICK SOCIETY
Corew Viscoe,
Leland Downs,
Hayle, Cornwall.

G24 Local History and Archaeology Societies.
The societies listed below are grouped under
modern county headings. Those which fell in
the area of Greater London are still listed under
that heading, but those which fell in the
metropolitan counties of Greater Manchester,
West Midlands, Merseyside and Tyne and
Wear which were abolished in 1986, are listed

under their historic counties. Yorkshire is treated as one entity. Current addresses may usually be obtained from the local library or record office, but the most useful publication for this information is *Historical, Archaeological and kindred societies in the United Kingdom,* published by Pinhorns, Hulverstone Manor, Isle of Wight in 1986.

Avon:
Almondsbury Local History Association
Avon Archaeological Council
Avon Local History Association
Banwell Society of Archaeology
Bath and Camerton Archaeological Society
Batheaston Society
Bristol and Avon Archaeological Research Group
Bristol and Gloucestershire Archaeological Society
Bristol Records Society
Bristol University Speleological Society
Chew Magna Local History Society
Clevedon and District Archaeological Society
Frampton Cotterell and District Local History Society
Keynsham and Saltford Local History Society
Nailsea Local History Society
Sodbury and District Historical Society
Thornbury Society
Weston-super-Mare Archaeological and Nat. Hist. Society
Whitchurch Local History Society
Yatton Local History Society

Bedfordshire:
Ampthill and District Archaeological and Local History Society
Bedford Archaeological Society
Bedfordshire Archaeological Council
Bedfordshire Historical Record Society
Biggleswade History Society
Luton and District Historical Society
Manshead Archaeological Society of Dunstable
Pitstone Local History Society
Potton History Society

Berkshire:
Berkshire Archaeological Society
Berkshire Field Research Group
Berkshire Local History Association
Bracknell and District Historical Society
Easthampstead Park Historical Association
Finchampstead Local History Society
History of Reading Society
Hungerford Historical Association

Maidenhead Archaeological and Historical Society
Mortimer Local History Group
Newbury Archaeology and History Section
Newbury District Field Club
Shinfield and District Local History Society
Thatcham Historical Society
Twyford and Ruscombe Local History Society
Wargrave Local History Society
Windsor Local History Group
Windsor and Wraysbury Archaeological Society
Wokingham Society History Group
Wraysbury History Group

Buckinghamshire:
Amersham Society
Beaconsfield and District Historical Society
Bletchley Archaeological and Historical Society
Buckingham Historical Society
Buckinghamshire Archaeological Society
Buckinghamshire Record Society
Chalfont St Peter and Gerrards Cross Local History Society
Chesham Society
Cholesbury-cum-St Leonards Local History Society
High Wycombe Society
Milton Keynes and District Archaeological Society
Woburn Sands and District Society
Wolverton and District Archaeological Society

Cambridgeshire:
Barrington Local History and Conservation Society
Brampton Historical Society
Cambridge Antiquarian Records Society
Cambridge Antiquarian Society
Cambridgeshire Local History Society
Ely and District Archaeological Society
Huntingdonshire Local History Society
Kimbolton Local History Society
Linton and District Historical Society
Peterborough Museum Society
St Neots Local History Society
Sawtry and District Local History Society

Cheshire:
Audlem Historical Society
Barrow Local History Group
Birkenhead History Society
Bowdon History Society
Bromborough Society
Burton and South Wirral Local History Society
Cheshire County Local History Committee

Chester Archaeological Society
Chetham Society
Congleton History Society
Frodsham Local History Group
Heald Green Historical Society
Historic Society of Lancashire and Cheshire
Hoylake Historical Society
Knutsford Historical and Archaeological
   Association
Lancashire and Cheshire Antiquarian Society
Longdendale Amenity Society
Lymm and District Local History Society
Macclesfield History Society
Marple Antiquarian Society
Merseyside Archaeological Society
Middlewich Archaeological Society
Nantwich Local Historical Society
North Cheshire Archaeology Group
Northwich Archaeological and Local Studies
   Society
Poynton Local History Society
Sandbach History Society
Stalybridge Historical Society
Stockport Historical Society
Wallasey and District Historical Society
Warrington and District Archaeology and
   Hist. Society
Widnes Historical Society
Wilmslow Historical Society
Winsford Local History Society

Cleveland:
Cleveland History Workshop
Cleveland and Teeside Local History Society
Guisborough and District Archaeological
   Society
Hartlepool Archaeological and Historical
   Society
Kirklevington Research Group
Norton Heritage Group
Teesdale Archaeology Group
Teesdale Record Society
Teesside Archaeological Society

Cornwall:
Budock Local History Group
Chacewater Old Cornwall Society
Cornish Buildings Group
Cornwall Archaeological Society
Cornwall Association of Local Historians
Cornwall Committee for Rescue Archaeology
Fal History Group
Federation of Old Cornwall Societies
Fowey History Group
Kea Old Cornwall Society

Lizard and Meneage Oral History Group
Luxulyan Old Cornwall Society
Mousehole Old Cornwall Society
Newquay Old Cornwall Society
Porthleven Old Cornwall Society
St Buryan Old Cornwall Society
St Columb Old Cornwall Society
St Germans History Group
St Ladoca Old Cornwall Society
Stithians Local History Group
Torpoint Old Cornwall Society
Truro Buildings Research Group
Wadebridge Old Cornwall Society

Cumbria:
Cumberland and Westmorland Antiquarian
   and Arch. Soc.
Sedbergh and District History Society
Workington Local History Society

Derbyshire:
Bakewell and District Historical Society
Belper Historical Society
Bolsover Local History Society
Buxton Archaeological and Natural Hist.
   Society
Derbyshire Archaeological Society
Derbyshire Record Society
Glossop and District Historical Society
Heanor and District Local History Society
Hunter Archaeological Society
Ilkeston and District Local History Society
Old Dronfield Society
Peakland Archaeological Society

Devon:
Beaford Local History Group
Bradworthy Historical Society
Brixham Museum and History Society
Culmstock Local History Group
Devon and Cornwall Record Society
Devon Archaeological Society
Devon History Society
Exmouth Historical and Archaeological
   Society
Hatherleigh History Society
Modbury Local History Society
Moretonhampstead and District Museum and
   Loc. Hist. Soc.
North Devon Archaeological Society
Okehampton Local History Society
Plymouth and District Archaeological Society
Sidmouth Local History Group
Teignmouth Museum and Historical Society
Totnes Museum Society
Tottington and District Society

G24 *(contd)*

Dorset:
Bournemouth Natural Science Society
Christchurch Conservation Society
Dorset Natural History and Archaeological Soc.
Dorset Record Society
Langton Maltravers Local History and Pres. Soc.
Sherborne Historical Society

Durham:
Architectural and Archaeological Society of Durham and Northumberland
Chester-le-Street Local History Society
Consett Local History Society
Darlington Historical Society
Durham County Local History Society
Gateshead and District Local History Society
Hurworth History Society
Ryton and District Local History Society
South Shields Archaeological and Historical Soc.
Surtees Society
Whickham and District Local History Society
Winlaton and District Local History Society

Essex:
Benfleet and District Historical Society
Billericay Archaeological and Historical Society
Braintree and Bocking Local History Society
Brentwood and District Historical Society
Chigwell and Loughton Historical Society
Colchester Archaeological Group
Essex Archaeological Society
Great Bardfield Historical Society
Halstead and District Local History Society
Mid Essex Archaeological and Historical Group
Rayleigh and District Antiquarian and Natural Hist. Soc.
Rochford Hundred Historical Society
Saffron Walden Historical Society
South-East Essex Archaeological Society
Southend-on-Sea Historical Society
Thurrock Local History Society
Waltham Abbey Historical Society

Gloucestershire:
Blockley Antiquarian Society
Campden and District Historical and Archaeology Society
Charlton Kings Local History Society
Cheltenham Local History Society
Cirencester Archaeological and Historical Soc.
Forest of Dean Local History Society

Gloucester and District Archaeological Research Group
Minchinhampton Local History Group
Moreton-le-Marsh and District Local History Society
Wotton-under-Edge Historical Society.

Greater London:
Barking and District Historical Society
Barnes and Mortlake History Society
Barnet and District Local History Society
Beddington, Carshalton and Wallington Arch. Soc.
Bexley Historical Society
Brentford and Chiswick Local History Society
Camden History Society
Carshalton Society
Charlton Society
Chingford Historical Society
City of London Archaeological Society
Clapham Antiquarian Society
Croydon Natural History and Scientific Society
Docklands History Group
Ealing Museum and History Society
East London History Society
Edmonton Hundred Historical Society
Eltham Society
Enfield Archaeological Society
Fulham and Hammersmith Historical Society
Greenwich and Lewisham Antiquarian Society
Hammersmith Historical Society
Hanwell Preservation Society
Harefield History Society
Hayes and Harlington Local History Society
Hendon and District Archaeological Society
Highgate Literary and Scientific Institution
Hornchurch and District Historical Society
Hornsey Historical Society
Hounslow and District History Society
Ilford and District Local History Society
Islington Archaeological and History Society
Kingston-upon-Thames Archaeological Society
Lamorbey and Sidcup Local History Society
Lewisham Local History Society
London and Middlesex Archaeological Society
London Feminist History Group
London History Workshop Centre
London Society
London Topographical Society
Merton Historical Society
Mill Hill Historical Society
Newham History Society
Middlesex Society
Orpington and District Archaeological Society
Pinner Local History Society

Potters Bar and District Historical Society
Romford and District Historical Society
Roxeth Local History Society
Ruislip, Northwood and Eastcote Local Hist. Soc.
St Marylebone Society
Shooters Hill Local History Group
Southall Local History Society
Southgate Civic Trust
Southwark and Lambeth Archaeological Society
Stanmore and Harrow Historical Society
Streatham Society
Tooting Local History Group
Twickenham Local History Group
Uxbridge Local History and Archives Society
Walthamstow Antiquarian Society
Wandsworth Historical Society
Wanstead Historical Society
Wembley History Society
West Drayton and District Local History Society
West London Archaeological Field Group
Willesden Local History Society
Woodford Historical Society
Woolwich and District Antiquarian Society

Hampshire:
Aldershot Historical and Archaeological Society
Alresford Historical and Literary Society
Alton Natural History Society
Alton Society
Andover Archaeological Society
Andover Local History Society
Basingstoke Archaeological and Historical Society
Bickton Conservation Society
Bosmere Hundred Society
Botley and Curdridge Local History Society
Bramdean Society
Bramshott and Liphook Preservation Society
Burley Village Protection Society
Crondall Society
Denmead History Group
Eastleigh and District Local History Society
Fareham Local History Society
Farnborough and District Historical Outings Society
Fawley Local History Group
Forest of Bere Natural History Society
Gosport Society
Hamble Preservation Society
Hampshire Field Club and Archaeological Society
Havant Local History Group

Itchen Valley Archaeological and Historical Society
Kingsworthy Local History Group
Lymington Historical Record Society
Lyndhurst Historical Society
Micheldever Archaeological and Local History Soc.
Milford-on-Sea Historical Records Society
New Forest Association
New Milton Local History Group
North-East Hampshire Archaeological Society
Odiham Society
Overton Society
Palmerston Fort Society
Petersfield Area History Society
Portsdown Local History Group
Portsmouth Royal Dockyard Society
Portsmouth Society
Portsmouth WEA Local History Group
Ringwood Historical Society
St Maryborune Conservation Society
Selborne Association
Sheet Preservation Society
Solent Protection Society
Somborne District Society
Test Valley Archaeological Society
Wellow History Society
Whitchurch Conservation Group
Wickham History Society
Yateley Society

Herefordshire and Worcestershire:
Alvechurch Historical Society
Belbroughton History Society
Bromyard and District Local History Society
Droitwich and District Historical Society
Hagley Historical and Field Society
Halesowen Local History Group
Hereford and Worcester Architectural Record Group
Kidderminster and District Archaeological and Hist. Soc.
Kilvert Society
Kington Local History Society
Leominster Historical Society
Lickey Mills Local History Society
Stourbridge Historical and Archaeological Society
Vale of Evesham Historical Society
Weobley and District Local History Society
Worcestershire Archaeological Society
Worcestershire Historical Society

G24 *(contd)*

Hertfordshire:
Berkhamsted and District Archaeological
  Society
Berkhamsted and District Local History
  Society
Bishops Stortford and District Local History
  Society
Bricket Wood Society
Codicote Local History Society
East Hertfordshire Archaeological Society
Elstree and Borehamwood Historical Research
  Group
Essendon Society
Harpenden Local History Society
Hatfield and District Archaeological Society
Hemel Hempstead Local History Society
Hertford and Ware Local History Society
Hertfordshire Archaeological Council
Hertfordshire Record Society
Hitchin Historical Society
Hunsdon Local History and Preservation
  Society
Kings Langley Local History and Museum
  Society
Little Berkhamsted Local History Group
Mundens and Sacombe Local History Society
North Hertfordshire Archaeological Society
North Mymms Local History Society
Pirton Local History Association
Radlett Local History Society
Rickmansworth Historical Society
Royston and District Local History Society
St Albans and Hertfordshire Architectural and
  Arch. Soc.
Stevenage Society
Watford and Sth-West Herts Archaeological
  Society
Welwyn Archaeological Society

Humberside:
Cottingham Local History Society
Haxey Heritage Society
Hedon and District Local History Society
Immingham and District History Society
Laceby History Group

Isle of Wight:
Isle of Wight Natural History and
  Archaeological Soc.
Ventnor and District Local History Society

Kent:
Ashford Archaeology and History Group
Association of Men of Kent and Kentish Men
Aylesford Society
Bearsted and District Local History Society

Biddenden Local History Society
Brenchley and Matfield Local History Society
Broadstairs and St Peter's Archaeological Soc.
Canterbury Archaeological Society
Chalk Parish History Group
Charing and District Local History Society
Chatham and District Historical Society
Chatham Dockyard Historical Society
Council for Kentish Archaeology
Cranbrook and District Local History Society
Crayford Manor Historical and Archaeological
  Society
Dartford District Archaeological Group
Dartford Historical and Antiquarian Society
Deal, Walmer and District History Society
Dover History Society
East Peckham Historical Society
Edenbridge and District Historical Society
Erith and Belvedere Local History Society
Faversham Archaeological Research Group
Faversham Society
Fawkham and Ash Archaeological Group
Fawkham Historical and Antiquarian Society
Fleur-de-Lis Heritage Centre, Faversham
Gillingham and Rainham Local History Group
Goudhurst and Kilndown Local History
  Society
Gravesend Historical Society
Hadlow Historical Society
Hawkhurst Local History Society
Headcorn Local History Society
Herne Bay Records Society
Ightham and District Historical Society
Isle of Thanet Archaeological Unit
Isle of Thanet Historical Society
Kent Archaeological Rescue Unit
Kent Archaeological Society
Kent County Local History Committee
Lamberhurst Local History Society
Leigh and District Historical Association
Lower Medway Archaeological Research
  Group
Lyminge Historical Society
Maidstone Antiquarian Society
Maidstone Area Archaeological Group
Manor House Historical and Arch. Soc.
  (Crayford)
Meopham Historical Society
Otford and District Historical Society
Otford District Archaeology Group
Paddock Wood Historical Society
Rainham Historical Society
St Margarets-at-Cliffe Local History Society
Sandwich Local History Society
Sevenoaks Society
Sheppey Local History Society

Shorne Local History Group
Sittingbourne Society
Southborough Society
Springhead Excavation Group
Swale Archaeological Research Group
Tenterden and District Local History Society
Thameside Archaeological Group
Tonbridge Historical Society
Wateringbury Local History Society
Weald History Group
West Kent Border Archaeological Group
Whitstable Historical Society
Wye Historical Society

Lancashire:
Accrington Naturalist and Antiquarian Society
Blackburn Society of Antiquaries
Blackburn Historical Society
Bolton and District Archaeological Society
Burnley and District Historical Society
Bury Archaeological Group
Bury and District Local History Society
Chorley Historic and Archaeological Society
Colne and District Local History Group
Crosby and District Historical Society
Eccles and District History Society
Fleetwood and District Historical Society
Fylde Historical Society
Garstang Historical and Archaeological
    Society
Greater Manchester Archaeological Unit
Haslingden Local History Society
Helmshore Local History Society
Historic Society of Lancashire and Cheshire
Huyton-with-Roby Historic Society
Kirkby Local History Society
Lancaster Archaeological Society
Lancashire and Cheshire Antiquarian Society
Leigh Local History Society
Leyland Historical Society
Lonsdale Historical Society
Nelson Local History Society
Newton-le-Willows District Historical Society
Oldham and District Historical and
    Antiquarian Society
Ormskirk and District Historical Society
Prescot Historical Society
Preston Historical Society
Prestwich and District Local History Society
Radcliffe Local History Society
Rainhill Civic Society
Rochdale Historical Society
Rossendale Local History Group
Saddleworth Historical Society
St Helens Historical Society
Salford Local History Group
West Lancashire Archaeological Society

Leicestershire:
Anstey Historical Society
Ashby-de-la-Zouch Local History Society
Barkby Local History Group
Bringhurst, Great Easton and Drayton Local
    History Group
Castle Cary and District Museum and Pres.
    Soc.
Castle Donington Local History Society
Coalville and District Local History Society
Croft Local History Group
Desford and District Local History Group
Dunton Bassett Local History Group
Earl Shilton Local History Group
Evington Local History Society
Fleckney Local History Group
Frisby-on-the-Wreake Historical Society
Glenfield and Western Park and District Arch.
    and Hist. Soc.
Greater Wigston Historical Society
Groby Village Society

Herrick and Beaumanor Society
Hinckley Local History Group
Husbands Bosworth Historical Society
Ibstock Historical Society
Kimcote and Walton Village History Society
Leicestershire Archaeological and Hist. Soc.
Leicestershire Local History Council
Loughborough and District Archaeological
    Society
Market Harborough Historical Society
Melton Mowbray and District Historical
    Society
Newbold Verdon Archaeology and Local
    History Group
Oadby Local History Group
Rearsby Local History Society
Rutland Local History Society
Rutland Record Society
Shepshed Local History Group
Somerby Local History Group
Vaughan Archaeological and Historical
    Society
Whitwick Historical Group

Lincolnshire:
Boston and District Archaeological Society
History of Boston Project
Burgh-le-Marsh Local History Society
Coningsby and Tattershall Local History
    Society
Crowland Historical Society
Grantham Local History Society
Horncastle Local History Society
Lincoln Record Society

G24 *(cont)*

Louth Naturalist, Antiquarian and Literary
  Society
Society for Lincolnshire History and
  Archaeology
Spalding Gentlemen's Society
Spilsbury and District History Society
Stamford and Rutland Arch. and Local History
  Soc.
Stamford Historical Society
Waddington Local History Group
Wainfleet and District Heritage Society

Norfolk:
East Suffolk and Norfolk Antiquaries
Fakenham Local History Society
Great Yarmouth and District Archaeological
  Society
Norfolk and Norwich Archaeological Society
Norfolk Archaeological Rescue Group
Norfolk Archaeological Unit
Norfolk Record Society
North Walsham and District Historical Society
Scole Archaeological Committee

Northamptonshire:
Bozeat Historical and Archaeological Society
Brackley and District History Society
Brigstock Historical Society
Duston Local History Group
Earls Barton and District Historical Society
Harlestone Local History Society
Long Buckby Local History Society
Middle Nene Archaeological Group
Midland Archaeological Research Society
Moulton Local History Group
Nene Valley Research Committee
Northampton Archaeological Society
Northamptonshire Local History Committee
Northamptonshire Record Society
Oundle Historical Society
Raunds and District History Society
Thrapston and District Historical Society
Towcester Local History Society
Upper Nene Archaeological Society
Weldon Local History Society
Wellingborough and District Archaeological
  Society
Woodford Halse History Society

Northumberland:
Acomb Local History Society
Allendale Local History Society
Aln and Breamish Local History Society
Alnwick and District Local Society
Architectural and Archaeological Society of
  Durham and Northumberland

Ashington and Newbiggin Local History
  Society
Bedlingtonshire Local History Society
Belford and District Local History Society
Bellingham and North Tyne Local History
  Group
Berwick-upon-Tweed Local History Society
Blyth Local History Society
Cramlington Local History Society
Cullercoats Local History Society
East Coquet Local History Society
Elswick Local History Group
Felton and Swarland Local History Society
Fenham Local History Society
Glendale Local History Society
Gosforth Local History Society
Haltwhistle Local History Society
Heaton and District Local History Society
Hexham Local History Society
Kenton Local History Society
Killingworth Local History Society
Morpeth Antiquarian Society
North Sunderland and Seahouses Local
  History Soc.
Ponteland Local History Society
Prudhoe and District Local History Society
Redesdale Society
Rothbury and Coquetdale History Society
Seaton Delaval and District Local History
  Society
Society of Antiquaries of
  Newcastle-upon-Tyne
Stannington Local History Society
Tynemouth Antiquarian and Historical Society
Walbottle and District Local History Society
Wallsend Local History Society
Westerhope Local History Society
Whitley Local History Society
Wylam Local History Society

Nottinghamshire
Basford and District Local History Society
Beeston and District Local History Society
Bingham and District Local History Society
Bleasby Local History Society
Bulwell Local History Society
Burton Joyce and Bulcote Local History Society
Caunton Local History Society
Cotgrave Local History Society
East Leake and District Local History Group
Eastwood Historical Society
Edwinstowe Local History Society
Gotham and District Local History Society
Hucknall Heritage Society
Lambley Historical Society
Lenton Local History Group

Newark Archaeological and Local History Soc.
Nottinghamshire Local History Council
Nuthall and District Local History Society
Old Mansfield Society
Retford and District Historical and Arch. Soc.
Ruddington Local History and Amenity
  Society
Sherwood Archaeological Society
Southwell and District Local History Society
Sutton Bonington Local History Society
Sutton-on-Trent Local History Society
Thoroton Society
Old Warsop Society
West Bridgford and District Local History
  Society
Wilford History Society
Worksop Archaeological and Local Historical
  Soc.

Oxfordshire:
Abingdon Area Archaeological and History
  Soc.
Banbury Historical Society
Blewbury Local History Group
Charlbury Local History Society
Chipping Norton Local History Society
Cumnor and District Historical Society
Didcot and District Arch. and Historical Soc.
Enstone Local History Group
Faringdon and District Historical and Arch.
  Soc.
Goring Local History Society
Henley-on-Thames Archaeological and Hist.
  Group
Kidlington and District Historical Society
Lewknor Hundred Historical Society
Oxford Archaeological Unit
Oxford Historical Society
Oxford University Archaeological Society
Oxfordshire Architectural and Historical Soc.
Shrivenham Local History Society
South Oxfordshire Archaeological Group
Thame Historical Society
Wallingford History and Archaeology Society
Wantage and District Field Club
Whitchurch Archives Committee
Woodstock Local History Society

Shropshire:
Bridgnorth and District Historical Society
Clun Historical Society
Ludlow Historical Research Group
Shropshire Archaeological Society
Telford Historical and Archaeological Society
Whitchurch Area Archaeological Group

Somerset:
Axbridge Archaeological and Local History
  Soc.
Bridgwater and District Archaeological Society
Burnham-on-Sea Archaeological and Natural
  History Soc.
Chard Museum and History Group
Crewkerne Local History Society
Exmoor Society
Frome Society for Local Study
Glastonbury Antiquarian Society
Ilchester and District Archaeological Society
Ilminster and District Historical Society
Kingston St Mary Local History Society
Milverton and Fitzhead Society
North Curry Local History Society
North Somerset Archaeological Research
  Group
Nynehead Historical Society
Shepton Mallet Local History Society
Somerset Archaeological and Natural History
  Society
Somerset Record Society
South-East Somerset Archaeological Society
South Petherton Local History Group
Stapleton Local History Society
Wells Natural History and Archaeological
  Society
West Somerset Archaeological and Natural
  Hist. Soc.
Wiveliscombe Historical Society
Yeovil Archaeological and Local History
  Society

Staffordshire:
Ashley and District Historical Society
Blythe Bridge and Forsbrook Historical Society
Brewood Civic Society
Burton-upon-Trent Natural Hist. and Arch.
  Soc.
Cheadle Historical Society
Cheddleton Historical Society
Kings Bromley Historians
Kinver Historical Society
Leek and District Field Club
Mid Staffordshire Field Club
North Staffordshire Field Club
Norton Canes Historical Society
Old Nortonian Society
Pattingham Local History Society
South Staffordshire Arch. and Historical Soc.
Stafford and Mid Staffordshire Arch. Soc.
Stafford Historic and Civic Society
Staffordshire Record Society
Staffordshire Parish Registers Society

G24 *(cont)*

Stoke-on-Trent Museum Archaeological
  Society
Tamworth Civic Society
Walsall Local History Society

Suffolk:
Beccles and District Historical Society
Boxford History Society
Bury St Edmunds Past and Present Society
East Anglian History Workshop
East Suffolk and Norfolk Antiquarians
Felixstowe History and Museum Society
Framlingham and District Local History
  Council
Haverhill and District Local History Group
Lowestoft Archaeological and Local Hist. Soc.
Newmarket Local History Group
Otley Local History Group
Southwold Archaeology and Natural History
  Society
Stour Valley Antiquarian Society
Sudbury and District Historical Research
  Group
Suffolk Institute of Archaeology and History
Suffolk Local History Council

Surrey:
Addlestone Historical Society
Albury History Society
Banstead History Research Group
Betchworth and Buckland Society
Bletchingley Conservation and History Society
Bourne Society
Cuckfield Society
Dorking and Leith Hill Preservation Society
Egham-by-Runnymede Historical Society
Frensham and Dockenfield Local History
  Group
Leatherhead and District Local History Society
Mayford and Woking District History Society
Newdigate Society
Nonsuch Antiquarian Society
Ockham Local History Society
Oxted and District History Society
Puttenham and Wanborough History Society
Send and Ripley History Society
Shere, Gomshall and Peaslake Local History
  Soc.
Sunbury and Shepperton Local History
  Society
Surbiton and District Historical Society
Surrey Archaeological Society
Surrey Local History Council
Walton and Weybridge Local History Society
West Surrey Society
Wood Street Village History Society

Sussex:
Ashurst Wood Historians
Battle and District Historical Society
Beeding and Bramber Local History Society
Billingshurst Local History Society
Bognor Regis Local History Society
Brighton and Hove Archaeological Society
Burgess Hill Local History Society
Chichester Local History Society
Climping Local History Group
Crawley Local History Group
Crawley and Mid-Sussex Arch. Soc.
Danehill Parish Historical Society
Eastbourne Local History Society
Federation of Sussex Local History Societies
Forest Row Local History Group
Friends of the East Sussex Record Office
Hailsham Historical and Natural History
  Society
Hartfield and District History Group
Hastings Local History Research Group
Heathfield and Waldron Community
  Association (History Section)
Horley Local History Society
Horsham Museum Society
Hurstpierpoint Historical Society
Iford Local History Society
Lewes Archaeological Group
Littlehampton and District Nat. Science and
  Arch. Soc.
Maresfield Parish History Society
Mayfield Local History Society
Mid Sussex Local History Society
Midhurst Society
Newhaven Historical Society
Northiam and District Historical and Literary
  Society
Ringmer History Study Group
Robertsbridge and District Archaeological Soc.
Rye Museum Association
Shoreham and Southwick Archaeological
  Society
Steyning Society
Sussex Archaeological Society
Sussex History Study Group
Sussex Record Society
Sussex Saxon Research Group
Warbleton and District History Group
Warnham Historical Society
Westbourne Local History Group
Worthing Archaeological Society

Warwickshire:
Alcester and District Local History Society
Birmingham and Warwickshire
    Archaeological Society
Chelmsley Local History Society
Coventry and District Archaeological Society
Dugdale Society
Kenilworth History and Archaeological
    Society
Kings Heath Local History Society
Rugby Local History Group
Shipston-on-Stour and District Local History
    Soc.
Warwickshire Local History Society
Wolvey Local History Group

Wiltshire:
Bourne Valley Historical and Records Society
Cricklade Historical Society
Hatcher Society
Highworth Historical Society
Melksham and District Historical Association
Salisbury Local History Group
Swindon Archaeological Society
Warminster History Society
Wilton Historical Society
Wiltshire Archaeological and Natural Hist.
    Soc.
Wiltshire Local History Forum
Wootton Bassett Historical Society

Yorkshire:
Ackworth and Hemsworth Historical Society
Beeston Local History Society
Bradford Historical and Antiquarian Society
University of Bradford Archaeological Society
Brompton Local History Society
Bronte Society
Calder Valley Archaeology and Research
    Group
Castleford and District Historical Society
Dewsbury and District Historical Society
East Riding Archaeological Society
East Yorkshire History Society
Garforth Historical Society
Greater Elland Historical Society
Halifax Antiquarian Society
Hebden Bridge Literary and Scientific Soc.
Elmsley Archaeological Society
Huddersfield and District Archaeological
    Society
Huddersfield Local History Society
Hutton Rudby and District Local History
    Society
Morley Local History Society
Olicana Museum and Historical Society
Ossett Historical Society

Otley Archaeological and Historical Society
Pontefract and District Archaeological Society
Pontefract and District Local History Society
Rotherham Archaeological Society
Scarborough Archaeological and Historical
    Society
Sherburn Local History Society
Shitlington History Research Group
Spen Valley Historical Society
Stokesley and District Local History Study
    Group
Thoresby Society
Todmorden Antiquarian Society
Wakefield Historical Society
Wensleydale Society
Wetherby Historical Society
York Archaeological Society
Yorkshire Archaeological Society

Scotland:
Aberdeen Natural History and Antiquarian
    Society
Abertay Historical Society
Ayrshire Archaeology and Nat. History
    Society
Banffshire Field Club
Buteshire Natural History Society
Cowal Archaeological Society
Dumfriesshire and Galloway Natural History
    and Antiquarian Society
East Kilbride History Society
East Lothian Antiquarian and Field Naturalists
    Society
Edinburgh Archaeological Field Society
Falkirk Archaeological and Natural History
    Soc.
Forfar and District Historical Society
Glasgow Archaeological Society
Hawick Archaeological Society
Kilmarnock and District History Group
Kincardine Local History Group
Kinross-shire Antiquarian Society
Kintyre Antiquarian and Natural History Soc.
Lorn Archaeological and Historical Society
Mid-Argyll Natural History and Antiquarian
    Soc.
Mull Historical Society
Saltire Society
Scottish History Society
Scottish Record Society
Society of Antiquaries of Scotland
West Lothian History and Amenity Society

G24 *(contd)*

Wales:

Clwyd:
Abergele Field Club
Clwyd Local History Council
Denbigh Local History and Museum Society
Denbighshire Historical Society
Dyserth and District Field Club
Flintshire Historical Society
Ruabon Field Club
Ruthin Local History Group

Dyfed:
Carmarthenshire Antiquarian Society
Ceredigion Antiquarian Society
Pembrokeshire Historical Society

Glamorgan:
Bridgend District Local History and Museum Society
Caerphilly Local History Society
Cynon Valley History Society
Gelligaer Historical Society
Glamorgan History Society
Llantrisant and District Local History Society
Merthyr Tydfil Historical and Civic Society
Neath Antiquarian Society
Penarth District Local History Society
Pontypridd Historical Society
Port Talbot Historical Society
Porthcawl Museum and Historical Society
Swansea Valley History Society

Gwent:
Abergavenny Local History Society
Abertillery and District Museum Society
Blaenavon Local History Society
Caerleon Local History Society
Chepstow Local History Society
Gwent Local History Council
Monmouth Field and Antiquarian Society
Pontypool and District Local History Society
Raglan Local History Group
Tredegar Local History Society

Gwynedd:
Anglesey Antiquarian Society
Caernarvonshire Historical Society
Merioneth Historical and Record Society

Powys:
Brecknock Local History Society
Builth Wells Local History Society
Crickhowell and District Civic Society
Hay-on-Wye Study Group
Knighton and District Local History Society
Llangynidr Local History Society
Offa's Dyke Association

Powysland Club
Presteigne Local History Society
Radnorshire Society
Talgarth Local History Society
Ystradgynlais Local History Society

SECTION H

Genealogy

PART ONE
GENERAL

H1 Genealogy. Genealogy is the study and tracing of ancestors from which a chart of descent may be compiled. It is usually begun with details of recent descendants and then traced backwards. Historically, genealogical charts have usually been traced through the male line: this bias towards the male blood has been bolstered by the continuity of surname and the male inheritance of property. The retention of the male surname through the generations inevitably makes research easier and renders the pedigree chart clearer, but if the object is to trace one's ancestors out of academic and family interest, there is no reason why research should be confined to the male line.

The researcher will use a wide variety of sources and documents, the principal ones being the General Registry of Births, Deaths and Marriages from 1837, the Parish Registers before that, the Probate registries, monumental inscriptions, vestry minutes, manor court rolls, rate books, bishops' transcripts and the census.

The nature and whereabouts of such records are dealt with in Section D.

The researcher should be methodical from the beginning. All information should be systemically transferred from notebook to an index system and the sources of that information recorded. Index cards may be obtained from the Society of Genealogists (qv) but if the project is a large one it may well be more economic to devise a tailor-made card and have it printed. Alternatively devise a detail sheet and print the required number of copies at an instant-print place or find someone who will let you use a photostat machine for the price of the paper involved; these sheets may be conveniently kept in a ring binder, which is easier to carry around for reference than a card index drawer. The drawback to this mobility, of course, is the possible loss of the research records.

Another method, growing in popularity is to keep your records on a personal computer system. These machines are now realistic in price and have good word-processing facilities so that updating of records is simple and quick. Furthermore, a print-out of relevant records may be made at any time so that they may be used as memory aids when visiting libraries. It is important to make floppy disc copies at frequent intervals of all material and to put these copies somewhere safe, and preferably in another building. This is to guard against accidental deletion on the machine, theft or fire.

Each person being researched should have a code number which should be duplicated on the draft family tree. The usual method is to allocate an alphabetical code to each generation and then a separate numerical reference to each person within that generation. The index card or the index sheet should then be filed under the generation letter. Personal computers vary but it should be possible to simulate this filing method on most of them so that information retrieval is fast and reliable.

H2 Individual histories. The information that should be obtained on each person in the family tree is more than can be included in the chart. However, the extra information quite often makes the pursuit of family history worthwhile and also provides clues when research has reached an *impasse*. The data for each person should include:

Full name.
Dates of birth, baptism, death and burial.
Date(s) of marriage(s) and full names of spouse(s) together with their code numbers within the filing system.
Details of children.
Residences.
Education and occupational career and qualifications if any.
Social status.
Public responsibilities or appointments.
Property or land ownership, together with dates.
Details of will.
Details of military service if any.
Details of immigration or emigration.
Details of monumental inscription.

It will be seen from this that the information recorded might well be more than one index card or sheet can carry, in which case additional cards or sheets should be used and be headed with the code number and a continuation number, such as B55/2.

H3 Duplication of research. It may well be that some of the people in the tree or of the family name in question have been researched already. Previously it was wise to consult the *National Pedigree Index*, housed at the Society of Genealogists, which acted as a central clearing house of information in such matters. However, this was discontinued from September 1986 as a result of the greatly improved sources of information elsewhere. There are now national and international directories published which contain information about family research and the magazine *Family Tree* has a computer-based directory of research. Furthermore, the individual family history societies each publish regular lists of their members' interests. The old National Pedigree Index has been transferred to the Society of Genealogists where it will be incorporated in its Index of Members' Interests.

In addition the College of Arms checks and registers completed pedigrees provided that they are submitted with appropriate evidence. A fee is charged for this, but the pedigree is available for permanent reference.

A large number of One-Name groups exists. To enquire if such a group exists for the surname in which you are interested, contact the Guild of One-Name Studies, Box G, 14 Charterhouse Buildings, London, EC1M 7BA, who will also advise you how to set up a group.

The Society of Genealogists has an index system which has millions of entries; this should also be consulted.

H4 The Society of Genealogists. The Society has a collection of over 45,000 volumes including transcripts of nearly half the pre-1837 parish registers in the country, in its library. It has documents relating to 12,000 families and an index featuring millions of entries. The Society also has *Boyd's Marriage Index* which includes the register entries from 17 counties and which contains between 6 and 7 million names. The Society publishes a quarterly journal entitled *The Genealogists' Magazine*. The Society also arranges courses for beginners.

Membership is by subscription, which varies according to whether a member comes from town, country or overseas. Non-members may use the library, which is closed on Sundays and Mondays, on payment of a fee which is based on the number of hours research involved.

The Society's address is 14 Charterhouse Buildings, London, EC1M 7BA (01 251 8799). The nearest Underground station is Barbican.

H5 The Institute of Heraldic and Genealogical Studies. The Institute, founded in 1961, provides facilities for study and training in family history research. It organises courses and publishes *Family History* six times a year. It also publishes maps and other publications of particular use to genealogists. Its address is Northgate, Canterbury, Kent.

H6 Federation of Family History Societies. The Federation began in 1974 in response to the growing number of local family history groups being formed. Membership is open to any Society or body specialising in family history or an associated discipline. Its Council consists of representatives of the member societies. The central offices are at the Birmingham and Midland Institute, Margaret Street, Birmingham where postal enquiries should be sent.

Branches exist for the following areas: Aberdeen and North-east Scotland, Avon, Bedfordshire, Berkshire, Birmingham and Midlands, Bristol & Avon, Bucks, Cambs, Channel Islands, Cheshire, North Cheshire, Cleveland, Clwyd, Cornwall, Cumbria, Derbyshire, Devon, Doncaster, Dorset, Durham, Dyfed, Essex, Folkestone, Glamorgan, Glasgow and West of Scotland, Glos, Gwent, Gwynedd, Hants, Herefordshire, Herts, Highlands, North of Ireland, Kent, North-west Kent, Lancs, Leics, Lincs, Liverpool, East of London, Isle of Man, Manchester & Lancs, Central Middlesex, North Middlesex, West Middlesex, Monmouthshire, Norfolk and Norwich, Northants, Northumberland and Durham, Notts, Oxon, Peterborough, Powys, Rossendale, Scotland, Sheffield, Shropshire, Somerset & Dorset, Suffolk, East Surrey, West Surrey, Sussex, Tay Valley, Ulster, Waltham Forest, Wilts, Windsor & Slough, Woolwich, East Yorkshire, York.

The Federation also has close contacts with many overseas family history groups.

H7 The Guild of One-Name Studies. The Guild was formed in 1979 to help those researchers who were concentrating on one surname. From time to time it publishes a *Register of One Name Studies* which includes details of all those surnames being researched. The Guild's address is c/o Box G, 14 Charterhouse Buildings, London, EC1M 7BA.

H8 The Association of Genealogists and Record Agents. Many people are unable, for one reason or another, to conduct their own research. About one hundred professional genealogical researchers now belong to this Association which seeks to uphold standards and protect the interests of those using the services of the members. A list of researchers may be obtained from the Association c/o Ms Jean Tooke, 1 Woodside Close, Caterham, Surrey. The Association of Scottish Genealogists and Record Agents is at 106 Brucefield Avenue, Dunfermline, KY11 4SY. It is advisable to obtain a clear understanding as to fees before work commences.

PART TWO
MISCELLANEOUS TERMS

H9 Alias. The Latin word for 'otherwise'. An alias may be adopted for perfectly innocent reasons, such as the perpetuation of a family name, quite often resulting in a hyphenated name.

H10 Ancestor. Strictly speaking, a person from whom others are descended, but the term is used to describe others related to the ancestor in question. Legally it is extended to apply to any person from whom an estate was inherited.

H11 Chanceling. An illegitimate child.

H12 Espousal. Engagement to be married. Before the 17th century it had almost as much significance as the actual marriage, so that it was by no means uncommon for a child to be born earlier than nine months after a marriage.

H13 Family. Strictly speaking, many genealogists insist that the term describes only the people of the same name and blood who descend from the same male ancestor. In documents up to the 17th century, the term could indicate the whole household, including servants.

H14 Generation. The average time span between the birth of the parents and their children. Genealogists, more specifically, use the term to denote the span between the birth of a male and his male-line descendant. It is unwise to generalise as to the number of years since it depends upon what was the usual age of marriage in a given period, and what class the ancestors belonged to. Thirty years is a commonly accepted generation average, and up to thirty-five if the calculation is based on the 'median' child of a marriage.

H15 German. A relationship in the fullest sense. Thus, brothers and sisters german have the same parents, and a cousin german is a first cousin.

H16 Half-baptised. A term to denote a child who has been baptised privately and not in a church.

H17 Half-blood. A relationship between two people who have one common ancestor.

H18 Pedigree. A term denoting a genealogical table illustrating a line of descent, sometimes interpreted as in the male line only (agnatic). The word is derived from the Old French *pie de grue*, meaning crane's foot, the shape of which resembled early pictorial representations of family lines. A Paragraph Pedigree is one in which the line of descent is set out in indented and numbered paragraphs.

H19 Total Descent. A genealogical chart which shows descent through both male and female lines. Alternatively called Birth Brief.

PART THREE
THE FAMILY TREE

H20 Construction of a Family Tree. The most common form of chart is one which has the earliest ancestors at the top and the most recent at the bottom, the reverse of a tree. It is important to fix the purpose of such a chart initially, for the inclusion of too much information can muddle a chart's presentation. Often the chart shows the descent through the male line; sometimes the tree shows how two families, through the male line, joined forces at the foot; a chart can show the female descent only. If a chart has a specific purpose, or if it is meant to be reproduced in a publication, it is better to restrict the detail on it to avoid clutter. On the other hand, if a chart is intended as a family record to show all the lines which have contributed towards a descendant, then the chart needs to be planned with some care and will, no doubt, go through several revisions to cope with the mass of information and relationships that will crop up.

This kind of chart may be in landscape form with the earliest ancestor placed to the left of the sheet, centrally, and the descent spreading out, generation by generation, to the right.

In a Total Descent chart ancestors, both male and female, are shown. One popular form of this consists of a series of concentric circles emanating from, say, two people in a centre circle. Each concentric circle is then divided into segments; the first concentric circle would have four segments, in which the parents of the two people in the centre circle are noted, and the next concentric circle would have eight segments noting the parents of the previous four people, and so on. This series of circles can, of course, be extended indefinitely, but the drawback of this method is that it can be restrictive of detail. Also, it merely shows parents, with other offspring going unnoticed. Quite often the function of this type of chart is to indicate the relationship between numerous families and this it does successfully, as by the time the chart has been taken back, say, seven generations it is possible that 64 different families have appeared.

Suitable sheets of paper and pre-printed pedigree charts may be obtained from the Society of Genealogists.

It is the convention to indicate a marriage by a short double-dash, a child by a short drop dash, and each child will be joined by a thin horizontal line. A wavy drop line indicates an illegitimate child and possible, but unconfirmed relationships indicated by a broken line. It is usual to abbreviate the words born, baptised, married and died by b,bp, m, and d respectively.

PART FOUR
NAMES

H21 Surnames. There are eight main derivation categories for surnames:

Place-names – Pangbourne, Thorpe etc
Location – Attwood, Byfield etc
Occupation – Baker, Shepherd etc
Status – Leader, Yeoman etc
Creature – Fox, Parrott etc
Patronymic – Richardson, Johnson etc
Nickname – Redhead, Whitehair etc
Personal name – Edwards, Williams etc

Hereditary surnames were probably introduced by the Normans and the incidence of them in early times is higher in those areas closest to the court itinerary. The inheritance of property was facilitated by hereditary names and therefore the better-off had surnames earlier than the poor. Some parts of Wales did not have hereditary surnames until the 19th century.

Changing a surname has always been legal although there have been various official ways of doing it, ranging from a private Act of Parliament to a Deed Poll. If the researcher should suspect a change of surname a first step would be to consult *An Index to Changes of Name 1760–1901*, by W. P. W. Phillimore and E. A. Fry (1905).

Before beginning research it is helpful to list the variations of a surname which could occur – this will become increasingly important as reference to parish registers and other rather illiterate records is required. As with foreign names, a name will often be spelt as it is pronounced.

In Scotland a woman retains her maiden name for legal purposes.

H22 Christian Names. There have been fashions in the giving of christian names. Among the landed classes Norman names such as William, Ralph and Walter were popular after the Conquest although the poorer people still clung to Anglo-Saxon names. Religious names such as Matthew, John, Simon were in vogue in Plantagenet times, and for girls the most popular were Elizabeth, Mary and Anne. During the Puritan era Biblical names were again important but those having connotations of post-Biblical saints and therefore of Catholicism, were less common. The Georgian period saw a revival of classical names, in particular for women – such as Olivia, Amelia etc. The later Romantic period brought a return of Anglo-Saxon names such as Alfred, Edwin, Edgar, Matilda and Ethel.

Before the 17th century it was uncommon for someone to have more than two christian names.

Some women have been christened with common men's names such as Alexander and Philip, and occasionally women's names have been interchangeable, such as Agnes and Anne, Esther and Hester, Mary Ann and Marion.

PART FIVE
BIBLIOGRAPHY

In Search of Ancestry, G. Hamilton Edwards (4th ed 1983)

Introducing Genealogy, A. J. Willis

How to record your family tree, Patrick Palgrave-Moore (1979)

The Family History Book, Stella Colwell (1st ed. 1980)

Family History Annual, ed Michael Burchall (1st ed. 1985)

Dictionary of Genealogy, Terrick V. H. FitzHugh (1985)

English Genealogy, Sir Anthony Wagner (1983)

Tracing Your Ancestors in the Public Record Office, J. Cox and T. Padfield (3rd ed. 1984 HMSO)

In Search of Scottish Ancestry, G. Hamilton Edwards (1983)

A Genealogist's Bibliography, C. Humphery-Smith (1985)

Computers in Genealogy, quarterly newsletter published by the Society of Genealogists.

Sources for Non-conformist Genealogy and Family History, D. J. Steel (1973)

In Search of Huguenot Ancestry, N. Currer-Briggs & Royston Gambier

My Ancestor was Jewish. How can I find more about him? Michael Gandy

My Ancestors were Quakers. How can I find more about them? E. Millington and M. J. Thomas.

World War One Army Ancestry, Norman Holding.

In Search of Army Ancestry, G. Hamilton-Edwards

British Military Records as Sources for Biography and Genealogy, leaflet pub. by the Public Record Office

Family Tree, magazine previously published six times a year, but to be monthly from 1987. For details contact 129 Great Whyte, Ramsey, Huntingdon, Cambs. (0487 814050)

The Genealogists' Magazine, published by the Society of Genealogists.

Family History, published by the Institute of Heraldic and Genealogical Studies.

Family History News and Digest, published twice a year by the Federation of Family History Societies

Publications from the Federation of Family History Societies

A useful and inexpensive series of booklets has

Bibliography *(cont)*

been produced for the Federation, mainly by Eve McLaughlin and J. S. W. Gibson. These explain in considerable detail how particular classes of records may be located and used for genealogical research. The list of titles includes:

Parish Registers, Eve McLaughlin (1986)

Annals of the Poor, Eve McLaughlin (1986)

Marriage, Census, and other Indexes for Family Historians, Jeremy Gibson (1986)

A Simplified Guide to Probate Jurisdictions: Where to Look for Wills, Jeremy Gibson (3rd ed. 1985)

St Catherine's House, Eve McLaughlin (1985)

The Censuses 1841–1881, Eve McLaughlin (1985)

Unpublished Personal Names Indexes in Record Offices and Libraries, J. S. W. Gibson (1985)

Wills before 1858, Eve McLaughlin (1985)

Hearth Tax Returns, other Later Stuart Tax Lists & the Association Oath Rolls, J. S. W. Gibson

Quarter Sessions Records for Family Historians, ed J. S. W. Gibson (2nd ed. 1983)

Somerset House Wills, Eve McLaughlin

Where to find the IGI, J. S. W. Gibson and Michael Walcot

SECTION J

Education

PART ONE
LEGISLATION

J1 Catholic Emancipation Act 1829. This Act removed discrimination against Roman Catholic teachers and schools.

J2 Legislation 1833. It was enacted that juveniles could be employed only if they also attended a school for a specified number of hours a week. This led to the establishment of Factory Schools.

J3 Poor Law 1844. Poor Law Commissioners were empowered to appoint a teacher for workhouse children. This led to the formation of District Schools (qv) serving several workhouses in a district, where children could be educated away from the workhouse buildings.

J4 Industrial Schools Act 1857. This Act enabled magistrates to send children found begging, or else needing care and protection, to Industrial Schools (qv) to learn a trade.

J5 Forster's Education Act 1870. This major Act provided that England should be divided into districts and that elementary schools be established in areas where school provision from other sources was insufficient. Boards were set up to manage these districts. Board Schools were the first local authority-run schools and were, at first, complementary and later competitive, to the voluntary and endowed schools. Board schools could be secular and undenominational but an amendment to the Act, called the Cowper-Temple Conscience clause, permitted school boards to provide religious instruction if they wished.

J6 Legislation 1876. The principle was established that all children should receive elementary education. The legislation established school attendance committees where no school boards existed, and imposed further restrictions on the employment of children.

J7 Education Act 1880. School attendance to the age of ten was made compulsory. At that age a child could obtain a certificate and leave but if his record of attendances did not meet a standard he was required to stay on at school longer.

J8 Education Act 1889. The Board of Education was set up. County Councils were empowered to levy a 1d rate to provide technical education.

J9 Legislation 1891. Elementary education was provided free.

J10 Legislation 1893 and 1899. The school-leaving age was raised to eleven and then twelve.

J11 Balfour's Education Act 1902. Local authorities were empowered to provide elementary and secondary education, thereby superseding the old School Boards. Usually the secondary education was not co-educational – the boys went to state grammar schools and the girls to high schools.

J12 Legislation 1918. The school-leaving age was raised to 14.

J13 Education Act 1944. Fees in state secondary schools were abolished. Elementary education was reorganised into infant and junior schools, and secondary education was graded into modern, grammar and technical schools. The school-leaving age was raised to 15.

PART TWO
TYPES OF SCHOOLS

J14 Adult School Movement. Founded by Quakers and later called the National Adult School Union, the movement provided undenominational, but religiously based, education in the 19th century.

J15 Board Schools. Forster's Education Act 1870 divided the country into educational districts each administered by a school board. The schools were secular and undenominational and as such were resented by the voluntary, usually religious, schools many of which had to close for want of pupils. The first Board School opened in St Austell, Cornwall, in 1872. In 1902 Board Schools became Council Schools.

J16 British Schools. In 1808 followers of the Quaker Joseph Lancaster, formed the Royal Lancastrian Society to carry out his educational ideas. The Society altered its name in 1810 to the British and Foreign School Society once Lancaster, an indifferent financial organiser, had cut himself off from the movement. The

special feature of the Society's education was the use of the monitorial system by which older children taught groups of younger ones under the supervision of paid staff. The method was cheap and was copied by other types of schools including those which later were part of the state system. In 1824 Parliament made a grant of £24,000 to elementary schools which was shared between the British and National (qv) schools. By 1851 there were 1500 British schools in the country, drawing their main support from Nonconformist families.

J17 Cathedral and Monastic Schools. The earliest schools were those attached to cathedrals and monasteries. The first one appears to have been at Canterbury in the early 7th century – King's School is its present-day successor. At the Reformation many went out of existence or were refounded as grammar schools (qv).

J18 Chantry Schools. In the Middle Ages it was common for a person to endow a chantry so that priests might, in perpetuity, pray for his soul. Sometimes a small school grew up from this bequest. Many went out of existence at the Reformation and some were refounded as grammar schools (qv).

J19 Circulating Schools. To cater for the sparse and scattered Welsh population in the late 17th century, the Rev. Thomas Gouge founded a society in order to instruct poor Welsh children in English. In 1730 the Rev. Griffith Jones of Llandowror in Carmarthenshire founded what was to be known as a Circulating School. The instruction was carried out by itinerant teachers who stayed in localities for three to six months. The schools were for adults as well as children and Welsh, rather than English, was used. It is estimated that by 1777 there were over 6,000 such schools in Wales.

J20 Common Day Schools. Private, low-fee, elementary schools for poor children.

J21 Dame Schools. Elementary schools run by women, the usual fee being 3d or 4d per week. These largely disappeared after the 1870 Education Act.

J22 District Schools. In 1844 the Poor Law Commissioners were empowered to educate workhouse children in District Schools large enough to cater for several workhouses. These schools declined after the 1870 Education Act.

J23 Factory Schools. An Act of 1833 made the employment of children dependent upon their receiving a certain amount of education at school. It is estimated that after ten years about 40% of the children in the manufacturing areas were attending factory schools. This type of school had been pioneered earlier by Robert Owen and David Dale.

J24 Grammar Schools. These schools have their origin in the Saxon ecclesiastical establishments which taught young men Latin for the priesthood. In the Middle Ages such schools were established by private benefactors, trade guilds or ecclesiastical bodies but many grammar schools date from the 1550s – a period when new foundations were being endowed to replace those schools lost at the Reformation. By the 17th century boarding and day grammar schools existed. Endowments provided free, or almost free, basic education; the terms of these gifts usually precluded extension of the curriculum away from classical subjects and by the 19th century it was common for the schools to charge fees for new subjects such as science. The Grammar Schools Act 1840 gave powers to grammar schools to teach subjects other than those stipulated in their statutes.

J25 Industrial Schools. The early Industrial Schools were for poor children, many of whom were sent to them by magistrates who felt that they needed to escape their family background and learn a trade. The name was also used to describe state-aided schools later in the 19th century in which boys were taught a craft and girls usually trained for domestic service.

J26 Junior Schools. These schools were established after the 1918 Education Act but were not common until after 1926. They taught children aged from seven to eleven, whereas the earlier elementary schools had catered for children from seven to fourteen.

J27 Mechanics' Institutes. The name did not derive from machinery but was a term to denote manual workers and craftsmen. A Mechanics' Institute was established in Chester in 1810 and a similar organisation existed in London in 1817. The London Mechanics' Institution was founded, very much the inspiration of Dr George Birkbeck, in 1823 and by 1825 there were about 70 institutions around the country. The educational results were rather mixed, and the institutes were not particularly well-supported by the men the founders had in mind; in part this was due to the institutes' specialisation in science.

J28 National Schools. The National Society for the Education of the Poor in the Principles of the Established Church was formed in 1811 and gradually absorbed the schools already established by the SPCK (qv). By 1851 the Society controlled over 17,000 schools and shared a government grant of £24,000 in 1824 with the rival British Schools (qv). The 1870 Education Act, which provided free education for poorer children, led to the Society's gradual decline.

J29 Pestalozzi Schools. Some schools were established in the 19th century whose teaching was based on the ideas of Johann Pestalozzi (1746–1827). In the curriculum the rote-learning of other schools was abandoned and pupils were encouraged to learn from direct experience instead; the subject list was also expanded to include science, architecture and astronomy.

J30 Preparatory Schools. The rejuvenation and new popularity of Public Schools (qv) in the second half of the 19th century encouraged the establishment of preparatory schools in which younger pupils could be prepared for admission.

J31 Public Schools. The term 'Public Schools' is now generally accepted as denoting about 200 independent schools, mainly in the south of England. Many derive from old grammar schools especially those which, in their early days, boarded scholars. Approximately one third of today's Public Schools were grammar schools founded between the 14th and 17th centuries. They became known as 'public' by their ability to attract pupils from outside their own locality.

In 1868 the Public Schools Act required each school to draw up a constitution and laid down conditions for the appointment of governors.

J32 Ragged Schools. These schools began with the work of a Portsmouth cobbler, John Pounds. From 1818 he provided a school which was entirely free for the poorest children. In 1844 Lord Shaftesbury helped to organise an official union of Ragged Schools; by 1869 there were about 200 establishments as well as allied night and Sunday schools.

J33 SPCK. The Society for the Propagation of Christian Knowledge was founded in 1698. It provided schools for the industrial poor and by 1750 there were at least 1500 of them supported by voluntary subscriptions. They set the pattern for 19th-century charity education with an insistence on subordination, frugality and gratitude. They declined in importance in the first half of the 19th century and many were taken over by the National Society (qv).

J34 Sunday Schools. The first Sunday School appears to have been in Catterick, Yorkshire, in 1763, but the movement was popularised by Robert Raikes who founded a school in Gloucester in 1780. He engaged four women to teach and charged pupils a penny each week. In 1785 a society was formed for the 'Establishment and Support of Sunday Schools throughout the Kingdom of Great Britain'. The Sunday School Union was founded in 1803 to improve such schools in the London area.

J35 Workers' Educational Association. The Association to Promote the Higher Education of Working Men, as it was first called, was founded in 1903 by Albert Mansbridge, the first branch being at Reading in 1904. The Association assumed its present name in 1905.

J36 Workhouse Schools. Education for workhouse children was encouraged by legislation in 1844 when Poor Law Commissioners were empowered to provide it. It was generally thought that the children should be educated outside the workhouse buildings and District Schools (qv) were established.

J37 Working Men's Colleges. In 1842 the Sheffield People's College was founded by the Rev. R. S. Bayley; it was open to both men and women at a fee of 9d per week. Classes were held at 6.30 am and 7.30 pm. Its successes inspired the foundation of the Working Men's College in Queen Square, London, in 1854, a venture closely connected with the Christian Socialist movement. Classes were open to all men over the age of 16 who were competent in the three Rs. Between 1855 and 1868 a dozen or more such colleges were formed in England and two in Scotland.

A Working Women's College was founded in 1864 in Queen Square, London which in 1874 changed its name to the College for Men and Women.

PART THREE
SCHOOLS AND UNIVERSITIES

J38 Schools. The following are the foundation dates of some old-established schools:

Beds: Bedford pre-1066, Bedford Modern 1566
Berks: Abingdon pre-1066, Blue Coat, Sonning 1646, Reading c1125
Bucks: Aylesbury Grammar 1598, Dr Challoner's Grammar, Amersham 1620, Eton 1440, Royal Grammar, High Wycombe c1548, Royal Latin, Buckingham 1540, Sir William Borlase's, Marlow 1624
Cambs: King's, Ely c970, Perse, Cambridge 1615
Cheshire: King's, Chester 1541, King's, Macclesfield 1502, Birkenhead 1860, Stockport Grammar 1487
Cornwall: Truro Grammar 16th century
Cumberland: St Bees 1583, Sedbergh 1525
Derbyshire: Ashbourne Grammar 1586, Repton c1556, Wirksworth Grammar 1584
Devon: All Hallows, Lyme Regis 1524, Ashburton Grammar 1314, Blundell's, Tiverton 1604, Exeter 1633
Dorset: Sherborne c8th century
Durham: Durham pre-1066
Essex: Brentwood 1557, Chelmsford 16th century, Chigwell Grammar 1629, Davenant, Loughton 1680, Felstead 1584, Saffron Walden by 1314, Bancroft's, Woodford Green 1727
Glos: Bristol Cathedral refounded 1542, Badminton 1852, Bristol Grammar by 1532, Cheltenham College 1841, Cheltenham Ladies' College 1853, Gloucester Grammar 12th century, Red Maids', Bristol 1634
Hants: Churcher's College, Petersfield 1722, King Edward VI, Southampton 1553, Portsmouth Grammar 1732, Winchester 1382
Herefordshire: Hereford Cathedral refounded 1381, Lady Margaret Hawkins Grammar 1625, Lucton 1708
Herts: Aldenham 1597, Berkhamsted 1541, Haberdashers' Aske's 1690 (in London), Christ's Hospital School for Girls, Hertford 1552 (in London), Richard Hale, Hertford 1617, St Albans c948, Stevenage Grammar 1558, Watford Grammar 1704
Hunts: Kimbolton 1600
Kent: King's, Canterbury c600, King's, Rochester by 604, Maidstone Grammar by 1450, St Edmund's, Canterbury 1749, St Olave's, Orpington 1749, Sevenoaks 1418, Sutton Valence, Maidstone 1576, Tonbridge 1553
Lancs: Bolton Grammar 1524, Burnley Grammar by 1532, Manchester Grammar 1515, Mer-

chant Taylor's, Liverpool 1620, Queen Elizabeth, Blackburn 1509, Stonyhurst College 1794, Queen Elizabeth, Wakefield refounded 1591, Hulme Grammar 1611, Bury Grammar 1634

Leics: Appleby Parva 1697, Loughborough Grammar by 1495, Old Grammar School, Market Harborough 1614

Lincs: Bourne Free 1768, Stamford 1532

London (GLC area): Battersea Grammar 1700, City of London 1442, Colfe, SE12 refounded 1652, Dulwich 1619, Emanuel 1594, Hampton, Middlesex 1557, Harrow 1571, Highgate 1565, Kingston Grammar by 1264, Latymer Upper by 1583, Merchant Taylors' 1561, Mill Hill 1807, North London Collegiate 1850, St Paul's refounded 1509, Trinity, Croydon 1596, Westminster by 1339, Whitgift, Croydon 1596

Norfolk: Gresham's, Holt 1555, Norwich by 1256

Northants: Oundle 1556, Wellingborough 1478

Northumberland: Dame Allan's, Newcastle 1705, Morpeth 16th century, Royal Grammar, Newcastle 1525, Shafto Trust, Haydon Bridge 1685

Notts: Newark High School for Girls 1623, Nottingham High School 1513

Oxon: Abingdon re-endowed 1563, Magdalen College School 1478, Radley 1847

Rutland: Oakham 1584, Uppingham 1584

Shropshire: Bridgnorth Grammar by 1503, Ludlow by 1553, Shrewsbury 1552

Somerset: King's College, Taunton 1522, King's, Bruton 1519, King Edward's Bath 1552, Kingswood 1748, Taunton 1847, Wells Cathedral by 12th century

Staffs: Wolverhampton Grammar 1512

Suffolk: Bungay 16th century, Debenham mid-17th century, Ipswich 1390, Woodbridge 1662

Surrey: Charterhouse, Goldalming 1611 (in London), King Edward's, Goldalming 1553 (in London), Reigate 1675, Royal Grammar, Guildford 1509

Sussex: Christ's Hospital, Horsham 1553 (in London), Lancing 1849, Roedean 1885

Warwickshire: Bablake, Coventry 1344, Bayley's 1733, King Edward's, Birmingham 1552, King Henry VIII, Coventry 1545, Rugby 1567, Solihull by 1560, Stratford-upon-Avon Grammar 1426, Queen Mary's Grammar School, Walsall 1554, Warwick by 914

Westmorland: Windermere 16th century

Wiltshire: Marlborough 1843, Pauntsey, Devizes 1543

Worcestershire: Bromsgrove re-endowed 1553, Dudley Grammar 1562, Hartlebury by 1558, King's, Worcester 1541, King Edward VI Grammar 1552, Malvern College 1865, Royal Grammar, Worcester 1290, Sebright, Wolverley 1618

Yorks: Archbishop Holgate's, York 1547, Ampleforth 1802, Bootham, York 1823, Bradford Grammar by 1548, Giggleswick 1512, Leeds Grammar 1552, Pocklington 1514, St Peter's, York 6th century, Sedburgh 1527, Woodhouse Grove, Bradford 1812.

J39 Oxford University. The foundation dates of the Oxford Colleges and Halls are as follows:

All Souls 1437, Balliol 1263, Brasenose 1509, Christ Church 1532, Corpus Christi 1516, Exeter 1314, Hertford 1874, Jesus 1571, Keble 1870, Lady Margaret 1878, Lincoln 1427, Magdalen 1458, Mansfield 1886, Merton 1264, New 1379, Nuffield 1937, Oriel 1326, Pembroke 1624, Queen's 1340, St Anne's 1952, St Anthony's 1950, St Catherine's 1962, St John's 1555, St Peter's 1929, Somerville 1879, Trinity 1554, University 1249, Wadham 1612, Worcester 1714

J40 Cambridge University. The foundation dates of the Cambridge Colleges and Halls are as follows:

Christ's 1505, Churchill 1960, Clare 1326, Corpus Christi 1352, Downing 1800, Emmanuel 1584, Fitzwilliam 1869, Gonville and Caius 1348, Jesus 1496, King's 1441, Magdalene 1542, Pembroke 1347, Peterhouse 1284, Queen's 1448, St Catherine's 1473, St John's 1511, Selwyn 1882, Sidney Sussex 1596, Trinity 1546, Trinity Hall 1350

J41 Other Universities. The foundation dates of other principal universities are as follows:

Aberdeen 1494, Belfast 1908, Birmingham 1900, Bristol 1909, Dublin (Trinity) 1591, Dundee 1967, Durham 1831, East Anglia 1963, Edinburgh 1582, Essex 1963, Exeter 1955, Glasgow 1450, Hull 1927–54, Keele 1949–62, Kent 1963, Lancaster 1694, Leeds 1904, Leicester 1918–57, Liverpool 1881–1903, London (University College) 1826, London (King's) 1829, London School of Economics 1895, Manchester 1851–80, Newcastle 1963, Nottingham 1881–1938, Reading 1892–1926, St Andrew's 1411, Sheffield 1905, Southampton 1862–1952, Surrey 1966, Sussex 1961, Wales 1893, York 1963.

Bibliography

PART FOUR
BIBLIOGRAPHY

A History of English Education from 1760, H. C. Bernard (1961)
Four Hundred Years of English Education, W. H. G. Armytage (1970)
History of Education in Great Britain, S. J. Curtis (1948 rev. 1967)
Blond's Encyclopedia of Education, ed. Edward Blishen
Education Charters and Documents AD598 to 1909, A. F. Leach (1911)
The History of Scottish Education, James Scotland (2 vols 1969)
Samuel Wilderspin and the Infant School Movement, Phillip McCann and Francis A. Young (1982)
Elementary Education in the Nineteenth Century, Gillian Sutherland (1971)
The Rise of the Public Schools, T. W. Bamford (1967)
The Public Schools, Brian Gardner (1973)
The Charity School Movement, M. G. Jones (1938)
The Education of the People, Mary Sturt (1967)
Secondary Education in the Nineteenth Century, R. L. Archer (1966)
A Centenary of Education 1808–1908, Henry B. Binns (1908). (A history of the British and Foreign School Society).

English Universities, Hastings Rashdall (1895 rev. 1936)
English Schools at the Reformation 1546–8, A. F. Leach (1896)
The Schools of Medieval England, A. F. Leach (1915)
The Educational Innovators 1750–1880, W. A. C. Stewart and W. P. McCann (1967)
Hope Deferred, (re education for girls), Josephine Kamm (1965)
A History of Adult Education in Great Britain, Thomas Kelly (1970)

SECTION K

Social Welfare

PART ONE
THE RELIEF OF THE POOR

K1 1388. An attempt was made to control vagrancy. If a parish could not maintain a beggar who was unable to work, out of its own resources, he was sent back to his birthplace. Vagrants capable of working were severely dealt with. A labourer was prohibited from leaving his own parish unless provided with a testimonial issued by authority of the Justices of the Peace.

K2 Statute of Mortmain 1391. In parishes where the Great or Rectorial Tithes were held by an ecclesiastical institution, such as a monastery, a proportion of the tithe income was to be used for the relief of the poor.

K3 1494. Vagrants capable of working were subjected to severe penalties such as whipping, the loss of ears and hanging.

K4 1530/1. Vagrants incapable of working were obliged to obtain a begging licence from the magistrates.

K5 1535/6. With the suppression of the monasteries the parishes were made responsible for the care of the impotent poor. Private alms-giving was made an offence, and carried a penalty of ten times the amount given; however, the priest and churchwardens were empowered to solicit charitable donations on Sundays. A start was made in setting capable beggars to work, and penalties similar to those of 1494 for able-bodied vagrants were re-imposed.

K6 1547. The measures of 1535/6 were modified. A vagrant who refused work was to be branded with the letter 'V' (for vagabond), and adjudged to be a slave for two years; if he ran away during that period he was branded with an 'S' on his cheek and adjudged a slave for life.

K7 Poor Law 1563. It was enacted that 'two able persons or more shall be appointed gatherers and collectors of the charitable alms of all the residue of people inhabiting in the parish'. Often the churchwardens were appointed Col-

147

lectors; the Act gave them limited powers to compel or encourage generosity.

K8 1572. The office of Overseer of the Poor was created. Overseers were elected by the vestry subject to the approval of the Justices of the Peace. They supervised endowments and other charitable funds.

K9 1597/8. Parishes were allowed to levy a poor rate and from this, some poorhouses were built. Work was to be provided for paupers and a stock of raw materials kept for this purpose. As far as possible pauper children were to be apprenticed.

K10 Poor Law Act 1601. This Act was the basis for Poor Law administration for two centuries. It divided the poor receiving relief into three categories: the able-bodied who were to be found work, the impotent poor, and people who were unwilling to work. This classification was still in evidence in the 20th century. It was enacted that in each parish the churchwardens and two or more substantial landholders should act as Overseers of the Poor and collect the poor rate. The rate was to be spent in four main ways: (a) 'for setting to work the children of all such whose parents shall not be thought able to maintain them'; (b) 'for setting to work all such persons, married or unmarried, having no means to maintain them, and who use no ordinary or daily trade of life to get their living by' [ie the able-bodied pauper]; (c) 'for providing a convenient stock of flax, hemp, wood, thread, iron and other ware and stuff to set the poor on work'; (d) 'for the necessary relief of the lame, impotent, old, blind, and such other among them being poor and not able to work.'

K11 Law of Settlement 1662. A stranger in a parish could be removed by the Overseers of the Parish if he had no prospect of work within 40 days, or if he did not rent property worth £10 per annum. A temporary worker, at harvest time for example, was required to obtain a certificate from his home parish guaranteeing to take him back. After 40 days a stranger could claim settlement and poor relief in his adopted parish.

K12 1691. It was enacted that a register of parishioners in receipt of poor relief should be kept.

K13 Settlement Act 1697. Strangers were allowed to settle in a new parish if they were armed with a certificate from their home parish guaranteeing to take them back if they became in need of poor relief. Paupers were to wear a capital P on their clothing followed by a letter indicating the name of their parish.

K14 Knatchbull's General Workhouse Act 1723.
Single parishes were empowered to erect workhouses; small parishes could form a union with others to make such a building viable. By 1776 there were about 2,000 workhouses in England. Generally the poor were restricted to the building except for Sundays. Vagrant children could be apprenticed against the wishes of their parents; illegitimate children did not necessarily receive a settlement certificate for the parish of their birth. The sheltering of vagrants outside the workhouse was forbidden.

K15 Gilbert's Act 1782. Parishes were encouraged to combine with others to form unions and independent inspectors were appointed. The able-bodied were provided with employment outside the workhouse; indoor relief in the workhouses was confined to the impotent poor. Children under seven were allowed to remain with their parents and orphan children were boarded out. Paupers of good character were not obliged to wear the pauper's badge.

K16 The Speenhamland System c1795. At a time of high prices and low wages parishes attempted to supplement earnings with an allowance related to the prevailing price of bread. Interpretation of this supplementary benefit differed from parish to parish, but its provision became generally known from the method adopted in the Berkshire village of Speenhamland. The system encouraged employers to reduce wages in the knowledge that the parish would make up the difference. A further consequence was a general depression of wages which threw even more people on to poor relief.

K17 Care of Lunatics 1815. Parish overseers were instructed to send lists of pauper lunatics to the Clerk of the Peace, who laid them before Quarter Sessions.

K18 Poor Law Amendment Act 1834. This Act was to be the basis for poor law administration in a period when poor relief was at its height. It minimised the provision of outdoor relief and made confinement in a workhouse the central element of the new system. While acknowledging that workhouses should receive the impotent and helpless poor as a haven and last resort, it also encouraged administrators to make workhouses as unpleasant as possible in an effort to deter people from seeking relief. Therefore, married couples were separated and children were taken from their parents; communication between them was not allowed in communal places such as chapel or refectory, and only infrequent reunions were permitted.

From 1834 to 1847 the Poor Law was administered by three Poor Law Commissioners who employed Assistant Commissioners for local inspection. The Commissioners actively encouraged or coerced parishes into unions so as to make the provision of large workhouse buildings viable. Boards of Guardians were appointed at local level to manage poor relief in the parish, although the vestry continued to levy the rate.

K19 Poor Law Board 1847. From 1847 to 1871 the Poor Law Board was responsible for the administration of the Poor Law although in effect the Board did not meet and its work was carried out by civil servants.

K20 Local Government Board 1871. This Board was set up to control a range of matters, especially public health, but it also administered the Poor Law until 1919 when the Ministry of Health became responsible.

K21 1913. The workhouse was officially retitled a 'Poor Law Institution'. Indoor relief was increasingly confined to the impotent poor.

K22 National Insurance Act 1911. This Act began the provision of social insurance; in 1946 the modern framework of benefits was established.

K23 Local Government Act 1929. Boards of Guardians were abolished as, too, was the term 'pauper'. The powers of the Guardians were transferred to local authorities such as county councils or county boroughs. Local boroughs were encouraged to convert workhouses into infirmaries.

PART TWO
HOSPITALS AND ASYLUMS

K24 Hospitals and Asylums. The foundation dates of some of the major hospitals and asylums are as follows:

Bath General	1738
Belgrave Hospital for Children	1866
Bethel (Norwich)	1713
Bethlem, London (as a priory)	1247
Brompton Hospital for Diseases of the Chest	1841
Cancer Hospital, Fulham Road	1851
Central London Ophthalmic	1843
Central London Throat and Ear Hospital	1876
Charing Cross (previously West London Infirmary)	1818
City of London Lying-in	1750
Colney Hatch Lunatic Asylum	1851
Devon and Exeter Hospital	1753
Durham, Newcastle-upon-Tyne and Northumberland Infirmary	c1745
East London Hospital for Children	1868
Eastman Dental Hospital	1930
Elizabeth Garrett Anderson (previously the New Hospital for Women)	1872
Exeter Eye Hospital	1806
Florence Nightingale (previously the Institute for Sick Governesses)	1850
Foundling Hospital, London	1739
General Lying-in	1765
Gloucester Infirmary	1745
Grosvenor Hospital for Women	1866
Guys Hospital	1721
Hanwell Asylum	1831
Hereford General Infirmary	1776
Hospital for Diseases of the Throat, London	1863
Hospital for Sick Children, London	1852
House of Recovery, London	1802
Hull Royal Infirmary	1784
Kensington Children's Hospital	1840
King Edward VIII Hospital for Officers	1899
King's College, London	1839
Leeds Hospital for Women	1853
Leeds Infirmary	1767
Leicester Infirmary	1771
Lincoln County	1769
Liverpool Infirmary for Children	1857
Liverpool Royal Infirmary	1745
Liverpool Royal Lunatic Asylum	1792
Lock Hospital for Women, London	1746
London Fever Hospital	c1801
London Homeopathic Hospital	1850
London Hospital	1740

London Skin Hospital	1887	Westminster Lying-in	1765
Magdalen	1738	Worcester Royal Infirmary	1746
Manchester Fever Hospital	1796	York County	1740
Manchester Hospital for Children	1829	York Lunatic Asylum	1777
Manchester Royal Infirmary	1752		
Manchester Royal Lunatic Asylum	1766		
Metropolitan Ear, Nose and Throat	1838		
Middlesex Hospital	1745		

K25 Medieval Hospitals. A comprehensive list of medieval hospitals, arranged under counties, is contained in Rotha Mary Clay's book *The Medieval Hospitals of England* (1909).

Moorfields Eye Hospital	1805
National Dental Hospital	1861
National Hospital for Diseases of the Heart	1857
National Hospital for Paralysis and Epilepsy	1859
National Temperance Hospital	1873
Nottingham General	1782
Poplar Hospital for Accidents	1855
Queen Charlotte's Hospital	1739
Queen's Hospital for Children	1867
Radcliffe Infirmary, Oxford	1770
Royal Dental, London	1858
Royal Ear, London	1816
Royal Eye, London	1857
Royal Free, London	1828
Royal Hospital for Diseases of the Chest	1814
Royal Hospital for Incurables	1854
Royal National Orthopaedic	1838
Royal Sea Bathing Hospital, Margate	1796
Royal Westminster Ophthalmic	c1816
Royal Waterloo Hospital for Children and Women	1816
St Bartholomew's, London	c1123
St Bartholomew's, Dover	c1141
St George's, London	1733
St John's, Oxford	c1180
Refounded	1233
St John's, Canterbury	c1084
St Leonard's, York (previously St Peter's)	c937
St Luke's Hospital for Lunatics, London	1751
St Mark's Hospital for Cancer	1835
St Peter's York (see St Leonard's)	
St Peter's, Bristol	1696
St Peter's Hospital for Stone, London	1860
St Thomas's, London	c1213
Samaritan Free Hospital for Women	1847
Sheffield Royal Infirmary	1832
Shrewsbury Infirmary	1745
Smallpox Hospital, Kings Cross, London	1767
Taunton and Somerset Hospital	c1810
University College Hospital, London	1828
Victoria Park Hospital for Diseases of the Heart and Lungs	1848
Wakefield Hospital	1787
Westminster Hospital	1720

PART THREE
PHILANTHROPIC BODIES

K26 Philanthropic Bodies. The foundation dates of the more important organisations are listed below:

Alleged Lunatics Friend Society	c1851
Anti-Slavery Society	1823
Association for Promoting the General Welfare of the Blind	1856
Association for the Christian and Domestic Improvement of Young Women	c1860
Association for the Relief of the Manufacturing and Labouring Poor	1811
Baptist Missionary Society	1793
Barnardo's Homes	1866
British and Foreign Bible Society	1814
British and Foreign School Society	1814
Charity Organization Society	1869
Church Building Society	1818
City Parochial Foundation (London)	1891
Destitute Children's Dinner Society	1864
Discharged Prisoners Aid Society	1857
East End Dwellings Company	1884
Edinburgh Society for Improving the Condition of the Poor	1867
Four Per Cent Industrial Dwellings Co.	1886
General Society for the Improvement of Dwellings of the Working Classes	1852
Guinness Trust	1889
Home Teaching Society for the Blind	1855
Improved Industrial Dwellings Co	c1863
Leeds Society for the Erection of Improved Dwellings	c1860
Liverpool Central Relief Society	1863
London Missionary Society	1795
London Society for the Prevention of Cruelty to Children (later National Society)	1884
London Society for Teaching the Blind to Read	1839
Marine Society	1756
Metropolitan Association for Improving	

the Dwellings of the Industrious Classes	1841
Metropolitan Drinking Fountain and Cattle Trough Association	1859
National Society for Promoting Education	1809
Peabody Trust	1862
Philanthrophic Society (for children)	1788
Ragged School Union	1844
Relief of the Infant Poor	1769
Royal National Lifeboat Institution	1824
Royal Society for the Prevention of Cruelty to Animals	1824
Society for Bettering the Condition of the Poor	c1800
Society for Improving the Condition of the Labouring Classes	c1844
Society for Promoting Christian Knowledge	1698
Society for the Propagation of the Gospel in Foreign Parts	1701
Society for the Relief of Distress	1860
Sunday School Society	1785
Thatched House Society (for those in debtors' prisons)	1773

PART FOUR
MISCELLANEOUS

K27 Almshouses. Buildings erected by private individuals, religious bodies, trade guilds and livery companies, to house old or infirm poor people. Alternatively called Bedehouses or Spital Houses.

K28 Badgers. A term derived from the Settlement Act 1697 (qv) which obliged paupers to wear a capital 'P' on their clothing. This practice was abolished in 1810. The term was later used loosely for pedlars and chapmen.

K29 Bareman. A pauper. Alternatively spelt Bairman.

K30 Bastardy. An Act of 1576 enabled Justices to imprison the parents of an illegitimate child. Another of 1610 allowed the mother to be sent to prison unless she could give securities for her future good behaviour. Usually the child would receive the same settlement rights as its mother but if the father was known to be from another parish the child and mother would be settled in the father's parish if the parents married.

An Act of 1733 obliged the mother to declare that she was pregnant with an illegitimate child, and to reveal the father's name. Parish officials would then attempt to obtain a maintenance sum from him by way of a Bond of Indemnity; this could be either a lump sum or moneys paid over a period.

K31 Cess. In this context, a donation from public funds to a poor parish.

K32 Collectioner. A pauper in receipt of relief from parish funds.

K33 Dole. In this context, the distribution of money or provisions to the poor.

K34 Hundred House. A workhouse erected by a union of parishes within a Hundred (qv).

K35 Leatherhouse. A London term for a poorhouse.

K36 Removal. This describes the removal of a pauper to the parish legally bound to maintain him.

K37 Second Poor. Poor people not in receipt of poor relief.

K38 Union. A combination of parishes formed to administer poor relief and to build workhouses.

PART FIVE
BIBLIOGRAPHY

Poor Law Administration
Early History of English Poor Relief, E. M. Leonard (1900)
Poor Relief in Elizabethan Ipswich, J. Webb (1966)
The Old Poor Law 1795–1834, J. D. Marshall (2nd ed. 1985)
The Poor Law in Nineteenth-century England and Wales, Anne Digby (1982)
The New Poor Law in the Nineteenth Century, ed. D. Fraser (1976)
The Anti-Poor Law Movement 1843–44, Nicholas Edsall (1971)
The English Poor Law 1780–1930, Michael Rose (1971)
English Poor Law History parts 1 and 2, Sidney and Beatrice Webb (3 vols 1963 edition)
The Workhouse System 1834–1929, M. A. Crowther (1981)
The Workhouse, N. Longmate (1974)
Reminiscences of a Workhouse Medical Officer, J. Rogers (1889)

Bibliography *(cont)*

A History of Vagrants and Vagrancy, C. Ribton-Turner (1887)
London Labour and the London Poor, Henry Mayhew (4 vols 1861–2)
Life and Labour of the People in London, Charles Booth (17 vols)
Poverty: A Study of Town Life, Seerbohm Rowntree (1901)
History of the English Poor Law. Vol 1 *924–1714*, G. Nicholls (1898), Vol 2 *1714–1853*, G. Nicholls (1898), Vol 3 *1834–1894*, T. Mackay (1899)

Public Health
Doctors and Disease in Tudor Times, W. S. C. Copeman (1960)
The Rise of the Medical Profession, N. Parry and J. Parry (1976)
The Medical Profession in Mid-Victorian London, M. J. Peterson (1978)
History of English Public Health 1834–1939, W. M. Frazer (1950)
Public Health in the Victorian Age, introduction by Ruth Hodgkinson (2 vols 1973)
Endangered Lives: Public Health in Victorian Britain, Anthony S. Wohl (1983)
Edwin Chadwick and the Public Health Movement 1832–1854, R. A. Lewis (1952)
Public Health in the Nineteenth Century, C. Fraser Brockington (1965)
The Sanitary Evolution of London, H. Jephson (1907)
A History of Epidemics in Britain, C. Creighton (2 vols 1891 repr. 1965)
The History of Diseases, F. Henschen (1966)
The Conquest of Smallpox, P. Razzell (1977)
Cholera 1832, R. J. Morris (1976)

Hospitals
Elizabeth Garrett Anderson, Jo Manton (1965)
The Medieval Hospitals of England, Rotha Mary Clay (1909)
The Story of England's Hospitals, Courtney Dainton (1961)
English Hospital Statistics 1861–1938, R. Pinker (1966)
The Hospitals, Brian Abel-Smith (1964)
Mr Guy's Hospital 1726–1948, H. C. Cameron (1954)
History of St Thomas's Hospital, F. G. Parsons (3 vols 1932)
A History of the Mental Health Services, Kathleen Jones (1972)
Museums of Madness, A. T. Scull (1979)
The Trade in Lunacy: A Study of Private Madhouses in England in the 18th and 19th centuries, William L. Parry-Jones (1972)
A History of the Royal College of Physicians, Sir George Clark (2 vols 1962)
The History of the Royal College of Surgeons, Z. Cope (1959)
The Story of the Growth of Nursing, Agnes Pavey (rev. 1959)

Philanthrophy
Charities, B. Nightingale
English Philanthropy, D. Owen (1964)
Philanthrophy in England 1480–1660, W. K. Jordan (1959)
History of English Philanthrophy, B. K. Gray (1905)
The Charities of London 1480–1660, W. K. Jordan (1960)
Charities of Rural England 1480–1660, W. K. Jordan (1961)

SECTION L

Law and Order

PART ONE
THE DEVELOPMENT OF THE POLICE

L1 Statute of Winchester 1285. This Statute rationalised the primitive system of policing and reaffirmed the obigation of a locality to keep its own law and order. In the towns it introduced the system called Watch and Ward. Watch was the term for the night guard of constables and Ward referred to their duties in the daytime. Up to sixteen men were to guard the walls through the night and place any wrongdoers in the hands of the parish constable the next day.

The Statute also introduced the system of Hue and Cry in which a person wishing to make an arrest could call on the rest of the parish to join him in pursuit. This system still has a modern application in the obligation of the public to assist the police, if requested, in making an arrest.

The third major innovation of the Statute was the establishment of the Assize of Arms. Each man aged between 15 and 60 had to keep weapons or effects with which to help keep the peace – the higher a person's rank, the more expensive the weapons. The High Constables in each Hundred inspected the arms twice a year.

L2 Parish Constable. Throughout the post-Norman period the unpaid parish constable or petty constable emerged as the local peace-keeper. His duties are noted under B148.

L3 Local Acts from 1750. From this date many areas promoted their own Acts of Parliament to obtain powers to levy a rate to pay for lighting and watching streets.

L4 Metropolitan Police Act 1829. This Act, which took effect from the beginning of 1830, set up one police force for the metropolitan area of London, but excluding the City of London. The force was under the jurisdiction of the Home Secretary.

L5 Lighting and Watching Act 1833. This Act permitted any town with a population of over 5,000 to appoint paid watchmen.

L6 Municipal Corporations Act 1835. Each of the 178 boroughs was required to appoint a watch committee which, in its turn, appointed constables. The committee was to include not more than one third of the town council plus the mayor.

L7 County Police Act 1839. This was a permissive measure which enabled the Justices of the Peace to set up paid county police forces. An Act the following year authorised the amalgamation of borough and county forces where it was thought desirable. The County and Borough Police Act 1856 required the Justices to establish a force for any parts of the county still not covered.

L8 County Police Forces The approximate dates for the formation of county police forces are as follows:

Anglesey	1856/7
Bedfordshire	1840
Berkshire	1856/7
Breconshire	1856/7
Buckinghamshire	1856/7
Caernarvonshire	1856/7
Cambridgeshire	1851
Cardiganshire	1844
Carmarthenshire	1856/7
Cheshire	1856/7
Cornwall	1856/7
Cumberland	1840
Denbighshire	1840
Derbyshire	1856/7
Devon	1856/7
Dorset	1856/7
Durham	1839
Essex	1839
Flintshire	1856/7
Glamorgan	1839
Gloucestershire	1839
Hampshire	1839
Herefordshire	1841
Hertfordshire	1841
Huntingdonshire	1856/7
Isle of Ely	1841
Kent	1856/7
Lancashire	1839
Leicestershire	1839

Lincolnshire	1856/7
Merionethshire	1856/7
Monmouthshire	1856/7
Montgomeryshire	1840
Norfolk	1840
Northamptonshire	1840
Northumberland	1856/7
Nottinghamshire	1840
Oxfordshire	1856/7
Pembrokeshire	1856/7
Radnor	1856/7
Rutland	1849
Shropshire	1840
Somerset	1856/7
Staffordshire	1840
Suffolk (East)	1840
Suffolk (West)	1856/7
Surrey	1851
Sussex (East)	1840
Sussex (West)	1856/7
Warwickshire	1840
Westmorland	1856/7
Wiltshire	1839
Worcestershire	1839
Yorkshire (East)	1856/7
Yorkshire (North)	1856/7
Yorkshire (West)	1856/7

L9 Local Government Act 1888. This Act abolished police forces run by boroughs with a population of less than 10,000.

L10 Police Act 1946. This Act abolished 45 non-county police forces, and the watch committees in those boroughs lost their police powers. The Brecon, Radnor and Montgomeryshire county forces were amalgamated.

L11 Police in Scotland. An Act of 1857 established county forces on the same lines as those outlined in the legislation for England and Wales in 1856.

PART TWO
PRISONS

L12 General. Imprisonment as a punishment had evolved by the reign of Henry VII but freedom could usually be bought. Even up to the 19th century prisons were not regarded as primarily for punishment or for the protection of society. This was because a great many offences were punishable by death or transportation, which were punishment and protection enough. Between 1688 and 1765 the number of offences for which the nominal penalty was death increased from about 50 to about 160 and by the early 19th century had reached over 200.

The main function of prisons was to hold prisoners awaiting trial or sentence, or to hold debtors until they or their families repaid their debts. The most important exception to this were the Houses of Correction established to cope with the increased amount of vagrancy. This had resulted from the suppression of the monasteries and their almsgiving function, and the establishment of the Elizabethan poor law which decreed that able-bodied vagrants were not entitled to poor relief. The Houses of Correction were an attempt, not just to punish, but to reform the prisoners by the imposition of hard labour and other ordeals.

Early prisons were located in castles, churches, large houses and fortified gateways. The first purpose-built prison appears to be that of Hexham, Northumberland in 1330.

L13 Early Prisons. Some early prisons, in castles, large houses or purpose-built, are as follows:

Bedfordshire: Bedford 1165
Berks: Faringdon 1238, Wallingford 1241, Windsor 1260
Buckinghamshire: Aylesbury 1165, Buckingham 1213, High Wycombe 13th century
Cambs: Cambridge 1165, Wisbech
Cheshire: Chester 1237
Cornwall: Bodmin 19th century, Callington, Helston 1184, Launceston 1186
Cumberland: Cockermouth 1394
Derbyshire: Bakewell 1286
Devon: Exeter 1296, Plymouth
Dorset: Dorchester 1305
Durham: Durham 1247, Sadberge 1303
Essex: Colchester 1274, Newport 1177, Rayleigh 1254
Glos: Bristol 1240, Gloucester 1184, Tewkesbury 1273
Hants: Portsmouth 1278, Southampton 1182, Winchester 1250
Herefordshire: Hereford 1300
Herts: St Albans 1220
Hunts: Huntingdon 1171
Kent: Canterbury 1165, Faversham 1254, Maidstone 1279, Rochester 1165
Lancs: Kirkham 1296, Lancaster 1196, Manchester 1187, Preston 1200
Leics: Leicester 1208, Rothley 1165
Lincs: Lincoln 1254, Grimsby 1260

London: Bridewell 1829, Clink 14th century, Fleet 1290, Holloway 1851, Marshalsea 11th century, Newgate 1200, Millbank 1821, Pentonville 1842, Wandsworth 1851
Norfolk: Great Yarmouth 1213, King's Lynn 1212, Norwich 1165
Northants: Northampton, Peterborough 1275
Northumberland: Hexham 1330, Newcastle
Notts: Newark, Nottingham 1177
Oxfordshire: Oxford 1231
Rutland: Oakham 1253
Shropshire: Bridgnorth 1234, Shrewsbury 1221
Somerset: Bath 1275, Ilchester 1166, Taunton 1243, Wells.
Staffs: Newcastle-under-Lyme 1198, Stafford 1185
Suffolk: Ipswich 1163, Orford 1244
Surrey: Dorking 1279, Guildford 1207, Kingston-upon-Thames 1220, Reigate 1279
Sussex: Chichester 1197, Lewes 1487, Steyning 1477, Winchelsea 1200
Warks: Kenilworth 1185, Kineton 1165, Warwick 1200
Westmorland: Appleby 1227
Wilts: Malmesbury 1166, Salisbury 1166, Westbury 1460, Wilton 1249
Worcs: Worcester 1216
Yorkshire: Hull 129, Halifax, Knaresborough, Sheffield, Tickhill 1165, York 1165

L14 Bridewell. A common term for a county gaol, but the name became synonymous with a London prison at Blackfriars.

L15 Cage. Many parishes had temporary lock-ups, called Cages, usually on the village green, for the temporary imprisonment of alleged offenders before conveyance to a securer place.

L16 Clink. A colloquial term for a prison or cell, but more commonly applied to a prison in Southwark, London.

L17 Compter. A debtor's prison under the supervision of a sheriff; a term most commonly found in London.

L18 Franchise Prison. In Plantagenet times the Crown granted lords the right, or franchise, to maintain prisons. Neither the owner of the prison nor the Crown undertook to maintain the prisoners and the owner exacted his expenses and profits from the relatives and friends of the inmates. The last franchise prisons, those of Halifax, Hexham, Knaresborough, Newark, Sheffield and Swansea, were abolished in 1858.

L19 House of Correction. A county gaol most commonly used to house vagrants, beggars and unmarried mothers, where they were given hard labour as a remedial measure.

L20 Marshalsea Money. Parishes were obliged, via a county rate, to contribute to the relief of the poor prisoners in the King's Bench and Marshalsea prisons.

L21 Pledgehouse. A prison where debtors were kept.

L22 Rogue Money. Parishes were obliged to contribute to the relief of poor prisoners in county gaols.

L23 Round House. A village lock up, usually with no windows, and with the light coming in from a domed roof. It was also called a Blind House, Cage or Lob's Pound.

L24 Toll Booth. Apart from its use as a market court building it could also be used as a town gaol.

PART THREE
JUDICIAL AUTHORITIES

L25 Hundred Courts. Hundred Courts appeared in the 10th century. They were essentially folkmoots presided over by the Hundred bailiff and met, at least in Saxon times, monthly. This would indicate that they may have been, at that time, more important than the shire courts which met only twice a year. Their use was reduced under the Norman legal system which was based on the county as the unit of administration.

L26 Sheriff's Tourn. Twice a year, within a month after Easter and Michaelmas, the sheriff presided at a special session of the Hundred Court (qv). His main function was to review the Frankpledge (qv) and to see that tithings were up to strength. He also dealt with minor criminal cases but the more serious offences were dealt with by the Justices in Eyre (qv).

After the Assize of Clarendon 1166 the sheriff also had the power to oversee the manorial courts in their management of the Frankpledge. The effective power of the Sheriff's Tourn came to an end in 1461 when the cases formerly presided over by the sheriff were transferred to the Justices of the Peace in Quarter Sessions. The Tourn was formally abolished in 1887.

L27 Shire/County Courts. Shire Courts in Saxon and early Norman times consisted of freemen of the county and were presided over by an earldorman. They met twice a year and dealt with civil and criminal cases, the suitors also being the judges. Local knowledge was important in arriving at a verdict, for defendants were judged by reputation rather than by evidence. Innocence could be established by compurgation, a practice whereby a defendant called sufficient good-character witnesses to warrant such a verdict.

The Normans established the sheriff in charge of these courts and gradually they became part of the king's justice and administration. Until 1072 bishops also sat in at the courts, assisting the ealdorman or sheriff but they were removed when separate ecclesiastical courts were established. As from 1166 Justices in Eyre (qv) sat in the county courts dealing with the more important cases with the sheriff as their subordinate. More restrictions were placed on the sheriff when coroners were first appointed in 1194.

The Shire Courts declined in importance from the 13th century with the rise of the importance of Quarter Sessions, but they were revised by the County Courts Act 1846 to deal mainly with disputes concerning land.

L28 Honorial Courts. An Honor was a collection of estates owned by a tenant-in-chief of the Crown, which could be scattered over a large area. The owners were permitted to maintain their own courts which dealt mainly with disputes concerning landholdings.

L29 Possessory Assizes. A collective name to describe the three Assizes of Novel Disseisin, Mort d'Ancestor, and Darrein Presentment (qv).

L30 Assize of Darrein Presentment. Established in the reign of Henry II, this Assize was concerned with the dispossession of advowsons (qv). The plaintiff was able to obtain a writ which called on the sheriff to summon a jury to pronounce if the plaintiff had the right to present a benefice. The Assize was formally abolished in 1833.

L31 Assize of Mort d'Ancestor. Established by the Assize of Northampton 1176, this was concerned with cases where the plaintiff claimed he had been dispossessed of a property that was his by inheritance. The plaintiff obtained a writ which obliged the sheriff to summon a jury to pronounce on the matter from its local knowledge. Cases of this nature arose most frequently where lords had repossessed property on the death of a tenant. The procedure was formally abolished in 1833.

L32 Assize of Novel Disseisin. Novel Disseisin means 'recent dispossession'. Under a procedure begun in 1166, a tenant unjustly ejected from a holding was able to obtain a writ instructing the sheriff to summon a jury to pronounce on his plea. Originally this action could only be brought in cases of recent dispossession but gradually the assizes dealt with cases involving longer periods. The procedure came in time to be used for fictional court cases to establish title. It was formally abolished in 1833.

L33 Justices in Eyre. As from 1166, and possibly earlier, the king's justices were sent on circuits, called Eyres, to sit at sessions of county courts for a short period. (The term 'Eyre' is derived from the Latin *itinere*, meaning 'on journey'). The responsibilities of the justices included an audit of the royal revenues, the hearing of Crown pleas, and the inspection of the administration of the county. Their main contribution was a standardised form of justice whereas in the county courts justice was usually administered to local standards. However, the justices appeared at the county courts very infrequently and this caused inconvenience to plaintiffs, defendants and witnesses.

L34 Court of Common Pleas. A court, otherwise known as the Court of Common Bench, which developed from the 12th century as a subdivision of the king's court. Unlike the Court of King's Bench (qv), it remained in London and, indeed, the Magna Carta stipulated that it should. Its jurisdiction was confined to civil cases between subjects.

L35 Court of King's (or Queen's) Bench. A court senior to the Court of Common Pleas with which it was contemporary. It dealt with criminal and civil cases, particularly those in which the king had an interest. Though based in London it travelled with the king, but from 1400 it rarely left the capital. In 1873 its jurisdiction was assigned to the Queen's Bench Division of the High Court of Justice.

L36 Court of Requests. Courts used for the recovery of small debts; they were superseded by the county courts.

L37 Commission of Oyer and Terminer. A Commission to 'hear and determine' cases dealing with treasons, murders and other misdemeanours. The Commission dealt only with cases within the county in question. The system of commissioning judges was less cumbersome than the Justices in Eyre (qv).

L38 Commission of Gaol Delivery. Indicted prisoners were held in gaols awaiting trial. Itinerant judges were commissioned by the Crown to try the prisoners and deliver them, (set them free), if they were found innocent.

L39 Grand Assize. An Assize which developed from the 12th century. Where a tenant had to defend his right to land a sheriff was issued with a writ of peace. He nominated four knights of the shire who elected twelve other knights. Their findings were conveyed to the Justices in Eyre. This Assize was formally abolished in 1833.

L40 Quarter Sessions. The meetings of the county justices held four times a year. Their origin stems from 1361 when Keepers of the Peace were made into Justices and empowered to determine cases as well as to bring them. From 1363 they began to meet quarterly. In 1461 the indictments which up to then had been heard at the Sheriff's Tourn (qv) were heard instead at Quarter Sessions. The courts had no power to hear civil cases but were able to deal with murder, riot, theft, assault, poaching etc. They could not deal with forgery or treason. From 1531 they also dealt with the administration of the Poor Law and in 1601 appointed the Overseers of the Poor for each parish.

The Sessions were usually attended by the High Sheriff or his deputy, and high and petty constables. The Clerk of the Peace was the officer and legal adviser of the court.

L41 Star Chamber. A court revived in 1487 to deal with perjury, serious misdemeanours and riots. It was abolished in 1640.

L42 Petty Sessions. A minor court presided over by two or more justices or magistrates.

L43 Brewster Sessions. The annual sessions to license victuallers held in the first fortnight of February. They were established in 1729.

L44 Barmote Courts. Courts having jurisdiction in Peak District mining areas in which the Crown is entitled to mineral duties.

L45 Stannaries Courts. A court for Cornwall and Devon which dealt with matters relating to tin mines and their workers. It was abolished in 1896 and its jurisdiction transferred to county courts.

L46 Courts of Commissioners of Sewers. Courts established by 1531 with jurisdiction over sea defences, navigation of rivers in specified areas, etc. They were formally abolished in 1930.

L47 Court of Hustings. A court in the City of London and some other cities which was the equivalent of a county court.

L48 Central Criminal Court. A court established in 1834 to try offences committed in London and Middlesex, and some parts of Essex, Kent and Surrey.

PART FOUR
JUDICIAL OFFICERS

L49 Clerk of the Peace. Clerks of the Peace were established by 1380 and possibly earlier. Their function was and is to keep the records of Quarter Sessions and to frame presentments and indictments. They have legal training so that they may advise the Justices.

L50 Coroner. See B149.

L51 Justices of the Peace. Keepers of the Peace were appointed to each county in 1277 and 1287. In 1361 the Keepers became Justices with power to hear cases as well as to bring them. In the 14th century there were four or five Justices to each county; an Act of 1388 allowed for six, another of 1390 for eight. By 1565 there were thirty or forty for each county.

In 1368 the Justices were made responsible for wage regulations and in 1461 the cases previously heard at the Sheriff's Tourn were transferred to Quarter Sessions. Gradually the Justices' civil functions increased: they enforced laws against Catholics, hawkers and brewers, and oversaw the administration of the Poor Laws. Matters which came before them are dealt with more fully in D177–229.

L52 Bailiff. In this context, a court official appointed to execute writs and processes and to distrain goods where necessary.

L53 Official Assignee. An officer of a bankruptcy court who acted in the winding up of a bankrupt's estate. He has been superseded by the Official Receiver.

L54 Puisne Judge. A junior judge in the courts of common law.

L55 Judge Ordinary. The judge of the former Court of Probate; he is now the President of the Probate, Divorce and Admiralty Division.

PART FIVE
CRIMES AND PUNISHMENTS

L56 Attainder. A person convicted of treason or other capital felony which also resulted in the forfeiture of his goods, was said to have had his blood corrupted, or attainted, by this punishment.

L57 Branding. The punishment by branding, of vagrants who refused to work, dated from at least 1547. An Act of 1650 allowed for the branding of the letter B on the forehead of women who were bawds or kept bawdy houses, and an Act of 1699 allowed for the branding of prostitutes on the cheek.

L58 Brawling. Acts of 1551 and 1553 made it an offence to brawl or quarrel in any churchyard, or to use force or to create a disturbance in church during divine service. Such offences could be punished by excommunication.

L59 Cucking Stool. A device commonly identified with that called a Ducking Stool (qv), but which was originally a primitive commode on which the victim was displayed ignominiously and subjected to abuse and missiles from the population. It was a punishment usually reserved for women.

L60 Deodand. An object, animal or inanimate, which contributed to the death of someone who had reached the age of discretion, was believed to share the guilt of his or her death. The object or its value was forfeited to the Crown, which applied it for charitable purposes. Deodands were formally abolished in 1846.

L61 Distraint. A term originally applied to the seizure of possessions, generally livestock, in compensation for an alleged breach of feudal service obligations. In modern times a landlord takes out a distress warrant to seize goods in lieu of unpaid rent.

L62 Ducking Stool. A caged seat at the end of a plank overhanging a pond or river, in which people were tied and then ducked in the water. The usual victims were women and dishonest tradesmen.

L63 Duelling. Duelling was prohibited and treated as a criminal offence in 1818.

L64 Hard Labour. A punishment introduced in 1706.

L65 Hidegild. A fine paid in lieu of flogging.

L66 Irons. The use of manacles and chains was known by the 12th century. Prisoners in irons were said to be held 'straitly'.

L67 Kinbote. A fine paid to the family of a murdered person.

L68 Larceny. Grand Larceny, where the goods stolen from a house were worth over twelve pence, was a capital offence. Petty larceny of goods worth less brought whipping, a sentence superseded in 1717 by transportation.

L69 Murder Fine. In Norman and Danish times it was necessary for the Hundred in which a man had been murdered to prove that he was English, and so escape the fine which would have been imposed if the victim had been Norman or Danish. Alternatively called Englishry.

L70 Outlawry. An absconded prisoner accused of a criminal charge could be declared an outlaw after being summoned at four consecutive courts without responding. He forfeited his goods and the protection of the realm, and could be killed on sight. The punishment was abolished in 1879.

L71 Scolding. The offence of brawling or disturbing the peace committed by a woman. She was usually punished by means of the ducking-stool.

L72 Stocks. A short spell in the stocks, a punishment known since Saxon times, was a normal reward for blasphemy, drunkenness, breaking the Sabbath etc. An Act of 1405 stated that stocks should be provided in each town and village. The punishment had lapsed by the 1830s.

L73 Suicide. It was the usual custom to bury a suicide at a crossroads in his parish. This procedure was abolished in 1823.

L74 Torture. Punishment by torture in prisons was permitted by royal warrant in 1310.

L75 Transportation. A punishment for vagrants and criminals which began in 1597 when they were shipped off, as prisoners, to America to work on the plantations as cheap labour. After the War of Independence 1776 convicts were transported to New South Wales instead.

L76 Trial by Battle. A method of settling a legal dispute in Saxon and Norman times. The accuser and the accused would do battle on the assumption that God would protect the person in the right. In civil disputes substitutes, called champions, were allowed. It was made illegal in 1819.

L77 Trial by Ordeal. A method of proving innocence or guilt in criminal cases on the assumption that God would protect the innocent.

In Ordeal by Fire, which was allowed to freemen, the accused had to carry a heated iron for a distance of 9 feet during mass; his hand was then bandaged and he was declared innocent if there were no scars after three days.

In Ordeal by Water, the accused was bound and lowered into cold water; if he sank he was innocent (and rescued), and if he floated he was guilty on the premise that the water had rejected him.

In 1215 clergy were forbidden to officate at Trials by Ordeal and the custom died out soon afterwards.

L78 Wergild. In effect, the monetary value of a man's life in Saxon times. Each class in the community was assigned a Wergild, and if one of its members was murdered this was the amount payable by the murderer or his family to the family of the deceased. A coerl's wergild was 2000s, and a gesith or thane was valued at 1200s. The wergild for a serf was paid to his master.

L79 Whipping. A punishment particularly imposed on women. Most parishes had whipping posts but offenders were often whipped at the tail of a cart through the main street. As late as 1740 prostitutes were whipped through the streets of London.

L80 Witchcraft. Under Acts of 1541 and 1603 Witchcraft was punishable by death and the last execution took place in 1716. The Witchcraft Act 1735 abolished the penalty.

PART SIX
LEGAL TERMS

L81 Abjuration of the Realm. From Saxon times criminals could seek Sanctuary (qv) in churches and churchyards. After forty days he could, in the presence of the Crown's agent, confess his crime, swear to abjure the realm and submit to banishment. He would travel to a named port, dressed in a white robe or sackcloth, and take the first available ship. His only hope of a return was the king's pardon.

L82 Affeerors. Jurors sworn to fix the amount of a fine.

L83 Affidavit. A sworn statement made in the presence of a person qualified to receive it.

L84 Allegation. An assertion by a party which he hopes to prove.

L85 Amercement. Convicted persons were in the 'king's mercy' and liable to a monetary penalty: they were therefore 'amerced'.

L86 Approver. A criminal turned informer who, to obtain a pardon, was required to fight five battles according to the customs of Trial by Battle (qv); he was hanged if he lost. The practice had largely disappeared by the 15th century.

L87 Benefit of Clergy. Originally the privilege granted to the clergy of being handed over from the civil to the ecclesiastical courts for trial for offences which carried a capital penalty. In England this was extended to all those who could read and who could therefore, theoretically, become clerics. Prisoners were usually tested in their ability to read a verse from a Latin bible but this was later relaxed by the use of an English text. The custom was extended and abused even further by courts in their willingness to avoid the legal capital sentence for minor offences. The test was abolished altogether in 1706 and the procedure itself in 1827.

L88 Capias. A warrant for arrest.

L89 Compurgation. The system by which an accused might call upon twelve others (called oath helpers) who would swear to his good character and innocence. The value of their oaths depended upon their wergilds (qv).

L90 Disseisin. The wrongful ejection of a person seized of a freehold property.

L91 Doctors' Commons. A college of lawyers in London. It had ceased to function by the 1830s and the building was demolished in 1867.

L92 Doom. The judgement of a court.

L93 Faitours. Villains.

L94 Forfang. A reward for the recovery of stolen property.

L95 Hue and Cry. The pursuit, using horn and voice, of a wanted felon; the responsibility for capture lay within the parish to which the criminal had fled. Abuse of this procedure could result in fine or imprisonment.

L96 Infangetheof. The right of a lord of the manor to try and punish a thief caught in his manor.

L97 Inns of Chancery. Collegiate houses for younger law students before their admittance to the Inns of Court in London. The Inns of Chancery were affiliated to specific Inns of Court as follows: Barnards (1454) and Staple (1378) affiliated to Gray's Inn, Clement's (1480) and Clifford's (1345) and Lyon's (1413) affiliated to Inner Temple, New Inn (1485) affiliated to Middle Temple, and Furnival's (1383) and Thavie's (1348) affiliated to Lincoln's Inn.

L98 Inns of Court. Collegiate houses in London which have the exclusive privilege of conferring the rank of barrister-at-law. There are four Inns – Gray's and Lincoln's, and Inner and Middle Temple.

L99 Jurat. A brief statement at the end of an affidavit detailing when, where and by whom it was sworn.

L100 Jurors. A property qualification for a juror was introduced in 1285, revised in 1664 and again in 1692 when it was fixed at the possession of copyhold, freehold or life-tenure of a property worth at least £10 per annum. From 1730 long-term leaseholders occupying property worth at least £20 per annum were eligible. From 1696 lists of eligible jurors were compiled and presented to Quarter Sessions.

The Jury Act 1825 limited jury service to those between 21 and 60 who possessed freehold property worth at least £10 per year, or leasehold property worth £20 per annum, or who were householders of houses worth £30 per year.

L101 Mainprise. A writ to the sheriff instructing him to collect sureties for a defendant's appearance. The sureties were collected from mainpernors.

L102 Oath Helpers. Defendants in medieval times could present witnesses – oath helpers – who would swear that they believed him innocent. The value of the oaths was dependant on the wergilds of the helpers.

L103 Outfangentheof. The right of a lord to pursue a thief outside his manor boundary and bring him back to his own court for trial.

L104 Presentment. The report of a jury concerning an offence brought to its notice, or the report of the homage of a manor court concerning alienations of land.

L105 Recognizance. A recorded pledge to appear at court, to keep the peace, to pay a debt etc.

L106 Replevin. An action to recover goods or property which had been distrained in lieu of alleged non-payment of rent or non-performance of feudal services.

L107 Sanctuary. A fugitive criminal had the right from Saxon times to take refuge in a church or churchyard. After 40 days there he could confess before the Crown's representative, abjure the realm and submit to banishment, rather than face trial. It was decided in 1486 that Sanctuary should not protect those charged with treason and in Tudor times Sanctuary areas were restricted to eight cities: Derby, Lancaster, Manchester, Northampton, Norwich, Wells, Westminster and York. Sanctuary for criminals was abolished in 1623 and for those involved in civil cases it was diminished and abolished in 1697 and 1723.

L108 True Bill. A bill of indictment was presented to the grand jury which, having heard the evidence, endorsed it as a 'true bill' if it considered that a *prima facie* case had been made.

PART SEVEN
BIBLIOGRAPHY

Police
Guardians of the Queen's Peace, George Howard (1953)
The Thief Takers, Patrick Pringle (1958)
A History of Police in England and Wales 900–1966, T. A. Critchley

Prisons
Imprisonment in Medieval England, R. Pugh (1968)
Pounds or pinfolds and lockups, B. M. Willmott Dobbie (1979)
The English Prisons, D. L. Howard (1960)
The Criminal Prisons of London, Henry Mayhew (1872)
English Prisons under Local Government, Sidney and Beatrice Webb (1922)
The English Prison Hulks, W. Branch Johnson (rev. 1970)
A Just Measure of Pain: The Penitentiary in the Industrial Revolution 1750–1850, Michael Ignatieff (1978)
Victorian Prison Lives: English Prison biography 1830–1914, Philip Priestley (1985)

Judicial Authorities
English Courts of Law, H. G. Hanbury (1967)
The Courts of Law, Peter Walker (1970)

Judicial Officers
The Justices of the Peace in England 1558–1640, J. H. Gleason (1969)

Crimes and Punishments
Elizabethan Life: Disorder, F. G. Emmison (1970)
Crime in England 1550–1800, J. S. Cockburn (1977)
Criminal and Victim; Crime and society in early nineteenth century England, George Rudé (1985)
Crime and Authority in Victorian England, D. Philips (1977)
Crime and Industrial Society in the Nineteenth Century, J. J. Tobias (1967)

Legal Terms and the History of the Law
A History of English Law, Sir W. S. Holdsworth (1903–66)
A Concise History of the Common Law, T. F. T. Pucknett (rev. 1961)
Historical Introduction to the Land Law, Sir W. S. Holdsworth (1927)
Oxford Studies in Social and Legal History, Sir Paul Vinogradoff (1921)

SECTION M
Utilities and Services

PART ONE
FIRE FIGHTING

M1 General history. The first organised fire-fighting groups were those employed by the fire insurance companies, each of which maintained its own liveried staff to deal with fires at premises insured by them. These brigades were mainly in the larger cities, but elsewhere the vestries maintained fire engines and placed ladders at strategic points. The earliest engines appear to have been those of the Hand-in-Hand (1707), Sun Fire Office (1716) and Westminster Fire Office (1720).

In London a combined brigade was begun in 1791 between the Phoenix, Sun Fire Office and the Royal Exchange Assurance Company and in 1833 ten London insurance companies formed the London Fire Engine Establishment. The Metropolitan Board of Works decided in 1855 to take over fire services and from 1856 the Metropolitan Fire Brigade, renamed the London Fire Brigade in 1904, was established.

It was normal for the fire insurance brigades to place a metal plate called a fire-mark on the wall of the property insured: this not only proved to the insurance brigade that their efforts were paid for but it also acted as an advertising plaque. The earlier ones were made of lead, quite often with the insurance policy number beneath the company device, and the later ones were of copper or iron.

M2 Fire Insurance Companies. The foundation dates of some of the earlier companies are shown below:

Aberdeen Assurance Company   1825
Aberdeen Fire Insurance Office   1801
Aegis Fire and Life Insurance Company   1825

Albert Insurance Company	1864	Essex and Suffolk Equitable Insurance	
Albion Fire and Life Insurance Company	1805	Society	1802
Alliance Assurance Company	1824	Etna Insurance Company (Dublin)	1866
Amicable Contributionship		Exchange House Fire Office	1708
(Hand-in-Hand)	1696	Fife Insurance Company	1800
Anchor Fire and Life Insurance		Friendly Insurance Society of Glasgow	1720
Company	1849	Friendly Society of Edinburgh	1720
Anchor Fire Office (Norwich)	1808	Friendly Society of London	1683
Athenaeum Fire Insurance Company	1852	General Accident	1885
Atlas Assurance Company	1808	General Insurance Company of Ireland	
Aylsham New Association	c1820	(Dublin)	1779
Bath Fire Office	1767	General Life and Fire Assurance	
Bath Sun Fire Office	1776	Company	1837
Beacon Fire Insurance Company	1821	Glasgow Insurance Company	1805
Berks and Glos and Provincial Life and		Globe Insurance Company	1803
Fire Insurance Company	1824	Great Britain Fire Company	1871
Birmingham District Fire Office	1834	Guardian Assurance Company	1821
Birmingham Fire Office Company	1805	Hand-in-Hand	1696
Bon Accord	1845	Hants, Sussex and Dorset Fire Office	1803
Bristol Crown Fire Office	1718	Hercules Insurance Company	1809
Bristol Fire Office	1769	Herts, Cambs and County Fire Office	1824
Bristol Union	1814	Hibernian Fire Insurance Company	
Bristol Universal Fire Office	1774	(Dublin)	1771
Britannia Fire Association	1868	Hope Fire and Life Assurance Company	1807
British Commercial Life and Fire		Imperial Fire Insurance Company	1803
Insurance Company	1818	Insurance Company of Scotland	
British Crown	1907	(Glasgow)	1821
British Dominions	1897	Irish Alliance Insurance Company	1824
British Fire Insurance Company	1908	Kent Fire Insurance Company	1802
British Fire Office	1799	King	1901
British and Irish United	1804	Lancashire Insurance Company	1852
British Union Fire and Life Insurance		Leeds Fire Office	1777
Company	1818	Leeds and Yorkshire Assurance	
Caledonian Insurance Company		Company	1824
(Edinburgh)	1805	Leicester Fire and Life Insurance	
Central Insurance Company (London)	1899	Company	1834
Church of England Life and Fire		Licences and General	1890
Assurance Institute	1840	Licensed Victuallers Fire and Life	
City of London Fire	1881	Assurance Co.	1836
Commercial Fire Insurance Company of		Lion Fire Insurance Company	1879
Dublin	1799	Liverpool and London and Globe	1836
Commercial Union Assurance Company	1861	Liverpool Fire Office	1777
Company of London Insurers (Sun Fire		London Assurance	1720
Office)	1710	London Fire Insurance Company	1879
County Fire Office	1807	London and Lancashire Insurance	
District Fire Office	1834	Company	1862
Dublin Insurance Company Against Fire	1782	London and Provincial Fire Insurance	
Dundee Insurance Company	1782	Company	1887
Eagle Insurance Company	1807	London and Westminster Insurance	
East Kent and Canterbury Economic Fire		Company	1905
Assurance	1824	Manchester Fire Insurance Company	1824
Eastern Counties	1890	Manchester Fire Office	1771
Economic Fire Insurance Company	1868	Middlesex Fire Insurance Company	1874
Empress Assurance Corporation	1895	Monarch Insurance Company	1907
Equitable Fire Insurance Company	1873	National Assurance Company of Ireland	
Essex Economic Fire Office	1824	(Dublin)	1822

M3

National British and Irish Millers Insurance Co.	1896
National Reliance	1898
National Union of Fire Office (Bedford)	1894
Newcastle-upon-Tyne Fire Office	1783
New Fire Office (Phoenix)	1782
Newport Association	c1811
North British and Mercantile Insurance Company	1809
Northern Assurance Company	1836
Norwich General Assurance Office	1792
Norwich Union Fire Insurance Society	1797
Notts and Derbyshire Fire and Life Assurance Co.	1835
Palatine Insurance Company (Manchester)	1886
Palladium	1824
Patriotic Assurance Company of Ireland	1824
Phenix	1680
Phoenix (New Fire Office)	1782
Property Insurance Company	1898
Protector Fire Insurance Company	1825
Queens Insurance Company (Liverpool)	1857
Reading Insurance Company	1822
Reliance	1881
Royal Exchange Assurance	1720
Royal Exchange of Ireland	1784
Royal Farmers and General Fire, Life and Hailstorm Insurance Company	1840
Royal Insurance Company (Liverpool)	1845
Royal Irish Assurance Company	1823
St Patrick Insurance Company	1824
Salamander and Western Fire Assurance	1822
Salop Fire Office	1780
Scottish Commercial Fire and Life Insurance Co	1865
Scottish Imperial Insurance Company (Glasgow)	1865
Scottish Union Insurance Company	1824
Sea Insurance Company	1875
Shamrock Fire and Life Assurance Company	1823
Sheaf of Arrows	1683
Sheffield Fire Office	1808
Shropshire and North Wales Assurance Co.	1837
South British	1872
Star Fire Insurance Company	1845
State Assurance	1891
Suffolk and General Counties	1802
Sun Fire Office (Company of London Insurers)	1710
Surrey, Sussex and Southwark Fire Assurance Co.	1825
Sussex County and General Fire and Life Ass. Co.	1825

Union Assurance Society (London)	1714
United British	1915
West of England Fire and Life Ass. Co. (Exeter)	1807
West of Scotland Insurance Office	1826
Western Fire	1863
Western Insurance Company of Plymouth	1887
Westminster Fire Office	1717
Winchester, Hants and South of England Fire and Life Insurance Company	1841
Worcester Fire Office	1790
York and North of England	c1834
Yorkshire Insurance Company	1824

Records of the Westminster Fire Office are with Westminster City Libraries. Those for the London Assurance and the Hand-in-Hand Companies are at the Guildhall Library, London. The Society of Genealogists has a 'collection of claims documents of the Sun Fire Office for 1770–88. Other towns which had Fire Insurance Brigades include Andover, Baldock, Bradford, Burnley, Bury St Edmunds, Cambridge, Canterbury, Chatham, Chelmsford, Chester, Coventry, Crayford, Darlington, Dartford, Gateshead, Grimsby, Hereford, Kidderminster, Loughborough, Ludlow, Maidstone, Middlesborough, Oxford, Ramsey, Rochester, Swansea, Whitchurch and Wootton-under-Edge.

PART TWO
THE POST OFFICE

M3 General. In the reign of James I a Postmaster of England was appointed to have 'the sole taking up, sending and conveying of all packets and letters concerning our service or business to be despatched to foreign parts'. A regular service between Edinburgh and London was begun in 1635 and in 1644 Edward Prideaux established a weekly post of letters to various parts of the country. An Act of 1656 established 'one general post office and one officer stiled the Postmaster-General of England and Comptroller of the Post Office'. A private Penny Post was begun in London in 1680, soon to be absorbed by the Post Office who then successfully fended off introduction of other private schemes.

Mail coaches were introduced in 1784 and in 1830 mail was first carried by rail – on the

Liverpool-Manchester railway. At this stage letters were charged by weight and distance but in 1840 the Penny Post, devised by Rowland Hill, introduced a standard charge whatever the distance. The first pillar box was erected in 1855, postcards were introduced in 1870, and postal orders issued in 1881

M4 Old Post Offices. The *Post Office Magazine* in 1966 held a competition to find the oldest post office in continuous use. The following were noted in the results:

Sanquhar Sub. (Dumfries) c1800
Donaghmore Sub., Dungannon c1834
Edderton Sub., Dinwall, probably 1843
Shipton-under-Wychwood, Oxford, c1845
Kings Worthy, Winchester 1845
Wormshill, Sittingbourne 1847
Dennington, Woodbridge, c1847
Banbury Head Post Office, 1849
Guyhirn, Wisbech, 1854
Penshurst, Tonbridge, 1861
Stoke Climsland, possibly 1839
Pottersbury, Towcester c1866
Darlington Head Post Office 1865
Edinburgh General 1866
Caergeiliog, Holyhead 1894, possibly 1840

PART THREE
WATER SUPPLIES

M5 General. Water supply has traditionally been the responsibility of both private companies and local authorities. The earliest charters enabling boroughs to provide piped water supplies appear to be those for Southampton (1420), Hull (1447), Bath (1500) and Gloucester (1542), but usually most towns relied upon wells and springs well into the 19th century.

Water was first supplied to London houses by *mechanical* means in 1581 from beneath an arch of London Bridge. The first major undertaking was that of the New River Company which constructed a supply from Hertfordshire to London between 1609 and 1614. Usually, wooden pipes were used but these were unpredictable in performance; cast-iron pipes became feasible from 1785. The Metropolitan Paving Act 1817 ordered that all new pipes were to be made of iron.

A Royal Commission, sitting in 1843–5, reported on the unsatisfactory and unhygienic nature of water supplies in populous areas. At that time water mains could only be built beneath main streets. The Public Health Act 1848 enabled a local authority to provide a water supply. In rural districts the position was more complicated as the rateable income of many administrative areas was not sufficient to finance expenditure on water supply. The Public Health (Water) Act 1878 stipulated that no new house should be built in a rural area unless it was within a reasonable distance of a water supply.

In London the Metropolis Water Act 1852 laid down new standards of hygiene, specifying that all reservoirs within five miles of St Paul's should be covered.

In 1871 the Board of Trade appointed a water examiner.

PART FOUR
CEMETERIES

M6 Burial Acts 1852 and 1853. Before the passing of these Acts most people were buried in church graveyards. By the middle of the 19th century, especially in those parishes whose populations had grown dramatically, churchyard overcrowding was a serious health risk.

Burial Acts were passed in 1852 for London, and in 1853 for the rest of the country, enabling local authorities to administer their own cemeteries. Vestries elected Burial Boards to manage them.

M7 Local Government Act 1894. The duties of the Burial Boards were transferred to District and Parish authorities.

PART FIVE
GAS

M8 General. Until the development of statutory regional boards gas supply was usually the responsibility of limited companies or municipal undertakings. The first company established was the Chartered Gas Light and Coke Co. (later commonly known without the word Chartered), in Westminster, which began in 1812. Its charter restricted its area to the City of London, Southwark, Westminster and adjacent areas. Its success stimulated the formation of other companies in London and elsewhere, each requiring permission from Parliament.

By 1815 it was estimated that there were 4,000 gas lights in London, and by 1819, 51,000. In 1822 there were seven gasworks in London and frequently three or four gas companies supplied the same street, each with their main pipes beneath the pavement.

By 1819 there was gas lighting in many towns including Bath, Birmingham, Brighton, Bristol, Cheltenham, Chester, Edinburgh, Exeter, Glasgow, Kidderminster, Leeds, Liverpool, Macclesfield, Manchester, Nottingham, Preston, and Sheffield.

The Gasworks Clauses Act 1847 consolidated legislation regarding construction, profits etc. By the middle of the century competition, particularly in London, was cutthroat with the companies making small profits. An agreement was reached between the major companies to parcel out London so that each area was served by one company to avoid duplication and to enable a higher charge for gas to be levied. This arrangement was approved by the Metropolis Gas Act 1860, which also imposed standards of illumination.

M9 Gas Companies.   A list of some gas companies follows:

Berks:
Ascot and District Gas and Electric Co. 1883
Bracknell Gasworks c1862
Hungerford Gas Co.
Lambourn Gas, Coal & Coke Co.
Maidenhead Gas Light & Coke Co. 1835
Windsor Royal Gas Light & Coke Co. 1827

Bucks:
Amersham Gas Light & Coke Co. 1851
Beaconsfield Gas Co. 1865
Burnham United Gas Light & Coke Co. 1863
Great Marlow Gas Co. 1845
High Wycombe Gas Light & Coke Co. 1848
Slough Gas & Coke Co. 1848

Devon:
Torquay & Paignton Gas Co.

Essex:
Barking Gas Co. 1837
Billericay Gas Co. 1892
Brentwood Gas Co. 1834
Chigwell, Loughton & Woodford Gas Co. 1863
Grays & Tilbury Gas Co. 1853
Ilford Gas Co. 1839
Ingatestone & Freyerning Gas Co. 1858
Laindon Gas and Water Co. 1896

Leigh-on-Sea Rural District Undertaking 1899
Rochford Gas Co. 1847
Romford Gas Co. 1847
Shoeburyness Gas Co. 1870
Shoeburyness RD Undertaking 1879
Southend-on-Sea District Gas Co. 1854
South Essex Gas Light & Coke Co. 1852
Stanford-le-Hope Gas Co. 1905

Glos:
Cirencester Gas Co.
Fairford Gas Co.
Tewkesbury & Winchcombe Gas Co.

London:
Aldgate Gas Light & Coke Co. 1815
British Gaslight Co. 1825
Chartered Gas Light & Coke Co. 1812
City of London Gas Light & Coke Co. 1816
Commercial Gas Co. 1847
County and General Consumers Co. (Lea Bridge) 1856
East London Gas Light & Coke Co. 1831
Equitable Gas Co. 1842
Gas Light and Coke Co. 1812
Great Central Gas Consumers Co. 1849
Imperial Gas Light & Coke Co. 1820
Independent Gaslight and Coke Co. 1829
Lea Bridge District Gas Co. 1868
London Gas Co. 1843
London Gaslight & Coke Co. 1833
North Woolwich Undertaking 1850
Phoenix Gaslight & Coke Co. 1824
Portable Gas Co. 1821
Ratcliff Gas Light & Coke Co. 1823
South Metropolitan Gaslight & Coke Co. 1842
Victoria Docks Gas Co. 1858
Walthamstow Gas and Coke Co. 1854
Western (Cannel) Gas Light & Coke Co. 1845
West Ham Gas Co. 1845
West London Junction Gas Co. 1865
West Suburban Gaslight & Coke Co. 1905
Whitechapel Road Gas Light & Coke Co. 1821

Middlesex:
Brentford Gas Co. 1821
Great Stanmore Gas Co. 1858
Harrow Gas Co. 1872
Hornsey Gas Co. 1857
North Middlesex Gas Co. 1862
Pinner Gas Co. 1868
Staines & Egham District Gas Co. 1833
Sunbury Gas Consumers Co. 1861
Uxbridge Gas Co. 1841

Oxon:
Bampton Gas Co.

Surrey:
Chertsey Gas Co. 1852
County and General Consumers Co. (Chertsey) 1858
Richmond Gas Co. 1847

Warks:
Birmingham Municipal Gas Undertaking 1874

Wilts:
Marlborough Gas Co.
Salisbury Gas Co.
Swindon Gaslight & Coke Co.
Swindon New Gas Co.
Swindon United Gas Co.

Worcs:
Pershore Gas Co.

Scotland:
Arbroath Gaslight Co. by 1834
Kilmarnock Gaslight Co. by 1826

PART SIX
ELECTRICITY

M10 Use of electricity. The first public lighting using electricity appeared in London 1877–79; in the latter year the reading-room of the British Museum was lit by electricity, and by 1881 the House of Commons used a combination of electricity and gas. The first public supply for street lighting was that for Godalming, Surrey in 1881, although the cables were laid in the gutters as permission had not been obtained to break up the pavements.

It is claimed that the first house to be lit by electricity was that of Sir Joseph Swan in Gateshead in 1880 although other authorities state that a house in Porchester Gardens, London was lit in 1879.

Electrical items such as vacuum-cleaners, refrigerators and washing-machines were introduced into this country in 1908, 1918 and c1917 respectively.

M11 Electricity Companies. Generally the supply of electricity was in the hands of local authorities before nationalisation. In 1878 companies introduced 34 Private Bills into Parliament seeking powers to supply electricity. The Electric Lighting Act 1882 enabled the Board of Trade to grant 7-year licences which were renewable, but at the end of 21 years the local authority had the option to purchase the enterprise – the Electric Lighting Act 1888 lengthened this period to 42 years.

M12 Municipalisation. Local authorities were, from the beginning, involved in public supply. The first municipal power station appears to have been that of Bradford in 1889; the first in London was that of St Pancras in 1890. The Electricity (Supply) Act 1919 established Commissioners to reorganise supply on a regional basis and a similar Act of 1926 introduced national co-ordination.

PART SEVEN
PUBLIC LIBRARIES

M13 Public Libraries Act 1850. This empowered boroughs with a population of over 10,000 to provide public libraries. However, the consent of two-thirds of the ratepayers in an assembled meeting was required; expenditure was limited to ½d per £1 rate. More importantly, it gave the authorities no power to buy books – only to lend those donated to them.

Warrington and Salford had already opened libraries in 1848 and 1849 using the Museums Act as their basis.

M14 Public Libraries Act 1854. This extended the provisions of the 1850 Act to Scotland.

M15 Public Libraries Act 1855. This Act increased the permitted expenditure to 1d in the £1 rate.

M16 Public Libraries Act 1892. This was the most important early Libraries Act. It enabled all local government units, except counties, to become library authorities but it was not until 1919 that more than 1d in the £1 rate could be spent. It was found that some of the authorities set up by the 1892 Act were spending only £10 a year on purchasing books.

M17 Public Libraries Act 1919. Limits on library expenditure were removed. County councils could become library authorities and serve rural districts. Further impetus was provided by the Carnegie United Kingdom Trust and the Passmore Edwards Foundation.

Bibliography

PART EIGHT
BIBLIOGRAPHY

Fire Fighting
A History of the British Fire Service, G. V. Blackstone (1957)
London's Noble Fire Brigades 1833–1904, Sally Holloway (1973)
A History of Fire-Fighting and Equipment, Arthur Ingram (1978)
History of Firefighting, ed John L. Kirk (1960)
The Early Days of the Sun Fire Office, Edward Baumer (1910)
Fire-marks, John Vince (1973)
A Gazetteer of English Urban Fire Disasters 1500–1900, E. L. Jones, S. Porter and M. Turner (for Institute of British Geographers 1984)
The British Fire Mark 1680–1879, Woodhead-Faulkner (1982)
British Firemarks and Plates: A Catalogue of the Institute and Bashall Dawson Collections, Chartered Insurance Institute (1971)
Fire Marks and Insurance Office Fire Brigades, B. Williams (1927)

Post Office
The Penny Post, Frank Staff (1964)
History of the British Post Office, J. G. Hemmeon (1912)
The British Post Office to 1925, C. F. Dendy-Marshall (1926)
The Post Office – an Historical Survey, HMSO (1911)
The Letter Box, Jean Farrugia (1969)
Picture Postcards and Their Publishers 1894–1939, Anthony Byatt (1978)
The Picture Postcard and its Origins, Frank Staff (2nd ed. 1979)

Water
Early Victorian Water Engineers, G. M. Binnie (1981)
The New River, Bernard Rudden (1985)
The Story of Water Supply, F. W. Robins (1946)
Water in England, Dorothy Hartley (rev. 1978)
The Lost Rivers of London, Nicholas Barton (repr. 1982)

Cemeteries
The Victorian Celebration of Death, James Stevens Curl (1972)

Gas
The History of the Gas Light and Coke Company 1812–1949, Stirling Everard (1949)
New Flame (How Gas changed the commercial, domestic and industrial life of Britain between 1813 and 1984), Hugh Barty-King (1984)

A History of the British Gas Industry, Trevor Williams (1981)
British Gas Industry before 1850, M. E. Falkus (Economic History Review Vol 20, 1967)

Electricity
A History of Electric Light and Power, Brian Bowers (1982)
Electricity Supply in Great Britain – its Development and Organisation, Sir Henry Self and Miss E. M. Watson (1952)
The British Electrical Industry 1875–1914, I. C. R. Byatt (unpub. thesis 1962)
Electricity Supply in Great Britain: a chronology Electricity Council (1977)
The Electric Revolution, R. A. S. Hennessey (1972)
Electricity before Nationalisation, Leslie Hannah (1979)

Libraries
History of the Public Library Movement in Great Britain, J. Minto (1932)

SECTION N

Roads and Transport

PART ONE
ROADS

Legislation

N1 Statute of Winchester 1285. This legislation affirmed the responsibility of the manors for the upkeep of the king's highways and, by implication, charged the manor constables with the duty of supervision.

N2 Repair of Bridges 1530. A county rate was permitted to finance the repair of bridges which were outside towns and not the responsibility of an authority or person.

N3 Highways Act 1555. This was the first legislation of any importance which affected roads. It transferred responsibility for the upkeep of the king's highways to the parishes. Each parishioner owning a ploughland in tillage, or keeping a draught or plough, was liable to supply a cart for four days a year for use in road repair. Each able-bodied householder or tenant was required to give four days' 'statute' labour a year (increased in 1691 to six). It was possible to pay a fine to commute this, or else to provide a substitute.

It was enacted that a surveyor or surveyors should be appointed by each parish. Usually the selection of such an officer was made in Easter week by the churchwardens, constable and some parishioners; from 1662 the selection was made by the majority of parishioners. The procedure was altered once more in 1691 when it was the custom for the parish officers to supply a suitable list of people, who could act as surveyors, to the justices who then made the appointment.

N4 Turnpike Roads. Wheeled traffic up to the 17th century was rare. For example, Elizabeth I was the first monarch to have a coach. The primitive system of road maintenance could cope with the wear and tear of horse traffic but by the latter half of the 17th century, with wheeled traffic common, the parishes were unable to maintain the sort of roads needed. The first Turnpike Act was in 1663 in Cambridgeshire on the London to York road and there was not another for about 30 years. By such an Act a defined stretch of road came under the jurisdiction of a trust which, in return for its proper maintenance, was entitled to collect a toll from which to defray its expenses. Nearly 2,000 particular Turnpike Acts were enacted in the 18th century until in 1773 a General Turnpike Act was passed which speeded up the whole process and took less of Parliament's time. As a precaution a trust was granted toll rights for 21 years only but permission was usually renewed. The term turnpike is derived from the toll bar which was in a shape resembling a pike.

N5 Highways Act 1835. This Act abolished statute labour and permitted the levy of a highway rate. It provided for the unification of parishes into highway district authorities and allowed the employment of a paid district surveyor.

N6 Highways Act 1862. This act empowered the justices to compulsorily unite parishes into highway authorities where they thought it necessary.

N7 Local Government Act 1888. The responsibility for main roads was transferred to the newly-established county councils.

N8 Local Government Act 1894. Minor roads were made the responsibility of local authorities.

Terms

N9 Borstal. A southern term for a path up a steep hill.

N10 Bridle Path. A path suitable for horses and pedestrians and from which vehicles are legally barred. Legislation has tended to make the pedestrian's right to the use of bridle-paths stronger than on a footpath. Also known as Halter Path, Sheergate, Sheerway, Wapple, Warple and Wobble.

N11 Causeway. A pavement or raised footpath. Also known as Causey.

N12 Chare. An alley; a term found in northern England, the Midlands and Glos.

N13 Chase. In this sense, a road leading to a field or farmhouse; a green lane.

N14 Chimin. A legal term for a road.

N15 Drang. A passage between two walls or hedges. Alternatively called Dring or Drong.

N16 Drove Road. A road of ancient origin not subject to toll and principally used for long-distance herding of cattle to market towns. It was not usually kept in repair by any authority. Alternatively called Drift Road.

N17 Easement. A right of way over adjoining property.

N18 Enclosure Roads. Before the period of large-scale enclosure of land, roads followed the contours of small holdings. Quite often an enclosure entailed the creation of a new road to replace an older one. Usually these are straight and have wide strips of grass on either side; enclosure awards usually stipulated that the distance from hedge to hedge should be 40 ft.

N19 Farrow. A road.

N20 Footpaths. The National Parks and Access to the Countryside Act 1949 defines a footpath as a 'highway over which the public has a right of way on foot only'.

Maps showing footpaths have to be available to the public at county council offices. Footpaths are shown (to distinguish them from Bridle Paths) on Ordnance Survey maps as lines of red dots. County councils, are able to close footpaths but the extinguishment order has to be approved at government level. Footpaths may be diverted if this leads to better land use; if the termination point is a road this may be altered, but otherwise the termination point must remain as before.

Liability for the maintenance of footpaths is often unknown, but parish councils are empowered to do the work. It is an offence to block a path with a gate and a walker has the right to follow the line of the path through crops if necessary.

N21 Ford. In some areas the term meant simply a road rather than a road through a watercourse.

N22 Fordraught. A path between two farms.

N23 Gate. A Middle English term for a road.

N24 Gatrum. A Lincolnshire term for a rough path between two fields.

N25 Gennell. A north-country term for a narrow passage between houses.

N26 Green Lane. A right of way sometimes synonymous with a Drove Road. As its name implies it is grassed and was probably a road to market.

N27 Hollow Way. A sunken road. Alternatively known as Howegait.

N28 Leet. A meeting point of roads. Also known as Releet.

N29 Ley Roads. Alfred Watkins in his book *The Old Straight Track* (1925) propounded the theory that the country was crossed by prehistoric ley tracks which were aligned over considerable distances, often directed towards mountain peaks, cairns etc, and which crossed at significant sites such as those of churches, mounds, burial places etc.

N30 List Road. A Kent term for a Green Lane (qv).

N31 Load. A lane, sometimes across a marshy area. Alternatively known as Loan or Lode.

N32 Loke. An East Anglian term for a lane, sometimes a private one.

N33 Marchway. A boundary road.

N34 Mear Path. A path between two holdings. Alternatively spelt Meer Path.

N35 Port Way. A path leading to a market town which would normally have a gateway.

N36 Raik. A cattle path. Alternatively spelt Rake.

N37 Ridding. A Green Lane (qv) through a wood.

N38 Ridgeway. A path along a ridge of land, chosen because it would dry quicker than other paths.

N39 Roman Roads. Roman roads were connections between garrison towns essential for the quick movement of troops and supplies. In addition there was a substantial network of subsidiary roads, much of which is still being discovered.

The most authoritative book on the subject is *Roman Roads* by Ivan Margary. The Ordnance Survey publish a map of Roman Britain on which most roads are shown.

The roads are usually straight between prominent points – at these they might well change direction. The raised, cambered platform of the roads – the agger – was bounded by a kerb and a V-shaped ditch on either side, the latter serving as a drain. The platform had a bed of large stones in an excavated ditch, smaller, bonded stones on top, and a surface of gravel, flints etc. The main roads could be as much as 80 ft wide, the smaller ones generally about 21 ft between ditches.

N40 Saltways. Roads found in salt-boiling areas such as Cheshire and Worcestershire. They lead from brine-pits where salt water was boiled.

N41 Signposts and Direction Stones. Legislation in 1697 required posts and stones to be placed at crossroads but this injunction was often neglected. Similarly the General Turnpike Acts of the 18th century laid down that posts or stones should be provided at turnpike crossroads. Mileposts were already provided, quite often erected to the distances shown on Ogilby's maps. Alternatively known as Handposts, Handingposts and Fingerposts.

N42 Smoot. A north-country term for a passage between two houses.

N43 Snicket. A narrow passageway.

N44 Tenantry Road. A Sussex term derived from the open-field farming system. It was a road of about 8 ft wide dividing several holdings in the fields.

N45 Turnpike Roads. The administrative history of these roads is described in N4. A feature of turnpike roads was the toll house, usually built projecting on to the road, and in which the toll collector (the pikeman) lived. A common toll would be a farthing per head of cattle and sixpence for a carriage horse. Local cart traffic and that to church or to a funeral was exempt from toll.

N46 Twissell. A narrow footpath between hedges; a path which forks. Alternatively called Twitten. In east Hertfordshire the term Twitchell describes an urban alley.

N47 Went. A narrow path.

N48 Wynd. An alley or court.

PART TWO
CARRIAGES AND COACHES

N49 Early road transport. Although slow stage wagons for passengers and goods existed in the 16th century, such traffic was insignificant. By 1605 long wagons ran between London and Canterbury, and a scheduled stage-coach ran on various routes, such as London to York and Oxford by 1640. The hackney carriage appeared in London c1610.

N50 Road transport in the 18th century and early 19th century. The growth of towns with paved roads and the improved surfaces of turnpike roads had a considerable effect on coach design. Suspension was improved and by the end of the century it was possible to 'shrink-on' the iron tyres, a development which led to a lessening of vibration.

The Landau was introduced from Germany c1757. It was a cumbersome vehicle, requiring two or four horses, which had the facility of closing both front and back hoods to form a completely enclosed vehicle.

Two fashionable vehicles were the cabriolet and curricle, both introduced at the turn of the 19th century. The cabriolet was of French design. It had two wheels, was drawn by a single horse and used for short journeys. It had two seats, including one for the driver, and the groom or servant had a platform at the rear. The vehicle was increasingly used as a hiring vehicle, hence the term 'cab'. The curricle, of Italian origin, also had two wheels but used two horses either side of a central pole. They were more comfortable than other two-wheeled vehicles but were more expensive due to the use of two horses.

In the early 19th century the gig was the most common vehicle – the term describes a range of two-wheeled vehicles. The Stanhope gig, built by a coachbuilder called Tilbury for the Hon. Fitzroy Stanhope, appeared c1815. Also at this time a version of a gig was constructed which had space for the carriage of dogs, but the name 'dog-cart' came to describe a kind of gig with back-to-back seats for the use of people only.

N51 The Hansom Cab. Joseph Aloysius Hansom introduced his cab in 1834; it was, originally, a clumsy, square-framed vehicle with wheels 7 ft 6 ins in diameter, and with the driver on the roof. Subsequently the Hansom had smaller wheels and the driver rode high on a platform at the rear, with the reins running over the roof. It has been claimed, with some justification, that this cab, as it evolved, was in fact, the invention of John Chapman who took out patents for vehicles which, despite his inventiveness, were still called Hansom cabs.

N52 Stage coaches. A vehicle drawn by four horses which could seat four or six inside and twelve on the roof. A stage was the point where the horses were changed; generally stages were at ten-mile intervals. Stage-coaches were of several kinds – stage coach proper, mail coach, road coach and private coach. The heyday of the vehicle was from 1784 when the Post Office began sending mail by this means.

N53 Decorative coaches of the 19th century. Closed carriages for town use were popular from the 1820s. Clarences, four-seater vehicles using two horses, were introduced in the 1820s. These were particularly used by cab drivers, as they were large enough to carry several passengers and their luggage. Lord Brougham in 1839 had built for himself a light two-seater, one-horse vehicle which became immensely popular and fashionable. Phaetons were carriages used for social occasions; they were low vehicles pulled by one horse, and often had a groom's rumble seat. In 1828 the mail phaeton appeared; this had nothing to do with the mail, and was much larger than the usual phaeton. It had seats for the driver, a passenger and two servants, and was capacious enough to take a good quantity of luggage. It was therefore a vehicle used for long journeys and consistent travelling The Victoria was a cab vehicle, seating one or two passengers, with the driver on a high box seat at the front; it was invented by David Davies in 1835, but became popular in this country only in the late 1860s.

PART THREE
CANALS

N54 Canal formations. The following are dates for completion of the more important canals. In some cases stretches of canal were opened before completion of the whole route and, where available, the range of dates is given.

Aberdare	1812
Aberdeenshire	1805
Andover	1794
Ashby-de-la-Zouch	1804
Ashton-under-Lyme	1792–6
Barnsley	1799
Basingstoke	1796
Birmingham & Fazeley	1790
Birmingham & Liverpool	1835
Birmingham & Warwick	1844
Bradford	1774
Brecknock & Abergavenny	1812
Bridgewater's (Duke of)	1761
Bridgwater & Taunton	1827–41
Bude	1823
Burnturk	c1800
Caledonian	1822
Campbeltown	1794
Carlingwark	1765–80
Carlisle	1823
Chard	1842
Chelmer & Blackwater	1796
Chester	1779
Chesterfield	1776
Coombe Hill	1796
Coventry	1790
Crinan	1801
Cromford	1794
Croydon	1809
Dearne & Dove	1804
Derby	1796
Donnington Wood	1765
Droitwich	1777
Droitwich Junction	1853
Dudley	from 1779
Edinburgh & Glasgow	1822–3
Ellesmere	1779
Fletchers	c1791
Forth & Clyde	1790
Fossdyke	Roman
Glamorganshire	1798
Glasgow, Paisley & Johnstone	1811
Glastonbury	1833
Gloucester & Berkeley	1822
Grand Junction	1793–1822
Grand Surrey	1810–26
Grand Union	1814
Grand Western	1812
Grantham	1797
Grosvenor	1825
Hackney (Devon)	1843
Hertford Union	1830
Huddersfield Broad	1811
Huddersfield Narrow	1798
Isle of Dogs	1805
Kennet & Avon	1798–1810
Kensington	1828
Ketley	1788
Kilbagie	c1780
Lancaster	1819–26
Leeds & Liverpool	from 1781
Leicester Navigation	1794
Liskeard & Looe	1828–31
Louth	c1765
Macclesfield	1831
Manchester, Bolton & Bury	1808
Manchester & Salford	1839
Manchester Ship	1894
Monkland	from 1793
Montgomeryshire	1797
Montgomeryshire (West)	1821
Newcastle-under-Lyme	c1800
Newdigate	1795
Newport Pagnell	1817
North Wilts	1819
Nottingham	1794–1842
Nutbrook	1795
Oakham	c1803
Oxford	1790
Par	1847
Peak Forest	1800
Portsmouth & Arundel	1823–31
Ravenhead	c1773
Regent's	1816–1820
Rochdale	from 1794
St Columb	1777–9
Sheffield	1819
Shrewsbury	1796
Shropshire Union	1792
Somerset Coal	1805–11
Staffs & Worcs	1772
Stourbridge	1779
Stourbridge Extension	1840
Stover	1792
Stratford-upon-Avon	1816
Stroudwater	1778–9
Tavistock	1817
Tennant	1790
Thames & Medway	1824
Thames & Severn	1789
Torrington	1827
Trent & Mersey	from 1777

Ulverston	1796
Walsall	c1798
Warwick & Birmingham	1800
Warwick & Napton	1800
Wey Navigation	1653
Wey & Arun	1816
Wilts & Berks	1803–19
Woodeaves	c1802
Worcester & Birmingham	1815
Wyrley & Easington	from 1795

PART FOUR
BUSES

N55 Horse-drawn buses. In 1829 George Shillibeer ran the first horse-drawn omnibus in this country, between Paddington and the Bank in London. The vehicle, whose name means 'for all' was introduced into France in the 1820s. Shillibeer's vehicle seated about 20 passengers and was drawn by three horses abreast. Later omnibuses were shortened (as indeed was the name for the vehicle) and only two horses were used. By 1840 some buses had a roof, reached by an iron ladder, on which there were more seats.

The Stage Carriage Act 1832 permitted buses, as well as cabs, to ply for hire in the London metropolitan area. In 1855 the Compagnie Generale des Omnibus de Londres, an amalgamation of about three-quarters of the London bus companies, was established in Paris. It was quickly known here as the London General Omnibus Company. A serious rival in the 1880s was the London Road-Car Co. Ltd. Birmingham had a regular horse-bus service by 1834.

In 1901 London had 3736 licensed horse-buses – this despite the growing popularity of the tram, and in 1905 the London General Omnibus Company had 17,000 horses. From the 1901 peak the end came quickly: the last horse-buses in regular service in London were withdrawn on 4th August 1914, a decision hastened by the wartime requisitioning of horses. Probably the last urban horse-bus service in the country was that across the High Level Bridge between Newcastle-upon-Tyne and Gateshead, which was finally withdrawn in June 1931.

N56 Steam buses. Steam buses were introduced by Goldsworthy Gurney between Cheltenham and Gloucester in 1831, and in 1833 Walter Hancock used steam-buses in London on the original Shillibeer route. Modified vehicles appeared intermittently during the rest of the century but the heyday of this vehicle was just before the 1st World War.

N57 Motor buses. The first motor-bus service, in 1898, was in Edinburgh. In the same year the vehicle was introduced into Clacton, Falkirk, Llandudno, Mablethorpe, Mansfield and Torquay. Services began in London in 1899 under the auspices of the short-lived Motor Traction Company. Southampton was the first local authority to operate a bus service, in 1901, when they used hired vehicles; Eastbourne, when they began their service in 1903, owned their own buses.

N58 Trolleybuses. The trolleybus was invented in Germany in 1882 and demonstrated in London in 1909. The first such buses in service were those in Leeds and Bradford in 1911, and it was in the latter city that the last trolleybus service in the country was abandoned – in 1972.

PART FIVE
RAILWAYS

N59 Railway formations. The following is a list of the railway lines built in England, Wales and Scotland, together with their dates of incorporation and opening dates where known, and also details of their later history.

	Inc.	Open	Other Information
Abbotsbury	1877	1885	1896 to GWR
Aberdare	1845	1846	1847 to Taff Vale
Aberdare Valley	1855	1856	1864 to Vale of Neath
Aberystwyth & Welsh Coast	1861	1863	1865 to Cambrian
Abingdon	1855	1856	1904 to GWR
Alcester	1872	1876	1878 to GWR and Stratford-upon-Avon

	Inc.	Open	Other Information
Alexandra (Newport) Dock	1865		1882 name change to Alexandra (Newport and South Wales) Dock and Railway
Alexandra (Newport & Sth. Wales) Dock and Railway	1882		1897 merged with Pontypridd, Caerphilly & Newport
Anglesey Central	1863	1867	1876 to LNWR
Ashover Light	1919	1925	1950 closed
Aylesbury & Buckingham	1860	1868	1890 to Metropolitan
Ayr and Wigtownshire	1887		1892 to G & SWR
Bala and Dolgelly	1862	1868	1877 to GWR
Bala and Festiniog	1873	1882	1910 to GWR
Banbury and Cheltenham	1873	1881	1897 to GWR
Bangor & Caernarvon	1851	1852	1852 to Chester & Holyhead
Barnoldswick	1867	1871	1899 to Midland
Barnstaple & Ilfracombe	1870	1874	1890 to LSWR
Barry	1884	1888	1922 to GWR
Bedford	1845	1846	1845 to London & Birmingham
Bedford & Cambridge	1860	1862	1865 to LNWR
Bedford & Northampton	1865	1872	1885 to Midland
Berks and Hants	1845	1847	1846 to GWR
Berks and Hants Extension	1859	1862	1882 to GWR
Birkenhead			1859 name change from Birkenhead, Lancs and Cheshire. 1860 to LNWR
Birkenhead, Lancs and Cheshire	1846	1850	1859 name change to Birkenhead
Birmingham & Derby Junction	1836	1839	1844 to Midland
Birmingham & Gloucester	1836	1840	1846 to Midland
Birmingham & Henley-in-Arden	1873	1894	1900 to GWR
Birmingham, North Warwickshire & Stratford-upon-Avon	1894	1907	1900 to GWR
Birmingham & Oxford Junction	1846	1852	1848 to GWR
Birmingham West Suburban	1871	1876	1875 to Midland
Birmingham, Wolverhampton & Dudley	1846	1854	1848 to GWR
Birmingham, Wolverhampton & Stour Valley	1846	1852	1847 to LNWR
Bishops Castle	1861	1865	1935 closed
Bishops Stortford, Dunmow & Braintree	1861		1865 to GER
Bishops Waltham	1862	1863	1932 closed
Blackburn	1857		Amalgam. of Blackburn, Darwen & Bolton, and Blackburn, Clitheroe & North Western. 1858 amalgamated with Lancs & Yorks, and the East Lancs
Blackburn, Clitheroe & North Western			1857 to Blackburn
Blackburn, Darwen & Bolton			1857 to Blackburn
Blackpool & Lytham	1861	1863	1871 to Preston & Wyre
Blythe and Tyne	1852		1874 to NER
Bodmin & Wadebridge	1832	1834	1846 to L&SW
Bolton and Leigh	1825	1828	1845 to Grand Junction
Bolton and Preston	1837		1843 to North Union
Bourne & Essendine	1857		1864 to GNR
Bourton-on-Water	1860	1862	1874 to GNWR
Bradford & Thornton	1871	1878	to GNR
Bradford, Eccleshill & Idle	1866		1871 to GNR
Brecon & Merthyr Tydfil Junction	1859	1863	1922 to GWR
Bridgwater	1882	1890	1923 to LSWR
Bridport	1855	1857	1901 to GWR

	Inc.	Open	Other Information
Brighton and Dyke	1877	1887	1938 closed
Bristol & Exeter	1836	1841	1876 to GWR
Bristol & Gloucester	1828	1835	1846 to Midland
Bristol & North Somerset	1863	1873	1884 to GWR
Bristol & Portishead	1863	1867	1884 to GWR
Bristol and South Wales	1857	1863	1868 to GWR
Bristol Port Railway & Pier	1862	1865	1890 to Midland and GWR
Briton Ferry Dock & Railway	1851	1861	1873 to GWR
Bromley Direct	1874	1878	1879 to SER
Brynmawr & Blaenavon	1866	1869	1869 to LNWR
Brynmawr & Western Valleys	1899	1906	1902 to LNWR and GWR
Buckfastleigh, Totnes & South Devon	1864	1872	1897 to GWR
Buckingham & Brackley Junction	1846		1847 to Buckinghamshire
Buckinghamshire	1847		Amalgam. of Buckingham & Brackley Jc, and Oxford & Bletchley Jc. 1847 to LNWR
Buckley	1860		1923 to Great Central
Bullo Pill	1809	1812	1826 to Forest of Dean
Burry Port & Gwendreath Valley	1865	1869	1922 to GWR
Bute Docks	1886		1897 name change to Cardiff
Caernarvon & Llanberis	1864	1869	
Caernarvonshire	1862	1867	
Caledonian	1845		Amalgam. of Scottish North Eastern, Wishaw & Coltness, Garnkirke, Glasgow, Perth, Almond Valley & Methven
Calne	1860	1863	1892 to GWR
Cambrian	1864		Amalgam. of Oswestry & Newtown, Oswestry, Ellesmere & Whitchurch, Llanidloes & Newtown, Newtown & Machynlleth, and Aberystwyth & Welsh Coast. 1922 to GWR
Cannock Chase	1860		1863 to LNWR
Cannock Mineral			1855 name change from the Derbys, Staffs and Worcs Jc. 1869 to LNWR
Canterbury & Whitstable	1827	1830	1844 to SER
Cardiff		1911	1897 name change from Bute Docks
Cardiff & Ogmore Valley	1873	1876	1876 to Llynvi & Ogmore
Cardiff, Penarth & Barry Junction.	1885	1887	1889 to Taff Vale
Carlisle & Silloth Bay	1855	1856	1880 to North British
Carmarthen & Cardigan	1854	1860	1881 to GWR
Caterham	1854	1856	1859 to SER
Central London	1891	1900	
Central Wales	1859	1862	1868 to LNWR
Central Wales & Carmarthen Junction	1873		1873 name change from Swansea and Carmarthen
Central Wales Extension	1860	1866	1868 to LNWR
Chard & Taunton	1861	1866	1863 to Bristol & Exeter
Cheddar Valley & Yatton	1864	1869	1865 to Bristol & Exeter
Cheltenham & Gt. Western Union	1836	1841	1843 to GWR
Cheshire Midland	1860	1862	1865 to Cheshire Lines Committee
Chester & Birkenhead	1837	1840	1847 to Birkenhead, Lancs & Cheshire Junction

	Inc.	Open	Other Information
Chester & Crewe	1837	1840	1840 to Grand Junction
Chester & Holyhead	1844	1846	1856 to LNWR
Chesterfield & Brampton	1870	1873	1871 to Midland
City & South London	1884	1890	previously known as London & Southwark Subway
Cleobury Mortimer & Ditton Priors Light	1901	1908	1922 to GWR
Cockermouth & Workington	1845	1847	1866 to LNWR
Coleford	1872	1883	1884 to GWR
Coleford, Monmouth, Usk & Pontypool	1853	1856	1887 to GWR
Colne Valley & Halstead	1856	1859	1923 to LNER
Conway & Llanrwst	1860	1863	1867 to LNWR
Cornwall	1846	1859	1889 to GWR
Cornwall Minerals	1872	1874	1896 to GWR
Corris	1858	1883	1930 to GWR
Corwen & Bala	1862	1866	1896 to GWR
Cowbridge	1862	1865	1889 to Taff Vale
Cowbridge & Aberthaw	1889	1892	1895 to Taff Vale
Cowes & Newport	1859	1862	1887 to Isle of Wight Central. 1923 to SR
Cromford & High Peak	1825	1831	1862 to LNWR
Culm Valley Light	1873	1876	1880 to GWR
Dare Valley	1863	1866	1889 to Taff Vale
Dartmouth & Torbay	1857	1859	1862 to South Devon
Deeside	1846/ 1852	1853	1875 to Great North of Scotland
Denbigh, Ruthin & Corwen	1860	1862	1879 to LNWR
Derbyshire, Staffordshire, & Worcestershire Junction	1847	1859	1855 name changed to Cannock Mineral
Devon & Cornwall	1873	1879	
Devon & Somerset	1864	1871	1901 to GWR
Didcot, Newbury & Southampton	1873	1882	1923 to GWR
Dore & Chinley	1884	1893	1888 to Midland
Dorset Central	1856	1860	1862 to Somerset & Dorset
Dover & Deal	1874	1881	Jointly vested in LCDR and SER
Duffryn, Llynvi & Porcawl	1825	1829	1847 to Llynvi Valley
Dulas Valley Mineral	1862		1863 name change to Neath & Brecon
Dunstable	1845	1848	1845 to London & Birmingham
Dursley & Midland Junction	1855	1856	1861 to Midland
Easingwold Light	1887	1891	Was not nationalised. Passenger service withdrawn 1948
East & West India Docks & Birmingham Junction	1846	1850	1853 name change to North London
East and West Junction	1864	1871	
East Anglian	1848	1848	Amalgam. of Lynn & Ely, Lynn & Dereham, and Ely & Huntingdon. 1852 to Eastern Counties
East Cornwall Mineral	1869	1872	1891 to Plymouth, Devonport & Sth Western Jc. Previously known as the Callington & Calstock
East Gloucestershire	1862	1873	1890 to GWR
East Kent Light	1911	1916	1948 closed to passengers
East London	1865	1869	1892 to LBSCR, Metropolitan and Metropolitan District
East Somerset	1856	1858	1874 to GWR

	Inc.	Open	Other Information
East Usk	1885	1898	1892 to GWR
Eastern & Midlands	1882		Amalgamation of Lynn & Fakenham, Gt Yarmouth & Stalham Light, and Yarmouth Union. 1893 to Midland & Gt Northern Joint Committee
Eastern Union	1844	1846	1867 took in Ipswich & Bury
Edinburgh & Dalkeith	1826		1845 to North British
Edinburgh & Glasgow	1838	1842	
Edinburgh & Northern	1844	1847	
Edinburgh, Leith & Granton	1836	1848	1847 to Edinburgh, Perth & Dundee
Edinburgh, Perth & Dundee	1847	1847/ 1848	1862 to North British
Ely & Clydach Valleys	1873	1878	1880 to GWR
Ely & Huntingdon	1845		1848 to East Anglian
Ely & St Ives	1864		1876 to GER
Ely Valley	1857	1860	1903 to GWR
Ely Valley Extension	1863	1865	1865 to Ogmore Valley
Epsom & Leatherhead	1856	1859	1860 to LSW
Erewash Valley	1845	1847	1845 to Midland
Evesham & Redditch	1863	1866	1882 to Midland
Exeter	1883	1903	1923 to GWR
Exeter & Crediton	1845	1877	1886 to GER
Exeter Valley	1874	1885	1875 to Bristol & Exeter
Faringdon	1860	1864	1886 to GWR
Felixstowe Ry & Dock	1875	1877	1886 to GER
Ffestiniog & Blaenau	1868		1910 to GWR
Findhorn	1859	1862	
Fleetwood, Preston & West Riding Junction	1846	1850	1867 to LNWR and L&YR
Forcett	1865		1873 to NER
Forest of Dean	1826		1847 to South Wales
Forest of Dean Central	1856	1868	1923 to GWR
Forth Bridge	1873	1890	1882 to Midland
Freshwater, Yarmouth & Newport	1873	1889	
Furness & Midland	1863	1867	1863 to Midland and Furness Rys jointly
Glasgow & Milngavie Junction	1861		1876 to North British
Glasgow & Sth Western	1850		Previously the Glasgow, Paisley, Kilmarnock & Ayr
Glasgow, Bothwell, Hamilton & Coatbridge	1874	1878	1878 to North British
Gloucester & Cheltenham	1809	1811	1837 to Birmingham & Gloucester
Gloucester & Dean Forest	1846	1851	1871 to GWR
Golden Valley	1876	1881	1899 to GWR
Grand Junction	1833	1837	1846 to LNWR
Gravesend	1881	1883	1883 to LCDR. 1953 closed
Great Marlow	1868	1873	1897 to GWR
Great North of Scotland	1849		
Great Western	1835	1838	
Great Western & Brentford	1855	1859	1871 to GWR
Great Western & Uxbridge	1846	1856	1847 to GWR
Great Yarmouth & Stalham Light	1876	1877	1882 to Eastern & Midlands
Gwendreath Valleys	1866	1871	1923 to GWR

	Inc.	Open	Other Information
Halesowen & Bromsgrove Branch	1865	1883	1876 name change to Halesowen. 1872 jointly worked by Midland and Gt Western
Hampstead Junction	1853	1860	1867 to LNWR
Harrow & Stanmore	1886	1890	1899 to LNWR
Hay	1811	1816	1860 parts to Hereford, Hay & Brecon
Hayle	1834	1837	1846 to West Cornwall
Helston	1880	1887	1898 to GWR
Hemel Hempstead	1863	1877	1886 to Midland
Henley-in-Arden & Gt Western Junction	1873		1884 name change to Birmingham & Henley-in-Arden
Hereford, Hay & Brecon	1859	1863	1874 to Midland
Hereford, Ross & Gloucester	1851	1853	1862 to GWR
Hertford & Welwyn Junction	1854	1858	1855 merged with Dunstable & Welwyn Jc to form Hertford, Luton & Dunstable
Hertford, Luton & Dunstable	1855		Formed from merger of Hertford & Welwyn Jc, and Dunstable & Welwyn Jc
Highland	1865		Amalgam. of the Inverness & Aberdeen Jc, and the Inverness & Perth Jc. Later took in Ross-shire, Sutherland & Caithness, and Golspie & Helmsdale
Huddersfield & Manchester Ry and Canal	1845	1847	1847 to LNWR
Hull & Barnsley	1880	1885	1922 to NER
Hull & Selby	1836		1846 to York & Nth Midland
Hunstanton & West Norfolk Junction	1874		Amalgam. of Lynn & Hunstanton and the West Norfolk Jc. 1890 to GER
Inverness & Aberdeen Junction	1856		1865 to Highland
Inverness & Nairn	1854	1855	1861 merged with Inverness and Aberdeen
Inverness & Perth	1861		1865 to Highland
Inverness & Ross-shire	1860	1863	1862 to Inverness & Aberdeen
Isle of Wight Central	1887		Amalgam. of Cowes & Newport, Isle of Wight (Newport Jc), and the Ryde & Newport
Keighley & Worth Valley	1862	1867	1881 to Midland
Keith & Portessie	1882	1884	
Kendal & Windermere	1845	1846	1857 to Lancaster & Carlisle. 1879 to LNWR
Kent Coast	1857		1871 to LCDR
Lambourne Valley	1883	1898	1905 to GWR
Lampeter, Aberayron & New Quay Light	1906	1911	1922 to GWR
Lanarkshire & Ayrshire		1888	1884 name changed from Barrmill & Kilwinning
Lancashire & Yorkshire		1854	An amalgam. of several Lancs and Yorks lines
Lancashire Union	1864	1869	1883 to LNWR
Lancaster & Carlisle	1844	1846	1859 to LNWR
Lancaster & Preston Junction	1837	1840	1849 to Lancaster & Carlisle
Lauder Light	1882	1901	
Launceston & Sth Devon	1862	1865	1869 to Sth Devon
Lee-on-Solent	1892	1894	1931 closed to passengers
Leeds & Bradford	1844	1846	1851 to Midland
Leeds, Dewsbury & Manchester	1845	1848	1847 to LNWR

	Inc.	Open	Other Information
Leicester & Swannington	1830	1832	1846 to Midland
Leominster & Bromyard	1874	1884	1888 to GWR
Leominster & Kingston	1854	1857	1898 to GWR
Leven	1852	1854	1861 to Leven & East of Fife
Leven & East of Fife	1861		Amalgam. of Leven and the East of Fife. 1877 to NBR
Liskeard & Caradon	1843	1844	1909 to GWR
Liskeard & Looe	1858	1860	1923 to GWR
Liverpool & Manchester	1826	1830	1845 to Grand Junction
Liverpool Central Station	1864	1874	1865 to Cheshire Lines Committee
Liverpool, St Helens & South Lancs			1893 name change from St Helens & Wigan Jc.
Liverpool, Southport & Preston Junction	1884	1887	
Llanelly & Myndd-Mawr	1875	1883	1923 to GWR
Llanelly Ry & Dock	1828	1833	1889 to GWR
Llangollen & Corwen	1860	1865	1896 to GWR
Llanidloes & Newtown	1853	1859	1864 to Cambrian
Llantrisant & Taff Vale Junction	1861	1863	1889 to Taff Vale
Llynvi & Ogmore	1866	1883	Amalgam. of Llynvi Valley, Ogmore Valley, and the Cardiff & Ogmore Valley
Llynvi Valley	1846	1861	1866 to Llynvi & Ogmore
London & Birmingham	1833	1837	1846 to LNWR
London & Croydon		1839	to LBSCR
London, Brighton, Sth Coast			Amalgam. of London & Croydon and London & Brighton. 1923 to SR
London & Greenwich	1833	1836	
London, Midland & Scottish	1923		
London & North Eastern	1923		
London & North Western	1846		Initially amalgam. of London & Birmingham, Grand Junction, and Manchester and Birmingham
London & South Western			Previously London & Southampton
London & Southampton	1834		Changed name to London South Western 1839
London, Tilbury & Southend	1862	1854	1912 to Midland
Lostwithiel & Fowey	1862	1869	1877 to Cornwall Minerals
Louth & East Coast	1872	1877	
Ludlow & Clee Hill	1861	1864	1892 to LNWR and GWR
Lydney & Lidbrooke	1809	1813	1810 name change to Severn & Wye Ry and Canal. 1879 to Severn & Wye and Severn Bridge Ry
Lynn & Dereham		1846	to East Anglian
Lynn & Ely		1846	to East Anglian
Lynn & Fakenham	1876	1879	1882 to Eastern & Midlands
Lynn & Sutton Bridge	1861	1865	1866 to Midland & Eastern
Maidens & Dunure Light		1906	Closed 1930. Reopened 1932. Closed 1933
Maidstone & Ashford	1880	1884	1883 to LCDR
Malmesbury	1872	1877	1880 to GWR
Manchester & Birmingham	1837	1840	1846 amalgam. with London & Birmingham to form LNWR
Manchester & Milford	1860	1866	1911 to GWR

	Inc.	Open	Other Information
Manchester & Stockport	1866	1875	1869 to Midland
Manchester, Buxton, Matlock & Midlands	1846	1848	1871 to Midland
Manchester, Sheffield & Lincs	1849		Amalgam. of Sheffield, Ashton-under-Lyne & Manchester, Grimsby & Sheffield Jc, Sheffield & Lincs, Sheffield & Lincs Extension, Manchester & Lincoln Union
Manchester Sth District	1873	1880	1877 to Midland
Manchester Sth Jc & Altrincham	1845	1849	1849 to LNWR and MS and LR
Mansfield	1910	1913	to GCR
Mansfield & Pinxton	1817	1819	(horse drawn); 1849 loco. 1848 to Midland
Marlborough	1861	1864	1896 to GWR
Marlborough & Grafton	1896	1898	1899 to Midland & Sth Western Junction
Marple New Mills & Hayfield Junction	1860	1865	
Maryport & Carlisle	1837	1840	
Mawddwy	1865	1865	1923 to GWR
Merthyr, Tredegar & Abergavenny	1859	1862	1862 to LNWR
Mid Hants	1861		1881 to LSWR
Midland	1844		Amalgam. of Midland Counties, North Midland, and Birmingham & Derby Jc, and other smaller lines
Midland & Sth Western Junction	1884		Amalgam. of Swindon Marlborough and Andover, and Swindon & Cheltenham Extension. 1923 to GWR
Midland and Eastern	1866		Amalgam. of Lynn & Sutton Bridge, and Spalding & Bourne. 1883 to Eastern & Midlands
Midland Counties	1836	1839	1844 to Midland
Mid Wales	1859	1864	1904 to Cambrian
Milford	1856	1863	1896 to GWR
Minehead	1871	1874	1897 to GWR
Mitcheldean Road & Forest of Dean Junction	1871	1885	1880 to GWR
Mold	1847	1849	1849 to Chester & Holyhead
Mold & Denbigh	1861	1869	
Monkland	1848		Amalgam. of Monkland & Kirkintilloch, the Ballochney, and the Slammannan. To NBR
Monmouthshire	1792	1798	Canal at first. 1880 to GWR
Morayshire	1846	1852	1880 to Gt North of Scotland
Morecambe Ry & Harbour	1846	1848	1871 to Midland
Moreton Hampstead & Sth Devon	1862	1866	1872 to Sth Devon
Much Wenlock & Severn	1859	1862	1896 to GWR
Nantlle	1825	1828	1867 to Caernarvonshire
Nantwich & Market Drayton	1861	1867	1897 to GWR
Narbeth & Maenclochog	1872	1876	1881 amalgamated with Nth Pembroke & Fishguard
Neath & Brecon	1863	1864	1869 to Swansea Vale & Neath & Brecon Jc.
Nerquis			1866 to LNWR
Newquay		1846	1873 to Cornwall Minerals
Newent	1873	1885	1892 to GWR

	Inc.	Open	Other Information
Newmarket & Bury Ext.	1846	1848	
Newport, Abergavenny & Hereford	1846	1854	1860 to West Midland
Newport Pagnell	1863	1867	1875 to LNWR
Newquay & Cornwall Junction	1864	1874	1884 to Cornwall Minerals
Newtown & Machynlleth	1857	1863	1864 to Cambrian
Norfolk	1845		Amalgam. of the Yarmouth & Norwich, and the Norwich & Brandon
Norfolk & Suffolk Joint	1898	1898	
North and Sth Western Junction	1851	1853	1871 to LNWR, Midland and North London. 1921 to LMS
North British	1844		Eventually included 50 lines
North Cornwall	1882	1886	
North Devon & Cornwall Light		1925	
North Eastern	1854		Amalgam. of many lines
North Lindsey Light	1900	1906	
North London		1850	1853 name change from East & West India Docks & Birmingham. 1909 to LNWR. 1921 to LMS
North Midland	1836	1840	1844 to Midland
North Pembrokeshire & Fishguard	1884		name change from Rosebush & Fishguard. 1898 to GWR
North Staffs	1847		Amalgam. of several lines
North Wales Mineral	1844	1846	1846 to Shrewsbury & Chester
North Western	1846	1849	1871 to Midland
Norwich and Spalding	1853	1858	1877 to Midland & Eastern
Nottingham Suburban	1886	1889	
Nuneaton & Hinckley	1859	1862	1860 name change to Sth Leics. 1867 to LNWR
Ogmore Valley	1863	1865	1865 to Llynvi & Ogmore
Oldbury	1873	1884	1894 to GWR
Oldham, Ashton-under-Lyne & Guide Bridge	1857	1861	1862 to LNWR and Manchester, Sheffield & Lincs
Oswestry & Newtown	1855	1860	1864 to Cambrian
Oswestry, Ellesmere & Whitchurch	1861	1864	1864 to Cambrian
Otley & Ilkley	1861	1865	
Oxford	1843	1844	1844 to GWR
Oxford & Bletchley Junction	1846	1850	1847 to Buckinghamshire
Oxford & Rugby	1845	1850	1846 to GWR
Oxford, Worcs & Wolverhampton	1845	1850	1860 to West Midland
Par (Cornwall)		1841	1873 to Cornwall Minerals
Pembroke & Tenby	1859	1863	1897 to GWR
Penarth Extension	1876	1878	1923 to GWR
Penarth Harbour, Dock & Railway	1856	1859	1922 to GWR
Pentewan		1829	Closed 1918
Peterborough, Wisbech & Sutton	1863	1866	1883 to Eastern & Midlands
Pontypool, Caerleon & Newport	1865	1874	1876 to GWR
Pontypridd, Caerphilly & Newport	1878	1884	1897 to Alexandra (Newport & Sth Wales) Dock & Railway
Port Talbot Ry & Docks	1894	1897	1922 to GWR
Portpatrick	1857	1861	1885 to Portpatrick & Wigtownshire Jt Ctte
Portpatrick & Wigtownshire Jt Ctte			1885 amalgam. of Portpatrick and Wigtownshire. 1885 to Midland

	Inc.	Open	Other Information
Preston & Longridge	1836	1840	1856 to Fleetwood, Preston & West Riding Jc
Preston & Wigan	1831	1838	1834 to North Union
Preston & Wyre	1835	1840	1847 to Lancs & Yorks and LNWR
Princetown	1878	1883	1922 to GWR
Ramsey	1861	1863	1875 vested in GER
Ramsey & Somersham Jc	1875	1889	1897 to GER and GNR
Ravenglass & Eskdale	1873	1875	
Redditch	1858	1859	1874 to Midland
Redruth & Chasewater	1824	1826	Worked by horse until 1854. Closed 1915
Rhondda & Swansea Bay	1882	1885	1922 to GWR
Rhondda Valley & Hirwain	1867	1878	1889 to Taff Vale
Rhymney	1854	1858	1922 to GWR
Rosebush & Fishguard	1878	1895	1884 name change to Pembrokeshire & Fishguard
Ross & Ledbury	1873	1885	1892 to GWR
Ross & Monmouth	1865	1873	1922 to GWR
Rugby & Leamington	1846	1851	1846 to London & Birmingham
Rumney	1825	1836	1863 to Brecon & Merthyr Tydfil Jc
Rye & Camber		1895	
St George's Harbour & Ry	1853	1858	1861 to LNWR
St Helens & Runcorn Gap	1830	1833	1845 to St Helens Canal & Ry
St Helens Canal & Ry	1845		1864 to LNWR
Scottish Central	1845	1848	1865 to Caledonian
Scottish Midland Junction	1848	1855	
Severn & Wye Railway & Canal			See Lydney & Lidbrooke
Severn & Wye & Severn Bridge	1879		1894 to Midland and GWR
Severn Bridge	1872	1879	1879 to Severn & Wye & Severn Bridge
Severn Valley	1853	1862	1870 to GWR
Sheffield & Rotherham	1838	1838	1845 to Midland
Shrewsbury & Birmingham	1846	1849	1854 to GWR
Shrewsbury & Chester	1846		1854 to GWR
Shrewsbury & Hereford	1846	1852	1862 to LNWR, GWR and West Midland. 1870 to GWR and LNWR jointly
Shrewsbury, Oswestry & Chester Junction	1845	1848	1846 to Shrewsbury & Chester
Sirhowy	1802	1805	Opened as Tramroad. 1860 name change to S. Railway. 1876 to LNWR
Solway Junction	1864	1869	
Somerset & Dorset	1862		Amalgam. of Somerset Central and Dorset Central. 1875 to Midland & LSWR. 1923 to SR and LMS
Somerset Central	1852	1854	1862 to Somerset & Dorset
South Devon	1844	1846	1878 to GWR
South Devon & Tavistock	1854	1859	1865 to South Devon
South Leicestershire	1860		Previously called the Nuneaton & Hinckley. 1867 to LNWR
South Staffordshire	1846	1847	Amalgam. of Sth Staffs Jc and Trent Valley, Midland and Grand Junction 1867 to LNWR
South Staffordshire Junction	1846		1846 to Sth Staffs
South Wales	1845	1850	1863 to GWR

	Inc.	Open	Other Information
South Wales Mineral	1853	1860	1923 to GWR
Southern	1923		
Southport & Cheshire Lines Extension	1881	1884	1881 to Cheshire Lines Ctte
Southsea		1885	To LBSCR and LSWR
Spalding & Bourne	1862	1866	1866 to Midland & Eastern
Staines & West Drayton	1873	1884	1900 to GWR
Stockport & Woodley Junction	1860	1863	1865 to Cheshire Lines Ctte
Stockport Timperley & Altrincham Junction	1861	1866	1865 to Cheshire Lines Ctte
Stocksbridge	1874	1876	
Stockton & Darlington	1821		1863 to NER
Stonehouse & Nailsworth	1863	1867	1878 to Midland
Stourbridge	1860	1863	1870 to GWR
Stratford & Moreton	1821	1826	1845 to Oxford, Worcs & Wolverhampton
Stratford-upon-Avon	1857	1860	1883 to GWR
Stratford-upon-Avon, Towcester & Midland Junction	1879	1882	
Swansea & Carmarthen	1865		1873 name change to Central Wales and Carmarthen Jc
Swansea & Mumbles		1806	Closed 1960
Swansea & Neath	1861	1863	1863 to GWR
Swansea Vale & Neath & Brecon Jc	1864	1875	1869 to Neath & Brecon. 1922 to GWR
Swansea Valley	1847		1855 to Swansea Vale
Swindon & Highworth	1875	1883	1882 to GWR
Swindon & Cheltenham Extension	1881	1883	1884 to Midland & Sth Western Jc
Swindon, Marlborough & Andover	1873	1881	1884 to Midland & Sth Western Jc
Taff Vale	1836	1840	1922 to GWR
Tanat Valley Light	1898	1904	1921 to Cambrian
Teign Valley	1863	1882	1923 to GWR
Tenbury	1859	1861	1869 to LNWR and GWR
Tenbury & Bewdley	1860	1864	1869 to GWR
Tewkesbury & Malvern	1860	1862	1876 to Midland
Tiverton & Nth Devon	1875	1884	1894 to GWR
Torbay & Brixham	1864	1868	1882 to GWR
Tottenham & Forest Gate	1890	1894	1914 to Midland
Tottenham & Hampstead Junction	1862	1868	1902 to Midland, and Gt Eastern
Treferig Valley	1879	1883	1889 to Taff Vale
Trent Valley	1845	1847	1846 to London & Birmingham, Grand Junction, and Manchester & Birmingham
Trent Valley, Midland & Grand Junction	1846		1846 to Sth Staffs
Vale of Clwyd	1856	1858	1867 to LNWR
Vale of Glamorgan	1889	1897	1922 to GWR
Vale of Llangollen	1859	1861	1896 to GWR
Vale of Neath	1846	1851	1863 to Swansea & Neath
Vale of Rheidol	1897	1902	1913 to Cambrian
Vale of Towy	1854	1858	1889 to GWR
Van		1871	1923 to GWR
Wakefield, Pontefract & Goole	1845	1848	Later to Lancs and Yorks
Wallingford & Watlington	1864	1866	1872 to GWR
Warrington & Altrincham Junction	1851	1853	1853 to Warrington & Stockport. 1859 to LNWR and St Helens

	Inc.	Open	Other Information
Warrington & Newton	1829	1831	1836 to Grand Junction
Warrington & Stockport			See Warrington & Altrincham Junction
Warwick & Leamington Union	1842	1844	1843 to London & Birmingham
Watford & Rickmansworth	1860	1862	1881 to LNWR
Watlington & Princes Risborough	1869	1872	1883 to GWR
Watton & Swaffham	1869	1875	1880 to GER
Wellington & Drayton	1862	1867	1864 to GWR
Wellington & Severn Junction	1853	1857	1892 to GWR
Welshpool & Llanfair Light	1899	1903	1923 to GWR
Wenlock	1861	1864	1896 to GWR
West Cheshire	1861	1869	1865 to Cheshire Lines Ctte
West Cornwall	1846	1852	1878 to GWR
West Lancs	1871	1878	1897 to Lancs and Yorks
West London Extension	1859	1863	Jointly held by LNWR, GWR, LSWR and LBSCR
West Midland	1860		Amalgam. of Oxford, Worcester & Wolverhampton and Newport, Abergavenny & Hereford, and Worcester & Hereford. To GWR 1863
West Somerset	1857	1862	1922 to GWR
Weston, Clevedon & Portishead Light	1885	1897	
Weymouth & Portland	1862	1865	
Whitby, Redcar & Middlesborough Union	1866	1883	1889 to NER
Whitechapel & Bow	1897	1902	1897 to London, Tilbury & Southend. 1912 to Midland
Whitehaven, Cleator & Egremont	1854	1856	1877 to LNWR. 1878 to LNWR and Furness
Whitehaven & Furness Junction	1845	1849	1866 to Furness
Whitehaven Junction	1844	1847	1866 to LNWR
Widnes	1873	1877	1875 to Sheffield & Midland Joint
Whitland & Cardigan	1869	1873	1890 to GWR
Wigtownshire	1872	1875	1885 to Portpatrick & Wigtownshire Jt Ctte
Wiltshire, Somerset & Weymouth	1845	1848	1851 to GWR
Witney	1859	1861	1890 to GWR
Wolverhampton & Walsall	1865	1872	1876 to Midland
Wolverhampton, Walsall & Midland Jc	1872	1879	1874 to Midland
Woodstock	1886	1890	1897 to GWR
Worcester & Hereford	1853	1859	1860 to West Midland
Worcester, Bromyard & Leominster	1861	1874	1888 to GWR
Wrexham & Ellesmere	1885	1895	1922 to GWR
Wrexham & Minera	1861	1862	1871 to GWR
Wrington Vale Light	1897	1901	Closed 1931
Wycombe	1846	1854	1867 to GWR
Wye Valley	1866	1876	1905 to GWR
Yarmouth & North Norfolk	1876	1877	1882 to Eastern & Midlands
Yarmouth Union	1880	1882	1882 to Eastern & Midlands
York and North Midland	1836	1839	1854 to NER
Yorkshire Dales	1897	1902	Later to Midland

PART SIX
TRAMS

N60 Tramways. An American, George Train, introduced the first horse-drawn tramway into the country, at Birkenhead in 1860. The following year he opened the first tramway in London from Marble Arch to Porchester Road to demonstrate the new vehicle and, subsequently, two others in the London area. All of these lines were failures. One reason for this was that despite the fact that rails which were flush with the road surface were available, Train chose to use rails which protruded slightly above that level and they were therefore a serious hazard. A second reason was that his experimental tracks were in areas where the population was less likely to take a tram and more likely to use its own private transport.

Interest in tramways revived later in that decade and a number of companies applied to the government for permission build them. It was decided that trams should not penetrate into the centre of the city but act, instead, as feeders from the suburbs. Thus the first proper tramway to open, in 1870, ran from Brixton to Westminster Bridge Road. That year the Tramways Act was passed which permitted local authorities to run their own concerns, but the usual practice was for the authority to establish a tramway and then lease it out to a private company.

By the 1890s trams were common in most provincial cities and in London alone there were a thousand of them. The vehicle was, despite the smooth running on the rails, heavier for the horse than was an omnibus. The horse-drawn tram had virtually disappeared by 1914, and electric trams had begun to take over from 1904.

A cable tramway was opened up Highgate Hill, north London, in 1884. On this route the carriages were attached to a continuous belt and were hauled up the steep hill by horses. A similar tramway was opened on Brixton Hill. These two lines were both electrified c1910.

PART SEVEN
MOTOR CARS

N61 Motor Cars. The first cars with internal combustion engines were introduced into the country in the 1880s. Their use was restricted by an Act of 1865 relating to steam vehicles, usually known as the Red Flag Act, which permitted speeds of only up to 4 mph in towns. This was repealed in 1896.

Motor car registration was introduced by the Motor Car Act 1903. The first car registered on January 1st, 1904, numbered A1, belonged to the Earl Russell.

The first car accident fatality appears to have been in Harrow in 1899.

PART EIGHT
BIBLIOGRAPHY

General
British Transport. An Economic Survey from the Seventeenth Century to the Twentieth, H. J. Dyos and D. H. Aldcroft (1969)
A History of Transport, T. C. Barker and Michael Robbins (2 vols 1963 and 1979)
The Transport Revolution from 1770, Philip S. Bagwell (1974)
A Hundred Years of Inland Transport, C. E. R. Sherrington (1969)
The Story of Passenger Transport in Britain, J. Joyce (1967)

Roads
A History of Roads, Geoffrey Hindley (1971)
Roman Roads in Britain, Ivan Margary (rev. 1967)
Roman Ways in the Weald, Ivan Margary (rev. 1956)
The Road System of Medieval England, F. M. Stenton (Economic History Review vol 7, 1936)
English Wayfaring Life in the Middle Ages, J. J. Jusserand (rev. 1950)
Roads and Their Traffic 1750–1850, John Copeland (1968)
English Local Government: the story of the King's Highway, Sidney and Beatrice Webb (1913)
Ancient Bridges of England, S. Jervoise (4 vols 1930–36)
The Turnpike road system in England 1663–1840, William Albert (1972)
Transport and Economy: the turnpike roads of eighteenth-century Britain, Eric Pawson (1977)
Vanishing Street Furniture, Geoffrey Warren (1978)

Carriages, Coaches and Cabs

Carriages at Eight, Frank E. Huggett (1979)
The Mail-Coach Men of the Late Eighteenth Century, Edmund Vale
Stage Coach to John O'Groats, Leslie Gardiner (1961)
English Pleasure Carriages, W. Bridges Adams (1837 repr. 1971)
A History of the London Taxicab, G. N. Georgano (1972)

Canals

The Canals of Britain, Charles Hadfield (1950)
The Canals of Britain, D. D. Gladwin (1973)
British Canals, Charles Hadfield (1969)
The Canal Age, Charles Hadfield (1968)
Lost Canals of England and Wales, Ronald Russell (1971)
Bradshaw's Canals and Navigable Rivers of England and Wales

Buses

The Omnibus, ed John Hibbs (1971)
Omnibuses and Cabs, H. C. Moore (1902)
London's Buses, K. C. Blacker, R. S. Lunn and R. G. Westgate (2 vols 1977 and 1983)
London's Trams and Trolleybuses, John R. Day (1971)
The History of British Bus Services, John Hibbs (1968)

Railways

Historical Geography of the Railways of the British Isles, E. F. Carter (1959)
A Regional History of the Railways of Great Britain:
Vol 1 *The West Country*, David St John Thomas
Vol 2 *Southern England*, H. P. White
Vol 3 *Greater London*, H. P. White
Vol 4 *The North East*, K. Hoole
Vol 5 *The Eastern Counties*, D. I. Gordon
Vol 6 *Scotland (Lowlands and Borders)*, John Thomas
British Railway History 1877–1947, Hamilton Ellis (1959)
The Midland Railway, Fred Williams (1876 repr. 1968)
The North Western, O. S. Nock (1968)
LMS Steam, O. S. Nock (1971)
History of the Great Western Railway, E. T. MacDermot (rev. C. R. Clinker 1964)
History of the London & North Western Railway, W. L. Steel (1914)
History of the Southern Railway, C. F. Dendy-Marshall and R. W. Kidner (2 vols 1963)
London's Underground, H. F. Howson (1951 rev. 1967)

Rails Through the Clays: A History of London's Tube Railways, Alan Jackson (1962)
The Railway Clearing House Handbook of Railway Stations, (1904 repr. 1970)
Bradshaw's Railway Timetable (1st published 1839)
The Railway Builders, Lives and Works of the Victorian Railway Contractors, R. S. Joby (1983)
The Railway Navvies, Terry Coleman (1965)
The Railway Mania and its Aftermath, Henry Grote Lewin (1936 repr. 1968)
The Railway-Lover's Companion, ed Bryan Morgan (1963)

Trams

London's Trams and Trolleybuses, John R. Day (1977)
The Golden Age of Tramways, Charles Klapper (1961)
Great British Tramways Networks, Wingate Bett and John Gilham (1962)
History of Tramways, R. J. Buckley (1975)
London's Trams and Trolleybuses, John R. Day (1977)

Motor Cars

The Motor Car and Politics 1896–1970, William Plowden (1971)

SECTION P

Religion

PART ONE
ADMINISTRATIVE AREAS

P1 Archdeaconry. A division of a Diocese (qv). It can itself be sub-divided into Rural Deaneries.

P2 Chapelry. A section of a large parish having its own chapel and, sometimes, a resident priest who was subordinate to the parish incumbent.

P3 Diocese. An area with a cathedral under the jurisdiction of a bishop, usually divided into archdeaconries. At the Reformation the number of dioceses was increased from 14 to 18, with an additional four in Wales.

P4 Donative. A parish wholly or partly exempt from the jurisdiction of the diocesan bishop.

P5 Parish. The smallest unit of ecclesiastical administration, with its own church and priest who is competent to administer the sacraments, and to whom the inhabitants used to pay tithes and other ecclesiastical dues. The term also came to denote a civil administration.

P6 Peculiar. A parish or church exempt from the jurisdiction of the archdeacon or bishop in whose diocese it lay. Usually it derived from the possession of land by a church dignitary lying within the diocese of another bishop.

P7 Province. A principal ecclesiastical division, containing several dioceses, under the jurisdiction of an archbishop. The Church of England has two provinces – Canterbury and York. The former consists of the territory south of the River Trent, the latter the remainder of the country to the north. The Province of

Wales, created in 1920, formerly came under the control of Canterbury.

P8 Royal Peculiar. A benefice, usually a royal chapel, where the Crown has the right to nominate the clergyman.

PART TWO
ADMINISTRATIVE BODIES

P9 Chapter. The governing body of a religious house having jurisdiction over its administration and the secular possessions and estates owned by the Chapter.

P10 Consistory Court. The court of a bishop which hears ecclesiastical causes.

P11 Court of Arches. The Appeal Court of the Province of Canterbury. Its name derived from its early location in Bow Church, London, which was the church of the 'Blessed Mary of the Arches'.

P12 Court of Augmentation. A body created in 1535 to administer the lands, possessions and revenues of the dissolved religious houses. It was abolished in 1554 and its functions transferred to the Exchequer.

P13 Court of Chancery. The Appeal Court of the Province of York.

P14 Court of Delegates. The Court which hears appeals against decisions of the Prerogative Courts of Canterbury and York.

PART THREE
CHURCH OFFICIALS AND OTHER APPOINTMENTS

P15 Archbishop. The bishop in charge of a province. The Archbishop of Canterbury, as Primate of All England, has precedence in the Church of England. The Archbishopric of Wales was established in 1920; before that the province was controlled by Canterbury.

P16 Archdeacon. The bishop's deputy in a diocese with a duty to regularly visit each parish to inspect the fabric of the church and any other church property, and to assess the general running of affairs in the parish.

P17 Beadsman. A person paid or endowed to pray for others.

P18 Bishop. A priest, whose appointment is vested in the Crown, having jurisdiction over a diocese.

P19 Canon. In this context, a priest on the staff of a cathedral, usually having a stipend (called a prebend) derived from the revenues of one or more cathedral estates. In pre-Reformation days the council of canons had the authority of electing the diocesan bishop.

P20 Cardinal. An immediate subordinate of the Pope and appointed by him. Pre-Reformation Archbishops of Canterbury were frequently created cardinals.

P21 Chaplain. a) In a pre-Reformation sense, a priest without a benefice who ministered to private bodies such as hospitals and nunneries, or else to private families. His modern equivalent ministers to the armed forces or to prisons,
  b) A priest in charge of a chapel
  c) Private secretary to a diocesan bishop.

P22 Churchwarden. See B145.

P23 Curate. Originally a term to denote a minister in charge of souls and synonymous, until the 17th century, with a parish incumbent. Since then the term has denoted an assistant to the incumbent. A Perpetual Curate is the incumbent of a parish church where the Great Tithes have been annexed by an ecclesiastical body or lay person. (See also Vicar).

P24 Deacon. A clergyman without the full status of a priest – he cannot, for example, perform marriages. He acts as an assistant to the beneficed incumbent.

P25 Dean. An official who presides over a cathedral chapter (qv).

P26 Incumbent. A rector, parson, vicar or minister of a parish.

P27 Lecturer. An unbeneficed clergyman employed to preach.

P28 Ordinary. An ecclesiastical superior, such as an archbishop, bishop or archdeacon.

P29 Parson. In its strictest sense, a rector rather than a vicar, but now used to denote either.

P30 Priest. In a pre-Reformation sense, the head of a province, usually an archbishop.

P31 Questman. An assistant to a church-warden; a sidesman.

P32 Rector. Originally the incumbent of a parish who received all the tithes and customary offerings and dues. He was responsible for the upkeep of the chancel and rectory, and for the provision of vestments and service books. When an ecclesiastical body, such as a monastery, annexed a benefice it became, nominally, the rector and appointed a deputy called a vicar to administer the parish. However, the Great Tithes went to the monastery as Rector, and the Small Tithes to the vicar. After the Reformation many monastic estates fell into lay hands and subsequently Lay Rectors became common; they had the right to nominate the vicar but had to seek the bishop's approval. They also inherited the obligation to keep up the chancel and vicarage.

P33 Rural Dean. A bishop's deputy in charge of several parishes, but inferior to an archdeacon.

P34 Suffragan Bishop. An assistant to a diocesan bishop.

P35 Surrogate. A clergyman or other person appointed by the bishop as his deputy to grant licences for marriages without banns.

P36 Vicar. An ecclesiastical body, such as a monastery, which annexed a living and became its Rector, appointed a deputy called a vicar to care for the parish. The religious house received the Great or Rectorial Tithes and the vicar the Small or Vicarial Tithes. This system continued after the Reformation when many monastic estates fell into lay hands.

P37 Vicar-General. A deputy of an archbishop or bishop.

PART FOUR
BUILDINGS AND MEETING PLACES

P38 Abbey. In its pre-Reformation sense, a religious community or building presided over by an abbot or abbess. Usually the abbot was elected by his brethren subject to the approval of the diocesan bishop.

P39 Cathedral. The principal church of a diocese, containing the bishop's throne (*cathedra*).

P40 Chantry. A chapel within a church, or built on its own site, established by a wealthy person or body, whose endowment supported the cost of building and the perpetual saying of mass for the souls of the founding family or body. In 1547 nearly 2,400 chantries were suppressed.

P41 Chapel. a) A small church subordinate to the parish incumbent, usually called a 'Chapel-of-Ease', located in populous areas at some distance from the parish church.

b) The meeting house of a non-conformist sect.

P42 Church House. A parish hall, normally adjoining the church or churchyard.

P43 Collegiate Church. A large and important church served by a community or 'college' of clergy. The endowments of many of these churches at the Reformation were used to found grammar schools.

P44 Convent. Originally a term to denote an actual community of monks or nuns, but now usually applied to a building which houses them.

P45 Conventicle. Originally a term denoting a meeting of monks in a monastery, but in the 17th century denoted a meeting, usually illegal, of non-conformists.

P46 Friary. A house occupied by friars. Usually Dominican houses were called Priories.

P47 Grange. The buildings and land of an outlying estate held by a monastery.

P48 Minster. Originally a monastic church, but now a name applied to some large churches or cathedrals.

P49 Monastery. The residence of a religious community, usually monks of friars. The Cistercians opened their first house in England in 1128, the Dominicans in 1221 and the Franciscans in 1224.

P50 Priory. A monastery in the charge of a prior rather than an abbot.

PART FIVE
ECCLESIASTICAL TERMS

P51 Advowson. The right to present a clergyman to a benefice, a nomination subject to the approval of a diocesan bishop. Strictly speaking, this is a Presentative Advowson to distinguish it from a Collative Advowson where the right to present is held by the bishop who also appoints.

Although Lay Advowsons existed from the 8th century they became common after the Reformation when monastic estates and holdings fell into lay hands. Since 1924 a Lay Advowson may not be sold after two vacancies have occurred, and in 1933 parochial councils were allowed to purchase an advowson except where it was in the gift of the Crown or a bishop.

P52 Advowson Appendant. An advowson (qv) annexed to an estate or manor.

P53 Advowson in Gross. An advowson (qv) belonging to a person.

P54 Annates. The profits of a benefice for the first year after a vacancy which were paid to the Pope. Also called First Fruits.

P55 Appropriation. The annexation by an ecclesiastical body of a benefice and the Great Tithes attached to it. See also Impropriation.

P56 Benefice. An ecclesiastical office or the income derived from it. It is a term usually denoting the incumbency of a parish church.

P57 Canon. In this context, an ecclesiastical law.

P58 Church Ale. A feast to commemorate the dedication of a church, at which ale was sold in aid of funds for church expenses.

P59 Collation. The institution of a clergyman to a benefice which the bishop has in his own gift, or in cases where the Presentative Advowson has lapsed after six months. (See Advowson).

P60 Conge D'Elire. Royal permission to a monastic body or cathedral chapter to fill up a vacant see or abbacy by election.

P61 Faculty. A licence or authorisation by an ecclesiastical superior to hold an office or perform a function otherwise forbidden.

P62 Impropriation. The annexation by a corporate body or a lay person of an ecclesiastical benefice and of the associated Great Tithes. Such an act carried the obligation to present a vicar to look after the parish, subject to the agreement of the diocesan bishop, and to keep up the chancel and vicarage.

P63 Institution. The ceremony by which the presentee of a living is given care of the souls in that parish.

P64 Litten. A churchyard or burial ground.

P65 Plurality. A simultaneous holding by a clergyman of two or more benefices.

P66 Prebend. The stipend granted to a member of a cathedral chapter for his support, usually derived from the revenues of chapter lands; the term also applies to the recipient of these revenues.

P67 Presentation. The nomination of a clergyman to a benefice by the holder of the advowson (qv).

P68 Recusant. One who declined to attend his parish church. After 1570 the term usually applied to Roman Catholics.

P69 Spiritualities. Ecclesiastical revenues and rights derived from tithes which were exempt from secular control.

P70 Temporalities. Secular sources of income for a religious house, such as buildings and lands.

P71 Wake. Originally an all-night vigil prior to a holy day, but later the term denoted the feast and celebration of the day itself.

PART SIX
NON-CONFORMIST SECTS AND OTHER RELIGIONS

P72 Anabaptists. A sect which appeared in Saxony early in the 16th century that repudiated infant, and promoted adult, baptism. It also encouraged common ownership of goods, equality of status, and the repudiation of secular interference in religious affairs.

P73 Baptists. A sect founded by John Smythe, an English refugee in Amsterdam. Like the Anabaptists they advocated that only adult believers should be baptised. Thomas

Helwys founded the first Baptist church in England in 1612, in Newgate Street, London. The General Baptists, of which Helwys was one, believed in the individual's responsibility to work for his soul's salvation, whereas the Particular (or Strict) Baptists formed in 1633, followed Calvin and believed in predestination and redemption only for particular believers.

As with other non-conformist sects the Baptists were persecuted until the Toleration Act of 1689. The General Baptists divided when the New Connexion was formed in 1770 and the Old Connexion became Unitarians. The Baptist Union in 1813 promoted closer cooperation between the various parts of the sect and in 1891 the Particular Baptists and the New Connexion merged to form the Baptist Union of Great Britain and Ireland.

P74 Barrowists. A Congregationalist sect in the reign of Elizabeth I. It was founded by Henry Barrow who was executed for his beliefs in 1593. Many Barrowists that year fled to Holland and New England.

P75 Bible Christians. A breakaway sect from the Methodists formed in 1815.

P76 Brownists. An early Puritan sect. They were followers of Robert Browne, a schoolmaster, who established a group in Norwich in 1580. He was imprisoned for denouncing the established Church, later went to the Netherlands with his followers but eventually he accepted a benefice in Northamptonshire within the Church of England. The sect, which opposed state intervention in religious matters, survived and was the basis for the Congregationalists.

P77 Catholic Apostolic Church. A church promoted by Edward Irving and alternatively called Irvingites, derived from a group founded in 1826 by H. Drummond. They believe in a 'Second Coming' and appointed twelve apostles and six prophets in preparation for the event. They founded a church in Gordon Square, London, and others in Cambs, Shropshire and Surrey.

P78 Congregationalists. A sect which derived from the Brownists (qv) and who were also known as Independents. They believed that there should be no state interference in religion and therefore were at odds with the Presbyterians. They were forced into nonconformity at the Restoration and after a relatively inactive period, expanded substantially in the 19th century. In 1831 the Congregationalist Union of England and Wales was established. In 1972 they amalgamated with the Presbyterians to form the United Reformed Church.

P79 Countess of Huntingdon's Connexion. A Methodist sect, of Calvanistic views, founded by Selina Hastings, Countess of Huntingdon in the 18th century. She appointed the noted Methodist preacher, George Whitefield, as her chaplain in 1751 and his popularity led to the establishment of a number of Connexion chapels which catered for the socially better-off. The principal chapel was Whitefield's Tabernacle in Tottenham Court Road, London.

P80 Free Church of England. A small Protestant sect formed in 1843 following a dispute with the established Church.

P81 Free Church of Scotland. In 1843 about a third of the Church of Scotland formed this new sect which, in 1910, joined with the United Presbyterian Church to form the United Free Church.

P82 Huguenots. The first Huguenot immigrants came to England in the reigns of Henry VIII and Edward VI, with concentrations of settlements in London, the Cinque Ports, Norwich and Bristol. The Revocation of the Edict of Nantes in 1685 caused at least another 40,000 Huguenots to flee to England.

P83 Independents. See Congregationalists.

P84 Inghamites. A small sect formed in 1754 by Benjamin Ingham in a breakaway from the Moravians (qv). What remains of the church is now in the north of England.

P85 Jews. Jews arrived in England in large numbers at the time of William the Conqueror although they were regarded as second-class citizens. They were not allowed to trade wholesale or retail, or to engage in agriculture. But they were useful to the Crown or lords because they were able to lend money at a time when usury was forbidden to Christians. Many Jews were massacred in 1189–90 and they were expelled in 1290 when their use to the Crown was minimal. Cromwell, despite opposition from Church and City, readmitted them in 1655. They were not granted political equality until the middle of the 19th century.

P86 Latter-Day Saints. Popularly known as the Mormons, the Church of Jesus Christ of

Latter-Day Saints was founded in 1830 by Joseph Smith in the USA and popularised by Brigham Young. The sect, after a controversial existence, settled at Salt Lake, Utah. A feature of the Church is its encouragment of members to discover their ancestors so that they might be posthumously admitted to membership. Because of this the study of genealogy in this country has been extensively funded and computerised.

P87 Methodists. John and Charles Wesley began a ministry in 1738 which sought to inspire an individual's communion with God without the need or intervention of a priest. Prevented from using Anglican churches they, together with George Whitefield, resorted to the use of open-air meetings. They established a Methodist Society in Moorfields in 1740 and later a governing body, called the Methodist Conference. There were several secessions from the Methodist church. In 1797 the Methodist New Connexion was formed by Alexander Kilham; this group joined with the United Methodist Free Churches in 1907 to form the United Methodist Church. The Independent Methodists were established in 1805. Primitive Methodists were formed in 1808 after a dispute about the role of the Conference; the Bible Christians, or Bryanites, broke away in 1815 and joined the United Methodist Church in 1907. Apart from the Independent and Primitive divisions, Methodism was reunited in 1932 in the Methodist Church of Great Britain.

Welsh Methodism was Calvinistic; it was founded by George Whitefield with an organisation based on that of the Presbyterians.

P88 Moravians. A protestant sect which claims to trace its origins to Bohemia and Moravia in the 15th century. In 1728 three Moravian societies came to London and Oxford and John and Charles Wesley were converts shortly before they launched the Methodists. The Congregation of the Unity of Brethren was established in 1742 as a separate Moravian sect in this country.

P89 Presbyterians. Presbyterians rejected the episcopal organisation of the Churches of England and Scotland and proposed, instead, a church governed by committees called presbyteries at local level, diocesan synods and a national assembly. This reflected the views of Calvin. This system was adopted in Scotland in 1560 and had much influence in 17th-century England, particularly during the Civil War, and in 1647 it was made the official church of the country. It was not, however, popular in England and was overthrown at the Restoration. In the 18th and 19th centuries many Presbyterians became Unitarians. In 1972 the Presbyterian Church of England, formed in 1876, amalgamated with the Congregationalists to form the United Reformed Church.

P90 Puritanism. A general term to describe a movement, basically Calvinist, dating from the reign of Henry VIII, which sought to purify certain aspects of the Church of England which it regarded as being Roman Catholic.

P91 Quakers. The Society of Friends stems from the activities of George Fox in 1647, and derives its cognomen from the spiritual 'trembling' manifested at their early meetings. They were opposed to formal services and paid preachers, refused to take oaths, and have since been closely identified with pacifism. The Society's system of organisation was established in 1666 and its library in 1673.

P92 Roman Catholics. Until the Reformation during the reign of Henry VIII, Roman Catholicism was the religion of England and Wales. The Acts of Uniformity of 1552 and 1559 made Catholics liable to fines, and as the political situation deteriorated, stricter anti-Catholic laws were introduced. During the reign of Charles I these laws were lightly enforced and in 1634 Maryland was formed as a Catholic colony. Catholics were tolerated during the Protectorate, but persecuted after the Restoration. The first Test Act, of 1673, excluded them from civil and military office, the second, of 1678, from Parliament; their cause was further disadvantaged by the deposition of James II. The 1778 Catholic Relief Act enabling Catholics to own land sparked off a series of disorders which culminated in the Gordon Riots of 1780; full emancipation did not come until 1829, although it was not until 1871 that Catholics were allowed to take university degrees or hold office in universities.

P93 Salvation Army. William Booth, then a member of the Methodist New Connexion, came to London in 1865 and with others he formed the evangelical Christian Revival Association; in 1878 this organisation changed its name to The Salvation Army, its primary aim to attract people to Christianity who had not previously been involved. From the beginning the Army gave equal status to its women workers; all Salvationists are expected to be total abstainers, and officers are expected to be non-smokers. Much of the Army's work has been among the most seriously deprived section of the community and it is justly renowned for its provision of hostels for the homeless.

P94 Swedenborgians. A sect founded in London in 1788 as the Swedenborgian New Church, based on the views of the Swedish theologian Emanuel Swedenborg. They are also loosely called the New Jerusalem Church.

P95 Unitarians. A sect which believes in Christ as prophet but not as divine. The Church seeks to combine belief in God, reason and scientific knowledge. The sect expanded considerably in the 17th and 18th centuries as Presbyterians joined it, but many chapels are Congregationalist based.

P96 United Free Church of Scotland. Formed in 1900 upon the merger of the Free Church of Scotland and the United Presbyterian Church. In 1929 it joined with the Church of Scotland.

P97 United Reformed Church. Formed in 1972 upon the amalgamation of the Presbyterian Church of England and the Congregationalists.

PART SEVEN
RELIGIOUS HISTORY SINCE TUDOR TIMES

P98 Significant Dates. The following are some of the dates important for local historians to bear in mind.

1535 Bishop Fisher and Sir Thomas More executed for denying the king's supremacy of the Church
1536 Suppression of the smaller monasteries
1539 Suppression of the larger monasteries
1545 Suppression of chantries began
1549 First *Act of Uniformity*, which required that the first *Book of Common Prayer* be used in Anglican worship. Clergy are permitted to marry

1552 Second *Act of Uniformity*, which required the use of the second *Book of Common Prayer*, and laid down severe penalties for non-compliance; it imposed fines for non-attendance at church
1553–8 Restoration of Roman Catholic forms of worship
1555 Persecution of Protestants begins
1559 Third *Act of Uniformity*, which restored Anglican worship; a new prayer book was introduced. Weekly fines were imposed for non-attendance at Anglican church
1563 The *Thirty-nine Articles* were published
1593 *Conventicle Act* passed, which imposed penalties on those who did not attend Anglican churches and met in secret assemblies
1580 The Brownist sect was formed
1604 The Hampton Court Conference between Puritans and the established church was held
1611 The new translation of the *Bible* was published
1633 *Particular Baptists* were formed
1644 The *Book of Common Prayer* was suppressed
1647 George Fox began his ministration which was to result in the formation of the Quakers
1655 Jews were readmitted into England
1662 The fourth *Act of Uniformity* was passed. Church services were to be conducted according to a revised prayer book and liturgy. About 2,000 clergy were ejected from their livings for not conforming to the Act

1664 *Conventicle Act* passed; this forbade meetings of more than five people who were not members of the same household
1665 *Five Mile Act* passed; this forbade non-conformist ministers who refused to take the non-resistance oath, to come within five miles of any corporation where they had previously preached
1667 Roman Catholics excluded from corporate office
1670 *Conventicle Act* passed which exacted severe penalties for attendance at unlawful assemblies
1673 First *Test Act* passed; this directed that all civil and military office holders receive the sacraments according to the forms of the Church of England, and take an oath which repudiated the Roman Catholic doctrine of transubstantiation, and affirm the monarch's supremacy as head of the Church of England
1678 Titus Oates's Popish plot
1678 Second *Test Act* passed; this excluded

Roman Catholics, other than the Duke of York, from Parliament

1685 Revocation of the Edict of Nantes in France, which led to an immigration of Huguenots into England

1689 *Toleration Act* passed; this granted non-conformists the right to have their own places of worship together with teachers and preachers. They were still excluded from public office although they were able to qualify for municipal office by 'occasional conformity' with Anglicanism

1704 The *Queen Anne's Bounty,* a fund to supplement the stipends of clergy, was established

1710 Disputes between high and low church led to the trial of Dr Henry Sacheverell

1711 *Occasional Conformity Act* was passed; this was designed to prevent non-conformists from receiving communion in the Anglican church so as to qualify themselves for civil or military office

1728 The *Moravian* sect arrived in England

1738 John and Charles Wesley commenced their ministry

1740 The *Methodist Society* was established in Moorfields

1770 The *Methodist New Connexion* was formed

1780 The anti-Catholic Gordon riots

1788 The *Swedenborgian* sect was formed

1815 The *Bible Christians* were formed

1829 The *Catholic Emancipation Act* was passed. The first Catholic MP since disqualification took his seat

1831 The *Congregationalist Union of England and Wales* formed

1836 The *Ecclesiastical Commissioners* were incorporated. The *Tithe Communation Act* was passed

PART EIGHT
BIBLIOGRAPHY

General Historical Works
History of the Church, ed Hubert Jedin, Konrad Repgen and John Dolan (10 vols 1962–79)
The English Church 1000–1066, F. Barlow (2nd ed. 1979)
The English Church 1066–1154, F. Barlow (1979)
Oxford Dictionary of the Christian Church, ed. F. L. Cross
Class and Religion in the Late Victorian City, Hugh McLeod (1974)
The Churches and the Working Classes in Victorian England, K. S. Inglis (1963)

Five Centuries of Religion, G. G. Coulton (4 vols 1913–50)
The Abbeys and priories of medieval England, Colin Platt (1984)
The English Reformation, A. G. Dickens (1964)

Church Officials and Other Appointments
History of the English Clergy 1800–1900, C. K. F. Brown (1953)
Origin of the Office of Churchwarden, C. Drew (1954)
Parish Priests and their People in the Middle Ages, E. L. Cutts (1891)
The Country Clergy in Elizabethan and Stuart Times, A. T. Hart (1958)

Buildings and Meeting Places
Vicarages in the Middle Ages, R. A. R. Hartridge (1930)

Non-conformist Sects and Other Religions
Sources for the History of Roman Catholics in England, J. H. Pollen (1921)
Catholic Community 1570–1850, John Bossy (1975)
Catholics in England 1559–1829, M. D. R. Levy (1961)
Recusant Records ed. C. Talbot (Catholic Record Society Vol 53 1961)
History of Presbyterianism in England, A. H. Drysdale (1889)
Origins of the Plymouth Brethren, H. H. Rowden (Ph.D 1965)
History of English Congregationalism, R. W. Dale (1907)
The Beginnings of Quakerism, W. C. Braithwaite (rev. 1955)
History of the Salvation Army, R. Sandall (1947)
History of English Baptists, A. C. Underwood (1947)
New History of Methodism, W. Townsend, W. J. Workman and G. Hayes (2 vols 1909)
The Moravian Communities in Britain, Article by W. H. G. Armytage in *Church Quarterly* No 158

Coins and Tokens

PART ONE
COINS

Where possible old values are expressed in decimal terms.

Q1 Angel. A gold coin worth 33⅓p minted in 1464/5; it replaced the Noble (qv). Often the coin, which derived its name from the depiction of the Archangel Michael on its obverse side, was pierced by a hole and used as a touch-piece to induce good health and in particular to cure scrofula. It was discontinued in the reign of Charles II. There was also a half-angel called an Angelet.

Q2 Atcheson. A Scottish coin struck in the reign of James VI, worth two-thirds of an old English penny.

Q3 Crown. A gold coin minted in 1526 and worth 22½p. In 1551 it appeared as a silver coin and was valued at 25p. The Crown was discontinued in Victorian times, although it has been revived for recent commemorative issues.

Q4 Dandiprat. A 16th-century coin worth about ½p.

Q5 Doit. A copper coin worth one old Scottish penny but only one-twelfth of an old English penny.

Q6 Farthing. A coin worth a quarter of an old penny – until 1279 it was obtained by cutting a penny into quarters. Silver farthings were issued from this date until the reign of Edward VI. Copper versions were minted in 1672; they were later made of bronze. The coin was discontinued in 1956.

Q7 Florin. A gold coin minted in 1344 and worth 30p. It took its name from Florence where Europe's first gold coin was introduced. In 1849 silver florins were first minted as a preliminary step towards decimalisation of the currency. In modern times it was the name of the two-shilling piece, superseded by the modern 10p piece. A double florin was minted in 1887 but discontinued three years later.

Q8 Groat. A silver coin introduced in 1279, and reintroduced from 1351 to 1662; its approximate value was 1½p. A small silver groat was later minted but discontinued in 1855. A half-groat was introduced in 1351.

Q9 Guinea. A gold coin worth £1, first minted in 1663. It took its name from the place where the gold was mined – Guinea in West Africa, later known as the Gold Coast. In 1717 it was revalued at 21 shillings (105p) and discontinued in 1813, although its use as a name persisted until decimalisation.

Q10 Half-Crown. A gold coin first introduced in the reign of Henry VIII, but later reissued by Edward VI as a silver coin. In modern times, before decimalisation, a half-crown piece was worth 12½p.

Q11 Half-Penny. Until 1279 a half penny was obtained by cutting a penny in half. Silver half-pennies were issued from this date until 1672 when they were minted in copper. In 1860, in common with the penny, it was made from bronze and in this form was used until decimalisation when the new ½p was introduced.

Q12 Half-Ryal. A gold coin, worth five shillings, introduced in the reign of Edward IV.

Q13 Helm. A quarter of a florin (qv), first issued in 1344.

Q14 Leopard. A gold coin issued in 1344 worth half a florin.

Q15 Mark. The Mark was not an English coin but it was used as a unit in accountancy, especially in the Danelaw counties (qv). It was a weight of metal originally valued at 128 silver pennies (53.3p), but later revalued at 66.6p.

Q16 Noble. A gold coin minted in 1344 worth 33.3p. It was superseded in 1464/5 by the Angel (qv).

Q17 Ora. This was not an English coin but was a monetary unit in Danelaw counties (qv). It represented 16 silver pennies (6.6p).

Q18 Penny. A silver coin first issued in the 8th century, probably in the reign of Aethelbert II of Kent. It was called a denier from the Roman silver coin, the *denarius*. For nearly 500 years it was the only coin struck in England and it remained a silver coin until 1797. The Saxon penny weighed 22½ grains, and there were 240 pennies to the Saxon pound weight of silver. By the tenth century a long cross appeared on the reverse side so that the coin could be broken accurately into half-pennies and farthings.

In 1180 a new series of pennies was issued now known, from the reverse side, as the shortcross coinage. In 1247 more longcross pennies were minted on which the ends of the cross reached to the edge of the coin in an attempt to deter clipping. In 1279 Edward I issued new designs and added groats, half-pennies and farthings to the coinage.

In 1797 a copper penny was introduced which weighed 1 oz, and in 1799 it was made smaller. It was reduced again in 1860 to its pre-decimalisation size, and made of bronze. These Victorian pennies are called 'Bun' pennies as the depiction of the Queen shows her hair in a bun. No pennies were issued in 1923–5, 1941–3, 1952 and 1954–60. Only a token supply was minted in 1933.

The present decimalised penny is worth 2.4 of the old coin.

Q19 Pound. Originally a pound weight of silver from which 240 pennies could be minted. The pound was the name of a short-lived coin in the reign of Charles I. Pound notes were first issued in 1797 and have been superseded by the decimalised £1 coin.

Q20 Ryal. A gold coin worth 50p which was introduced 1464/5.

Q21 Sceat. A mid 7th-century gold coin, particularly found in southern Anglo-Saxon settlements.

Q22 Shilling. A silver coin first minted in 1504 and then called a Testoon. It had a chequered career due to its continual debasement. Its modern equivalent was superseded by today's 5p coin.

Q23 Sixpence. A silver coin introduced in 1551. In 1947 it was made of cupro-nickel although the 'silver' coin had for some time been made of debased metal. It was worth 2½p and was demonetarised after decimalisation.

Q24 Sovereign. A gold coin minted in 1489 which, by the reign of Elizabeth I was worth 30 shillings. It was discontinued by James I in favour of the Unite (qv), but reintroduced from 1817 to 1917 when it was worth twenty shillings.

Q25 Three Farthings. A silver coin issued in 1561 and discontinued the following year.

Q26 Threepenny piece. A silver coin first minted in 1551 and issued only spasmodically. It became most popular in Victorian times and in this form was discontinued in 1937. A twelve-sided nickel-brass coin then appeared which was discontinued in 1967.

Q27 Thrysma. An Anglo-Saxon gold coin.

Q28 Twopenny piece. Issued in the years 1797–1799. It was very large, weighed 2 ozs, and was nicknamed a 'cartwheel'.

Q29 Unite. A gold coin minted early in the 17th century which was named after the union of England and Scotland. It replaced the sovereign for the time being and was worth £1.

PART TWO
MINTS

Q30 Mints. Mints have existed at the following places:

Beds: Bedford
Berks: Reading, Wallingford
Bucks: Aylesbury, Buckingham, Newport Pagnell
Cambs: Cambridge
Cheshire: Chester
Cornwall: Launceston, Truro
Cumberland: Carlisle
Derbys: Derby
Devon: Barnstaple, Exeter, Lydford, Totnes
Dorset: Dorchester, Sherborne, Wareham, Weymouth
Durham: Durham
Essex: Colchester, Horndon, Maldon
Glos: Berkeley, Bristol, Gloucester, Winchcombe
Hants: Southampton, Winchester
Herefordshire: Hereford
Herts: Hertford
Hunts: Huntingdon
Kent: Canterbury, Dover, Hythe, Lympne, Rochester, Romney, Sandwich
Leics: Leicester
Lincs: Caistor, Horncastle, Lincoln, Stamford, Torksey
London: Tower of London, Tower Hill, Durham House in the Strand, Southwark
Norfolk: Castle Rising, King's Lynn, Norwich, Thetford
Northants: Northampton, Peterborough
Northumberland: Corbridge, Newcastle-upon-Tyne

Notts: Newark, Nottingham
Oxon: Oxford
Shropshire: Bridgnorth, Shrewsbury
Somerset: Axbridge, Bath, Bridport, Bruton, Cadbury, Crewkerne, Ilchester, Langport, Milbourne Port, Petherton, Taunton, Watchet
Staffs: Lichfield, Stafford, Tamworth
Suffolk: Bury St Edmunds, Ipswich, Sudbury
Surrey: Guildford
Sussex: Bramber, Chichester, Cissbury, Hastings, Lewes, Pevensey, Rye, Steyning
Warks: Birmingham, Coventry, Warwick
Wilts: Bedwyn, Chippenham, Cricklade, Malmesbury, Marlborough, Salisbury, Warminster, Wilton
Worcs: Droitwich, Pershore, Worcester
Yorks: Hedon, Kingston-upon-Hull, Pontefract, Scarborough, York
Wales: Aberystwyth, Cardiff, Llantrisant, Rhuddlan, Swansea.

PART THREE
NUMISMATIC TERMS

Q31 AE. A term applied to coins made of brass, bronze or copper.

Q32 Broke Money. Coins in the Middle Ages which were cut in halves or quarters to make smaller denominations.

Q33 Clipping. The practice of cutting pieces from the coinage; at times this was a capital crime.

Q34 Grades of Coin. Coins are graded according to their condition. The terms used are:

Proof: specially struck coin.
FDC: Fleur-de-coin; in perfect mint condition.
UNC: uncirculated coin.
EF: extremely fine, unworn but not perfect.
VF: very fine, slight wear.
F: fine, worn but with the image distinct.
Fair: considerably worn or damaged.
Mediocre
P: poor

In describing the condition of both sides of a coin the obverse (face) side is given first.

Q35 Hoard. A large cache of coins. Probably the largest hoard in this country was one of 20,000 coins of Edward I and Edward II found at Tutbury.

Q36 Jettons. Metallic or card counters, sometimes resembling coins, generally used in gambling.

Q37 Jugate. The overlapping of heads on a coin.

Q38 Legend. The wording around the coin inside the border.

Q39 Longcross. Refers to the penny struck from 1247–1272 on which the cross extended to the edge of the coin to discourage clipping.

Q40 Maundy Money. Specially minted sets of silver coins, 1d, 2d, 3d and 4d pieces, distributed by the monarch on Maundy Thursday to poor people. The number of recipients is equivalent to the age of the sovereign.

Q41 Milled. A term now applied to the serrated edge around a coin.

Q42 Obverse. The face side of a coin.

Q43 Reverse. The reverse of the face side of the coin.

Q44 Shortcross. Refers to the penny struck from 1180–1247 with a short cross on the reverse; this facilitated the cutting of the coin into halves and quarters.

Q45 Tealby. Refers to the first coinage of Henry II.

Q46 Tokens. Issued in times of monetary change or shortage and used within a locality in exchange for goods. The three main periods of their use were the mid-17th, the late 18th and early 19th centuries.

PART FOUR
BIBLIOGRAPHY

Coins and Tokens

English Coins from the 7th Century to the Present Day, G. C. Brooke (1932)
Story of the English Coinage, P. J. Sealby (1985 ed)
Anglo-Saxon Coins, ed. R. H. M. Dolley
The Scottish Coinage, I. H. Stewart (1955)
Kenyon's Gold Coins of England, R. L. Kenyon (1884 repr. 1969)

Seventeenth Century Tokens of The British Isles and their Values, Michael Dickinson (1986).
The Eighteenth Century Token-Coinage, R. Dalton and S. H. Hamer (1910–18, repr. 1967).

19th Century Token Coinage of Great Britain and Ireland, W. J. Davis (1904)
Trade Tokens, Jim Newark (1981)

SECTION R

The Militia

PART ONE
THE MILITIA UP TO TUDOR TIMES

R1 The Fyrd.   In Anglo-Saxon times military service was connected with the feudal ownership of land. The military force was called the Fyrd and the obligation to serve, the fyrd-bote – one of the three duties of the thegns under the *Trinoda Necessitas* (qv). King Alfred divided the Fyrd into two parts, one under arms, one resting, alternating with each other.

It was unusual for a county Fyrd to fight outside its own boundaries.

R2 Knight Service.   In 1070 William I introduced a system, now called Knight's Service, whereby he negotiated with his tenants-in-chief for a number of knights to be equipped and available for duty. In peacetime the amount of service was normally 40 days each year.

R3 Assize of Arms 1181.   In 1181 Henry II issued an Assize of Arms which set down the weapons and equipment required of each knight, freeman and burgess. For example, each possessor of a Knight's Fee was obliged to

provide a coat of mail, helmet, shield and lance, and a free layman, owning effects or rents of the value of 16 marks and over, was obliged to find a similar suit. A free layman whose property was not above ten marks, had to find a haubergeon (a small coat of plate or mail), a chapelet of iron (skull cap) and a lance. The sheriff was responsible for raising the levy and justices were sent round to the shires to enforce the Assize. It was provided that juries from towns and hundreds should make the assessments of military obligation. By the 13th century the unfree were liable for military service as well. This legislation was consolidated by the Statute of Winchester 1285 and the provisions remained in force until 1558.

R4 Scutage.   By the reign of Henry I it was established that knights could excuse themselves from military service and pay 'shield-money' instead – this was commonly called Scutage; the tenant-in-chief recouped this money from his tenants. Scutage was last levied in 1327.

R5 Commissions of Array.   The king exercised control by appointing Commissions of

Array which compiled the Muster Rolls – these showed the men available for service in each shire.

R6 The Tudor Militia. In Tudor times the Lord Lieutenant was nominally head of the county militia though usually he delegated his responsibilities to the Deputy Lieutenant, who made sure that the parish constables raised the required local levy. The county force was sometimes called the *posse comitatus*. Able-bodied men between 16 and 60 were liable for service.

A number of enactments reorganised the militia in the Tudor period. The first described the provision of equipment. The community was divided into ten classes ranging from those who were required to keep a coat of armour, a helmet and a longbow, to those who had to provide as many as 16 horses, 80 suits of light armour, 40 pikes, and 30 longbows.

Trained Bands were established. This term does not necessarily mean that the force was trained but only that it was liable for training. Many units acquired a bad reputation for discipline and application.

General musters – formal inspections of county forces – were held at least every three years and more frequently in disturbed times. The musters, which were also largely social occasions, were held over two days with an interval between each day so that defects found on the first day could be remedied by the second.

PART TWO
EVOLVEMENT OF MODERN FORCES

R7 Evolvement of the standing army. Up to 1660 the county militias were the principal defence force of the kingdom and there was no standing army. The deficiencies of the system were exposed in the Civil War of the 1640s when both sides tended to rely on the early volunteer companies whose soldiers were flexible, unlike the militia whose members declined to cross county borders. Successive Acts after the Restoration, including the Militia Act 1672, abolished the feudal basis for levying and financing the defence of the realm and substituted instead a system whereby people contributed according to their income and property. Rules were laid down as to the period and frequency of musters and a further Act provided for a county rate to help train the militia.

Fear of a French invasion in the 1750s led to the Militia Bill 1757 which, in essence, was the basis for the modern army; it had, then, a quota of about 32,000 men.

R8 Volunteer Companies. The earliest recorded volunteer company was the Guild of St George, incorporated in 1537, and which became today's Honourable Artillery Company. The raising of volunteer companies was permitted in 1758 and by 1778 some had the same allowances for arms and uniforms as those allowed to the compulsory militia. The volunteer companies came from the better-off population and they tended to train and have their headquarters separate from the common soldiers. An Act of 1782 formalised the division between the two.

The volunteer companies existed only during a war or threat of war. They were disbanded in 1783 at the cessation of hostilities, reformed in the 1790s, disbanded after the Peace of Amiens 1802, reformed in 1803 and lost popularity in the next decade. In the late 1850s relations with France again became strained and volunteer forces were once more formed. In 1859 the formation of volunteer rifle companies was authorised; these companies at first paid the cost of their arms, uniforms, accommodation etc, a factor which limited their membership to more affluent residents.

R9 The Local Militia. The Local Militia Act 1807 raised battalions of Local Militia in the counties. Most of the old Infantry Volunteers transferred into the new force, but those who preferred not to were allowed to resign. Any shortfall in the required quota was made up by ballot. Unlike the County Militia, the Local Militia was not liable to serve outside their own or adjacent counties, and whereas the County Militia continued in service after the end of the Napoleonic Wars, the Local Militia was disbanded in 1816. The Local Militia may be likened to the Home Guard of World War 2, a purely local defence force. The County Militia, on the other hand, was more akin to the Territorial Army of recent times, and could be called upon to serve in any part of the country, or to act as reliefs for the regular troops in the garrisons.

R10 Territorial Army. The Territorial And Reserved Forces Act 1907 allowed for the combination of volunteers and yeomanry as a force with its main responsibility home defence, but able to serve abroad as first line reserve for the

Bibliography

regular forces. The territorials were equipped with modern weapons and organised into 14 divisions.

PART THREE
BIBLIOGRAPHY

The English Militia in the Eighteenth Century, J. R. Westland (1965). This includes dates for the formation of each county militia between 1758–78 (pp 447/8)

Elizabeth's Army, C. G. Cruickshank (1946)

A History of the Volunteer Force: From earliest times to the year 1660, C. Sebag Montefiore (1908)

The Elizabethan Militia 1558–1638, Lindsay Boynton (1967)

Cromwell's Army, Charles Firth (1902 rev. 1962)

The English Militia in the Eighteenth Century, J. R. Western (1965)

Rifleman form: a study of the Rifle Volunteer movement 1859–1908, I. F. W. Beckett (1982)

A History of the Formation and Development of Volunteer Infantry, R. Potter Berry (1903)

A Register of the Regiments and Corps of the British Army, ed. Arthur Swinson (1972)

History of the Uniforms of the British Army, Cecil Lawson (5 vols)

A Bibliography of regimental histories of the British Army, A. S. White (1965)

SECTION S

Architecture and Housing

PART ONE
GENERAL ARCHITECTURAL TERMS

S1 Abacus. The slab on the top of a classical column which separated it from the entablature.

S2 Abutment. Part of a pier or wall which supports an arch by taking the lateral thrust of the arch.

S3 Acanthus. A representation of leaves found in the capitals of the Corinthian and Composite Orders. (see Classical Orders)

S4 Angel Beam. Hammer beams (qv) were sometimes carved at the ends with a representation of an angel or human being.

S5 Architrave. The entablature on a Classical Order (qv) is divided into three parts, the lowest of which is the architrave.

S6 Atrium. The central court of a Roman house.

S7 Baluster. A pillar supporting a handrail, usually slender at the top and thicker at the base.

S8 Balustrade. A row of balusters supporting a coping, on terraces, balconies etc.

S9 Bargeboard. A board covering the rafters of a roof which overlap the walls of the house.

S10 Bartizan. A battlemented turret overhanging a tower.

S11 Bas-Relief. An abbreviation of *Basso-relievo* in which the figures of a carving project from the wall to less than half their true proportions.

S12 Belvedere. A turret projecting from the roof of a house designed to provide extensive views.

S13 Boss. An ornamental projection placed to disguise the intersection of ceiling ribs.

S14 Bracket. An ornamental projection off a wall which supports a statue or horizontal feature.

S15 Cantilever. A beam which is supported at only one end, mainly used to hold balconies etc.

S16 Capital. The carved or moulded head of a column.

S17 Cartouche. A stone tablet in the shape of a scroll or paper, bearing an inscription.

S18 Caryatid. A column in the form of a female figure; the most famous examples are on the Erectheum in Athens.

S19 Classical Orders. In Classical architecture an Order is an entire column consisting of base, shaft, capital and entablature. The three Greek kinds are Doric, Ionic and Corinthian; Composite and Tuscan are Roman developments of the Greek originals. Doric, Ionic and Corinthian capitals are shown below. The Composite uses the ram's horns volutes of the Ionic and the acanthus leaves of the Corinthian; the Tuscan Order is a larger version of the Doric.

| Doric | Ionic | Corinthian |

S20 Clerestory. An upper storey or wall near the roof of a high building or church pierced with a row of windows.

S21 Cloister. A covered way around a quadrangle, especially in a monastery or college.

S22 Coffering. Recessed panelling in ceilings etc, mainly for decoration but it had the advantage of lessening the weight of the ceiling.

S23 Collar-beam. A horizontal beam connecting the mid-points of the sloping rafters of a pitched roof.

S24 Colonnade. A range of columns.

S25 Column. A round pillar. It includes the base, shaft and capital and other named features which, in Classical architecture, have precise proportions.

S26 Console. A bracket or corbel, usually decorated, in Classical architecture.

S27 Coping. Sloped capping, either brick or stone, on top of a wall to prevent water penetration.

S28 Corbel. A bracket, or projecting beam, supporting a weight.

S29 Cornice. A horizontal moulding at the top of a column beneath the frieze, or else an ornamental moulding at the top of a wall directly beneath the ceiling.

S30 Cove. A concave moulding at the junction of ceiling and wall.

S31 Crocket. A carving representing leaves to be found on spires and pinnacles of Gothic buildings.

S32 Cruck-beams. A pair of curved timbers taken from a single tree which hold up the ridge-beam of the roof in a timber-framed house.

S33 Cupola. A dome covering a square, circular or polygonal base.

S34 Cusps. The projecting points in a Gothic arch which separate the foils.

S35 Dado. a) The cube forming the body of a pedestal between the base and the cornice;

b) The lower part of a wall when coloured differently from that above.

S36 Decorated. English Gothic architecture of the first part of the 14th century.

S37 Diapered. A lozenge-shaped pattern on a wall, carved or painted. The term is applied also to brickwork where the use of different coloured bricks forms the same shape.

S38 Dormer. A window in an upper floor which projects from the roof. It was named by being usually a window of a bedroom.

S39 Dovecote. Free-standing dovecotes were introduced from Normandy and were only allowed to the aristocracy.

S40 Dressed Stone. Smoothly finished stonework.

S41 Drum Columns. The cylindrical sections of a stone column.

S42 Early English. English Gothic architecture of the 13th century.

S43 English Bond. A method of laying bricks with alternate courses displaying long and short faces of the bricks.

S44 Entablature. The superstructure above a row of columns. It is divided into architrave, frieze and cornice.

S45 Entasis. A device originally used by the Greeks to correct the optical illusion of columns curving inwards. The columns were made thicker at the top to correct this.

S46 Fan Vault. Vaulting used mainly in Late Perpendicular architecture in which the ribs have the same equal curve giving an effect like the bones of a fan.

S47 Fillet. A narrow flat band between mouldings.

S48 Finial. An ornamental feature at the head of pinnacles, canopies etc in Gothic architecture.

S49 Flemish Bond. A method of laying bricks in which each course consists of alternately broad and narrow faces of the brick

S50 Fluting. Semi-circular channels cut into the shafts of columns.

S51 Foils. The interior arches between the cusps of a window.

S52 Frieze. The centre section of an entablature in Classical architecture. In the Ionic, Corinthian and Composite Orders it is usually ornamented, in the Doric Order it has slight projections and in the Tuscan Order it is plain.

S53 Gable. The triangular upper part of a wall immediately beneath a ridge roof.

S54 Garderobe. The privy in a castle or medieval house of some size. Usually it was placed at the end of a Z-shaped passage and was built into the thickness of a wall with a shaft underneath.

S55 Gargoyle. An ornamental spout projecting from gutters to carry water away from the wall. It is usually carved in the form of a human's, demon's or animal's mouth.

S56 Gazebo. A tower or turret overlooking a garden view.

S57 Hammer beams. Beams supported by brackets which project at right-angles from the walls. They eliminated the need for a tie beam.

S58 Header. The narrow face of a brick.

S59 Herringbone. A wall style in which the bricks, masonry or timber blocks are laid diagonally to form a zig-zag pattern.

S60 Hipped roof. A roof with sloped instead of vertical ends.

S61 Inglenook. A seat built into a wall next to a fireplace.

S62 Keystone. A wedge-shaped stone positioned at the head of an arch.

S63 King Post. A post standing on the tie beam and reaching to the roof ridge.

S64 Lintel. A horizontal piece of wood, stone or steel placed over a doorway, window etc, supporting the wall above.

S65 Loggia. A covered verandah open on one or more sides.

S66 Long Houses. Early forms of thatched houses which provided accommodation for people at one end and animals at the other.

S67 Long and Short Work. Corner stones of stucco work laid alternately horizontal and vertical.

S68 Mansard. A roof which has two slopes, the lower one steeper than the upper.

S69 Moulding. Ornamental projections or carvings on walls and ceilings. There are many kinds, such as billet, cable, chevron, cove, hood, plain and roll.

S70 Mullion. A vertical division of stone, wood or metal, separating the lights of a window.

S71 Newel Post. The central post, sometimes extending to the roof, in which the steps of a winding staircase are set.

S72 Oculus. A round window.

S73 Oriel. Originally part of a room set aside for prayer, quite often above an oratory, and from which the service below could be followed. The term was later applied to any projecting part of a room, and then to a projecting window supported by corbels.

S74 Palladian. A style of architecture inspired by Andreo Palladio (1518–80).

S75 Pantile. An S-shaped roof tile with one curve larger than the other.

S76 Parapet. A low wall on the roof of a building, or a wall at the edge of a balcony.

S77 Pargetting. Ornamental plasterwork, especially on a timber-framed house.

S78 Parlour. A room originally used for conversation.

S79 Pebble-dash. A result obtained by embedding small pebbles to surface rendering while it is still wet. Sometimes called rough-cast.

S80 Pediment. The triangular feature above a portico.

S81 Pele/Peel Tower. A small fortress most often found in northern England.

S82 Pier. A vertical support, especially that for a bridge.

S83 Pilaster. In Classical architecture, a rectangular pillar inset into a wall but projecting from it; a decorative feature.

S84 Pinnacle. In Gothic architecture a pointed turret terminating a buttress or tower.

S85 Plinth. The square projecting base of a column.

S86 Portico. A range of columns supporting a roof, forming the entrance to a building.

S87 Quatrefoil. In Gothic architecture an opening in tracery in the shape of four leaves.

S88 Quoin. The external corner stones of a building.

S89 Refectory. A dining hall.

S90 Revet. To face with masonry.

S91 Rib. A projecting band of a ceiling.

S92 Rococo. The later phase of the Baroque architectural style, c1720–60.

S93 Romanesque. A style of architecture which preceded Gothic; in England it is usually called Norman.

S94 Rose Window. A circular window with tracery resembling the petals of a rose. Alternatively called a Wheel window.

S95 Rotunda. A domed circular building.

S96 Rustication. Masonry joints made conspicuous by chiselling grooves or channels.

S97 Saddle-backed roof. A tower roof shaped like a gabled timber roof.

S98 Shaft. The part of a column between base and capital.

S99 Shingle. A flat, wooden tile used in churches, particularly in south-east England.

S100 Solar. A quiet room in an upper storey, usually on the sunniest side of the house.

S101 Stanchion. A vertical bar or strut.

S102 Stretcher. The long face of a brick.

S103 String Course. A projecting ornamental band running round the face of a building.

S104 Tesselated Pavement. Pavement made from small pieces of stone, marble, brick etc.

S105 Tie Beam. A horizontal beam between the ends of two rafters.

S106 Tile Hanging. Overhanging tiles vertically pegged onto a timber-frame structure.

S107 Tracery. Ornamental stonework in the upper part of Gothic windows.

S108 Transom. A horizontal bar in a window which separates panes of glass.

S109 Tympanum. The space between a lintel and an arch above.

S110 Vault. An arched roof or ceiling.

S111 Vestibule. An entrance hall or anteroom.

S112 Vise. A spiral staircase with steps inset into a newel post.

S113 Voussoirs. Wedge-shaped stones forming an arch.

S114 Wall Plate. A wooden or steel member laid along the walls on which the roof rests.

PART TWO
CASTLE ARCHITECTURE

S115 Bailey. Space between fortified walls of a castle; it can also be called a court or ward. There could be two or three baileys between the outer wall and the central keep.

S116 Barbican. A defensive outer tower before the gate of a castle or fortified settlement. It could also be used as a watch-tower.

S117 Bastion. A fortified projection, usually an irregular pentagon, on a wall.

S118 Battlement. An indented parapet on castles which provided both cover and facility for archers.

S119 Castellated. Description of a building on which there are Battlements (qv).

S120 Curtain wall. The part of a castle wall between fortified towers.

S121 Embrasure. An opening in a Battlement (qv) through which weapons might be fired.

S122 Garderobe. A privy, usually at the end of a Z-shaped passage, built into the thickness of a wall with a shaft underneath.

S123 Gatehouse. A tower over the entrance to a castle.

S124 Keep. The principal inner tower of a castle. Alternatively called Donjon.

S125 Machiolation. Openings in the floor of a projecting parapet through which missiles might be dropped.

S126 Merlons. The teeth of an embattled parapet.

S127 Motte and Bailey. The Normans introduced the Motte and Bailey castle. The bailey, a forecourt, was surrounded by an earth rampart. The motte was a mound upon which stood the lord's house or keep. The remainder of the castle's inhabitants lived in a wooden hall in the bailey and the whole was enclosed by a wooden fortification. This layout was used in the later stone castles.

S128 Portcullis. A defensive gateway made of heavy grating, which could be raised and lowered from the inside.

S129 Rampart. A wall of earth around a castle, or a stone wall built on it.

S130 Ravelin. A pointed, defensive screen placed outside the walls of a castle.

PART THREE
CHURCH AND CHURCHYARD ARCHITECTURE

S131 Aisle. A division of a church running parallel to the nave and pillars. In England it is rare to find more than two in a church.

S132 Altar. The raised table or platform used for the Holy Sacrament. The Council of Epone 509AD instructed that it should be made of stone but most stone altars were removed at the Reformation. Rails to protect the altar from desecration were widely introduced in early Elizabethan times.

S133 Apse. A semi-circular or polygonal part of a church at the end of the choir or aisles, usually with a domed or arched roof.

S134 Bale Tomb. Basically a Chest Tomb (qv), but in a semi-cylindrical shape which may have represented bales of wool or reflected the custom of shrouding the dead in wool for burial. These tombs are particularly common in the wool-producing Cotswolds.

S135 Belfry. The tower in which the church-bells are hung; it could be a detached building.

S136 Bell Gable. In the absence of a belfry, a turret holding a bell.

S137 Bench Ends. It was the practice in the 15th and 16th centuries to carve the ends of the church benches.

S138 Broach Spire. Usually an octagonal shape rising from the top of a square tower.

S139 Buttress. A projecting support to a wall which in Classical architecture was disguised as a pilaster. The Norman churches had buttresses which were broad with a low projection, but the Early English style had greater projection and less breadth – familiarly known as Flying Buttresses.

S140 Campanile. A detached bell tower.

S141 Chancel or Choir. The eastern part of a church which includes the main altar used by the clergy and choir. It is separated from the nave by a screen or rails.

S142 Chantry Chapel. It was common from the Middle Ages for a wealthy person to endow a chapel within a church in which priests could say masses for the souls of him and his descendants.

S143 Chapter House. The assembly room in which the governing body of a cathedral or monastery transact business.

S144 Chest. All churches were once obliged to possess a strong chest in which the records of the church were kept.

S145 Chest Tomb. A hollow rectangular chest of stone resting on a plinth above the place of burial.

S146 Churchyard. A circular churchyard, particularly one on a natural mound, could indicate a very old settlement within a fortified enclosure.

S147 Churchyard Cross. It was the custom before the Reformation to erect a large cross in the centre of the churchyard. Few survive, except in the west of England.

S148 Cressets. Metal holders for the grease or oil used for early lighting. It is common now to apply this name to the cresset stones which contain these holders.

S149 Crossing. The space at the intersection of the chancel, transept and nave.

S150 Crypt. A vault, usually found under the east end of a church. It was built beneath the holiest part of the building to hold tombs and relics, or else to house pilgrims.

S151 Dorter. A first-floor dormitory in a monastery, connected to the south transept by a night-stairway.

S152 Font. Vessels in which to hold the consecrated water for the baptism of infants. Old fonts are deeper so that the child might be fully immersed; in 1236 it was ordered that fonts should be fitted with locked covers to prevent the theft of the holy water.

S153 Headstones. The practice of erecting memorial headstones became common from the beginning of the 17th century; they were generally undecorated apart from a figure of an angel. By the end of that century classical motifs and shapes were incorporated. Earlier stones used local materials; variety only came when transportation made the use of 'imported' stone or marble feasible. The fashion to celebrate death ostentatiously in Victorian times, with very elaborate headstones, allowed a bereaved family to make a statement of affluence, and to identify the grave plot emphatically.

S154 Lairstal. A grave within a church.

S155 Lancet window. A tall pointed arch window in a church found in Early English architecture.

S156 Ledgers. Black marble slabs laid over graves in the floor of a church, usually in the chancel. Particularly used in the 17th and 18th centuries.

S157 Lychgate. A roofed gateway at the entrance to the churchyard through which the coffin is carried and which contains seats for the bearers; the structure also provides shelter for those involved in the service. The word is derived from the Anglo-Saxon word *lich*, meaning corpse.

S158 Misericord. A projecting bracket on the underside of stalls in a church; they were fitted with a hinge which when turned up formed a projection which could be used as a rest for the tired or infirm during long services.

S159 Nave. The main body of a church from the inner door to the choir, in which the congregation assembles.

S160 Needle spire. A thin spire rising from the centre part of the tower roof.

S161 Piscina. A basin for washing the Communion or Mass vessels, usually placed in a wall south of the altar.

S162 Presbytery. The part of the church east of the choir used by those who minister the services.

S163 Reredos. An ornamented wall or screen at the back of the altar.

S164 Rood. A crucifix; a name generally applied to the large cross at the entrance to the chancel in Roman Catholic churches.

S165 Sacristy. A room in a church in which vestments, vessels etc are stored. Also called the Vestry.

S166 Sedilia. Seats for the priests on the south side of the chancel.

S167 Slype. A covered passage from transept to chapter-house in a cathedral.

S168 Transept. The short arms of a cruciform church crossing the line of nave and chancel.

PART FOUR
BUILDING MATERIALS

S169 Ancaster Stone. An easily-cut and carved limestone quarried on Wilsford Heath in Lincolnshire. It can be of various colours but weathers as grey.

S170 Ashlar. Square stones applied as facing for a wall, usually covering irregularly-cut stone.

S171 Bath Stone. A yellow stone, easily cut, quarried around Box and Corsham in Wiltshire.

S172 Bricks. The Romans brought brickmaking skills to Britain but the knowledge seems to have left with them. The earliest English brick known of is that used to build a house at Little Coggeshall, Essex, in 1190, although a claim is made that Polstead church, Suffolk is made from bricks of thirty years earlier. Brickmaking was still on a small scale in this country by the 13th century, however, as in 1278 over 200,000 bricks were imported from Ypres for building work on the Tower of London. The industry began seriously with the immigration of Flemish weavers to East Anglia. First regulations concerning the size of bricks were introduced in 1477 and there was further standardisation in 1625 when the dimensions of the brick were fixed at approximately their present sizes. The building regulations enacted after the Great Fire of London promoted the expansion of the industry and mass production began at the end of the 18th century. In the mid 1830s it was discovered how to cut the face of bricks with a wire, so as to give a smoother surface.

S173 Cement. Cement is a combination of various aluminates and silicates of calcium obtained by heating chalk or limestone. James Parker of Northfleet, Kent, introduced 'Roman Cement' in 1796. Joseph Aspidin, of Leeds, patented what he called 'Portland Cement', from its resemblance to Portland stone, in 1824, but Portland cement, as we know it today, was first manufactured in the works of John Bazley White in Swanscombe Kent, c1845.

S174 Clipsham Stone. A honey-coloured limestone quarried at Clipsham, in what was then Rutland.

S175 Clunch. Chalk generally used for internal carving work.

S176 Cob. A mixture of unburnt clay and straw used for walls and domestic dwellings.

S177 Cotswold Stone. A grey limestone quarried in the Cotswolds.

S178 Gallets. Pebbles or chips of stone inserted into the pointing of walls to give more strength. Generally found in south-east England.

S179 Glass. Glass is a mixture of pure silica sand, lime and soda. The earliest glass of quality in this country was imported from France and Germany; by the 13th century many churches had glass windows but only the very wealthy had them in their houses by the 15th century. Substitutes for glass included thin slivers of horn, lattice-work of stone, wood or wickerwork. When sash windows were introduced at the end of the 17th century glass was still blown. Plate glass, invented in France, was made at St Helens in 1773, but the cheaper sheet glass was made as from 1838. The laborious processes of grinding and polishing were made unnecessary by the invention of floating the glass mix across a 'bath' of liquid tin, in 1959.

S180 Hopton Wood Stone. A grey limestone quarried in Derbyshire. It polishes well and is used in particular for floors.

S181 Ironstone. Limestone or sandstone coloured by iron oxide. It has a brown or green colour.

S182 Kentish Rag. A greyish-green, sandy limestone quarried in Kent. It is very hard, resists moisture and is used extensively for facing buildings.

S183 Ketton Stone. A cream limestone quarried in what was Rutland.

S184 Moorstone. A granite found in the west of England. Used for buildings, monuments and paving.

S185 Portland Stone. A limestone which turns white on exposure, found in south-west England, and particularly in Dorset. It was too hard for common use until improved cutting tools were made in the 17th century.

S186 Purbeck Marble. A dark limestone containing fossils, mined near Swanage and used particularly for monuments.

S187 Slate. The main slate quarry areas are Cornwall, Devon, Wales, Cumberland, north Lancashire, Westmorland, Argyllshire and Perthshire. Welsh slates can be green, blue, purple, red or grey; Westmorland's are usually green, Cornwall's bluish-grey.

A tax was imposed on slates in 1831 but soon removed.

S188 Stucco. A rendering of lime, gypsum or cement applied to a wall surface, or applied to architectural decorations. It was used in England in the 16th century but it became most popular when the Adam brothers introduced their own concoction, known as Adams' Cement. In the United States the term 'stucco' denotes what in England is called pebble-dash.

S189 Weldon Stone. A creamy, easily-cut stone, quarried in Northants.

PART FIVE
CONSERVATION AND PRESERVATION

S190 Early legislation. Public opinion was aroused in the cause of preservation by the formation, in 1877, of the Society for the Preservation of Ancient Buildings. The first legislation passed, the Ancient Monuments Protection Act 1882, listed 29 monuments in England and 21 in Scotland. The Ancient Monuments Consolidation and Amendment Act 1913 provided for an Ancient Monuments Board with Inspectors and Commissioners of Works to list buildings of national importance. They were also empowered to list other monuments of lesser importance but which should be retained in the public's interest.

The Historic Buildings and Ancient Monuments Act 1931 empowered the Ministry of Works to issue interim preservation notices on the recommendation of the Ancient Monument Boards.

S191 Later legislation. The Town and Country Planning Act 1944 began a system by which the Ministry prepared lists of historic buildings for local authorities, and classified the buildings in grades of importance. Those grades are:

Grade 1: of such great value and interest that in no circumstance should demolition be allowed;

Grade 2: not to be demolished without very good reason.

Grade 3: generally applies to more modest buildings. The Historic Buildings and Ancient Monuments Act 1953 extended the range to include industrial buildings. The Local Authority (Historic Buildings) Act 1962 enabled local authorities to make grants for the upkeep of historic buildings whether graded or not.

The Ancient Monuments and Archaeological Areas Act 1979 redefined what could be preserved in such a way that almost any edifice may be a monument. The wording includes any 'building, structure or work, below or above ground and any cave or excavation'.

PART SIX
HOUSING TERMS

S192 Ancient Messuage. In theory, a house erected before the time of legal memory, that is, before the reign of Richard I. However, the term was used quite commonly to describe houses built before living memory.

S193 Backside. A Midland term for the backyard of a house.

S194 Biggin. A Scottish and northern term for a rough house or cottage.

S195 Bottle. A northern term for a house.

S196 Capital Messuage. A term commonly found in manor court rolls, wills and other legal documents for a large house.

S197 Claybiggin. A widespread term for a rough cottage or hut made of clay and wood.

S198 Cob/Cot House. A cottage built of clay and straw (cob).

S199 Cote. A small cottage, isolated farmhouse or hut. In northern counties a term for an animal shed.

S200 Curtilage. The yard and outbuildings of a house. Alternatively spelt, in the westcountry, courtledge.

S201 Erding. A medieval term for a dwelling. Alternatively spelt Earding.

S202 Garth. A yard or enclosure.

S203 Garthstead. A house and its land.

S204 Hallhouse. A dwelling.

S205 Messuage. A house and the ground around it. Alternatively spelt Mese.

S206 Tenement. Rented land or dwelling.

S207 Town Place. The buildings and cottages belonging to a farm.

PART SEVEN
HOUSING PROVISION

S208 Philanthropic Housing. Slums in towns, particularly in London, prompted the formation of many charitable housing organisations who took the lead in the development of tenement blocks. The principal organisations were as follows:

Metropolitan Association for Improving the Dwellings of the Industrious Classes, formed in

1841. The Association's first development was a block of flats in Pancras Road, London in 1847.

The Society for Improving the Condition of the Labouring Classes was established in 1844; its first development was of 2-storey buildings in the King's Cross area of London, followed by a tenement block in Streatham Street, Holborn, in 1849;

The General Society for the Improvement of Dwellings of the Working Classes was formed in 1852;

The Peabody Trust, which became the best-known of the various charities, was established in 1862 by a gift of £150,000 from George Peabody, to help the poor of London. Its first estate opened in Commercial Street, London, in 1864.

The Improved Industrial Dwellings Company was formed by Sidney Waterlow in 1865. By 1871 it had 1,000 occupied dwellings and a further 200 in the course of construction.

The Artisans, Labourers and General Dwellings Company was formed in 1867.

The East End Dwellings Company was formed in 1884.

The Guinness Trust was established by a gift from Sir Edward Guinness of £250,000 in 1889.

S209 Model Villages. Edward Akroyd built two model villages at Copley, Yorkshire in 1849–53. Price's Candle Company built Bromborough Pool, Wirral in 1858. The best known villages, (although some were as large as towns), were Saltaire, Bradford built by Titus Salt 1853–63, Bourneville near Birmingham, developed by the Cadbury company for its workers, 1893–1912, and Port Sunlight built by the soap company owned by Lever, from 1888. Joseph Rowntree built New Earswick near York.

S210 Lodging Houses. The Labouring Classes Lodging Houses Act 1851 enabled local authorities to appoint commissioners and borrow money for the erection or purchase of lodging houses for the working classes. The Act was largely ignored. Further legislation in the following years established a system of registration of private lodging houses.

S211 Slum Clearance. The Artisans and Labourers Dwellings Improvement Act 1875 permitted local authorities compulsory powers to buy up slum property and demolish or improve it.

S212 Local Authority Housing. The Housing Act 1890 enabled local authorities to provide working-class houses with a public subsidy. The national subsidy was adjusted in 1923 and 1924. Liverpool was the first authority to build council houses in 1869. The London County Council began provision in 1892 in the East End, and Manchester's first was in 1896.

S213 Building Societies. Building clubs existed by the end of the 18th century; these generally consisted of groups of tradesmen who built their own houses. The Building Societies Act 1874 permitted a limited company status and a permanent existence. Early societies included the Leeds Permanent 1848, the Woolwich Equitable 1847, Abbey National 1849, Bradford Equitable 1851 and the Halifax 1853.

S214 Freehold Land Societies. These societies were popular from 1840 to the 1860s. They had a political basis in that the organisers sought to provide cheap freeholds for the artisan classes so that they became enfranchised to vote. The societies declined after the franchise was generally extended in 1867.

PART EIGHT
BIBLIOGRAPHY

Architecture

English Medieval Architects, a Biographical Dictionary down to 1550, John Harvey

A Biographical Dictionary of English Architects 1660–1840, H. M. Colvin (1954)

The Architecture of England, D. Yarwood (1963)

A History of Building Types, Nikolaus Pevsner (1976)

Architecture in Britain 1530–1830, Sir John Summerson (Pelican rev. edition 1983)

English Medieval Architecture, C. E. Power (2 vols 1923)

Timber Building in Britain, R. W. Brunskill (1985)

Buildings of England series, Nikolaus Pevsner rev. B. Cherry

Introduction to Tudor Architecture, J. H. Harvey (1949)

Early Victorian Architecture, H. R. Hitchcock (2 vols 1954)

A History of Architecture on the Comparative Method, Sir Banister Fletcher

English Architecture since the Regency, H. S. Goodhart-Rendel (1953)

Bibliography *(cont)*

Church Architecture
The English Medieval Parish Church, G. H. Cook (1954)
Collins Guide to English Parish Churches, ed. John Betjeman
English Parish Churches, G. Hutton and E. Smith (1952)
The Architecture of Scottish Post-Reformation Churches, George Hay (1957)
A Guide to London's Churches, Mervyn Blatch (1978)

Building Materials
Innovations in Building Materials, Marian Bowley (1960)
Building Stones for England and Wales, Norman Davey (1976)
Stone for Building, Hugh O'Neill (1965)
Bricks to Build a House, John Woodforde (1976)
History of English Brickwork, N. Lloyd (1925)
The Pattern of English Building, Alec Clifton-Taylor (1962)
The Cement Industry 1796–1914: A History, Major A. J. Francis (1977)

Conservation and Preservation
Listed Buildings: The Law and Practice, Roger W. Suddards (1982)
Conservation of Buildings, John Harvey (1972)

Housing Provision
A Social History of Housing 1815–1970, John Burnett (1978)
House and Home in the Victorian City: Working Class Housing 1850–1914, M. J. Daunton (1983)
Middle-class Housing in Britain, ed. M. A. Simpson and T. H. Lloyd (1977)
The Making of a Model Village, S. M. Gaskell
The Eternal Slum, Anthony S. Wohl (1977)
Five per cent Philanthrophy: an account of housing in urban areas between 1840 and 1914, J. N. Tarn (1973)
Homes fit for heroes: the politics and architecture of early State housing in Britain, M. Swenarton (1981)
Housing and Local Government, J. B. Cullingworth (1966)
Cruel Habitations: A History of Working Class Housing 1780–1918, Enid Gauldie (1974)
The History of Working Class Housing, ed. Stanley Chapman (1971)
Working Class Housing in 19th-century Britain, J. N. Tarn (1971)
Dunroamin: The Suburban Semi and Its Enemies, Paul Oliver (1981)

SECTION T

Heraldry

PART ONE
THE COMPONENTS OF A
COAT-OF-ARMS

T1 General. Heraldry, or more properly Armory, began in England in the 12th century. Most probably it arose from the need to identify important individuals when they were in armour and their faces obscured. By the 13th century armorial bearings were applied to the linen surcoat over the armour, and from this came the term 'coat-of-arms'. In addition crests were emblazoned on helmets.

By the 14th century the number of families entitled to bear arms had grown to the extent that the heralds, who supervised tournaments etc, were given responsibility for regulating the design and the wearing of armorial bearings. This duty was consolidated in 1485 in the College of Heralds. By then bearings had become hereditary.

T2 College of Arms. The College, alternatively called the College of Heralds, was established 1485; it is responsible for the granting, control and confirmation of coats-of-arms in England. At its head is the Earl Marshal, an hereditary title held by the Duke of Norfolk. He has thirteen principal officers: three Kings of Arms – Garter, Clarenceux and Norroy, six heralds – Chester, Lancaster, Somerset, Richmond, Windsor and York, and four pursuivants – Rouge Croix, Rouge Dragon, Portcullis and Bluemantle. The Harleian Society has printed lists of those who received grants of arms from 1687 to 1898.

T3 Visitations. From 1529/30 the College of Arms made visitations to parts of the country to establish if coats-of-arms were being used correctly, and also to investigate new applications. The last visitation was in 1686. Many of the visitation records have been printed by the Harleian Society.

T4 Components of a Coat-of-Arms.

a) *The Shield*

A shield's right or left hand is how it is viewed by the wearer of the shield, *ie* the opposite to a person looking at it. The right is called Dexter, the left Sinister.

A shield's main points are shown as under:

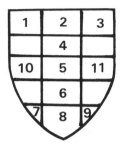

1   Dexter Chief Point
2   Middle Chief Point
3   Sinister Chief Point
4   Honour Point
5   Heart Point
6   Navel Point
7   Dexter Base Point
8   Middle Base Point
9   Sinister Base Point
10   Right Flank
11   Left Flank

The area of the shield is known as its ground or field and whatever is emblazoned upon it is said to be charged upon it. As a general rule descriptions of a coat of arms refer to the upper part of a shield first.

b) *Divisions of a Shield*

Some common divisions of the field of a shield are as follows:

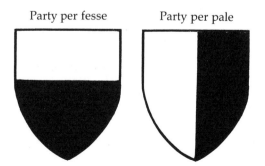

Party per fesse   Party per pale

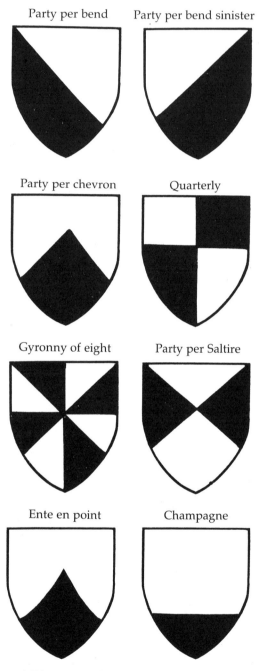

Party per bend   Party per bend sinister

Party per chevron   Quarterly

Gyronny of eight   Party per Saltire

Ente en point   Champagne

c) *Tinctures*

The tinctures which are used in coats-of-arms may be colours, metals or furs. In black and white illustrations these are denoted by a system of dots and lines. The most common tinctures are as follows:

Colours:

azure – blue (horizontal lines)

gules – red (perpendicular lines)

vert – green (diagonal lines from dexter chief to sinister base)

sable – black (horizontal and perpendicular lines crossing each other

purpure – purple (diagonal lines from dexter and sinister crossing each other.

Metals:

or – gold (dots)

argent – silver (plain white)

Furs:

ermine – white field with black spots or tufts

ermines – black field with white spots or tufts

erminois – gold field with black spots or tufts

pean – black field with gold spots

vair – argent and azure pattern in rows

counter-vair – same as vair except that figures are placed base against base, point against point

vaire – when the figures forming the vair are of more than two tinctures

potent – resembles the heads of crutches placed head to head.

The term 'proper' is used when the object is depicted in its natural colour.

A field is 'counter-charged' when it is made up of two tinctures – metal and colours, with the metallic part of the charge falling upon the field colour and the coloured part of the charge falling upon the metal field.

d) *Charges:*

Charges are the devices blazoned upon the shield's field. The most commonly used charges are called 'Ordinaries'; some of them are depicted as follows:

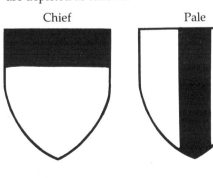

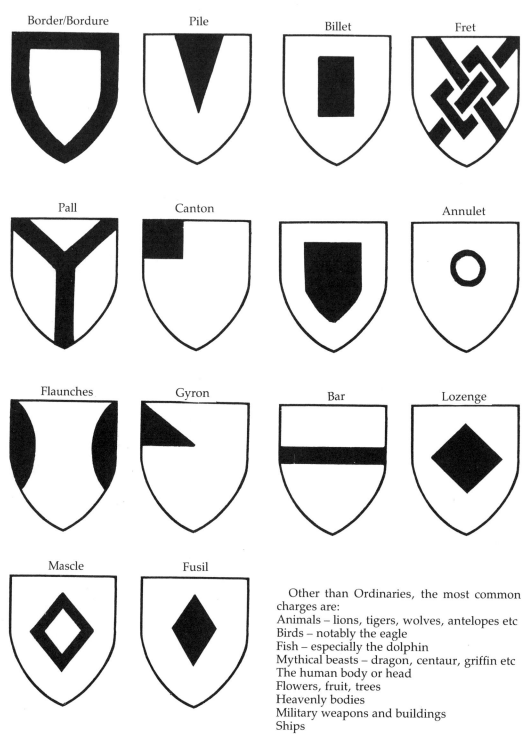

Border/Bordure   Pile   Billet   Fret

Pall   Canton   Annulet

Flaunches   Gyron   Bar   Lozenge

Mascle   Fusil

Other than Ordinaries, the most common charges are:
Animals – lions, tigers, wolves, antelopes etc
Birds – notably the eagle
Fish – especially the dolphin
Mythical beasts – dragon, centaur, griffin etc
The human body or head
Flowers, fruit, trees
Heavenly bodies
Military weapons and buildings
Ships

e) *Supporters*
The term refers to the two figures, usually animals, on either side of the shield. They are used in England only by the Crown, peers and some orders of knighthood.

f) *Mottoes*
A family motto may appear beneath or above the shield.

T5 Coats-of-Arms for Women. An unmarried woman bears her father's arms upon a lozenge instead of on a shield. On marrying, her arms are placed on the sinister side of a shield and her husband's on the dexter. This is called impalement. If she is an heraldic heiress, (an eldest daughter without brothers), her arms are depicted on a small shield known as 'escutcheon of pretence' in the middle of her husband's arms which occupy the remainder of the shield. A widow bears her late husband's arms on a lozenge, with her father's arms on an escutcheon of pretence, or else her late husband's arms are impaled with her father's.

T6 Coats-of-Arms for Children. Children may quarter their shields with the paternal arms in the top dexter and bottom sinister quarter, and the maternal arms in the other quarters.

PART TWO
HERALDIC TERMS

T7 Achievement. This describes a coat-of-arms with all its features displayed.

T8 Annulet. A ring, a device probably derived from chain mail. It can, in particular, denote a fifth son.

T9 Argent. Silver, represented by plain white in drawings.

T10 Armed. Describes the showing of claws, horns, hoofs etc., of an animal or bird.

T11 Armiger. One entitled to bear arms.

T12 Armory. The study of coats of armorial bearings, now usually called Heraldry.

T13 Augmentation. An addition to a coat-of-arms, usually granted as an honour.

T14 Azure. Blue, represented by horizontal lines in drawings.

T15 Badge. A distinctive insignia worn by soldiers and retainers.

T16 Bar. The area between two horizontal lines drawn across the shield.

T17 Barry. Describes a shield divided by horizontal lines.

T18 Bearing. A general term for an heraldic device.

T19 Bend. A charge consisting of the area between two parallel lines drawn from top right to bottom left of a shield. A shield is divided Per Bend when a single line is drawn in the same direction.

T20 Bend Sinister. A charge consisting of the area between two parallel lines drawn from top left to bottom right of a shield. A shield is divided Per Bend Sinister when a single line is drawn in the same direction.

T21 Border/Bordure. A charge which consists of a border around the edge of the shield.

T22 Cadency. The distinctions between members of a family depicted by various symbols. For example, the eldest son displays a device called a label, and the second son a crescent moon.

T23 Cadet. A junior member or branch of a family.

T24 Canton. A charge consisting of a box in the top right hand part of a shield.

T25 Charge. A device emblazoned on the face of a shield; it may be an Ordinary or a figure.

T26 Checkered/Checky. Describes a shield divided into chess-board squares.

T27 Chevron. A charge consisting of an inverted V-stripe. A field is divided Party Per Chevron when it is divided by a single line in the same shape.

T28 Chevronels. Small Chevrons (qv).

T29 Chief. The upper part of the shield.

T30 Cinquefoils. Five leaves of grass emerging from a central point.

T31 Coat-of-Arms. The shield, crest, mantling and helmet.

T32 Couchant. Describes an animal lying down but with its head up.

T33 Counter-charged. Describes a field where two tinctures are used.

T34 Crescent Moon. Denotes a second son.

T35 Crest. An insignia fixed to the helmet by a wreath.

T36 Crowned. Describes a crowned animal.

T37 Dexter. The right-hand side as viewed by the wearer of the shield.

T38 Displayed. Describes the spread of wings of a bird.

T39 Dormant. Describes an animal lying with its head down.

T40 Ermine. A fur tincture, depicted as white with black spots or tufts in drawings.

T41 Ermines. A fur tincture, depicted as a black field with white spots or tufts in drawings.

T42 Fesse. The area between two parallel lines drawn across the centre of the shield, slightly wider than a Bar (qv). A shield is divided Per Fesse when a single line crosses it in the same direction.

T43 Fesse Point. The centre point of a shield.

T44 Field. The surface of a shield or escutcheon. Alternatively called Ground.

T45 Fleur-de-lis. A lily. A common heraldic device and used in particular to denote a sixth son.

T46 Garb. A sheaf of wheat or corn.

T47 G(u)ardant. Describes a beast full-faced.

T48 Gules. Red, depicted by perpendicular lines in drawings.

T49 Gyronny. The division of the shield into triangles. The most common device is called Gyronny of Eight.

T50 Hatchment. The arms of a deceased person displayed on the front of his or her house. Originally the actual shield, helmet etc were shown but these were superseded by a pictorial representation of them.

T51 Impalement. A shield is impaled when it is divided into two equal parts and, for example, the arms of the husband are shown on the right and those of the wife on the left.

T52 In Escutcheon. Describes the placing of the armorial bearings of an heraldic heiress (see T5) on a lozenge within the arms of her husband.

T53 Label. A charge with three points which denotes an eldest son.

T54 Leopards. In France these figures are leopards, but in England they are royal lions.

T55 Lozenge. A diamond shape.

T56 Lozengy. A term to describe a field of a shield covered with diamond-shapes.

T57 Martlet. A device which denotes a fourth son.

T58 Mascle. A diamond-shaped charge through which the field of the shield may be seen.

T59 Mullet. A rowel of a spur used to denote a third son.

T60 Or. Gold, depicted by dots in drawings.

T61 Ordinaries. The most commonly used charges.

T62 Ordinary of Arms. An heraldic index consisting of armorial bearings classified according to their principal charges.

T63 Pale. Describes the area between two parallel perpendicular lines drawn in the centre of a shield. A shield divided Per Pale has a single perpendicular line in the same direction.

T64 Party. Divided or parted.

T65 Passant. Describes a beast in a walking position.

T66 Pile. A V-shaped charge drawn from the top of the shield.

T67 Proper. The natural colour.

T68 Purpure. Purple, depicted by diagonal lines drawn from top right to bottom left in drawings.

T69 Quarterings. Partitions of a shield holding armorial bearings.

T70 Quarterly. Describes the division of the field of the shield into four parts by one horizontal and one perpendicular line.

T71 Rampant. Describes an upright animal.

T72 Regardant. Describes an animal facing backwards.

T73 Roundel. A charge in the shape of a disc.

T74 Sable. Black, depicted by horizontal and perpendicular lines crossing each other in drawings.

T75 Saltire. Party Per Saltire is the division of the field of a shield into four equal parts by two diagonal lines crossing each other.

T76 Segreant. Describes a griffin on its hind legs with its wings back to back.

T77 Sinister. The left-hand side as viewed by the wearer of the shield.

T78 Supporters. Figures, usually animals, on either side of the shield. Their use is restricted to the armorial bearings of the Crown, peers and some orders of knighthood.

T79 Torteaux. Red roundels.

T80 Trick. A method of quickly depicting a coat-of-arms using a generally recognised shorthand to describe tinctures, charges etc.

T81 Vert. Green, depicted by diagonal lines from the top right to the bottom left in drawings.

PART THREE
BIBLIOGRAPHY

Boutell's Heraldry ed. by J. Brooke-Little
Heraldry Simplified, W. A Copinger (1910)
An Heraldic Alphabet, J. P. Brooke-Little (1985)
An Encyclopaedic Dictionary of Heraldry, Julian Franklyn and John Tanner (1970)
A Complete Guide to Heraldry, A. C. Fox-Davies rev. J. P. Brooke-Little (1969)
British Armorials, J. W. Papworth and A. W. Morant (1874 repr. 1961)

Trades and Occupations

PART ONE
CITY LIVERY COMPANIES

U1 General. The City Livery Companies developed from the craft guilds or 'misteries' of the 12th-15th centuries. A guild was entitled to regulate who was able to follow its own particular craft within the City and, to an extent, control wages, working conditions, quality of goods and prices. Over the years each company acquired charters which ratified or amended its privileges. Occasionally there were disputes as to which company had jurisdiction over a particular aspect of a trade, just as there can be today between trade unions. The word 'livery' originally meant the distinctive uniform granted to each company, but is now also used to denote the collective membership. The companies also admitted apprentices to their own trades who, on completion of their training, could become freemen of the company and then of the City of London.

With the spread of manufacture outside of the City the powers and functions of the companies became fewer and irrelevant. Increasingly the companies became organisations of the principal employers in the various industries they represented and involved themselves, instead, with educational and charitable projects. Since the companies publish no accounts it is difficult to judge how much of their revenue is spent in this way. What is apparent is that the loss of real functions has encouraged a preoccupation with ceremony and precedence, which is not to everyone's taste.

The records of the companies are important to local historians. Their whereabouts are detailed in D287.

U2 City Livery Companies. Listed below are the present livery companies. Their order of precedence is shown in brackets after the name of the company.

Actuaries (91)
5 New Bridge Street, EC4.
Livery granted 1979.

Air Pilots and Air Navigators (81)
30 Eccleston Street, SW1.
Established 1929, livery granted 1956.

Apothecaries (58)
Blackfriars Lane, EC4.
Charter granted 1617.

Arbitrators (93)
75 Cannon Street, EC4.
Livery granted 1981.

Armourers and Brasiers (22)
81 Coleman Street, EC2.
Established by 1322, charter 1453.
Brasiers were incorporated in 1708.

Bakers (19)
Harp Lane, EC3.
Established by 1155, originally for white-bread bakers only. The brown-bread bakers were included as from 1569. Charter granted 1486.

Basketmakers (52)
87–95 Tooley Street, SE1.
Established 1569, charter 1937.

Blacksmiths (40)
Established by 1494, charter 1571. Spurriers were included from 1571. The early blacksmiths were also toothdrawers.

Bowyers (38)
7 Chandos Street, W1.
Established by 1371, charter 1621. Originally included with the Fletchers.

Brewers (14)
Aldermanbury Square, EC2.
Established by 1292, first charter 1437.

Builders Merchants (88).
128 Queen Victoria Street, EC4.
Livery granted 1977.

Butchers (24)
87 Bartholomew Close, EC1.
Established by 1179, first charter 1605.

Carmen (77)
81–87 Gresham Street, EC2.
Established 1516, charter 1946.

Carpenters (26)
Throgmorton Avenue, EC2.
Established by 1333, first charter 1477.

Chartered Accountants (86)
81–87 Gresham Street, EC2.
Livery granted 1977.

Chartered Secretaries and Administrators (87)
16 Park Crescent, W1.
Livery granted 1977.

Chartered Surveyors (85)
12 Great George Street, SW1.
Livery granted 1977.

Clockmakers (61)
2 Greycoat Place, SW1.
Charter granted 1631. Originally part of blacksmiths.

Clothworkers (12)
Dunster Court, EC3.
Established 1528, charter 1528. An amalgamation of Fullers (inc. 1480 and Shearmen inc. 1508).

Coachmakers and Coach Harness Makers (72)
9 Lincoln's Inn Fields, WC2.
Charter granted 1677.

Cooks (35)
49 Queen Victoria Steet, EC4.
Established 1311, charter granted 1482.

Coopers (36)
13 Devonshire Square, EC2.
Established by 1396, charter granted 1501.

Cordwainers (27)
30 Fleet Street, EC4.
Established by 1272, charter 1439. Workers in Cordoba leather originally.

Curriers (29)
43 Church Road, Hove, Sussex.
Established by 1389, charter 1605. (Leather dressers).

Cutlers (18)
Warwick lane, EC4.
Established by 1389, charter 1416.

Distillers (69)
1 Vintners Place, EC4.
Charter granted 1638.

Drapers (3)
Throgmorton Street, EC2.
Established by 12th century, charter 1364.

Dyers (13)
Dowgate Hill, EC4.
Established by 1188, charter 1471.

Fan Makers (76)
107–111 Fleet Street, EC4.
Charter 1709, livery granted 1809.

Farmers (80)
7–8 King's Bench Walk, EC4.
Established 1946, charter 1955.

Farriers (55)
3 Hamilton Road, N14.
Established by 1356, charter 1674.

Feltmakers (63)
53 Davies Street, W1.
Charter 1667. (Mainly hatmakers).

Fishmongers (4)
Fishmongers Hall, London Bridge, EC4.
Established by 1154, charter 1272.

Fletchers (39)
College Hill Chambers, EC4.
Established 1371 as breakaway from Bowyers.

Founders (33)
13 St Swithins Lane, EC4.
Established by 1365, charter 1614.

Framework Knitters (64)
51 Dulwich Wood Avenue, SE19.
Charter 1657.

Fruiterers (45)
1 Serjeants Inn, EC4.
Established by 1292, charter 1606.

Furniture Makers (83)
Grove Mills, Cranbrook Road, Hawkhurst, Kent.
Established by 1952, livery granted 1963.

Gardeners (66)
College Hill Chambers, EC4.
Established by 1345, charter 1605.

Girdlers (23)
Basinghall Avenue, EC2.
Established by 1332, charter 1449.

Glass Sellers (71)
6 Eldon Street, EC2.
Charter granted 1664.

Glaziers (53)
9 Montague Close, SE1.
Established by 1368, charter 1637.

Glovers (62)
Bakers Hall, Harp Lane, EC3.
Established 1349, charter 1639. In 1498 joined by Pursers, and in 1502 joined by Leathersellers who separated again in 1639.

Gold and Silver Wyre Drawers (74)
40a Ludgate Hill, EC4.
Established by 1464, charter 1693.

Goldsmiths (5)
Foster Lane, EC2.
Established by 1180, charter 1327.

Grocers (2)
Princes Street, EC2.
Established 1180, charter 1428.
Originally called Pepperers and included the Apothecaries who broke away in 1617.

Gunmakers (73)
48–50 Commercial Road, E1.
Charter 1637.

Haberdashers (8)
Staining Lane, EC2.
Established by 1371, charter 1448. Originally part of the Mercers Co.

Horners (54)
Established by 1284, charter 1638. (Manufacturers of horn articles).

Innholders (32)
Dowgate Hill, EC4.
Established by 14th century, charter 1514.
Originally called Hostellers.

Insurers (92)
Chartered Insurance Institute, 20 Aldermanbury, EC2.
Established 1979.

Ironmongers (10)
Aldersgate Street, EC2.
Established by 13th century, charter 1463.

Joiners and Ceilers (41)
8 West Heath Road, SE2.
Established by 1375, charter 1571. (Ceilers were wood carvers).

Launderers (89)
34 Broadhurst, Ashtead, Surrey.
Established 1960, livery granted 1977.

Leathersellers (15)
St Helens Place, EC3.
Established by 1372, charter 1444.

Loriners (57)
2–5 Benjamin Street, EC1.
Established by 1261, charter 1711. (Makers of bits for horses).

Marketors (90)
25 Pebworth Road, Harrow.
Established 1975.

Masons (30)
9 New Square, Lincoln's Inn, WC2.
Established by 1356, charter 1677.

Master Mariners (78)
Headquarters on a ship named the Wellington,
Victoria Embankment
Established 1926, charter 1930.

Mercers (1)
Ironmonger Lane, EC2.
Established by 1347, charter 1394.

Merchant Taylors (7 or 6)
30 Threadneedle Street, EC2.
Charter 1327.
They alternate yearly with the Skinners in
precedence.

Musicians (50)
4 St Pauls Churchyard, EC4.
Established by 1350, charter 1469.

Needlemakers (65)
4 Staple Inn, Holborn WC1.
Charter 1656.

Painter Stainers (28)
9 Little Trinity Lane, EC4.
Stainers est. by 1268, Painters est. by 1283.
United in 1502. Charter 1581.

Pattenmakers (70)
6 Raymond Buildings, Grays Inn, WC1.
Established by 1379, charter 1670. (Pattens
were a kind of shoe).

Paviors (56)
Cutlers Hall, Warwick Lane, EC4.
Established by 1479, charter 1672.

Pewterers (16)
Oat Lane, EC2.
Established by 1348, charter 1473.

Plaisterers (46)
1 London Wall, EC2.
Charter 1501.

Playing Card Makers (75)
Charter 1628.

Plumbers (31)
218 Strand, WC2.
Established by 1365, charter 1611.

Poulters (34)
7–8 Kings Bench Walk, EC4.
Established by 1368.

Saddlers (25)
Gutter Lane, EC2.
Charter ?1272.

Salters (9)
Fore Street, EC2.
Established by 1394, charter 1599.

Scientific Instrument Makers (84)
9 Montague Close, SE1.
Established by 1955, charter 1964.

Scriveners (44)
4 Wilton Mews, SW1.
Established by 1373, charter 1617.

Shipwrights (59)
Ironmongers Hall, Aldersgate Street, EC2.
Established 1388, charter 1612.

Skinners (6 or 7)
8 Dowgate Hill, EC4.
Charter 1327. They alternate yearly with the
Merchant Taylors in precedence.

Solicitors (79)
Cutlers Hall, Warwick Lane, EC4.
Established 1908, charter 1944.

Spectacle Makers (60)
Apothecaries Hall, Blackfriars Lane, EC4.
Charter 1629.

Stationers and Newspaper Makers (47)
Stationers Hall, Ave Maria Lane, EC4.
Established by 1403, charter 1557.

Tallow Chandlers (21)
4 Dowgate Hill, EC4.
Charter 1462.

Tinplate Workers (als Wireworkers) (67)
Charter 1670. Evolved from Ironmongers.
Joined with Wireworkers in 1425.

**Tobacco Pipe Makers and Tobacco Blenders
(82)**
Established by 1619. Re-established 1954.
154 Fleet Street, EC4.

Turners (51)
1 Serjeants Inn, EC4.
Established by 1478, charter 1604.

Tylers and Bricklayers (37)
6 Bedford Row, WC1.
Charter 1568.

Upholders (49)
56 Kingsway, WC2.
Established 1360, charter 1626. (Makers of
upholstery and bedding).

Vintners (11)
Upper Thames Street, EC4.
Charter 1364.

Wax Chandlers (20)
Gresham Street, EC2.
Established by 1330, charter 1483.

Weavers (42)
1 The Sanctuary, SW1.
Established by 1155.

Wheelwrights (68)
Greenup, Milton Avenue, Gerrards Cross, Bucks.
Charter 1670.

Woolmen (43)
192–198 Vauxhall Bridge Road, SW1.
Established by 1297, charter 1552.

U3 Non-livery City Companies.
Two important companies which do not have a livery are:

Company of Parish Clerks,
14 Dale Close, Oxford.
Established by 1274, charter 1442.

Watermen and Lightermen of the River Thames,
18 St Mary-at-Hill, EC3.
Established by 1555.

PART TWO
MILLS AND MILLING

U4 Watermills. At least 6,000 watermills are recorded in Domesday Book. They were introduced to the British Isles during the Roman occupation. Four main types – horizontal, undershot, overshot and breastshot, have existed.

Horizontal: This type was brought here by the Saxons. The wheel was positioned across a stream and it used all the available water, which was directed by a chute on to the paddles of a horizontally-placed wheel; the shaft directly drove the grinding stone on the floor above. There were no gears and production was slow. Examples may be found in the Orkneys and Shetland.

Undershot: This type was introduced by the Romans and reintroduced sometime before the Norman Conquest. It consisted of a vertically-mounted wheel with flat blades around its circumference. The water came into contact with the wheel only at the bottom. The flow of water turned the blades but only limited control of the energy extracted could be

obtained. Where a mill was sited on an artificial watercourse called a leat much better control was possible since the excess water remained in the main stream by means of a weir and sluice gate. By this system the miller could adjust or cut off the water supply when necessary.

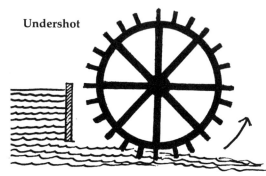

Undershot

Overshot: In the Middle Ages the Overshot watermill was introduced, which extracted more power from a given amount of water. By means of a leat the water was supplied to the mill wheel at the top of its circumference and the paddles were replaced by buckets, thereby using the motion of the water and its weight. This type was particularly well suited to hilly countryside.

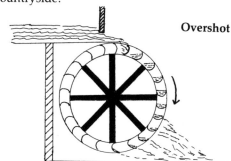

Overshot

Breastshot: Wheel construction is similar to that of the Undershot type, but by means of a sluice, water is directed into the buckets at or about the level of the axle. If there is a millpond behind, the effect of the weight of the water is added to the overall force applied to the wheel.

Except in the case of the Horizontal type the millstones are driven by a series of gears, usually at about 150rpm. The turbine was introduced in the 19th century. This is a development of the Horizontal wheel but has scientifically-shaped blades and works in a fully-enclosed chamber with controlled inflow and outflow ports.

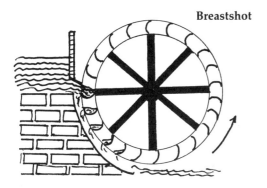

Breastshot

U5 Tidemills. This kind of mill probably dates from the late 14th century. It was situated on low-lying estuaries on which a large, but shallow millpond was constructed on the landward side of the mill. The pond was filled via a sluice at high tide, the sluice being then closed; a period of about three hours then had to elapse before there was a sufficient fall of water to work the mill. At best these mills could be worked for two six-hour periods each day. Examples may be seen at Eling near Southampton, and Woodbridge in Suffolk.

U6 Windmills. The earliest type of windmill was the post mill. It has been suggested that these were introduced into England from the East during the Third Crusade; the earliest record in this country is that of the illegal mill of Dean Herbert's at Bury St. Edmunds in 1191.

Post mills: The earliest kind was a fixed structure usable only when the wind was blowing in the right direction. Originally it had no roundhouse beneath it, to protect the trestles upon which the mill was supported from decay, but later types had an exterior housing which helped to preserve the trestles and provided storage space within. In the Middle Ages the body of the mill, which contained the machinery which drove grinding stones and sails, was balanced on a central post and could be turned into the wind by means of a pole at the back of the mill. The oldest surviving example of this kind is at Bourn, Cambridgeshire, and was erected in 1636. In 1745 a method was patented which used a fantail and gears for keeping the mill facing into the wind. Many post mills were built upon a raised mound to gain extra wind-power.

Post Mill

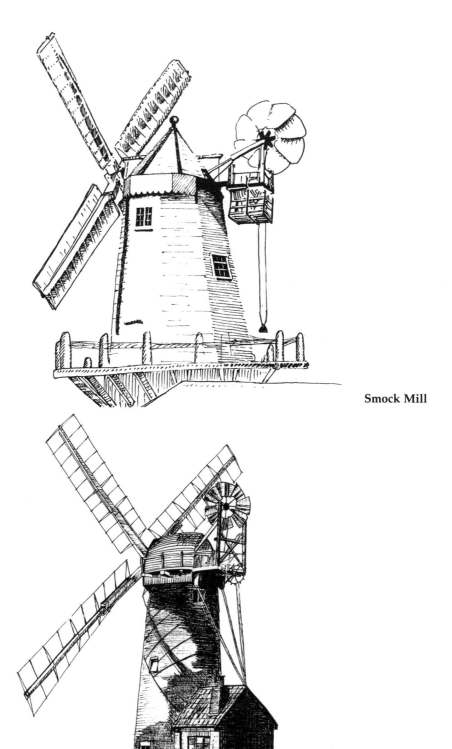

Smock Mill

Tower Mill

Smock mills: In a smock mill only the cap with the sails revolved on a circular track. They were built of wood, were usually octangular in plan and had sloping (battered) sides. They were introduced in the 17th century, one of the oldest being at Lacey Green, Bucks, built in 1650. Some versions were placed on a brick base – one at Cranbrook, Kent, is an example.

Tower Mills: While a smock mill was built of wood a Tower mill was constructed of either brick or stone. Most were round in plan but some were octagonal. As in smock mills, only the cap revolves to face the wind. Weaknesses in the structure often developed when the windows on the various floors were placed one above the other instead of being staggered around the tower.

U7 Sails or Sweeps. There are three main types of sails – Common, Spring and Patent. *Common* sails are the earliest type and consist of a sailcloth which can be stretched across the timber frame of each sweep. They were difficult and slow to adjust. *Spring* sails consist of a series of movable shutters pivotted at right-angles to the length of the sweep. They are connected by a long rod and tensioned by a spring which the miller can set and determine at what wind force the shutters shall open. This device was introduced in 1772. *Patent* sails have movable shutters which open from a system of weights and pulley. This was introduced in 1807. Windmills can work on two sails but four is the most usual number.

U8 Other Mills. *Gunpowder Mills:* Extensive use was made of water power from the 17th century onwards to grind and incorporate the various ingredients. The type of stones used were of the bedstone with two vertical runners, the kind used for preparing apples in the cider industry. Early sites were confined to the south-east of England. Ruined, but recently excavated sites, exist at Chilworth, Dartford, Faversham and Bedfont.

Marsh Mills: These were built to drain the fenlands and may drive a pump or a scoop-waterwheel. They are usually in the form of either a Tower or Smock mill of the 18th century.

Paper Mills: Water is essential to the production of paper from rags etc. As early as 1490 a paper mill was set up on the River Lea west of Hertford. Until the 19th century when steam power became the prime mover, there were hundreds of small paper mills scattered along clean rivers all over the country.

Threshing Mills: A mill for beating the seeds from the ear, used before the introduction of the combine harvester.

Miscellaneous Terms.

U9 Bedstone. The lower and fixed stone in a mill, usually fixed to the floor.

U10 Bere. An old form of barley, still grown today in the Orkney Isles because it is adapted to the cold climate. Alternatively spelt Beir.

U11 Corn Exchange. These stem from the medieval practice of all purveyors having to bring their wares for sale into the market town on the prescribed market day. The ones we see today date mainly from the 19th century and originally contained a number of stalls on which merchants displayed samples of corn.

U12 French Burr Stones. These were constructed from pieces of a hard quartz mined in the Paris basin mainly along the River Marne near La Ferte sous Jouarre. The lumps of freshwater quartz were not large enough to make a four-foot millstone, hence selected pieces were trimmed and keyed together, being held in place by a cement, and finally iron bands were shrunk around the circumference. These stones are still the preferred ones for milling wheat since they are hard and produce a very clear separation of the flour from the bran. Alternatively called Wheat Stones.

U13 Grist. The name for the material fed to the millstone.

U14 Mill Mound. An artificial mound on top of which there was a post mill.

U15 Mill Pond. An upstream area usually adjacent to the watermill where water was allowed to collect overnight to provide power for milling.

U16 Mill Race. The part of the river immediately downstream of the water mill.

U17 Millstones. Circular stones having the lower one fixed to the floor. The top stone is driven round and has a hole in the centre for the introduction of the unground wheat. The distance between the upper and lower stones can be adjusted to vary the fineness of the grind. The main kinds of stone which have been used are Millstone Grit, French Burr, Granite and Cullin Stone from Germany.

U18 Quern. A stone device for the hand milling of cereal into flour and meal. The earliest, in the Neolithic period were saddle querns, consisting of a saddle or saucer-shaped lower stone and a bun-shaped upper rubbing stone. These continued in general use until some time in the 3rd century BC when rotary querns were introduced in the Mediterranean area.

U19 Tail Pole. A long pole attached to the body of a Post mill by which it could be turned to face the wind. It was superseded by the Fan Tail and its associated gearing from 1745.

U20 Water Rights. The miller had a right to receive a constant supply of water without hindrance. To an extent these rights still exist.

PART THREE
BREWING AND PUBLIC HOUSES

U21 General. By the 19th century there were three main types of retail outlets selling ale: *Alehouses* (sometimes called tippling houses) in which beer and ale were brewed and sold on the premises, *Taverns* in which wine could also be sold, and *Inns* which provided food and shelter as well.

U22 Types of Beer. Ale was the only choice available until hops were introduced from Flanders c1400, when beer was then produced. Pale Ale was sold from the early 18th century and Porter was retailed first in London c1720.

Legislation

U23 Magna Carta 1215. Standardisation of measures of ale was introduced for the first time.

U24 Assize of Bread and Ale 1267. From this date a periodic announcement by the civic authority in each locality laid down the price of bread and ale, based upon the prevailing prices of corn and malt.

U25 Licensing Statute 1495. This legislation gave Justices of the Peace power to supervise and suppress local ale sellers.

U26 Ecclesiastical Brewing 1529. Legislation this year suppressed breweries attached to ecclesiastical organisations.

U27 Additional Licensing powers 1552. Justices were given additional powers to license as well as suppress – a power they still hold.

U28 Limitation of Taverns 1553. Legislation limited the number of taverns permitted. Towns allowed more than one were Bristol 6, Cambridge 4, Canterbury 4, Chester 4, Colchester 3, Exeter 4, Gloucester 4, Hereford 3, Hull 4, Ipswich 3, Lincoln 3, London 40, Newcastle-upon-Tyne 4, Norwich 4, Oxford 3, Salisbury 3, Shrewsbury 3, Southampton 3, Westminster 3, Winchester 3, Worcester 3, York 9.

U29 Limitation of Taverns 1590. An extra tavern was permitted (see U28) in Brightling-sea, Bristol, Colchester, Coventry, Exeter, Greenwich, Harwich, Hull, Ipswich, Lowestoft, Norwich, Sandwich, Southampton and Worcester.

U30 Brewster Sessions 1729. The Brewster Sessions, at which Justices of the Peace license retailers, were instituted.

U31 Second Gin Act 1736. One of a series of enactments, the aim of which was to reduce the consumption of gin and the social disorder it caused. This Act required a retailer to take out a licence for £50 and pay a duty of £1 on every gallon sold. It also restricted licences to victuallers.

U32 Alehouse Act 1828. This Act consolidated previous legislation and re-defined the role of the Justices of the Peace.

U33 Beerhouse Act 1830. This allowed a householder, assessed to the poor rate, to retail beer and cider from his own house, on payment of 2 guineas. The purpose of this legislation was to popularise beer at the expense of spirits. The Act was repealed in 1869.

U34 Opening Hours. In 1839 public houses in London were required to close between midnight Saturday and noon on Sunday; in 1848 this restriction was extended over the rest of the country. An Act of 1854 restricted Sunday opening hours to 1–2.30 pm and 6–10 pm, and in 1855 this was amended to 1–3 pm and 5–11 pm. Sunday closing came to Scotland in 1853, Ireland in 1878 and to Wales in 1881.

Miscellaneous Terms

U35 Ale Silver. A fee or gift paid to the Lord Mayor of London for the privilege of selling ale in London.

U36 Aletaster. The first record of the appointment of an aletaster (or aleconner in some parts of the country) is in the City of London in 1377. Elsewhere he was appointed either by a manor or vestry and his duties included the proclamation of the permitted price for selling beer and ale, and also the sampling of the product for strength. When brewers wished him to call they put up an ale-stake at the front of their premises.

U37 Bede-Ales. Drinking parties at which money was raised for someone who had fallen on hard times.

U38 Bride-Ales. On her wedding-day the bride's parents provided ale for which guests made a contribution.

U39 Brew-creech. A term found in Cumberland, Lincs, Warks, Worcs and Scotland, meaning a duty paid by brewers.

U40 Brew farm. A fee for a licence to sell ale.

U41 Custom pottes. A fee paid to the lord of the manor at brewing time.

U42 Host house. An inn.

U43 Hucksters. Street sellers of ale, usually women.

U44 Hush-shop. A house in which spirits were illegally sold.

U45 Jigger. An illegal distillery.

U46 Kidley-wink. A west-country term for an illicit alehouse.

U47 Scot-ale. A drinking party to which guests were expected to bring their own drink or else share in the expenses of the occasion.

U48 Shebeen. A Scottish and Irish term for a house in which beer or spirits are illicitly brewed, distilled or sold.

U49 Temperance. The Temperance movement originated in England in the 1820s. In 1831 the British and Foreign Temperance Society was formed and extended its influence over the country in a decade. In 1847 the Band of Hope, a temperance organisation for young people, was founded. In 1853 the United Kingdom Alliance, founded in Manchester, aimed to persuade politicians, national and local, into a policy of prohibition. It was an aggressive organisation and not always popular with less militant societies. The Church took up the cause in 1862 when the Church of England Total Abstinence Society was established.

U50 Tippler. An alehouse-keeper.

PART FOUR
FAIRS AND MARKETS

U51 General. Until the concentration of population into towns and the advent of good transport services, fairs and markets were the most important means of trading. Many are of ancient origin, pre-dating the earliest known grant or charter. After the Norman Conquest most were regularised by the Crown. In the 13th century 3,300 charters were granted, in the 14th century 1560. In practice this profusion of grants raised revenue for the Crown and enabled landowners to receive market tolls.

Fairs took place at specified dates in the year, and markets on a particular day or days each week. Frequently a charter granted both together. Strictly speaking the charter permitted the receipt of revenue from a fair or market rather than the right to hold one.

Some of the older sites for fairs are by funeral barrows, or else at junctions of old tracks or drove roads. They may also be at boundaries or on hilltops.

U52 Legislation. In 1285 it was made an offence to hold fairs in churchyards although this legislation was ignored in places for some time afterwards. In the reign of Henry VI it was made illegal to hold fairs on Good Friday, Ascension Day, Corpus Christi, Assumption of the Virgin Mary, All Saints and on any Sunday except the four at harvest time.

In the reign of Edward II it was made illegal to buy goods on the way to market in order to resell them at a profit at the market. Such an offender was called a regrator or forestaller. This legislation was not totally repealed until 1844, although by then it had long fallen into disuse.

U53 Administration. The fair or market was usually under the jurisdiction of the lord of the manor's steward, or else the representative of a religious house. He presided over the 'Pie Powder Court', which was empowered to dispense immediate justice in cases relating to prices, quality, or any other matter concerning the market. The name of this court is a corruption of *'pieds poudreux'* – the 'dusty-footed'.

The court met in a building called a tolbooth or tolsey – this word survives in a number of areas for a building used for local administration. During the period of the market the judicial powers of the local courts were suspended and precedence given to the market's court.

Often the local traders had the right to trade first and outsiders waited their turn. Alternatively the latter, called variously stallingers, censers or chensers, paid a fee to achieve equal status.

Fairs were opened by proclamation, sometimes by a customary local ceremony, such as the pinning-up of a glove. Any merchant found trading after the end of the fair was liable to forfeit to the Crown double the value of all that he had taken all day.

U54 Aulnager. A Crown official responsible for examining the size and quality of woollen cloth. Standards were first established in 1196 and aulnagers first appointed in the reign of Edward I. The regulations as to size were repealed in 1381 but those relating to quality continued until 1699.

U55 Clerk of the Market. Originally this was a post in the King's household which was concerned with market supply to the royal retinue, and with weights and measures. As the Court travelled the country he went with it and exercised authority over all markets within the Verge, that is, within 12 miles of the residence of the Court. For a time his responsibility was enlarged to cover the whole country and he farmed out this role as a concession to local landowners. An Act of 1640 restricted his power once more to the Verge and elsewhere gave it to local mayors, lords of the manors etc.

On market days the Clerk attended from 10 am to sunset, and trading commenced and ceased on his announcement.

U56 Overseers of the Market. Sometimes called market-lookers, they were the mayor's representatives.

U57 Ponderator. A person responsible for weighing goods at market.

U58 Charters. In 1889 the government published two volumes entitled *Market Rights and Tolls* which examined the history and existing position of fairs and markets. The Report showed those fairs and markets noted in Owen's *New Book of Fairs* (1792), and gave its own list for 1888. This Report may be seen in the House of Lords library and in other major libraries. The lists of 1792 and 1888 were reprinted in the first edition of this *Encyclopedia*.

U59 Hiring Fairs. These were held annually in market towns. Domestic servants, farmhands etc were interviewed by employers and taken on for a year.

PART FIVE
OLD NAMES FOR TRADES AND OCCUPATIONS

U60 Old occupational names.
Ackerman – oxherd
Ale Draper – innkeeper or publican
Backster/Baxter – baker, occasionally a female baker
Badger – pedlar of food; corn dealer, miller
Barker – tanner
Blaxter – bleacher
Bowyer – maker of, and dealer in, bows
Brewster – brewer
Buckler – buckle maker
Bunter – rag and bone man
Cadger – carrier; pedlar of small wares
Cafender – carpenter
Caffler – rag and bone man
Capper – cap maker
Carman – a driver of small carts
Carter – wagoner, stable headman
Cashmarie – fish pedlar
Chambermaster – boot and shoe maker
Chapman – pedlar; dealer in small wares
Collier – charcoal seller
Copeman – dealer; in the 18th century it came to mean a receiver of stolen goods
Cordwainer – shoemaker
Costermonger – originally an apple seller
Couper – dealer in cattle and horses
Currier – a leather dresser or colourer
Cursitor – a clerk in the Court of Chancery who drew up writs
Dexter – a dyer
Eggler – egg dealer
Elliman – oil man
Farandman – itinerant merchant
Fellmonger – dealer in hides
Flesher – butcher
Fletcher – maker of, and dealer in, bows and arrows
Fogger – pedlar, headman on a farm; groom; manservant
Frobisher – armour polisher
Furner – baker
Gaffman – bailiff
Garthman – yardman; herdsman
Greave/Grieve – bailiff; foreman
Hacker – maker of hoes, mattocks etc.
Haymonger – hay dealer
Higgler – itenerant dealer, generally with a horse and cart
Hillier – slater, tiler of roofs.
Hind – farm labourer
Hooker – reaper

Jagger – itinerant fish pedlar

Kempster – comber of wool, usually a woman

Lavender – washerwoman

Leightonward – gardener

Litster – dyer

Lorimer or Loriner – maker of bits and spurs for horses

Lotseller – street-seller

Malender – farmer

Navigator – a labourer who dug canals, then railways. Nowadays called a navvy

Neatherd – cowherd

Pigman – crockery dealer

Pikeman – assistant to a miller

Rippier – fishmonger

Roper – rope and net maker

Salter – maker of, and dealer in, salt

Scrivener – clerk, specialising in drawing up bonds

Spurrier – spur maker

Swaller/Swealer – miller; dealer in corn

Tasker – reaper, thresher

Tucker – fuller

Webster – weaver

Wetglover – maker of leather gloves

Whig – Scottish horse drover

Whitesmith – a worker in 'white' iron; tinsmith or one who polishes and finishes metal goods as distinguished from one who forges them. Sometimes called Whitster.

Whitster – bleacher of clothes. Alternative name for whitesmith

Whittawer – saddler

Wood-collier – charcoal burner

Wright – constructor

PART SIX
WORKING CONDITIONS AND TRADE UNIONS

U61 Ordinance of Labourers 1349. This was the first statute to regulate wages; it fixed a maximum for different kinds of labour.

U62 Statute of Labourers. This reinforced the 1349 Ordinance and attempted to hold wages at the levels pertaining before the Black Death. There were penalties for infringement but the shortage of labour after the plague meant that the Statute was largely ignored.

U63 Statute of Artificers 1562/3. This laid down that wages were to be assessed by Justices of the Peace, and that all able-bodied men between the ages of 12 and 60 were obliged to do agricultural work if required. Servants were to be hired for at least a year and apprentices were to serve seven years. A master who infringed this Statute was fined and a servant who did was imprisoned. Hours of work were fixed at 12 in the summer and for all of daylight in winter. Unmarried women were liable for domestic work.

This legislation was not repealed until 1813 by which time working conditions were so harsh that workers were pressing the government to ensure that the employers kept, at least, this Elizabethan law.

U64 Legislation 1947. Disputes between master and servant could now be referred to the Justices of the Peace. The legislation allowed for the cancellation of an apprentice's indentures if he was ill-treated.

U65 Legislation 1793. An Act was passed which permitted the punishment of masters found guilty of ill-treatment of servants and apprentices.

U66 Early trade unions. Despite about forty Acts of Parliament which were intended to prohibit the combination of workers, a number of skilled crafts, such as printers, bootmakers, woolcombers etc., had some sort of trade union in the 18th century. Fear of Radical movements following the French Revolution of 1789 encouraged the government to bring in repressive General Combination Acts in 1799 and 1800 which, in effect, made such trade unions liable to prosecution upon complaint. Theoretically masters could also be convicted of combination but none were. Not all trade unions were made illegal – it sometimes suited local masters to deal collectively with workers and in such situations the union could exist.

The Combination Acts were repealed in 1824, largely due to the campaigning of Francis Place, but although unions obtained a measure of legal freedom to strike on matters of hours and wages, a new repressive Act of 1825 provoked an outburst of strikes. The spinners organised a Grand General Union in 1829 and unions in the north of England launched a National Association for the Protection of Labour in 1830, the first important attempt at a general union of all trades. In 1833 Robert Owen succeeded in launching a still larger body, the Grand National Consolidated Trades Union, in effect a federation of trade unions of all sorts throughout the country.

However, trade unionism was overshadowed in this period by the agitation for reform of the franchise, but when the Reform Bill failed to provide the vote for the majority of the working population membership of trade unions increased substantially.

In 1834 the government successfully prosecuted the Dorset farm workers called, subsequently, the 'Tolpuddle Martyrs', for admitting members to a union by the uttering of unlawful oaths, and they were sentenced to transportation.

U67 Health and Morals of Apprentices Act 1801/2. It was enacted that apprentice children from workhouses were to work for no more than 12 hours a day and were to have cleaner and better ventilated accommodation. The Overseer of the Poor was to keep a register of apprentices and the magistrates were to supervise the working of the Act. It was also laid down that apprentices should receive elementary education.

U68 Factory Act 1819. This first Factory Act applied only to cotton mills. It prohibited the employment of children under nine years of age, and limited the hours of workers under sixteen to 9 hours a day, exclusive of mealtimes.

U69 Truck Act 1831. This Act aimed to curtail the practice whereby certain workers, particularly navvies, were paid partly in goods and partly in tokens exchangeable only at shops owned by the employers. Workers, other than domestic servants, were to be paid wholly in coin.

U70 Althorpe's Factory Act 1833. This Act, applicable to textile mills, laid down hours of work for young people. The maximum number of hours of work permitted each day for children aged 9–12 was 9 with a maximum of 48 hours a week, for those aged 13–18 the maximum was 12 hours and 69 hours a week. Children were to have 2 hours of schooling each day. The first factory inspectors were appointed.

U71 Factory Act 1844. This Act, applicable to textile mills, laid down that women were not to work more than 12 hours a day and that children were to spend half their day at school.

U72 Beginning of modern trade unions. The Amalgamated Society of Engineers was founded in 1851. It is generally regarded, because of its twin role in representing its workers and in providing benefits and sickness insurance for them, as the forerunner of modern trade unions.

U73 Factory Act 1853. This Act, applicable only to textile mills, laid down that children were to be employed only between 6 am and 6 pm, with 1½ hours for meals.

U74 Factory Act 1867. This Act began the modern period of factory legislation. It included the provision of fans to extract dust and gases from industrial premises, and proper sanitary conveniences. The Act consolidated and extended previous factory legislation.

U75 Workshop Regulation Act 1867. This Act introduced the inspection of workshops by local authorities. Employment of children under 8 was prohibited and those between 8 and 13 were to work only half a day. The employment of women and children was to fall within the provisions of previous Factory Acts.

U76 Trades Union Congress. What became the Congress was first convened in 1868.

U77 Trade Union Act 1871. Trade Unions were made legal but at the same time they were considerably restricted in their activities by the passing of the Criminal Law Amendment Act 1871 which laid down drastic penalties for picketing etc. After strong agitation the latter Act was replaced by the Conspiracy and Protection of Property Act of 1875.

U78 Factory Act 1874. It was enacted that the minimum working age should be 9 (and in 1875 this was amended to 10). Women and young people were to work no more than ten hours a day and children aged up to 14 were to work only half a day.

U79 Factory and Workshop Act 1891. The minimum working age was increased to eleven.

U80 Factory Act 1901. This consolidating Act raised the minimum working age to twelve.

U81 Employment of Women, Young Persons and Children Act 1920. Among other provisions this Act raised the minimum age of employment in industrial undertakings to 14 years, except in some businesses where only members of the same family were employed.

U82 Factory Act 1937. It was enacted that young people under 16 were to work no more than 44 hours a week, and that those between 16 and 18, and women, were restricted to 48 hours a week.

PART SEVEN
BIBLIOGRAPHY

City Livery Companies
The Livery Companies of the City of London, William Hazlitt (1892)
The Guilds and Companies of London, George Unwin (1963)

Mills and Milling
The Watermills of Britain, L. Syson (1980)
Discovering Watermills, John Vince (Shire Books)
The English Windmill, Rex Wailes (1977)
Essex Windmills, Millers and Millwrights, K. G. Farries (5 vols 1981–)
Windmills and Millwrighting, S. W. Freese (1971)
History of Corn Milling, R. Bennett and J. Elton (4 vols 1898)
Windmills and Watermills Open to View, Society for the Protection of Ancient Buildings

Brewing
A History of English Ale and Beer, H. A. Monckton (1966)
British Taverns: Their History and Laws, Lord Askwith (1928)
The Brewing Industry in England 1700–1830, P. Mathias (1959)
History of Liquor Licensing in England 1700–1830, Beatrice and Sidney Webb (1903)
The English Alehouse: A Social History 1200–1830, Peter Clark (1983)
Old Inns of England, C. G. Harper (2 vols 1906)
English Inn Signs, J. Larwood and J. C. Hotten (1951)
Some Sources of Inn History, W. B. Johnson article in *Amateur Historian* Vol 6 No 1 (1963)
Drink and the Victorians, Brian Harrison (1971)

Fairs and Markets
English Fairs and Markets, William Addison (1953)
Discovering English Fairs, Margaret Baker
Royal Commission on Market Rights and Tolls (2 vols 1889)
Markets of London, Cuthbert Maughan (1931)

Working Conditions and Trade Unionism
The Early English Trade Unions, A. Aspinall (1949)
The History of Trade Unionism, Sidney and Beatrice Webb (1894)
A History of British Trade Unionism, Henry Pelling (1963)
The Making of the English Working Class, E. P. Thompson (rev. 1968)
The Village Labourer 1760–1832, J. L. and B. Hammond (1948 ed.)
The Town Labourer 1760-1832, J. L. and B. Hammond (1917)

SECTION V

Archaeology

PART ONE
PREHISTORIC PERIODS AND CULTURES

V1 Dating. The table on the next page puts in order of time the headings in V2–V20. It will be seen that the earliest periods were by far the longest. Dating in years can only be very approximate, particularly for the Palaeolithic; with improvement in dating techniques revisions often have to be made. In any event, the time boundaries were never sharply defined and new phases did not begin suddenly, nor in all parts of the country at the same time.

Some of the cultural changes (see V140) may have been influenced by groups of people arriving in Britain from different parts of Europe, but it is likely that most immigrants merged with the native population whose traditions continued. Many innovations could have come about by normal development and the spread of ideas rather than invasions.

In the table, chronological divisions are shown on the left and cultural divisions, which may cut across them, on the right.

V2 Acheulian. The main stone industry of the Lower Palaeolithic, continuing for perhaps 200,000 years. The characteristic tool was the handaxe (V75); there were also flake tools (V67). Artefacts have been found mainly in southern England, especially in the Thames valley. Acheulian people probably lived in Britain only during the milder periods (see Palaeolithic, V18) and seem to have preferred lowland areas near water. At Swanscombe, Kent, part of a human skull about 250,000 years old was found with Acheulian tools.

V3 Arras Culture. Immigrants – sometimes referred to as Marnians or Parisi – from eastern France settled in East Yorkshire in the middle phase of the Iron Age from about 400 BC. (Arras is a deserted medieval village in the area). They buried their dead in large cemeteries of small round barrows with square ditches. The graves of the chief men and women contained their chariots or carts with horse-trappings and personal possessions, some decorated in the La Tène (Celtic) style (see V13).

showing approximate chronological divisions on the left and cultural stages on the right

		Years ago		*Years ago*
Palaeolithic:	Lower	300,000 – 100,000	Clactonian	300,000 – 230,000
			Acheulian	260,000 – 100,000
	Middle	100,000 – 35,000	Mousterian	90,000 – 35,000
	Upper	35,000 – 11,000	Creswellian	25,000 – 10,000
		Years BC		*Years BC*
Mesolithic:	Earlier	10000 – 8000	Maglemosian	9000 – 7000
	Later	8000 – 4500		
Neolithic:	Earlier	4500 – 3200	Windmill Hill	4000 – 3000
	Later	3200 – 2400	Beaker	2600 – 1800
Bronze Age:	Early	2400 – 1400	Wessex	2000 – 1400
	Middle	1400 – 950	Deverel-Rimbury	1700 – 700
	Late	950 – 700		
Iron Age:	Early	700 – 450	Hallstatt C & D	700 – 450
	Middle	450 – 150	La Tène I	450 – 250
			La Tène II	250 – 150
	Late	150 BC – AD 43	La Tène III	150 BC – AD 43

V4 Aylesford-Swarling Culture. This late Iron Age culture, named from two places in Kent, may have been influenced by Belgic settlers in the Kent-Hertfordshire-Essex area. It is notable for the grave goods which accompanied cremation burials; they include elegant wheel-made pedestal urns, with brooches, spoons and other personal belongings. A group of especially rich burials in the Welwyn area contained imports such as glass dishes and amphorae (V23).

V5 Beaker Period. Some authorities think that groups of immigrants arrived from the Rhine basin in the Late Neolithic, bringing beaker drinking vessels (V30) and, amongst other innovations, copper knives and daggers and perhaps woven cloth. However, it may be that these new things were simply adopted as a fashion which also included new burial customs, generally with round barrows for single inhumations. A beaker was placed with the body, often with archery equipment (arrowheads, bow and wristguard) and ornaments such as ear-rings and pendants. This typical group of objects could have been intended to signify high status. If beaker-using people were newcomers, it seems they soon joined with the existing Neolithic communities in enlarging monuments such as henges and stone circles.

The beaker phase extends into the Bronze Age.

V6 Belgae. Immigrants from Belgium and northern France may have come to Britain in the late Iron Age (see Aylesford-Swarling culture, V4). Other Belgic influence is seen in the Sussex-Hampshire-Berkshire area. In preference to hillforts the Belgic people lived in semi-urban centres protected by complex dykes.

They probably introduced the potter's wheel and rotary quern for grinding corn. The first British coins were made by a Belgic tribe.

V7 Bronze Age. The Early Bronze Age was a time of drier climate than today, with long warm summers. This was important for the Wessex culture (V20) with its open ritual sites and their use for astronomical observations.

There were rich grave goods not only in Wessex, for example a gold cup in a cairn in Cornwall and a gold ritual cape in Flintshire.

In the north a less specialised social structure developed from Neolithic and Beaker traditions. As well as farming the people traded in metals and jet. Food Vessels of decorated coarse pottery were used. The dead were buried in flat graves or under mounds, sometimes in cists (V47) decorated with cup-and-ring symbols (V58), which were also carved on standing stones and boulders.

Flint and stone continued to be used in the Early Bronze Age for artefacts such as arrowheads (V25) and battle-axes (V29). In the Middle Bronze Age metal-working developed (see Bronze, V37) with new kinds of tool and weapon including palstaves, swords, looped spear heads and socketed axes.

The old ritual monuments had been further developed, with extensive changes at Stonehenge in the Wessex phase. In the Middle Bronze Age however it seems that they were abandoned, perhaps a result of worsening climate making the sites waterlogged and causing people to move to different areas. It has been suggested that a new religion evolved based on water; areas such as the Thames valley, North Wales and the fens became important.

Deverel-Rimbury communities (see V10) are known from about 1700 BC. Farming settlements in the Middle and Late Bronze Age consisted of round houses inside banked enclosures, surrounded by fields. A number have survived where stone is plentiful. On Dartmoor an extensive system of reaves (V107) marked the land boundaries.

Building of simple hillforts started in the Late Bronze Age. New land divisions were marked by long dykes. Social changes were taking place, perhaps through a growing need to safeguard food supplies, and there was less emphasis on ritual burial. The Bronze Age merged into the Iron Age with no clear division.

V8 Clactonian. A Lower Palaeolithic flint industry known from the Essex coast and north Kent. It consists of chunky flake tools (V67) often with secondary working, and chopping tools (V46). Some of them seem suitable for use on wood, scraping bark for instance, suggesting that the people lived in forested areas. The shaped tip of a wooden spear was found at Clacton-on-Sea.

V9 Creswellian. A late Upper Palaeolithic blade (V32) industry named from Creswell Crags in Derbyshire where the people lived in caves; other sites are in south-west England, Wales and Yorkshire. There was a gradual change over several thousand years from larger to microlithic (V91) blade tools. Bone and antler artefacts have also been found, including a few engraved with pictures or designs.

V10 Deverel-Rimbury. A cultural phase mainly of the Middle and Late Bronze Age, named after two cremation sites in Dorset. Urns of thick pottery were used for the burials either under small barrows or simply in pits; there were also globular urns of finer ware. Grave goods are few – but may have been of perishable materials. The people lived in round houses with palisaded enclosures often associated with fields and dykes. The basic Deverel-Rimbury farming tradition continued in some areas into the Early Iron Age.

V11 Hallstatt. The first iron-using culture in central and western Europe, named after a site in Austria. Traders and settlers reached Britain around 700 BC (see Iron Age, V12). Hallstatt equipment included iron daggers, long bronze slashing swords and scabbards with winged chapes (V44), bronze cauldrons, pins and brooches. Iron gradually replaced bronze as the main material for tools and weapons, and was worked locally in each community. The main kinds of pottery were large jars thought to be modelled on bronze vessels, and shallow angular bowls.

V12 Iron Age. In the Early Iron Age Hallstatt (V11) traders and settlers introduced iron weapons and tools, and by 600 BC iron-working had started in Britain. For a time bronze was still used for basic tools, but deposits of scrap metal show that it was no longer wanted.

Hillforts (see V77) were built in large numbers – over 2,000 are known. They were not however suitable for all areas, for example the lowlands of eastern England. Farming communities continued in many places as in the Bronze Age, with circular houses in an enclosure and fields around. New kinds of cereal were grown, and the grain stored in pits. Sheep provided wool for clothing. Iron domestic equipment included sickles, hammers, adzes and ploughshares, and wood was used for many purposes such as bowls, loom-frames, ladders and dug-out boats.

About 450 BC a new phase began in southern England with the arrival of Celtic La Tène people (V13). Wheels and the lathe are now in evidence. This was a period of outstanding artistic achievement in the design and decoration of a wide range of objects from cauldrons and armour to jewellery.

Hillforts were strengthened with more defences, which suggests rivalry between different communities, some farmers becoming local chieftains in control of considerable resources. Their territories were defined by natural features such as rivers, or dykes were constructed. In Scotland various types of defended homestead were built (see Broch V36, Dun V63, Wheelhouse V128). Stone-built villages may be seen in Cornwall, for example Chysauster.

During the La Tène phase immigrants from eastern France settled in east Yorkshire: see Arras culture (V3). There were, no doubt, refugees from the Gallic wars. In general the native way of life continued and developed, influenced at times by new contacts. England was eventually divided into tribal territories with, for example, the Iceni in part of East Anglia and the Brigantes in the north.

The climate in the Iron Age was decidedly cool and wet. Religion connected with water may account for ritual deposits of weapons in marshes and other wet places. Temple sites of the late Iron Age are known, some under later Roman temples. Chalk figurines have been found.

Increasingly, imported goods came from the Roman world – France, Germany, Spain and Italy – to the ports of Colchester, Hengistbury Head and Mount Batten in Dorset.

The Roman invasion of AD 43 ended the Iron Age in southern Britain and the conquest of the north was completed in AD 84, but the Iron Age way of life did not immediately end, especially in northern Britain.

V13 La Tène. Iron Age culture of central and western Europe, named after a Swiss site. Its influence first reached Britain about 450 BC. The art and craft work of the La Tène people is especially remarkable. They used flowing designs with scrolls, tendrils and animal motifs to decorate large and small objects including helmets, shields, scabbards, torcs (V123), mirrors and brooches.

V14 Maglemosian. See Mesolithic.

V15 Mesolithic. The Middle Stone Age, starting about 10000 BC. An improvement in climate after the last glaciation meant that by then most of the ice had disappeared. The sparse vegetation was replaced by low bushes and trees and eventually forest. Separation of Britain from the Continent took place around 6000 BC; before this people could reach Britain overland from northern Europe.

The Maglemosian culture of the earlier Mesolithic originated in Denmark and the Baltic. Living sites, which were probably occupied seasonally, are known in many parts of Britain. People fished with bone harpoons, ate plant foods such as nuts, and hunted animals. Many of their flint tools were finely made from blades (V32) and included scrapers, obliquely-blunted points and awls; some were microliths (V91). They also had larger tools. mainly trans-

versely sharpened axes and 'picks'. The best known site is Star Carr, east Yorkshire (dated about 7600 BC by radiocarbon), where a range of objects including some of antler and wood had been preserved in wet ground.

In the later Mesolithic new forms of microlith were made in geometric shapes such as triangles, crescents and rods, also transverse arrowheads (V25).

Living sites in west Scotland show how late Mesolithic people lived in these coastal areas: they left large middens containing shells and other food remains, with bone and antler artefacts and tools known as limpet scoops.

V16 Mousterian. Middle Palaeolithic industry named from a site in France. It may derive from the Clactonian (V8) also influenced by the Acheulian (V2), bringing together flake and core traditions. The flint tools include heart-shaped axes, broad triangular points made from flakes, and scrapers. The way of striking flakes left disc-shaped cores (V52). There were bone tools and ornaments.

The early Mousterian people lived in an interglacial period, and later groups in colder conditions. Sites are known in Derbyshire, Wales and at several places in southern England, in caves and rock shelters.

V17 Neolithic. The New Stone Age, which began around 4500 BC and lasted for about 2,000 years. Groups of people able to grow crops and keep animals arrived from western Europe and spread around the country. These early communities lived in semi-permanent camps, clearing land for cultivation and moving within their own areas when the land was exhausted. The wheat was cut with flint sickles, and saddle querns used for grinding. In the late Neolithic the ard (V24) was in use for preparing the ground. It appears that large areas of forest were cut or burned down by Neolithic farmers to make more space for crops.

Pottery was an important innovation. The first pots were plain and round-bottomed, probably in imitation of leather bags. Pottery of the Windmill Hill culture, named after a settlement in Wiltshire with a large causewayed camp (V41), is similar in shape but decorated with lines and dots. The Peterborough pottery mainly found in the south was a later development: thick with heavy rims and decorated by impressions of bird bones, finger tips and twisted cord. The contemporary Grooved Ware, in flat-bottomed bucket shapes with patterns of grooves and applied strips of clay, is found in northern Scotland as well as southern England.

Near their settlements Neolithic people constructed henge monuments (V76), stone circles (V119) and long barrows (V28), connected with ritual and burial of the dead: see also Chambered Tombs (V43). The construction of these monuments involved a tremendous amount of communal labour with only simple equipment.

Flint tools, used for a variety of purposes, included scrapers (V113) and arrowheads (V25). Good quality flint was obtained by mining (see Flint Mines, V69) using antler picks. Stone axes were made from hard rocks in highland areas (see Axe Factory, V27); some were ground and polished, probably for ritual use. Their distribution suggests a network of trading routes all over the country. Local trackways with interlaced timber foundation were made to cross over marshy ground; they have been found mainly in the Somerset Levels where the ground has been continuously wet.

Neolithic living sites are known in various parts of Britain, generally isolated farmsteads. In the later period there were village communities, as at Skara Brae, Orkney. Some defended settlements suggest that rivalry was developing.

V18 Palaeolithic. The Old Stone Age, by far the longest archaeological period, usually divided into Lower, Middle and Upper Palaeolithic.

From geological and dating evidence we know that early man was living and making flint tools in Britain more than 250,000 years ago. In the long period of the Lower and Middle Palaeolithic gradual climatic changes took place: there were glacial times when ice covered most of Britain, alternating with interglacials when the climate was at least as warm as it is today. In all the cold periods Britain was joined to the continent – sea levels have varied by hundreds of feet – so that by stages man could move to a warmer area and return when the ice melted.

Early peoples collected plants and grubs to eat and hunted animals for food, also making use of the bones and skins. The animals and vegetation varied with climatic conditions: plants and trees at different periods are known from pollen analysis (V101).

People lived in natural shelters such as caves or camped in the open. They made tools of stone, wood and bone. The earliest flint tools known are of two kinds suggesting different culture groups, the Clactonian (V8) and Acheulian (V2).

In the Middle Palaeolithic there was a late Acheulian industry as well as the Mousterian which represents the last early type of man before the coming of modern man around 35000 BC.

The Upper Palaeolithic was mainly a time of cold climate, improving about 14000 BC. The characteristic flint tools were made from blades (V32, V33). Bone tools included harpoons and needles. Sites are known in various parts of southern Britain and in Derbyshire (see Creswellian, V9).

V19 Welwyn Burials. See Aylesford-Swarling Culture (V4).

V20 Wessex Culture. The notably rich culture of the Early Bronze Age in Wiltshire and Dorset. This area may have been particularly favourable for agriculture, supporting quite a large population. Metallurgy and craftsmanship were well developed; there were wide trading contacts. Few traces of living sites have been found.

Many graves are known, under round barrows (V28). In the earlier Wessex period burial was usually by inhumation and in the later phase cremation. Objects in the richest graves include bronze axes, decorated bronze daggers, gold-bound amber discs, faience beads (V65), amber cups and neck ornaments. Many of the materials came from Ireland and various parts of Europe. The monuments and grave goods suggest an organised society with wealthy chieftains. The final remodelling of Stonehenge was carried out in the late Wessex period, about 1550 BC.

The Wessex culture came to an end rather suddenly, perhaps affected by worsening of the climate (see Bronze Age, V7), and by a decline in the favourable trading conditions which had enabled it to flourish.

PART TWO
ARTEFACTS, MONUMENTS AND ACTIVITIES

V21 Adze. A hafted tool of stone or metal, with a substantial blade fixed at right-angles to the line of the handle. Used for trimming timbers; very suitable for hollowing out a tree trunk to make a boat.

V22 Agger. The raised foundation of a Roman road, usually with ditches on each side for drainage. An agger can sometimes be traced in a grass field.

V23 Amphora. Large elongated two-handled container of plain pottery, usually with a pointed base. Amphorae were used for importing liquids such as wine and oil into Roman Britain.

V24 Ard. A primitive kind of plough which was used in several forms from the Neolithic into Roman times. It cut and stirred the soil but did not turn a furrow. Cross-ploughing (V57) helped to break up the ground.

V25 Arrowheads. Prehistoric flint arrowheads had characteristic forms at different periods. In the Mesolithic they were either wide at the end (to stun the prey) or microliths (V91) mounted in bone or wood. Many Neolithic arrowheads were leaf-shaped, surface-flaked on both sides; others had a broad sharp edge to the front. In the early Bronze Age they were mainly tanged and barbed (pointed with central stem or tang and a pronounced barb on each side). From the Iron Age onwards iron was used for a variety of types.

V26 Awl, Borer. A pointed tool of bone, flint or metal for piercing holes.

V27 Axe Factory. Outcrops of fine-grained hard rock in highland areas provided the material for Neolithic polished axes, the sites being identified by quantities of flakes and discarded rough-outs. We know that finished axes and partly-shaped blanks were widely traded, as axes found in many parts of the country can be traced to their original axe factories by studying the stone: see Petrological Identification (V155).

V28 Barrow. A mound of earth or stones covering one or more burials.
Long barrows were constructed in the Neolithic period, the later ones incorporating megalithic burial chambers. The non-megalithic barrows are the longest, 65 to 400 feet, a few which are even longer being classed as bank barrows. One important group of chambered long barrows is in the Cotswold-Severn area; some have been partly restored. The disposal of skeletal remains found in long barrows suggests they were placed there after the bodies had decayed: see Mortuary Enclosure (V94). In many cases the mounds which formerly covered chambered tombs have completely disappeared, leaving the stones.
Round barrows are nearly all of Bronze Age date. The following types are associated especially with the Wessex culture (V20):
Bowl barrow – a mound with surrounding ditch.
Bell barrow – having a berm or platform between the mound and its surrounding ditch.
Disc barrow – a small mound on a wide platform surrounded by a ditch and outer bank.
Saucer barrow – a very low mound with ditch and outer bank.
Pond barrow – a circular depression surrounded by an outer bank.

V29 Battle-axe. Essentially an axe with a shaft-hole, for use in warfare. In the Late Neolithic and Early Bronze Age hard igneous rocks were used, worked to shape by surface pecking (this type of stone does not flake).
Battle-axes made of iron were used by the Vikings and in medieval times.

V30 Beaker. A pottery vessel first appearing in Britain about 2300 BC, normally without a handle, and decorated by impressed cord or a notched tool. There were local variants, for instance a long-necked shape in eastern England. Beakers have been mainly found in barrows (V28) with distinctive grave goods (see Beaker Period, V5).

V31 Bell Barrow. See Barrow (V28).

V32 Blade. A parallel-sided flake, commonly of flint, which has been struck from a prepared core (V52) using a punch of bone, wood or stone. The length of a blade is at least twice its width.

V33 Blade Tool. Selected flint blades were retouched to make special purpose tools such as end-scrapers and burins (V38). Blades with one side blunted by removing tiny flakes could have been used as cutting tools by applying finger pressure to the blunt edge.
Blade tools are an essential part of Upper Palaeolithic cultures. Mesolithic people specialised in very small blades (see Microlith, (V 91).

V34 Borer. See Awl (V26).

V35 Bowl Barrow. See Barrow (V28).

V36 Broch. A circular stone-built tower originally 30 ft or more in height with hollow walls containing stairs and narrow chambers. It is an extreme form of defended homestead. Brochs are numerous in north-east Scotland and were occupied in the Late Iron Age and Roman period. The best preserved are in Shetland and Orkney.

V37 Bronze. An alloy of copper with 10–12 per cent tin and a very small amount of lead in the Early Bronze Age, and containing more lead in the Late Bronze Age. Bronze is more versatile than stone and more durable than copper, and was used for making weapons, tools and ornaments; it can be beaten, engraved and (because of its low melting point) cast in moulds.

V38 Burin, Graver. A flint blade tool worked at the end to produce a narrow but strong transverse edge suitable for engraving on bone and antler. Used especially in Upper Palaeolithic times.

V39 Cairn. A mound constructed of stones to cover single or multiple burials, usually of Neolithic or Bronze Age date.

A pile of stones termed a cairn may have been built – especially in Scotland – as a landmark or memorial.

V40 Cart Burial. See Chariot Burial (V45).

V41 Causewayed Camp. An enclosure of the Neolithic period in southern England, constructed with up to four concentric ditches with internal banks, both with a number of gaps or causeways. Some are situated in valleys, others on hilltops, and many are of large size. They cannot have been easily defensible, and may have been meeting places for people from the surrounding area.

V42 'Celtic' Fields. An indefinite term covering systems of squarish fields cultivated in the Bronze Age and through the Iron Age and Romano-British period (the time of maximum use) until the Saxons changed the settlement pattern. Prehistoric 'Celtic' fields are most clearly seen in chalk upland.

V43 Chambered Tomb. A barrow (V28) containing a burial structure built of large stones or drystone walling, or both, and roofed with stone slabs. Most belong to the late Neolithic and early Bronze Age. There are many variations in design and scale.

Gallery graves are usually set in long barrows. A parallel-sided passage leads to a burial chamber of the same width. A transepted gallery grave has side chambers to left and right of the central passage. A segmented gallery grave is divided by low walls into sections, the passage becoming narrower at each dividing wall. Stalled cairns are found in the Orkney Islands: lateral slabs divide the gallery into 'stalls' and help to support the roof.

Passage graves are generally set in circular mounds. The passage is lower and narrower than in a gallery grave and leads to a wider and higher burial chamber. In Orkney are well-constructed passage graves with large square or rectangular chambers built of drystone walling, reached by a long low passage. Maes Howe is the best example, with high corbelled roof.

Portal dolmens are the remains of burial chambers approached through two upright slabs forming a sort of porch; the capstone usually rests on a shorter upright stone at the rear. They are mainly in Cornwall and Wales.

The design of many chambered tombs, particularly those in the Cotswold-Severn area, suggests that funeral rites took place in a forecourt just outside the entrance.

V44 Chape. A protective metal case for the tip of a sword scabbard, first used in the Late Bronze Age.

V45 Chariot (or Cart) Burial. Some Iron Age burials of the early 4th century BC were accompanied by a chariot or cart and harness trappings. The chariot was either buried upright in the grave or dismantled and the wheels placed flat beside the body and grave goods. These burials are found in East Yorkshire; see Arras Culture (V3).

V46 Chopping Tool. A characteristic tool of very early stone industries, made by striking off a few flakes from one side of a lump of flint in opposite directions, often resulting in a zig-zag edge.

V47 Cist. A small burial structure of stone slabs set on end, with a covering stone sometimes decorated with symbols. Cists may be below ground level or on the surface covered by a mound. Usually Early Bronze Age.

V48 Clay Tobacco Pipes. Clay pipes, first used in the 16th century, can be dated to within 25 years or so by their shape and sometimes by the maker's mark. Changes in size, style and decoration were frequent as pipes were inexpensive items, quickly thrown away when damaged. Manufacture continued to about the mid-19th century.

V49 Cleaver. A Palaeolithic stone tool related to the handaxe (V75) with a wide straight cutting edge at one end and a thick butt.

V50 Cliff Castle. See Hillforts (V77).

V51 Contour Fort. See Hillforts (V77).

V52 Core. A lump of flint from which flakes or blades have been struck. See Flint Knapping (V68).

V53 Core Tool. An artefact such as a handaxe or chopping tool formed by trimming a block of flint, the shaped core being the tool.

V54 Coulter. An iron knife fixed vertically to the beam of a plough; it cuts through the sod and helps break up land under grass. Probably first used around the middle of the Roman period.

V55 Crannog. Small artificial island in a lake or estuary, made of brushwood and stones kept in place by vertical piles and surfaced with timbers. A single homestead stood on it, with access to the shore by causeway. Crannogs are mainly Iron Age but continued to be used in Saxon and even medieval times. See also Lake Village (V82).

V56 Cromlech. A megalithic chambered tomb (V43) especially one which has lost its covering mound. The term is now used only in Wales.

V57 Cross-ploughing. The ploughing of an area twice, the second time with the cuts or furrows roughly at right-angles to those already made by the ard (V24) or plough.

V58 Cup-and-ring Marks. These are patterns of cup-shaped hollows and concentric circles with radial lines and other variations, carved in the Late Neolithic and Bronze Age. In Northumberland, Yorkshire and Scotland are huge natural boulders decorated in this way. Cup-and-ring marks are found also on standing stones and other Bronze Age monuments. Their meaning is not known.

V59 Currency Bars. Strips of iron used perhaps as units of exchange in the Iron Age, many of them sword-shaped and 'pinched' at one end for easier handling. There are regional variations. The commonest length is 2–3 feet

and smaller ones may indicate different standard units. Most have been found in the southern half of England.

V60 Cursus. An elongated earthwork of the later Neolithic period, about 100 yards wide with parallel banks and outer ditches. Some are several miles long, the largest being the Dorset cursus which continues for about 6 miles. The monuments probably had a ceremonial purpose; some incorporate or are close to long barrows.

V61 Deserted Medieval Villages Former villages can sometimes be traced in open fields as crop marks or by a pattern of raised platforms and narrow hollows which indicate the layout. There were many reasons for abandonment including the Black Death, expansion of sheep farming with more land enclosed for pasture, and deliberate replanning by a landowner to improve his view or create a park. So far about 3,000 deserted medieval villages have been discovered, many through aerial photography.

V62 Dolmen. Term used by early antiquaries for a megalithic burial chamber (V89) originally covered by a mound.

V63 Dun. The term covers various types of fortified stone dwelling in western and northern Scotland. Galleried duns, circular or oval, have very thick walls about 10 feet high containing small rooms and passages. There are also duns without galleries, and a larger type more like a small hillfort. The oldest belong to the late Iron Age, but duns were built or reoccupied in post-Roman and medieval times.

V64 Dyke. A linear earthwork consisting of a bank and ditch or multiple banks and ditches continuing more or less straight for a long distance. The earliest are of Bronze Age date and may be field or ranch boundaries. Dykes constructed in the later Iron Age and post-Roman periods may be either boundaries or defence works.

V65 Faience. A sand and clay material with a fused glass surface coloured blue or greenish by adding copper salts. It originated in the Middle East but was widely imitated. Segmented faience beads probably made in Britain have been found in Bronze Age barrows.

V66 Fibula. An ornamental brooch of safety-pin form. There were many design variations in the Iron Age La Tène period; fibulae were later made by the Romans and Saxons. The idea was then lost until Victorian times.

V67 Flake and Flake Tool. A flake is a fragment removed from a larger piece of stone by striking or pressure. Flint is particularly suitable for the purpose as it is very fine-grained and can be worked in any direction. Flakes may serve as tools as they are, or may be reworked by removing tiny flakes to make implements such as scrapers and arrowheads.

Flake tools of different kinds were used in all prehistoric periods.

V68 Flint Knapping. To knap is to shape flint by striking it, using various techniques. A flint nodule has first to be struck forcibly to expose a flat surface usable as a striking platform. Blows on its edges knock off large primary flakes which are discarded. The aim is then to produce flakes or blades useful, after some further working, as tools. See also Blade (V32); Blade Tool (V33); Core (V52); Core Tool (V53); Flake and Flake Tool (V67).

V69 Flint Mines. Deep shafts were dug in chalk areas by Neolithic people to obtain fresh high-quality flint, which occurs in bands at different levels. Some shafts were tunnelled at the lowest level. Antler picks were hammered into fissures in the chalk and then used as levers. There was also open-cast mining.

V70 Fogou, Souterrain. A long, narrow underground chamber lined and roofed with stone slabs, in late Iron Age settlements; it is called a fogou in Cornwall and a souterrain in Scotland. All may have been primarily for food storage, but also at times places of refuge.

V71 Gallery Grave. See Chambered Tomb (V43).

V72 Graver. See Burin (V38).

V73 Halberd. An Early Bronze Age weapon with a pointed blade fixed at right-angles to the shaft.

Halberds with protruding hooks and spikes, mounted on a handle 5–7 feet long, were used in the Middle Ages.

V74 Hammer-pond. A relic of the Wealden iron industry. Streams in narrow valleys were dammed, so providing water-power to work hammers for crushing ore, bellows for blast furnaces, and sometimes forges.

V75 Handaxe. A core tool characteristic of Lower Palaeolithic stone industries, especially the Acheulian. The most usual form is a flattish pear-shape with rounded butt but there are many variations including sharply pointed and oval (ovates). See also Cleaver (V49).

V76 Henge. A circular ritual monument of the Late Neolithic and Early Bronze Age. Henges have a ditch all round and a bank outside it, and may be 30 to as much as 1,600 feet across. The earlier have one entrance, the later and larger two to four. Many henges have stone settings, notably Stonehenge. Some had settings of wooden posts, perhaps for roofed buildings. More than 70 henge monuments are known in Britain, Avebury in Wiltshire being the largest.

V77 Hillfort. Hillforts are fortified settlement sites of the Late Bronze Age and (mainly) Iron Age, defended by earth ramparts or stone walls, with external ditches. In some cases stone walls were strengthened with layers of horizontal timbers. It is likely that most hillforts were continuously occupied, and the defences strengthened as needed in times of crisis, for instance by additional earthworks and guard chambers at the entrance. Traces of houses and other buildings have been found in a number of hillforts. In their final pre-Roman stage some of them were virtually towns. The surrounding area was part of the economic unit, used for farming.

Classes of hillfort include:

Contour fort – the commonest type, with defences following the contours of the hill top.

Plateau fort – a contour fort in generally low-lying country.

Promontory fort – built on a spur of land with steep natural slopes so that defences were only needed across the neck of the promontory, or on a coastal headland where it is sometimes called a cliff castle.

Univallate fort – having a single rampart and ditch.

Multivallate fort – having more than one bank and ditch, often with complex entrances. The best example is Maiden Castle, Dorset.

V78 Hollow-way. A sunken lane between higher fields, often medieval, mainly the result of treading by cattle and water erosion on a slope. Occasionally evidence of pre-Conquest estate boundaries.

V79 Hypocaust. The Roman system of heating. Hot air passed from a furnace to space under a floor supported by low pillars, then through hollow box tiles to warm the walls of the room above.

V80 Ice-house. A chamber constructed underground or partly under an artificial mound, to store ice and keep food refrigerated. Late 17th to mid-19th century.

V81 Kitchen-midden. Any heap of food refuse, for instance the huge mounds of sea shells and small bones left by Mesolithic food-gathering people. They provide evidence of diet, size of community and seasonal occupation.

V82 Lake village. Iron Age settlement on the edge of a lake. A number of houses were built on a platform of brushwood, stones and timber and supported by piles, with a surrounding wooden palisade. The best known site is near Glastonbury where woodwork, pottery, textiles and iron objects were excellently preserved. See also Crannog (V55).

V83 Long Barrow. See Barrow (V28).

V84 Longhouse. A rectangular house with accommodation for animals at one end and a dividing passage giving access to both parts. Some had an upper storey to extend the living quarters. Longhouses were mainly built in early medieval times.

V85 Lunula. Crescent-shaped sheet-gold neck ornament with chased decoration. Lunulae were made in the Early Bronze Age in Ireland and Scotland and traded to southern England.

V86 Lynchets. Low banks of earth on sloping ground giving the appearance of shallow steps, formed gradually as a result of ploughing. A negative lynchet is the hollowed-out dip below a lynchet. They may be as old as the Middle Bronze Age but are mainly connected with Iron Age and Roman agriculture.

Strip lynchets are long terraced fields laid out on sloping ground in post-Roman and medieval times.

V87 Marl-pit. Marl – decayed chalky soil – was used as fertiliser from the Iron Age to the 19th century. Pits to obtain marl were 30 to 50 feet across, in regular lines, and originally several feet deep.

V88 Megalith. A large block of stone, part of a megalithic structure such as a chambered tomb, stone circle or alignment.

V89 Megalithic Tomb. A term sometimes used for chambered tombs (V43) built of stones of any size.

V90 'Megalithic Yard'. A length of 2.72 feet believed by the late Professor Alexander Thom and others to be the unit of measurement originally used for laying out stone circles.

V91 Microlith. A very small flint artefact of the Mesolithic period, made from a tiny blade or part of a blade specially divided for the purpose. Microliths were used as arrow tips or to form composite tools by mounting a series in wood or bone, as harpoons for example.

V92 Monolith. A large single standing stone.

V93 Mortarium. Roman food-mixing bowl, shallow with a fairly small base and spreading broadly to a heavy rim incorporating a wide spout for pouring; sometimes with gritted inside surface. Mortaria were often stamped with the maker's name.

V94 Mortuary Enclosure. A structure of earth, wood or stone in which corpses were stored before collective burial. Usually associated with Neolithic barrows (V28).

V95 Mosaic Pavement. Roman decorative floor of coloured tesserae (V122). Designs developed from simple patterns in two colours to intricate interwoven effects and naturalistic pictures with plants, animals and human figures.

V96 Multivallate Fort. See Hillforts (V77).

V97 Ogam (or Ogham) Script. Celtic alphabet consisting of vertical and sloping strokes on or across a straight line. Many examples are on stones with incised lines at right-angles to the edge, some with Latin inscriptions as well so that they can be read. The script was in use from about the 3rd to 9th century. Inscribed stones are found in Scotland, Wales and Cornwall.

V98 Orthostat. A large stone slab set vertically. Orthostats were often used in the walls of chambered tombs (V43).

V99 Palstave. A type of bronze axe used in the Middle Bronze Age. It had a transverse ridge which reduced the risk of splitting the haft; some had side loops.

V100 Passage Grave. See Chambered Tombs (V43).

V101 Pictish Symbol Stones. Stones incised or carved in relief with Pictish symbols, believed to be of 7th to 9th century date, are found in north and east Scotland. The symbols include animals, birds and fishes, a stylised beast known as the 'Elephant', and various abstract motifs such as the 'Crescent and V-rod' and the 'Horseshoe'. Some stones also have Ogam inscriptions (V97). The later sculptures include Christian elements.

V102 Pillow-mounds. Low oblong mounds, usually 15 to 30 yards long, found mainly in southern England. Their purpose is not known but they are generally believed to be artificial rabbit warrens and may date from the 12th to 19th century.

V103 Plateau Fort. See Hillforts (V77).

V104 Pond Barrow. See Barrow (V28).

V105 Pot Boiler. Roundish stones which have been heated to high temperature in a fire; flint pot boilers are white or greyish with cracked and broken surface. They are thought to have been used in most prehistoric periods to heat water for cooking purposes.

V106 Promontory Fort. See Hillfort (V77).

V107 Reaves. Linear stone banks on Dartmoor, used to mark land boundaries in the late Bronze Age.

V108 Ridgeway. Ancient trackway on high ground, following the line of a ridge. The best-known ridgeway is the Icknield Way in Norfolk which continues to Berkshire and Salisbury Plain.

V109 Round-house. An aisled wheelhouse (V128) with radial divisions free-standing but connected to the wall by stone lintels.

V110 Samian Pottery (*Terra sigillata*). Roman high-quality tableware, usually glossy brick-red and decorated in relief by pressing the clay into a patterned mould. It was mainly imported from southern and central Gaul. There is also black-coated samian.

V111 Saucer Barrow. See Barrow (V28).

V112 Saxon Shore Forts. Roman forts with massive stone walls built from the mid-3rd century in strategic places along the coast of south-east England from the Wash to the Solent, for defence against Saxon pirates.

V113 Scraper. Flint scrapers, large and small, were used for many thousands of years from the Lower Palaeolithic to the Bronze Age. The worked scraping edge may be along the side of the flake or at the end, and may be straight, rounded or hollowed.

V114 Shell Mound. See Kitchen-midden (V81).

V115 Ship Burial. A burial in a ship or boat covered by a mound. The chief site in Britain is Sutton Hoo, Suffolk, where one of the mounds contained the remains of a rowing boat with a central burial chamber. The rich grave goods may have belonged to the Anglo-Saxon king Redwald who died in AD 625.

V116 Souterrain. See Fogou (V70).

V117 Staddle-stones. Stone supports of mushroom shape with separate base and top, placed under wooden farm buildings, especially granaries, to keep rats out.

V118 Stewpond. A medieval fishpond, where fish were kept alive for food during the winter.

V119 Stone Circle. Stone circles not associated with henges are mainly in highland areas, and belong to the Late Neolithic or Bronze Age. They vary greatly in size. In many cases the stones are set in a ring bank of piled stones, with one entrance. Some circles are in groups, some have outlying single stones or an alignment close by. There are recumbent stone circles in Aberdeenshire.

These monuments were originally laid out with great care and there has been much discussion about the method, and possible connection of the layout with observations of the sun, moon and stars marking the seasons.

V120 Stone Rows. These are often associated with stone circles and barrows. They are common in Devon, in single or multiple rows, some of considerable length.

V121 Strigil. A narrow curved implement of horn or metal, used by a bather (or his slave) in a Roman bath-house to scrape and cleanse the skin.

V122 Tesserae. Small blocks of coloured material such as stone, tile or glass laid in cement, to form a decorative mosaic pavement (V95) or sometimes a plain tessellated floor.

V123 Torc. A circular neck ornament of the Bronze Age and (chiefly) the Iron Age La Tène period. Torcs found in graves or hoards are of gold, silver, electrum and bronze. They were formed of twisted or plaited rods or of tubular metal and richly decorated.

V124 Tranchet Axe. A Mesolithic core-axe with a transversely struck cutting edge.

V125 Tumulus. A mound covering a burial. The term includes barrows (which are mainly earthen) and cairns (stone).

V126 Univallate Fort. See Hillfort (V77).

V127 Villa. Roman country house, the centre of an agricultural estate. The various types include the courtyard villa, winged corridor house, and small aisled building. The most palatial known is at Fishbourne in Sussex.

V128 Wheelhouse. A circular stone dwelling of the later Iron Age in Scotland and used into the Roman period. It had partition walls like the spokes of a wheel but leaving the central space open for a hearth.

PART THREE
ARCHAEOLOGICAL CONCEPTS, TECHNIQUES AND DATING METHODS

V129 Absolute Dating. The dating of objects or events in years, using an accepted base year: see Dating Conventions (V141). Radiocarbon analysis (V165) and dendrochronology (V142) are among the methods which (within limits) can provide absolute dates.
See also Relative Dating (V166).

V130 Aerial Photography. Photographs taken from the air have been of enormous help in detecting archaeological sites. These appear as shadow marks when low banks are photographed obliquely, soil marks indicating where ground has been disturbed, and crop marks (V139). Traces of monuments and other features of different periods may be superimposed, so careful study is needed to sort them out. Locating the sites on the ground may be difficult if there are no landmarks.
The right conditions are very important, for example in drought or light snow sites may show up clearly though on other occasions nothing can be seen.

V131 Archaeomagnetism. See Magnetic Dating (V148).

V132 Assemblage. A group of different kinds of artefact found together and belonging or thought to belong to a single group of people in one period. The objects may be of one material or several.

V133 Augering, Boring. An auger is a tool with a screw point for boring in the ground to bring up samples of soil. It must be used with caution on archaeological sites to avoid damage to layers and artefacts. A special type (Hiller) is used to extract cores of peat and clay to a depth of 60 feet or more, for studying ancient pollen and plant remains.

V134 Baulk. A strip of earth left standing between different parts of an excavation so that vertical sections can be studied, and for convenience of access.

V135 Boring. See Auguring (V133).

V136 Bosing. A method of locating buried features by sound. The ground is struck by a heavy wooden mallet or weighted stick: over undisturbed ground the sound is dull, and over a ditch or pit more resonant.

V137 Box Plan Excavation. A box plan is generally used where sites are too large or otherwise unsuitable for complete stripping. The site is marked out in a square grid and selected squares excavated. A baulk (V134) is left if two adjoining squares are dug.

V138 Charcoal. Charcoal, which is partly-burned wood consisting mostly of carbon, is found on practically every archaeological site. It may be the remains of structural timbers, wooden objects, firewood or vegetation such as grain. In some cases it is possible to determine the species of wood. Charcoal is the best material for radiocarbon dating (V165).

V139 Crop Marks. Archaeological features may be traced by differences in the growth and colour of a crop, observable sometimes from ground level and showing up much more clearly in air photographs. Buried ditches and pits, with deeper soil and extra moisture, enable the crop to grow taller and greener; and where soil is shallow, say above a wall or roadway, the crop is stunted. The differences are best seen in a dry summer.

V140 Culture. The way of life and pattern of thought of a people as reflected by material remains of different kinds recurring in a limited area. Features of everyday life may be revealed by the range of objects used, food remains, traces of dwellings and the like; beliefs and practices are suggested by (for example) stone circles and burials. Material culture thus expresses the needs and desires of a community at a particular time. Changes take place from various causes, as when one group of people adopts the cultural traits of another.

V141 Dating Conventions. AD – Years since the birth of Christ, or a calibrated radiocarbon date (see Radiocarbon Dating, V165).

BC – Years before the birth of Christ, or a calibrated radiocarbon date.

BP – Years before the present, assumed to be AD 1950; or a calibrated radiocarbon date.

ad, bc, bp – used for uncalibrated radiocarbon years.

V142 Dendrochronology. The dating of wood by tree-rings, which vary in thickness season by season (the wetter the thicker) forming patterns which overlap those from other timbers. The longest series has been obtained from the Californian bristlecone pine going back about 9,000 years. Elsewhere, for instance in Ireland, there are floating chronologies not continuing to the present time. The method has been used in Britain to date timber, mostly oak, in Roman and medieval structures.

V143 Dowsing, Divining. Dowsing has often been used to discover sources of water, and some dowsers using the normal Y-shaped stick have been able to detect archaeological features such as buried ditches, also the presence of metal. The scientific explanation is not known. Findings need to be followed up by excavation.

V144 Field Walking. Systematic survey on foot, after collecting information about the area and using large-scale maps, may lead to discovery of archaeological sites, mainly through surface finds such as pottery fragments and flint.

V145 Fluorine Content of Bone. A method of relative dating (V166). Buried bones gradually absorb fluorine from ground water, so that in general older bones contain more fluorine. The rate of change depends very much on local conditions and fluorine measurement is mainly useful for comparing bones found close together.

V146 Hedge Dating. Old boundaries often took the form of hedges. Study of hedges dateable from documents suggests that age can be estimated from the average number of shrub species found in 30-yard lengths, each species representing about 100 years. A hedge found in this way to contain eight species may thus be around 800 years old.

V147 Industry. A group of artefacts of one material (such as flint) occurring in several places, and thought to have been produced by a single society.

V148 Magnetic Dating. A dating method for clays in hearths and kilns. Changes in the direction and intensity of the earth's magnetic field (archaeomagnetism) over the last 2,000 years have been measured and recorded. Fired clay objects preserve a record of the magnetic field at the time of cooling, and provided they have not been moved their magnetic field may be matched with the dated series for hearths and kilns.

V149 Metal Detector. An electronic device used to locate buried metal objects by emitting a sound. In some circumstances metal detectors can be very helpful to archaeologists.

Many however are in the hands of amateur 'treasure hunters', who have at times caused serious damage by using them on archaeological sites. In any location, metal detection by amateurs is likely to destroy all real archaeological evidence, and efforts are being made to stop the practice. Co-operation is possible in the case of chance finds. There should be minimal disturbance of the ground, and the finds should be reported at once with full details to the local or county museum.

V150 Molluscs. Snails and other molluscs are useful indicators of former climate and environment: they show changes, for example from woodland to grassland. Marine molluscs which were a source of food are found in kitchen-middens (V81).

V151 Nitrogen Content of Bone. The nitrogen in buried bones is gradually lost. Analysis shows the relative age of bones found near together, as the older ones contain less nitrogen. Comparison with bones from other locations is not reliable.

V152 Open Excavation. The gradual removal of deposits over a whole site layer by layer, organised on a grid plan but leaving no baulks or sections. This of course results in total destruction of the site.

V153 Palaeobotany. The study of ancient plant remains. Plant fragments and pollen found on archaeological sites and through boring are a guide to former vegetation, environmental conditions and food resources. See also Pollen Analysis (V160).

V154 Palynology. See Pollen Analysis (V160).

V155 Petrological Identification. Neolithic stone axes from many find spots, and some stone artefacts of the Bronze Age, have been studied by special sampling techniques to discover where the stone originally came from: see Axe Factory (V27). Querns and building stones have also been analysed for this purpose.

Similar techniques are applied to pottery to trace the likely areas of origin.

V156 Phosphate Analysis. Phosphates from decayed animal matter and excrement remain as a residue in the soil over a long period, and high concentrations may indicate old settlement and farm sites. They are traced by chemically testing soil samples taken at intervals over the area.

V157 Pits. Former rubbish pits are a useful source of information as they generally contain food refuse, plant remains and a range of objects which help to date the occupation of the site in prehistoric or historic times.

V158 Plant Remains. See Palaeobotany (V153).

V159 Ploughmarks. Series of scratches made by early ploughs, sometimes crossing in two directions (see Ard, V24) have been detected on old soil surfaces beneath prehistoric monuments (such as barrows and embankments) and Roman structures.

V160 Pollen Analysis, Palynology. Pollen preserved in wet ground and buried soils provides useful information about vegetation and climate in former times. Trees and plants can be identified as their pollen grains vary in shape and the outer coat is remarkably resistant to decay.

The composition of pollen samples from different layers in a deposit shows the proportion of various plants at each stage. The information is usually set out in a graph called a pollen diagram. Some of the variations are due to climatic changes, others to man's influence: there is evidence for example that in the Neolithic tree pollen was much reduced, suggesting deliberate clearance of forests.

V161 Post and Stake Holes. Posts set in the ground in early times may have been removed soon afterwards or rotted away, but always the former holes are traceable in excavation. Some contain packing stones. When set out on plan they may show the position of early structures.

V162 Potsherd, Sherd. A broken piece of pottery. Even small fragments are useful as they show the type of fabric, and scraps of rims and bases reveal the shape of the complete pot.

V163 Probing. A probe is a metal rod with a T-handle for pressing into the ground until it meets harder material. It may be useful in tracing features such as a wall or a filled-in ditch.

For taking soil samples an auger is used (see Auguring, V133).

V164 Quadrant System. A method of excavating a circular feature such as a barrow (V28), by removing two alternate quarters leaving complete transverse sections.

V165 Radiocarbon (Carbon-14) Dating. Carbon absorbed by plants and animals (including man) is of two kinds: ordinary, carbon-12, and radioactive carbon-14 from the upper atmosphere, in fixed proportion. After an organism dies the carbon-14 decays at a known rate while the carbon-12 is unchanged, so the comparative amounts indicate the length of time since death. Half the carbon-14 disappears in about 5,730 years, half the remainder in the next 5,730-year period, and so on.

Radiocarbon is used for dates in the past 40,000 years. Charcoal and bone are the best materials. Although the dates cannot be exact this is a very important method of absolute dating (V129).

There is evidence that production of radiocarbon in the upper atmosphere has not always been constant so a deviation occurs in the date series. Carbon-14 dates are calibrated (adjusted to make allowance for irregularities) particularly by reference to tree ring dates for the past 10,000 years. See also Dating Conventions (V141) and Dendrochronology (V142).

V166 Relative Dating. Means that one event or object is older, or more recent, than another, without reference to calendar years. Relative dating methods include nitrogen and fluorine content of bones (V151 and V145) and stratified deposits (V174), the lower being older than the higher – but objects in them may have been displaced by activities of animals or worms (V180), or by tree roots.

V167 Resistivity Surveying. Measurement of the electrical resistance of the soil, using a resistivity meter, to locate buried features such as pits.

Rocks and soils conduct electricity in proportion to the amount of water in them. Resistivity is relatively high above a stone wall, and low above a pit or ditch which contains more moisture than the surrounding soil.

V168 Robber Trench. The trench, later filled in, where a wall has been removed; sometimes called a ghost wall.

V169 Section. A vertical face left during an excavation to show stratified layers of deposits; also the drawing of the vertical face.

V170 Sherd. See Potsherd (V162).

V171 Sieving. Sieves of various meshes are used on excavations to ensure that nothing is missed.

Wet sieving, by agitating a sieve full of soil in a container of water, helps to recover organic matter such as seeds, insects and charcoal.

V172 Snails. See Molluscs (V150).

V173 Soil Resistivity. See Resistivity Surveying (V167).

V174 Stratification The successive deposits which make up a site, revealed for example in a vertical section (V169). The relationship between layers may be very complicated, for instance when pits or channels have been cut into lower layers.

V175 Thermoluminescence (TL) Dating. A technique for dating pottery and also burnt material including flint found in hearths. The minerals in clay accumulate energy from radiation in the soil and when pottery is fired (or in the case of flint when heated above 500°C) the energy is given off as light and reduced to zero. With time new radiation builds up. By heating the material to measure its thermoluminescence and examining the soil where it was found, the length of time since the previous heating can be calculated.

V176 Timber-slot. A trench dug to contain a horizontal (or sleeper) beam for the foundation of a building, Roman or later. The slot can be traced in excavation when the timber has disappeared.

V177 Tree Rings. See Dendrochronology (V142).

V178 Type-site. Usually the site where an industry or cultural group was first recognised; in some cases one where the remains occurred in a particularly characteristic way.

V179 Wear Marks. Flint and bone tools are studied under a powerful microscope for traces of edge damage and polish to discover if possible the uses to which the tools were put, such as cutting up meat.

Sickles which were used to cut cereal plants show a distinctive gloss even to the naked eye.

V180 Worms. In some soils the worm population is ½ to 1 million or more per acre and over thousands of years they have burrowed down and transported fine soil from lower levels to the surface as worm casts. This causes stones and other objects to sink deeper into the ground, which has to be allowed for when associating finds with a structure or with one another.

PART FIVE
BIBLIOGRAPHY

General
Celtic Britain, L. R. Laing (1979)
Collins Field Guide to Archaeology in Britain, E. S. Wood (1979)
Discovering Archaeology in England and Wales, James Dyer (Shire, 1976)
Handbook of British Archaeology, L. and R. Adkins (1983)
Life in Roman Britain, A. R. Birley (1981)
Prehistoric Britain, Ian Longworth (British Museum, 1985)
Reconstructing the Past, Alan Sorrell (1981); reconstruction drawings of British sites
Roman Britain, T. W. Potter (British Museum, 1983)

Site Guides
A Guide to the Archaeological Sites of Britain (Peter Clayton 1985)
Guide to Prehistoric England, Nicholas Thomas (1976)
Guide to Prehistoric Scotland, R. Feachem (1977)
A Guide to the Roman Remains in Britain, R. J. A. Wilson (1980)
The Penguin Guide to Prehistoric England and Wales, James Dyer (1982)
The Shell Guide to British Archaeology, Jacquetta Hawkes with Paul Bahn (1986)
Wales: An Archaeological Guide, C. Houlder (1975)

Maps

Ancient Britain: A Map of the Major Visible Antiquities of Great Britain older than AD 1066 (Ordnance Survey, 1982)
Map of Roman Britain (Ordnance Survey, 1978)

Archaeological Techniques and Landscape Study

Aerial Archaeology in Britain, D. N. Riley (Shire, 1982)
A Dictionary of Terms and Techniques in Archaeology, ed. S. Champion (1980)
Field Archaeology in Britain, J. Coles (1972)
Fieldwork in Medieval Archaeology, C. C. Taylor (1974)
The History of the Countryside, Oliver Rackham (1986)
Interpreting the Landscape: Landscape Archaeology and Local Studies, Michael Aston (1985)
The Making of the English Landscape, W. G. Hoskins (1977)
Science and Archaeology, David Wilson (1975)
Techniques of Archaeological Excavation, Philip Barker (1982)

Particular Topics

Ancient Agricultural Implements, Sian Rees (Shire, 1981)
Barrows in England and Wales, L. V. Grinsell (Shire, 1984)
Bronze Age Metalwork in Southern Britain, Susan Pearce (Shire, 1984)
Celtic Art, I. M. Stead (British Museum, 1985)
Circles and Standing Stones, E. Hadingham (1978)
Clay Tobacco Pipes, Eric G. Ayto (Shire, 1979)
Deserted Villages, Trevor Rowley and John Wood (Shire, 1985)
The Farming of Prehistoric Britain, P. J. Fowler (1983)
Flint Implements of the Old Stone Age, Peter Timms (Shire, 1980)
A Guide to the Hill-forts of Britain, A. H. A. Hogg (1984)
Hedges and Local History, M. D. Hooper and others (Standing Conference for Local History, 1976)
Later Stone Implements, M. W. Pitts (Shire, 1980)
The Lost Villages of England, M. W. Beresford (1983)
Neolithic and Early Bronze Age Pottery, Alex Gibson (Shire, 1986)
Pottery in Roman Britain, V. G. Swan (Shire, 1980)
Rock Carvings of Northern Britain, Stan Beckensall (Shire, 1986)

Roman Forts in Britain, D. J. Breeze (Shire, 1984)
Roman Villas, D. E. Johnston (Shire, 1983)

Journals

Current Archaeology, from 9 Nassington Road, London, NW3
Popular Archaeology, from Vallis House, 57 Vallis Road, Frome, Somerset

INDEX

Cantilever S15
Cantle A77
Cantrev B58
Capias L88
Capital S16
Capital Messuage S196
Cardinal P20
Carl B8
Carlot B8
Carr A78, A330
Carriage Tax C2
Carriages N49–53
Cart Burial V45
Cartbote A304
Cartographer D140
Cartouche (maps) D141
Cartouche S17
Cartulary D2
Carucage C3
Carucate A9
Caryatid S18
Castellated S119
Castelry B59
Castle Architecture S115–130
Catchland A79
Catch-meadow A80
Catchpole Acre A79
Cathedral P39
Cathedral Schools J17
Catholic Apostolic Church P77
Catholic Emancipation Act 1829
   J1
Catholic records D70, D298
Catholics P92
Cattlegait A305
Cattlegate A10, A305
Causeway N11
Causewayed Camp V41
Caveat D119
Cavel A257
Celtic Fields V42
Cement S173
Cemeteries M6–7
Cemetery Registers D71
Census D98–105
Central Criminal Court L48
Ceorl B8
Cess C50, K31
Chain A11
Chambered Tomb V43
Champion A258
Chancel S141
Chanceling H11
Chancery Rolls D34
Chantry P40, S142
Chantry Schools J18
Chape V44

Chapel P41
Chapelry P2
Chaplain P21
Chapter P9
Chapter House S143
Charcoal V138
Chare N12
Chariot Burial V45
Charities – records of D184,
   D263, D271
Chart A331
Charter D3
Chartered Boroughs B212
Charterland A418
Chase A81, N13
Chattels A381
Chest S144
Chest Tomb S145
Chevage C51
Chief Pledge B148
Chief Rents C52
Childwite C53
Chimin N14
Chiminage C54
Chirograph D4
Chivalry A421
Choir (Architecture) S141
Chopping Tool V46
Christian names H22
Church Ale P58
Church Architecture S131–168
Church Commission C129
Church House P42
Church Rates C114
Church Reeve B145
Church Trustees – records of
   D272
Churchman B145
Churchmaster B145
Churchtown B60
Churchwarden B145
Churchyard S146
Churchyard Cross S147
Churl B8
Circle D142
Circulating Schools J19
Cist V47
City Livery Companies D287,
   U1–3
Clachan B61
Clactonian V8
Clapman B146
Classes of Society B1–49
Classical Orders S19
Clay Tobacco Pipes V48
Claybiggin S197
Cleaver V49

Clerestory S20
Clerical records D307
Clerk of the Market U55
Clerk of the Peace L49
Cleugh A82
Clink L16
Clipping Q33
Clipsham Stone S174
Clister S21
Clocks and Watches – taxation
   C4
Close A83
Close Parish B62
Close Rolls C35
Clough A82
Clunch S175
Coaches N49–53
Coal Industry records D292
Coat-of-Arms components
   T4–6
Cob S176
Cob/Cot House S198
Cockshoot A84
Cockshut A84
Codicil D120
Coffering S22
Coins Q1–29
Coins, grades of Q34
Coldharbour A85
Collar-beam S23
Collation P59
Collectioner K32
Collector of the Poor B147
College of Arms T2
Collegiate Church P43
Colonia B63
Colonnade S24
Column S25
Commissary Court D121
Commissions of Array R5
Common Appendant A306
Common Appurtenant A307
Common Day Schools J20
Common Fine C55
Common in Gross A308
Common of Pasture A309
Common of Piscary A310
Common of Shack A311
Common of Turbary A312
Common of Vicinage A313
Common Pleas, Court of L34
Common Rights A302–328
Common Terms A329–354
Commons A302–367
Commons Legislation
   A355–367

Commons Preservation Society A363
Commote B58
Compotus Rolls D36
Compter L17
Compurgation L89
Conditional Surrender A370, A372
Conductio Sedilium C115
Conge D'Elire P60
Congregationalist records D72, D299
Congregationalists P78
Conservation of Buildings S190–191
Consistory Court D122, P10
Console S26
Constable B148
Constablewick B64
Contours D143
Convent P44
Conventicle P45
Conveyance of Land A369–379
Conyearth A86
Conygarth A86
Conyger A86
Conygree A86
Conyhole A86
Conywarren A86
Co(o)mbe A87
Co-oration A259
Coping S27
Copyhold A422
Copyhold conveyance A370
Corbel S28
Core V52
Core Tool V53
Corn Exchange U11
Corn Rents D185
Cornage C56
Cornice S29
Coroner B149
Corporeal Hereditaments A382
Costume History D330
Cot-town B65
Cote A88, S199
Cotswold Stone S177
Cottar B9
Cottier A423
Coulter V54
Council Housing S212
Countess of Huntingdon's Connexion Registers D73
Countess of Huntingdon's Connexion P79
Counties, formation of B66
Countour B150

Country Life D315
County B66
County Courts L27
County Maps D152
County Police Act 1839 D211
County Police Act 1839 L7
County Police Forces – formation of L8
County Rate C57
County Record Offices F6
Court Baron B68
Court Leet B69
Court of Arches P11
Court of Augmentation P12
Court of Chancery P13
Court of Commissioners of Sewers L46
Court of Common Pleas L34
Court of Delegates P14
Court of Hustings L47
Court of King's Bench L35
Court of Requests L36
Court Rolls B218
Courts – types of L25–48
Couture A260
Cove S30
Cow Leaze A315
Cowgate A305
Crannog V55
Cressets S148
Cresswellian V9
Crew(e) A89
Croad A90
Crocket S31
Croft A90
Cromlech V56
Crop Marks V139
Cross-ploughing V57
Crossing S149
Croud A90
Crowd A90
Crown (coin) Q3
Cruck-beams S32
Crypt S150
Cucking Stool L59
Culture V140
Cunner A86
Cup-and-ring Marks V58
Cupola S33
Curate P23
Curation D123
Currency Bars V59
Cursus V60
Curtain wall S120
Curtesy of England A383
Curtilage S200
Cusps S34

Custom pottes U41
Customary Court Baron B68
Customary Freehold A424
Customs and Excise records D286
Custos Parci B183
Custos Rotulorum B170
Custumal B219

Dado S35
Dales A333
Dalt A332
Dame B10
Dame Schools J21
Dandiprat Q4
Danegeld C5
Danelaw Counties B70
Davoch A12
Day-Math A13
Day Work A14
Deacon P24
Dean P25
Death Certificates D92
Decennarius B163
Decimation C6
Decimer B153
Decorated S36
Decree D124
Deed Poll D5
Deedland A418
Defaulter B220
Dell A261
Demesne A91, A425
Demise A373
Dendrochronology V142
Denizen B11
Denn A92
Deodand L60
Deserted Medieval Villages V61
Deverel-Rimbury Culture V10
Devise A384, D125
Diapered S37
Diem Clausit Extremum A385
Diocesan Registries D296
Diocese P3
Direction Stones N41
Director of the Poor B151
Directories D322
Dispensaries D266
Disseisin A426, L90
Dissenters – registration of D186
Distraint L61
Distributor B152
District Councils B71
District Schools J22
Ditchsilver C58

253

Flint Mines V69
Flockrake A107
Flonk A108
Florin Q7
Fluorine content V145
Fluting S50
Fogou V70
Foils S51
Fold A109
Fold Course C66
Foldage C65
Foldbote A320
Folk Land A335
Folk Moot B76
Folklore records D331
Font S152
Food Rents C9
Footpaths N20
Ford N21
Fordraught N22
Fore-Acre A266
Foreigner B15
Foreman of the Fields B157
Forestaller U52
Forfang L94
Forical A266
Forschel A110
Forstal A111
Foss(e) A112
Fother A267
Foundlings – records of D265
Franchise B234–256
Franchise – Burial Boards B255
Franchise – Local Government B241–250
Franchise – Parliamentary B234–240
Franchise – Poor Law B251–254
Franchise – School Boards B256
Franchise – Women B238, B239, B249
Franchise Prison L18
Frank Fee A433
Frank Tenement A437
Frank Tenure A424
Frankalmoign A434
Franklin B16, B158
Frankmarriage A435
Frankpledge B77
Free Church of England P80
Free Church of Scotland P81
Free and Voluntary Present to Charles II C10, D282
Free Services C67
Free Warrant A436
Freebench A389

Freedom A321
Freehold A437
Freehold conveyance A368
Freehold Land Societies S214
Freeland A437
Freeman B17
Freemasons – registration of D189
Freemen's Rolls D332
Freeth A113
French Burr Stones U12
Friary P46
Friendly Societies – registration of D190
Frieze S52
Frith A114
Fumage C11
Furhead A268
Furlong A18, A269
Furnage C68
Furrow A270
Fyrd R1
Fyrdbote C104

Gable S53
Gair A271
Gale C69
Gallery Grave V43
Gallets S178
Game Duty C12, D191
Gannock B159
Gaol Delivery D192, L38
Garderobe S54, S122
Gargoyle S55
Garston A116
Garth S202
Garthstead S203
Gas Companies M8–9
Gate N23
Gatehouse S123
Gatrum N24
Gauger B160
Gavel B58
Gavelacre C70
Gavelerthe C71
Gavelkind A390
Gavelsed C72
Gavol C73
Gazebo S55
Gebur B18
Geld C13, C74
Gemote B78
Geneat B19
General Enclosure Act 1801 A259
General Register Office D89

Generation H14
Gennell N25
Gentleman B20
Gentleman's Magazine D313
Geographical Features A51–250
Geological Maps D155
George Rose's Act 1812
German H15
Gesith B21
Gilbert's Act 1782 B251, K15
Gill A117
Glass S179
Glebae Adsciptitii A439
Glebe A118, A438
Goad A28
Godbote C118
Gore A271
Gospel Tree A119
Gracious Aid C31
Grammar Schools J24
Grand Assize L39
Grand Serjeant A456
Grange A120, P47
Grasson A376
Graver V38
Great Tithes C134
Green Lane N26
Green Village B79
Greeve A121
Gregorian Calendar D26
Gressom C75
Grip A122
Grist U13
Groat Q8
Ground A123
Groundage C76
Guardian of the Poor B161
Guild of One-Name Studies H7
Guinea Q9
Gunpowder Mills U8
Guns – taxation on C14
Gustator Cervus B131
Gut A124
Gypsey A125

Hachuring D146
Hade A126
Hafood A127
Hagg A128
Hair Powder Duty C15
Halberd V73
Hale A129
Half A130
Half-baptised H16
Half-blood H17
Half-Crown Q10

Half-Penny Q11
Half-Ryal Q12
Half-Year Close A131
Half-Year Land A339
Hall A129
Hallhouse S204
Hallstatt Culture V11
Halmot B80
Ham A132, A336, B81
Hamil B82
Hamlet B83
Hammer beams S57
Hammer-pond V74
Hamstal A133
Handaxe V75
Hanger A134
Hanging Field A135
Hansard D40
Hant A136
Hard Labour L64
Hardwick B84
Hardwicke's Marriage Act 1754 D56
Harrage C77
Harrial A391
Harve A137
Hatch A138
Hatchet A139
Haughland A140
Haw A141
Hay A142
Haybote A322
Hayward B162
Head-Right A440
Headborough B77, B148, B163
Header S58
Headland A143, A272
Headstones S153
Heaf A144
Hearth Penny C119
Hearth Tax C16, D193, D283
Heater A145
Hedge Dating V146
Hedgebote A322
Hedgelooker B162
Helm Q13
Hempland A146
Hendre A147
Henge V76
Heraldic Terms T7–81
Hereditament A392
Heregeld C5
Hereyeld A393
Heriot A394
Heritor C120
Hern A148

Herringbone S59
Heusire C78
Heybote A322
Hide A19
Hideage C3
Hidegeld C3
Hidegild L65
Hield A149
High Constable B164, D194
Highway records D195, D333
Highways Act 1555 B200, N3
Highways Act 1835 N5
Highways Act 1862 N6
Hill (measurement) A20
Hillfort V77
Hipped roof S60
Hiring Fairs U59
Hirn A148
Historical Maps G156
Hitched Land A273
Hoard Q35
Hobhouse Vestries Act 1831 B244
Hock Day C79
Hogringer B165
Hogslease A150
Hold B22
Hollow Way N27, V78
Holme A151
Holograph Will D127
Holt A152
Homage B226
Home B85
Home Close A153
Home Office Records D41
Honorial Courts L28
Honour B86
Hookland A273
Hop Acre A21
Hop(e) A154
Hoppet A155
Hopton Wood Stone S180
Horngeld C56
Horse-buses N55
Horse-trams N60
Horsegate A305
Horselease A156
Horses – taxation on C17
Hospitals K24
Hospitals – records of D74, D279
Host house U42
House of Correction L19
Housebote A323
House-Duty C18
House-row B227

How(e) A157
Hucksters U43
Hue and Cry L95
Huguenots P82
Huguenot records D75, D300
Hundred B87
Hundred Constable B164
Hundred Courts L25
Hundred House K34
Husbandland A22
Husbandman B23
Hush-shop U44
Husting B87
Huvvers A274
Hypocaust V79
Hyrne A148

Ice-house V80
Illustrated London News D314
Immigration Records D255
Impression D147
Impropriation P62
In-by Land A158
Income Tax C19
Incorporeal Hereditaments A382
Incumbent B166, P26
Independent Methodists P87
Independents P78
Industrial Schools J4, J25
Infangetheof L96
Infield A158
Infield-Outfield A275
Inghamite Registers D76
Inghamites P84
Inglenook S61
Ings A159, A337
Inhams A160
Inheritance A380–409
Inhomes A160
Inhook A276
Inland A161
Inlandes A162
Innings A163
Inns of Chancery L97
Inns of Court D242, L98
Inquisitiones Post Mortem A395, D42
Inship B89
Insolvent Debtors D196
Institution of Incumbent P63
Intake A164
Inter-Common A338
Intestate D128
Intrante B24
Inventory D8

Inwood A165
Irish Mile A23
Irish Parish Registers D66
Irish Registration D97
Irish Wills D115
Iron Age V12
Irons L66
Ironstone S181
Irvingite Registers D77
Issue D148

Jack A166
Jack's Land A343
Jettons Q36
Jewish records D78, D301
Jews P85
Jigger U45
Joclet B90
Joint Enfeoffment A441
Jointure A396
Judge Ordinary L55
Jugate Q37
Julian Calendar D25
Junior Schools J25
Jurat B167, L99
Jurors D197, L100
Justices in Eyre L33
Justices of the Peace D198, L51
Juvenile Offenders – returns
    D199

Keep S124
Keld A67
Kentish Rag S182
Ketton Stone S183
Keystone S62
Kidders – licences D180
Kidley-wink U46
Kinbote L67
Kinegate A305
King Post S63
King's Bench, Court of L35
King's Widow A442
Kintra B91
Kirk Clachan B92
Kirkmaster B145, B168
Kirktoun B92
Kitchen-midden V81
Knap(p) A168
Knatchbull's Workhouse Act
    K14
Knight B25
Knight's Fee A24, A443, B86,
    B93
Knight's Service A443, C20, R2
Knocknobbler B169

Kyrle Society A363

La Tène Culture V13
Lache A169
Lackland B26
Ladder Farm A170
Lady Court B94
Laet B27
Laighton A171
Laine A277
Laird B28
Lairstall S154
Lake A172
Lake village V82
Lammas Lands A339
Lamplands C121
Lancet window S155
Land A278
Land Measurement A1–50
Land Registration D334
Land Tax C21, D200, D284
Landgable C80
Landyard A25
Langate A173
Larceny L68
Last Heir A397
Lathe B95
Latin Names D32
Latter-Day Saints P86
Law List D243
Law of Property Act 1925 A366,
    D7, D22
Lawn A279
Lay A175
Lay Advowson P51
Lay Fee A444
Lay Subsidies C22, D280
Laystall A174
Lea A175
League A26
Leah A175
Lease A176, A340
Lease and Release A368
Leasehold A445
Leasow A177
Leat A178
Leatherhouse K35
Leaze A176, A340
Lecturer P27
Ledgers S156
Lee A175
Leet (waterway) A178
Leet (road junction) N28
Legal Records D242–246
Legal Terms L81–108
Legend (on coin) Q38

Leighton A171
Leopard (coin) Q14
Letters Close D9
Letters of Administration
    D129–130
Letters Patent D10
Levant and Couchant A324
Lewis's Topographical
    Dictionaries D320
Lewn(e) C122
Ley A175
Ley Roads N29
Leywrite C81
Liberate A27
Liberty B96, B117
Libraries F3–5
Licences D201
Lieutenancy records D335
Lighting and Watching Act
    1833 L5
Limited Probate D131
Linch Land A179
Linchet A280
Lintel S64
List Road N30
Literary and Scientific Societies
    D202
Litten P64
Livery Companies D287, U1–3
Livery of Seisin A368, A398
Lloyd's, records of D239
Load N31
Local Authority Housing S212
Local Government Act 1888
    B67, D176, L9, N7
Local Government Act 1894
    B71, B105, B247, M7, N8
Local Government Act 1899
    B248
Local Government Act 1929
    K23
Local Government Act 1972
    B105
Local Government Board K20
Local History Publications
    D321
Local History Societies G24
Local Militia R9
Local Officials B128–211
Lodging Houses S210
Loggia S65
Loke N32
London Gazette D312
Long and Short Work S67
Long Houses S66
Longcross Q39

Longhouse V84
Loon A281
Lord Lieutenant B170
Lordship B97
Lot Meadows A341
Lowe A180
Lugg A28
Lunatics – care of K17
Lunatics – returns of D203
Lunula V85
Lychgate S157
Lynchets V86

Machiolation S125
Maenol B58
Maglemosian Culture V15
Magnetic Dating V148
Mail C82
Mailing A181
Mainport C123
Mainprise L101
Mains A182
Male Servants – taxation on C23
Mandate 1538 D49
Manor B98
Manor customs B213–233
Manorial Records D256
Mansard S68
Manuel Rent C83
Map Makers D160–173
Maps D140–173
March A183
Marchet C84
Mark Q15
Markets U51–59
Markland A29
Marksoil A184
Marl-pit V87
Marquess B33
Marriage Act 1823 D59
Marriage Act 1836 D60
Marriage Certificates D91
Marriage Licences D62
Marrows A282
Marsh Mills U8
Marshalsea Money L20
Master of the Parish B171
Matchway N33
Math A30
Maundy Money Q40
Mayor B172
Mayor's Brethren B99
Mear A283
Mear Path N34
Mechanics' Institutes J27
Medical records D275

Meer A283
Megalith V88
Megalith Tomb V 89
Membrane D11
Memoranda Rolls D43
Merchet C84
Mere A283
Meresman B173
Merestake A185
Merestone A185
Merlons S126
Mesnalty A446
Mesne Lord B29
Mesolithic V 15
Messor B157
Messuage S205
Metal Detectors V 149
Methodist New Connexion P87
Methodist Registers D79, D302
Methodists P87
Metropolis Management Act
    1855 B246
Metropolitan Commons Act
    1866 A362
Metropolitan Police Act 1829 L4
Metropolitan Public Gardens
    Association A363
Microlith V91
Mile A31
Militia R1–6
Militia Returns D204
Mill Ham A186
Mill Mound U14
Mill Pond U15
Mill Race U16
Milled Q41
Milling U4–20
Millsoke C85
Millstones U17
Ming Land A284
Minnis A342
Minster P48
Mints Q30
Misericord S158
Miss B30
Missionary Society Records
    D306
Mixed Tithes C134
Model Dwellings S208
Model Villages S209
Moiety A399
Molluscs V150
Monastery P49
Monastic Schools J17
Monolith V92
Monumental Brasses D174

Monumental Inscriptions D175
Moorstone S184
Moot B100
Moravian Registers D80
Moravians P88
Mormons P86
Mort D'Ancestor, Assize of
    A400
Mortarium V93
Mortgages A370
Mortmain A447
Mortuary C124, C130
Mortuary Enclosure V94
Mosaic Pavement V95
Moss Reeve B174
Moss Rooms A285
Mote B100
Motor buses N57
Motor cars N61
Motoring records D336
Motte and Bailey S127
Moulding S69
Mousterian V16
Mr B30
Mrs B30
Mullion S70
Multure C86
Municipal Corporations Act
    1835 B17, B54, B104, B245, L6
Municipal Corporations Act
    1882 B54
Muniment D12
Murage C87
Murder Fine L69
Murenger B175
Museums – general F1
Museums – specialist F2
Mysgather B176
Myslayer B177

Nailbourne A187
Narrow Oxgang A32
National Insurance Act 1911
    K22
National Pedigree Index H3
National Schools J28
National Society, records of
    D250
Nave S159
Navy Records D95, D234–239
Neatgeld C56
Neatherd B178
Needle spire S160
Neife B32
Neolithic Age V17
New Jerusalem Church P94

New Jerusalemite Registers D81
Newel Post S71
Newspapers D311
Nitrogen content of bone V151
Nobility, degrees of B33
Noble Q16
Noman's Land A343
Non-Parochial Registers D67–87
Nonage A401
Nook A33, A188
Notes and Queries D316
Numismatic terms Q31–Q46
Nuncupative Will D111

Oath Helpers L102
Oaths of Allegiance D205
Oblata Rolls D39
Obverse Q42
Occupation names U60
Oculus S72
Official Assignee L53
Og(h)am Script V97
Oldland A189
Open Excavation V152
Open Field Farming A251–301
Open Parish B101
Open Vestry B102
Ora Q17
Order Books of Quarter Sessions D206
Ordinance 1644/5 D51
Ordinary P28
Ordnance Survey D157
Organisations – national and regional G1
Organisations – specialist G2–23
Oriel S73
Orientation D149
Orteyard A190
Orthostat V98
Outlawry L70
Outfangentheof L103
Outfield A191
Overland A448
Overseer of the Highways B200
Overseer of the Market U56
Overseers of the Poor B179, D260
Oxgang A7, A34
Oxgate A305
Oyer and Terminer, Commission of D207, L37

Pace A35
Paddle A192
Palaeobotany V153
Palaeographic Abbreviations E85–91
Palaeographic Scripts E68–84
Palaeographic terms E1–67
Palaeolithic Age V18
Palatinate B103
Palimpsest D13
Palladian S74
Palstave V99
Palynology V160
Pannage A325, C88
Pantile S75
Paper Mills U8
Parapet S76
Pargetting S77
Parish B104, P5
Parish Clerk B190
Parish Constable L2
Parish Councils B105
Parish Records D267–272
Parish Registers D49–66
Park A193
Parker B181
Parliamentary records D44
Parliamentary representation B234–240
Parlour S78
Parrock A194
Parson P29
Parsonage C125
Parts B111
Passage C89
Patent Rolls D45
Paull A286
Pavage C90
Paving Board records D269
Pavior B182
Pawn D14
Pebble-dash S79
Peculiar P6
Peder B34
Pedigree H18
Pediment S80
Peerage directories D323
Pele/Peel Tower
Pell D15
Pendicle A195
Penny Q18
Pentecostals C126
Perambulation of the Bounds B228
Perch A36, A38
Perpetual Calendar D31

Personal Tithes C134
Personalty A402, D132
Pestalozzi Schools J29
Peter's Pence C126
Petitions at Quarter Sessions D208
Petrological Identification V155
Petty Constable B148
Petty Serjeant A456
Petty Sessions D209, L42
Pharmacists – records of D278
Philanthropic Bodies K26
Phosphate Analysis V156
Physicians – records of D276
Pictish Symbol Stones V101
Pier S82
Pightel A196
Pightle A196
Pigtail A196
Pike A197
Piking A198
Pilaster S83
Pilch A199
Pill A200
Pillow-mounds V102
Pin Fallow A201
Pinder B183
Pinfold B229
Pingle A196, A202
Pinnacle S84
Pipe Rolls D46
Piscina S161
Pit Money C127
Pits V157
Place Names – publications D337
Plack A203
Plantation Indentures D210
Plashet A204
Playstow A344
Pleck A345
Pledgehouse L21
Plight A449
Plinth S85
Plough Alms C128
Plough Duty C91
Ploughgate A19, A37
Ploughland A37
Ploughmarks V159
Plurality P65
Pole A38
Police – development of L4–11
Police – records of D211
Police Act 1946 L10
Political records D310
Poll Books D252

Poll Tax C24, D281
Pollen Analysis V160
Ponderator B184, U57
Pontage C92
Poor Law Act 1563 K7
Poor Law Act 1597/8 B179
Poor Law Act 1601 B179, K10
Poor Law Amendment Act 1844 B161, B252, B253, K18
Poor Law Board K19
Poor Law Records D261
Poor Rate Returns D212
Poor Relief K1–23
Port Way N35
Portcullis S128
Portico S86
Portland Stone S185
Portsoken B106
Portsoone B106
Possessory Assizes L29
Post and Stake Holes V161
Post Office M3–4
Post Office records D273
Postcards D274
Pot Boiler V105
Potsherd V162
Pound B229
Pound (coin) Q19
Poundkeeper B183
Praedial Tithes C134
Prebend P66
Precentor B185
Preparatory Schools J30
Presbyterian records D82, D303
Presbyterians P89
Presbytery S162
Presentation of Incumbent P67
Presentment L104
Preservation of Buildings S190–191
Priest P30
Primer Seisin A403
Primitive Methodists P87
Primogeniture A404
Printing Presses – licensing of D213
Priory P50
Prisoners – returns of D215
Prisons – records of D83, D214, D246
Prisons L12–24
Probate Act D133
Probate Courts D107–110
Probate since 1858 D113
Probing V163
Process Registers D216

Protestation Oath Returns 1641–2 D47
Proved D134
Province P7
Provost B186
Public Health Act 1848 B254
Public Houses U21–50
Public Libraries – legislation M13–17
Public Schools J31
Public Schools, records of D249
Public Undertakings – records of D217
Puisne Judge L54
Punder B183
Purbeck Marble S186
Puritanism P90
Purlieu A205
Purpresture A450
Purveyance C25

Quadrant System V164
Quaker records D84, D304
Quakers P91
Quarentena A287
Quarter (allotment) A206
Quarter B107
Quarter Days D27
Quarter Sessions L40
Quarter Sessions Records D176–228
Quarterage C93
Quatrefoil S87
Queen Anne's Bounty C129
Quern U18
Questman B187, P31
Quia Emptores A377
Quillet A207
Quillet A288
Quit Rent A451, C94
Quoin S88

Racehorses – taxation on C26
Rack-rent A452
Radiocarbon Dating V165
Radknight B19, B35
Ragged Schools J32
Ragman D16
Raik N36
Railway formations N59
Rampart S129
Rand A208
Rap A209, A289
Rape B108
Rate Books D270

Rating and Valuation Act 1925 B179
Ravelin S130
Reading A210
Reaves V107
Recognizances D218, L105
Recovery Rolls D48
Recto D17
Rector P32
Rectorial Tithes C134
Recusant P68
Recusants – returns of D219
Reeding A210
Reen A211
Reeve B188
Refectory S89
Reform Bill 1832 B235
Regality B109
Regardant Villein B36
Regarder B189
Registration of Births etc D88–97
Registration Tax C27
Regnal Years D30
Regrant A405
Regrator U52
Reguard B110
Relationship terms D139
Relative Dating V166
Release A368
Relief A368, A378, A406
Religious history P98
Religious records D295–307
Remainder A407
Removal Orders D220, K36
Rent Days D27
Rental D18
Renunciation D135
Replevin L106
Representation of the People Act 1867 B236
Representation of the People Act 1884 B237
Representation of the People Act 1918 B238, B250
Representation of the People Act 1928 B250
Representation of the People Act 1945 B250
Representation of the People Act 1948 B240
Reredos S163
Resistivity Surveying V167
Reveland A453
Reverse Q43
Revet S90

Statute of Westminster 1285 A356

Statute of Winchester 1285 B148, L1, N1

Steam buses N56

Steel Industry records D293

Stetch A297

Steward B199

Stewpond V118

Stint A305, A326

Stitch A297

Stitch-meal A298

Stocking A230

Stocks L72

Stone Circles V119

Stone Rows V120

Stoneman B200

Stonewarden B200

Stranger B42

Stratification V174

Stray A328

Stretcher S102

Strigil V121

String Course S103

Stubbing A230

Stucco S188

Sturges Bourne Act 1819 B102, B243

Sturges Bourne Vestries Act 1818 B242

Suffragan Bishop P34

Suicide L73

Suit of Court B231

Suit of Mill C85

Suling A41

Sulung A41

Sunday Schools J34

Surcharge A350

Surgeons – records of D277

Surnames H21

Surplice Fees C132

Surrender A379

Surrogate P35

Surveyor of the Highways B200

Swainmote B118

Swale A231

Swang A232

Swanimote B118

Swedenborgian Registers D85

Swedenborgians P94

Sweeps U7

Swineherd B201

Tail Pole U19

Tallage C101

Taxation records D280–286

Taxes – ecclesiastical C111–135

Taxes – local C31–110

Taxes – national C1–30

Tealby Q45

Team B119

Teinds C120

Telephone directories D324

Temperance movement U49

Temporalities C133, P70

Tenancies A410–463

Tenancy at Will A459

Tenancy by copy A422

Tenancy by the Verge A422

Tenant-in-Capite A460

Tenant-in-Chief A460

Tenantry Acre A42

Tenantry Field A351

Tenantry Road N44

Tenement A233, S206

Tenths C22

Termor A461

Territorial Army R10

Tesselated Pavement S104

Tesserae V122

Testamentary Peculiar D136

Testator D137

Thane B43

Theam B119

Theatrical records D308–309

Theow B44

Thermoluminescence Dating V175

Third Penny C102

Thirdborough B77, B148, B202

Thirling Mill C85

Thrall B45

Three Farthings Q25

Threepenny piece Q26

Threshing Mills U8

Thrysma Q27

Thwaite A234

Tidemills U5

Tie Beam S105

Tile Hanging S106

Timber-slot V176

Time Immemorial D21

Times The D311

Tippler U50

Tithe Act 1925 C129, C134

Tithe Act 1936 C134

Tithe Commutation Act 1836 C134

Tithe Maps D159

Tithe records D338

Tithes C134

Tithing B120

Tithingman B77, B148, B203

Title Deeds D22, D258

Toft A235

Tokens Q46

Tolbooth U53

Toll C103

Toll Booth L24

Tolsey U53

Tontine A462

Torc V123

Torture L74

Total Descent H19

Town Husband B204

Town Place S207

Townland A236

Township A237, B121

Tracery S107

Trade Unions U66, U72, U76–77

Trading Company records D288

Tramways N60

Transept S168

Transom S108

Transportation L75

Transportation records D225, D254

Trev B58

Trial by Battle L76

Trial by Ordeal L77

Trinoda Necessitas A434, C104

Trolleybuses N58

Troner B205

Truck Act 1831 U69

True Bill L108

Tuition D138

Tumulus V125

Turnpike Roads N4, N45

Twissell N46

Twitchell N46

Twopenny piece Q28

Tyburn Ticket D227

Tye A238, A352

Tympanum S109

Tyning A239

Type-site V178

Undersettle A463

Union K38

Unitarian records D86, D305

Unitarians P95

Unite Q29

United Free Church of Scotland P96

United Methodist Church P87

United Reformed Church P89, P97
Universities, foundation of J39–41
Universities, records of D248
Urban District Councils B122

Vaccary A240
Vagrants K3–6
Valor B232
Vassal B46
Vault S110
Vavassor B47
Velge A241
Verderer B148, B206
Verge A43
Verso D23
Vestibule S111
Vestry B123
Vestry Customs B213–233
Vestry Minutes D268
Vicar P36
Vicar-General P37
Vicarial Tithes C134
Victoria County History D37, D319
Victuallers – licences D226
Victuallers – records of D291
View of Frankpledge B77
Vill B124

Villa V127
Villein B48
Villein in Gross B48
Virgate A8, A44
Viscount B33
Vise S112
Visitations T3
Volunteer Companies R8
Voryer A242
Voussoirs S113

Waif B233
Wake P71
Wall A299
Wall Plate S114
Wandale A300
Wapentake B125
Ward A353
Ward Money C105
Wardman B207
Wardmote B126
Wardship and Marriage A409
Wardwite C106
Waste A354
Water Bailiff B208
Water Rights U20

Water Supplies M5
Water-Gavil C107
Watermills U4
Wath A243
Waver A244
Wax Scot C135
Waymaker B200
Wayman B200
Waywarden B200
Weald A245
Wear Marks V179
Webster B209
Weights and Measures, Inspectors of D228
Weldon Stone S189
Wellmaster B210
Welsh Methodists P87
Welsh Records D327
Welwyn Burials V19
Went A246
Went (path) N47
Wentin A246
Wergild L78
Wessex Culture V20
Wet Boon C108
Wheelhouse V128
Whip Land A45
Whipping L79
Wick (farm) A247
Wick B127
Wills D106–139
Windmills U6
Window Tax C30
Window Tax records D285
Winterbourne A248
Wista A46
Witchcraft L80
Wite C109
Women's Franchise B238, B239, B249
Wong A249, A301
Wood Acre A47
Wood Penny C110
Wood Reeve B211
Woodward B211
Workers' Educational Association J35
Workhouse Act 1723 K14
Workhouse Records D262
Workhouse Schools J36
Working conditions – legislation U63–82
Working Men's Colleges J37
Worms V180
Wray A250
Wynd N48

Yard A48
Yardland A8, A49
Yeoman B16, B49
Yoke A50